THE LAW OF DISABILITY DISCRIMINATION FOR HIGHER EDUCATION PROFESSIONALS

LEXISNEXIS LAW SCHOOL ADVISORY BOARD

THE LAW OF DISABILITY DISCRIMINATION FOR HIGHER EDUCATION PROFESSIONALS

Ruth Colker
Distinguished University Professor and Heck-Faust Memorial Chair in Constitutional Law
Moritz College of Law
The Ohio State University

Paul D. Grossman
Adjunct Professor
Hastings College of Law, University of California
Member AHEAD Board of Directors

ISBN: 978-1-63280-763-2
Ebook ISBN: 978-1-63280-764-9

Library of Congress Cataloging-in-Publication Data

Colker, Ruth, author.
The law of disability discrimination for higher educational professionals / Ruth Colker, Distinguished University Professor and Heck-Faust Memorial Chair in Constitutional Law, Moritz College of Law, The Ohio State University; Paul D. Grossman, Adjunct Professor, Hastings College of Law, University of California, Member AHEAD Board of Directors.
pages cm.
Includes index.
ISBN 978-1-63280-763-2
1. College students with disabilities--Legal status, laws, etc.--United States. 2. People with disabilities--Education (Higher)--Law and legislation--United States. 3. Education, Higher--Law and legislation--United States. 4. College administrators--United States--Handbooks, manuals, etc. I. Grossman, Paul D. (Lawyer) author. II. Title.
KF4244.P58C65 2014
344.73'07911--dc23
2014030931

This publication is designed to provide authoritative information in regard to the subject matter covered. It is sold with the understanding that the publisher is not engaged in rendering legal, accounting, or other professional services. If legal advice or other expert assistance is required, the services of a competent professional should be sought.

NOTE TO USERS
To ensure that you are using the latest materials available in this area, please be sure to periodically check the LexisNexis Law School web site for downloadable updates and supplements at www.lexisnexis.com/lawschool.

Editorial Offices
121 Chanlon Rd., New Providence, NJ 07974 (908) 464-6800
201 Mission St., San Francisco, CA 94105-1831 (415) 908-3200
www.lexisnexis.com

MATTHEW BENDER

(2014–Pub.3271)

ACKNOWLEDGMENTS

The Higher Education Edition of this text was made possible, in part, by generous research support at the Ohio State University College of Law. Paul Grossman has joined Ruth Colker in writing the Eighth Edition of ***The Law of Disability Discrimination***, as well as this special edition. We would like to acknowledge the contributions of Bonnie Poitras Tucker and Adam A. Milani, who assisted Ruth Colker in the preparation of previous editions of this book. We would like to thank Rebecca Bond, Irene Bowen, Marc Brenman, Jane Thierfeld Brown, Wilbert Francis, Michael Hing, Howard Kallem, David LaDue, Mary Beth McLeod, Alan Konig, Chris Kuczynski, Scott Lissner, Jo Anne Simon, Kim Swain, Rachel Weisberg, John Wodatch, and Stephanie Ziegler for their assistance in helping us keep abreast of the latest developments in the field. We would also especially like to thank Lexis-Nexis, and particularly our editor Keith Moore, for continuing to recognize the need for comprehensive and timely materials for a course on the law of disability discrimination, and for helping to endow the Adam A. Milani Writing Competition in Disability Law.

The Higher Education Edition, which focuses on disability discrimination issues in higher education, was made possible through a collaboration between the Association on Higher Education and Disability ("AHEAD") and LexisNexis. This version will be available pursuant to the DAISY Standard. The DAISY consortium seeks to make books accessible for everyone by contributing to the development of open accessible standards. We thank AHEAD, especially its Executive Director, Stephen Hamlin-Smith, for using its technical expertise to help make this special edition possible.

PREFACE

Few American institutions are more important than its colleges and universities. They help prepare our current and future citizens to participate in our democracy. They produce the research that keeps America the worlds' technological leader. Post-secondary institutions, at all levels, offer their participants the best chance in their lives for upward mobility, economic security, self-sufficiency and independence.

No discrete group benefits more from the post-secondary experience than individuals with disabilities. A good education is a prerequisite to many areas of employment. For a job candidate with a known disability, nothing can remove the cobwebs of prejudices and stereotypes more quickly than a good GPA from a respected college or technical program. Even if higher education does not lead to conventional forms of employment, it can be the most affirming and rewarding experience in an individual's life.

The United States Supreme Court has repeatedly recognized the "compelling interest" America has in maintaining diversity in its post-secondary classrooms. Ethnic and gender diversity benefits all students in the classroom and subsequently furthers diversity in the professions. This truth is no less compelling for individuals with disabilities, who can broaden the perspectives of their classmates by speaking authentically to their experiences growing up and living with disabilities. Moreover, the presence of individuals with disabilities in the classroom can spur innovation. At some institutions, provision of class-recordings, distributing PowerPoints, and exams that emphasize content over speed — once reserved for students with disabilities — are now universal practices.

Children with disabilities have the same needs as all other children to see successful individuals, like themselves, with their disabilities, employed in a wide variety of professions. The illustrative story of Bonnie Tucker, a deaf inhalation therapist (who later became a lawyer and an early co-author of this casebook), who had the unique ability to read the lips of her patients with laryngectomies, is featured in Chapter 1. Our society needs mechanics with disabilities because they are the individuals most likely to take the additional training necessary to learn how to prepare an adaptive van. We want teachers who "get" why accommodations are necessary because they benefitted from them while in elementary and secondary school as well as in college. Similarly, doctors' offices and hospitals need deaf nurses and doctors because they can often sign to deaf patients.

Nothing guarantees that government, even a democracy, will respect the interests of individuals with disabilities. Sometimes out of animus, often out of ill-informed paternalism, the United States has engaged in systemic discrimination against individuals with disabilities. As explained in Chapter 1, for many years, the law was not used to protect individuals with disabilities, but to segregate them and exclude them from effective participation in our governance. Given this history, it comes as no surprise that the moniker of the disability rights movement has been, "nothing about us without us." Access to higher education is essential to the ability of individuals with disabilities to ensure that government policy develops in a manner consistent with their interests.

Only when the number of individuals with disabilities who had earned college degrees achieved a critical mass were these individuals able to build upon the race, national origin and gender civil rights lessons of the recent past (lessons many of them had learned first-hand as participants in those movements) to organize and speak for themselves. It is not an exaggeration to say that the modern American disability rights revolution had at its heart a group of discontented UC Berkeley graduate students with disabilities. These individuals, whose story is mentioned in Chapter One, had no intention of living out their futures isolated, at the margins of American society. We watch with anticipation as more individuals with disabilities, including wounded warriors, directly enter the political process no longer just as protesters, but as political office holders and high-level policymakers. Individuals with disabilities in America have come a long way; they have a long way to go.

The law can achieve little, and advance no further, without its application in an insightful, knowledgeable and authoritative manner. The objective of this publication is to provide to all those persons who are responsible for implementing federal disability, anti-discrimination laws on our campuses, the support and guidance necessary to achieving these goals.

In 2013, LexisNexis published Colker and Grossman, ***The Law of Disability Discrimination, Eighth Edition*** (ISBN 978-0-7698-8201-7). This edition is a "remix" of that popular law school textbook, updated in several important respects, and refocused to address more specifically the needs of the many individuals who are responsible for disability equality in higher education: disabled student services directors, ADA officers, house and contract counsel, human resource directors, college grievances officers, ombudspersons, federal and state compliance agents, organizational advocates, health and counseling service personnel, deans and faculty, etc.

The unemployment rate for individuals with disabilities is several times that of nondisabled individuals. According to the United States Department of Labor, as of May 2014, the labor force participation of people with disabilities is 19.5% as compared to 68.7% for people without disabilities. Students of disability law and those responsible for its implementation are now watching with much interest to see whether the scale of this inequity will diminish in light of the Americans with Disabilities Act Amendments Act of 2008 (ADAAA). As discussed at some length in Chapter Two, the demanding definition of disability that has so long made it nearly impossible for individuals with disabilities to bring suits that addressed the merits of their claims is no longer the law. More recent employment decisions, reported in Chapter Three, are now focusing on the contours of what are essential job functions and effective job accommodations. Similarly, post-secondary decisions, as discussed in Chapter Four, are getting beyond the question of disability, and addressing how to determine if a student is "otherwise qualified," and which academic adjustments and auxiliary aids must be provided to such students as necessary, effective, and neither a fundamental alteration nor an undue burden.

The authors of this textbook recognize the importance and complexity of your mission. We sincerely hope this text will make your position more effective and your career more rewarding.

A DAISY-accessible version of this casebook will be made available upon request to individuals with disabilities.

Ruth Colker
Paul Grossman
June 2014

SUMMARY TABLE OF CONTENTS

TABLE OF CONTENTS

Chapter 3 EMPLOYMENT DISCRIMINATION

Chapter 1

OVERVIEW OF THE LAW OF DISABILITY DISCRIMINATION

The American legal system has not always been a viable tool for challenging discrimination. In fact, until the twentieth century our legal system was more likely to be used to legitimize discrimination than to prevent it. In more modern times, successive groups of individuals have turned the law into a device for their protection from discrimination and their inclusion in our common shared society. At the moment, the most advanced and tailored set of protections arguably pertains to individuals with disabilities. This book is about those laws, who they cover, what they provide, and their limitations.

A. HISTORICAL DISCRIMINATION AGAINST INDIVIDUALS WITH DISABILITIES

To understand how far the law has come, one need only consider the example of how, for many years, court decisions reflected the worst forms of animus, stereotypes, and fears concerning persons with psychiatric and intellectual disabilities, resulting in state sponsored segregation, institutionalization and worse with little or no due process. Two themes predominate in these cases: (i) eugenics measures to control reproduction; and (ii) forced institutionalization (even over the objections of parents).

Eugenics refers to a social movement intended to improve the qualities of individuals born in society. Literally, "eugenics" means "well born." Sir Francis Galton first coined the term in 1883 in his work INQUIRIES INTO HUMAN FACULTY AND ITS DEVELOPMENT. By the early twentieth century, the eugenics movement began what has been called "the hunt for the feebleminded," which arose from the conviction that "mental deficiency" was the cause of most social problems. As one commentator explained: "The eugenic and social alarms did not fall on deaf ears. The nation was aroused. The hunt for the feebleminded began. The more thoroughly the mental defective was searched for and found, the more completely was he apparently involved in all manner of offences against the social order." *See* STANLEY POWELL DAVIES, SOCIAL CONTROL OF THE MENTALLY DEFICIENT 76 (1930).

The eugenics measures and the institutionalization measures that developed in the early twentieth century emerged from a similar social concern. Many people believed that "feeble-minded" individuals should be prevented from reproducing and should be institutionalized because they posed dangers to society. Until recently, classification as "feeble-minded," could be a justification for forced sterilization. *See* Miss. Code Ann. § 99-13-1 (1999). Thirty thousand lobotomies were performed in the United States in 1936. The last state eugenics laws were repealed in 1968. Nazi Germany used Virginia's eugenic law as a model for its eugenics laws.

Another mechanism sometimes used to deal with people categorized as "feeble minded" was institutionalization. One rationale for institutionalization was avoiding sexual relations, especially for women. For example, in *In re Masters*, 13 N.W.2d 487 (Minn. 1944), the Minnesota Supreme Court was faced with a case in which a "feeble-minded" woman was committed to a state institution (called a "school") after she and her husband bore 10 "apparently normal" children. Because the "housekeeping was very poor," the family was broken up. Five of the children were sent to an orphanage, three were placed in county boarding facilities, and two eventually entered the Army. The mother was committed to the "School for Feeble-Minded"; the record is silent as to what happened to the father, who is also described as "feeble-minded." The court was careful to note that the mother was not institutionalized as punishment for having had 10 children, but only because of her "neglect of them after they arrived." *In re Masters*, 13 N.W.2d at 489. The Minnesota court did grant a new trial in the case due to some due process problems; however, the plaintiff had already spent two years in the state institution before the new trial was granted.

In cases involving forced institutionalization of men or boys, the focus is typically on their "danger" to society rather than their sexual relations. For example, in *Ex parte Ziegler*, 15 N.W.2d 34 (Wis. 1944), parents sought a writ of habeas corpus to have their son Carl released from Southern Wisconsin Colony and Training School. In denying the writ, the court noted Carl's need for commitment for the "protection of society." In support of that conclusion, the court noted that the mother admitted that the boy (who had epilepsy) "had stolen stamps from a dime store; had violated a bicycle ordinance; attempted to take a purse from a small boy; started a fire in a lavatory of a theater. Probation reports before the court showed Carl had set a fire on railroad property." *Id.* at 36. For such transgressions, children could lawfully be taken from their parents and institutionalized for life.

Although the institutions at which these children were kept were often labeled "schools," they were, in practice, often not at all educational. A New York court described one such "school" as follows:

> [Plaintiff] was put to work as though he were in a penal institution. Instead of going to school as the name of the institution would imply, he was assigned to the service building where he remained daily from 6:30 o'clock in the morning until 7 in the evening, working most of the time with only half-hour interruptions for his meals and perhaps some brief recreation periods for reading and playing cards.

Shattuck v. State, 2 N.Y.S.2d 353 (Ct. Cl.), *aff'd*, 5 N.Y.S.2d 812 (App. Div. 1938).

Two leading constitutional cases involved people who were considered "feeble-minded." In the first case, *Buck v. Bell*, 274 U.S. 200 (1927), the Supreme Court considered the constitutionality of a state statute providing that if the superintendent of certain institutions determined "that it is for the best interests of the patients and of society that an inmate under his care should be sexually sterilized, he may have the operation performed upon any patient afflicted with hereditary forms of insanity [or] imbecility." Plaintiff Carrie Buck lived at the State Colony for Epileptics and Feeble

Minded. In the Court's words, she was "the daughter of a feeble minded mother in the same institution, and the mother of an illegitimate feeble minded child." *Id.* at 205. At 18 years of age, Buck was about to be subjected to compulsory sterilization. She challenged the state statute as violating her right to both procedural and substantive due process. The Supreme Court, in an 8-1 decision authored by Justice Holmes, held that the statute was constitutional. In a well-known phrase, Justice Holmes upheld the forced sterilization, saying: "Three generations of imbeciles are enough." *Id.* at 207.

Buck v. Bell has never been explicitly overturned. The Supreme Court cited the decision with approval in *Roe v. Wade*, 410 U.S. 113, 154 (1973), although the statute at issue in *Buck* was repealed in Virginia in 1974. Litigation involving involuntary sterilization continues. *See, e.g., Poe v. Lynchburg Training School and Hospital*, 518 F. Supp. 789 (W.D. Va. 1981). Nonetheless, some states, as a matter of common law, have concluded that guardians and parents cannot consent to the sterilization of a ward in their care or custody without obtaining a judicial order. *See, e.g., In re Moe*, 432 N.E.2d 712 (Mass. 1982); *In re Terwilliger*, 450 A.2d 1376 (Pa. Super. Ct. 1982).

A second leading case was *City of Cleburne v. Cleburne Living Center*, 473 U.S. 432 (1985). In this case, a group home was denied a special use permit. Such permits were required for "hospitals for the insane or feeble-minded." When the group home's application for a special use permit was denied, it filed suit in federal court arguing that the zoning ordinance discriminated against the "mentally retarded" in violation of the Equal Protection Clause of the Fourteenth Amendment. The group home lost its case in the district court but won on appeal, with the Fifth Circuit concluding that mental retardation was a quasi-suspect class and that it should assess the validity of the zoning ordinance under intermediate-level scrutiny. The Supreme Court affirmed the holding of the Fifth Circuit that the zoning ordinance was unconstitutional but also determined that the mentally retarded should not benefit from heightened scrutiny.

The Supreme Court offered three reasons for denying heightened scrutiny to what it called "the mentally retarded." First, it concluded that the mentally retarded are genuinely different from others so that "how this large and diversified group is to be treated under the law is a difficult and often technical matter, very much a task for legislators guided by qualified professionals and not by the perhaps ill-informed opinions of the judiciary." *Id.* at 442. Second, it found that lawmakers have begun to address problems faced by those with mental retardation and was concerned that some of those laws might face legal challenges if heightened scrutiny were used to assess their constitutionality. "Especially given the wide variation in the abilities and needs of the retarded themselves governmental bodies must have a certain amount of flexibility and freedom from judicial oversight in shaping and limiting their remedial efforts." *Id.* at 445. Finally, the legislative response "negates any claim that the mentally retarded are politically powerless in the sense that they have no ability to attract the attention of the lawmakers." *Id.* at 445.

Although the Supreme Court used "rational basis" scrutiny to evaluate the constitutionality of the city zoning ordinance, it struck it down as unconstitutional because it found the ordinance was based "on an irrational prejudice against the mentally retarded." *Id.* at 451.

In one of his most eloquent opinions, Justice Marshall dissented from the view that discrimination against individuals with intellectual disability should not be subject to heightened scrutiny. His dissent provides a very different summary of the history of the treatment of individuals with disabilities than the one provided by the majority:

> [T]he mentally retarded have been subject to a "lengthy and tragic history," of segregation and discrimination that can only be called grotesque. During much of the 19th century, mental retardation was viewed as neither curable nor dangerous and the retarded were largely left to their own devices. By the latter part of the century and during the first decades of the new one, however, social views of the retarded underwent a radical transformation. Fueled by the rising tide of Social Darwinism, the "science" of eugenics, and the extreme xenophobia of those years, leading medical authorities and others began to portray the "feeble-minded" as a "menace to society and civilization . . . responsible in a large degree for many, if not all, of our social problems." A regime of state-mandated segregation and degradation soon emerged that in its virulence and bigotry rivaled, and indeed paralleled, the worst excesses of Jim Crow. Massive custodial institutions were built to warehouse the retarded for life; the aim was to halt reproduction of the retarded and "nearly extinguish their race." Retarded children were categorically excluded from public schools, based on the false stereotype that all were ineducable and on the purported need to protect nonretarded children from them. State laws deemed the retarded "unfit for citizenship."

Id. at 462–63.

The *City of Cleburne* decision was also important in drawing national attention to the housing problems often faced by individuals with disabilities and helped provide the impetus for the passage of the Fair Housing Amendments of 1988, as we will see below. The *City of Cleburne* decision is also important as recognizing the principle that discrimination against individuals with disabilities is only subject to rational basis rather than strict scrutiny. That ruling, in turn, limits the scope of Congress' authority to prohibit disability discrimination under Section 5 of the Fourteenth Amendment.

NOTES AND PROBLEMS FOR DISCUSSION

1. What are the implications of mere rational basis scrutiny for individuals with disabilities? Do you think that a policy of a state employer that it will not provide individuals with disabilities with costly reasonable accommodations would survive scrutiny under a rational basis standard?

2. Which recounting of the history of individuals with intellectual disabilities do you think is most accurate — that of the majority or that of Justice Marshall?

B. EARLY CIVIL RIGHTS PROTECTION

The protections afforded individuals with disabilities under the Americans with Disabilities Act of 1990 (ADA), as amended (ADAAA), Section 504 of the Rehabilitation Act of 1973 (Section 504) and the Fair Housing Act Amendments of 1988 (FHA) currently represent the furthest advances in our understanding of what inclusion and equal treatment mean for this group. This book is about these laws. The insights into the nature of discrimination and how to prevent it for individuals with disabilities, reflected in these three laws, would not be here for us to study if prior civil rights advances and laws did not exist with regard to race, gender, and national origin.

Since the time of the Civil War, the United States has adopted Constitutional Amendments, statutes, regulations, and Executive Orders to protect discrete groups of individuals (people of color, women, older persons, individuals with disabilities, and gay men and lesbians) from discrimination. The path to these legal protections has been the result of considerable political and legal struggle. Each new civil rights movement and responsive law has built on the principles established by predecessor movements and laws. Consequently, these legal protections carry some themes that are consistent, such as protecting people from biases based on negative stereotypes and myths. Nonetheless, over time, differences in the forms of protection afforded these discrete groups have developed, as well. Each new form of protection has had to take into account what are the new and unique needs of the group under consideration, as well as the political reality of what legal protections the government is willing to put in place.

For African Americans, one of the first important legal advances was the abolition of slavery through the ratification of the Thirteenth Amendment in 1865. The ratification of the Fourteenth Amendment in 1868 introduced the term "equal protection" into the Constitution and the ratification of the Fifteenth Amendment in 1870 made it unconstitutional to deny the right to vote on the basis of race, color or previous condition of servitude. With the ratification of the Nineteenth Amendment in 1920, it became unconstitutional to deny women the right to vote. It was not until the 1950s that the federal courts began to enforce the principle of racial nondiscrimination vigorously by concluding that the concept of nondiscrimination requires the absence of state-sponsored segregation. *See Sweatt v. Painter*, 339 U.S. 629 (1950) (law school); *Brown v. Board of Education*, 347 U.S. 483 (1954) (public, elementary and secondary schools).

In the 1950s and 1960s, civil rights organizations sought to build on these new judicial precedents by seeking broad federal statutory protection. They proposed and supported the Civil Rights Act of 1964 ("CRA"). Title VII of the CRA greatly expanded the concept of nondiscrimination to cover race, color, religion, sex, and national origin in the employment context. Title II of the CRA banned discrimination on the basis of race, color, religion or national origin at places of public accommodation, and Title VI of the CRA banned discrimination on the basis of race, color and national origin at entities receiving federal financial assistance, such as public elementary and secondary schools and most colleges and universities. In 1965, the Voting Rights Act was enacted; it prohibited states from imposing voting rules that deny or abridge the right to vote on account of race or color. In 1968, the Fair Housing Act ("FHA") became law; it prohibited discrimination in the sale, rental and financing of dwellings based on race, color, religion, sex and national origin. (Congress amended the FHA in 1988 to prohibit discrimination on the basis of disability and familial status.) In 1972, Title IX of the Education Amendments made it unlawful for educational entities that received federal financial assistance to engage in sex discrimination. These laws also made it easier for individuals and the United States to address discrimination through actions in the Federal courts.

Two advances in the definition of "equal treatment" important to individuals with disabilities are associated with Title VII. The first is that similarly-situated or similarly-qualified individuals ought to be treated in the same manner (e.g., hired, promoted, or fired) irrespective of race, color, national origin, sex, or religion. *McDonnell Douglas v. Green*, 414 U.S. 811 (1973).

The second principle, affirmed by the Supreme Court in *Griggs v. Duke Power Company*, 401 U.S. 424 (1971), was that identical treatment, in some instances, would not constitute equal treatment. In *Griggs*, the Supreme Court concluded that the consistent application to African American and white job applicants of facially-neutral selection criteria, even absent an intent to discriminate, could violate Title VII of the CRA due to its disparate impact against African Americans. In adopting the principle that the consistent application of neutral criteria is not deemed inherently sufficient to satisfy Title VII, Chief Justice Burger, writing for a unanimous Court, articulated the test that has become a central doctrine to the employment discrimination law: "The Act proscribes not only overt discrimination but also practices that are fair in form, but discriminatory in operation. [G]ood intent or absence of discriminatory intent does not redeem employment procedures or testing mechanisms that operate as 'built-in headwinds' for minority groups and are unrelated to measuring job capability." *Griggs*, 401 U.S. at 432. Although it is highly unlikely that Justice Burger had persons with disabilities in mind when he wrote those words, that concept will become basic to the concept of equal treatment under disability law.

The legal treatment of students who are non-English speakers under the Civil Rights laws is also worth examining closely because it will eventually set the stage for the development of the concept of "reasonable accommodation" under disability law. Coming after *Griggs*, it is the last step in the development of pre-disability law concepts of equal treatment.

In 1970, the U.S. Department of Health, Education and Welfare (HEW), at the urging of its San Francisco Office, issued "the May 25th Memorandum," interpretative guidance for public elementary and secondary schools with regard to non-English speaking language (national origin) minority children. 35 Fed. Reg. 11,595. This guidance posited that schools violated Title VI if they provided non-English speaking language-minority (national origin) groups with merely the same services as their nonminority, English-speaking peers. Schools needed to offer special programs, such as classes that teach the acquisition of English language or a combination of these classes and bilingual education, to their non-English speaking population.

The validity of OCR's May 25th Memorandum was directly tested in *Lau v. Nichols*, 414 U.S. 563 (1974). *Lau* concerned 1800 students of Chinese ancestry in the San Francisco Unified School District (SFUSD) who did not speak English and who received no supplemental services to enable them to acquire English language skills. Both the District Court and the 9th Circuit concurred with the position of the SFUSD that as it was providing these children the same services as all other children in the District, SFUSD was not violating the rights of such children under the Fourteenth Amendment or Title VI. The Supreme Court, in a set of concurring opinions, declined to reach the Fourteenth Amendment question, but concluded that the Department's Title VI regulation and interpretations with regard to non-English speaking children were valid and that the SFUSD was not in compliance with these requirements. Justice Douglas delivered the opinion of the Court, writing in pertinent part:

> Under these state-imposed [compulsory education] standards there is no equality of treatment merely by providing students with the same facilities, textbooks, teachers, and curriculum; for students who do not understand English are effectively foreclosed from any meaningful education.
>
> Basic English skills are at the very core of what these public schools teach. Imposition of a requirement that, before a child can effectively participate in the educational program, he must already have acquired those basic skills is to make a mockery of public education. We know that those who do not understand English are certain to find their classroom experiences wholly incomprehensible and in no way meaningful.

Lau, 414 U.S. at 566.

He concluded: "It seems obvious that the Chinese-speaking minority receive fewer benefits than the English-speaking majority from respondents' school system which denies them a meaningful opportunity to participate in the educational program — all earmarks of the discrimination banned by the regulations." *Id.* at 568. *Lau* provided the basis for the affirmative concept of reasonable accommodation that was eventually developed under the disability law. But for historic advances under Title VI of the CRA, disability law's most important conceptual breakthrough would not exist.

C. EVOLUTION OF DISABILITY RIGHTS PROTECTION

The first significant statute enacted to provide greater public access to individuals with disabilities was the Architectural Barriers Act of 1968. Hugh Gregory Gallagher, who was a legislative assistant, drafted this statute to require that all buildings constructed, altered, or financed by the federal government be physically accessible. He was instrumental in making the Library of Congress and other buildings in Washington accessible (but not the United States Capitol).

In 1972, Senator Hubert H. Humphrey proposed an amendment to the Civil Rights Act of 1964 that would have added "disability" as a protected class; this proposal had limited support. Some of his concern for this issue grew out of his personal experience of having a grandchild with Down Syndrome.

Despite Humphrey's inability to persuade Congress to amend the Civil Rights Act of 1964, legislation to benefit individuals with disabilities was enacted in 1972 as part of Section 504 of the Rehabilitation Act. *See* 29 U.S.C. §§ 791–797. Passage of the Rehabilitation Act was highly contentious because the Nixon administration thought it was a waste of money. Nixon provided a "pocket veto" of the bill by refusing to sign it into law while Congress was out of session. Congress passed the law again in 1973 and President Nixon vetoed it again, because of the costs of the bill. Once again, Congress passed the bill, but this time with less financial support for independent living facilities. This time, Nixon signed the bill into law. During all these deliberations, however,

Section 504's nondiscrimination provision was never mentioned.

Section 501 required federal agencies to develop affirmative action programs for the hiring, placement, and advancement of individuals with disabilities. Like Section 501, Section 503 required parties who were contracting with the United States to use affirmative action to employ qualified individuals with disabilities. Section 502 established the Architectural and Transportation Barriers Compliance Board, which had authority to enforce the Architectural Barriers Act of 1968. Finally, Section 504 prohibited discrimination on the basis of disability in any program or activity receiving federal financial assistance. Although Section 504 has ultimately been an extremely important provision for the disability community, it was not introduced upon the request of the disability community. It was quietly added to the legislation at the end of the legislative session and was never mentioned in any committee or on the floor of Congress.

Political activism, however, was necessary for Section 504 to be enforced. Although Congress enacted Section 504 into law in 1973 and the United States Department of Health, Education and Welfare ("HEW") drafted implementing regulations within a year of adoption, they were not issued under Presidents Nixon or Ford. In 1976, the federal district court for the District of Columbia ordered HEW to issue the regulations, but the district court failed to provide a specific date for their issuance. *Cherry v. Secretary Mathews*, 419 F. Supp. 922 (D.C.D.C. 1976). HEW shared draft regulations with Congress, an unprecedented step, and Congress formed advisory committees, without a member from the disability community, but HEW issued no regulations.

Regulations were needed to define crucial concepts like the definition of disability and scope of reasonable accommodation requirements. Without regulations to guide them, courts issued inconsistent decisions. Jimmy Carter, while campaigning for President, made a commitment to disability leaders to issue the regulations but his Secretary of HEW, Joseph Califano, failed to issue them. Moreover, disability advocates feared that the regulations that Secretary Califano might issue would be very watered down.

On April 5, 1977 the American Coalition of Citizens with Disabilities, the Emergency 504 Coalition, and other organizations began demonstrations at each of HEW's regional offices. Most of these demonstrations did not persist for very long. Nonetheless, a wide range of students with disabilities, some with experience in early civil rights movements and many attending the University of California at Berkeley, engaged in a 28-day occupation of the HEW offices in the Old Federal Building at 50 United Nations Plaza.[1]

Some medically fragile students risked their lives to remain in the occupied building. This event, attended at times by up to 150 persons, garnered significant local and national press coverage and community support including the Mayor of San Francisco, labor organizations, churches, and the black and gray panthers. Civil rights

---

[1] To learn more about these protests, see *The Power of 504: Parts I and II* (available at http://www.youtube.com/watch?v=HMC5UuiIQkI; http://www.youtube.com/watch?v=5vOM0-IOrKg) (DREDF videos) (produced by The Section 504 Sit-in 20th Anniversary Committee) (last viewed on Apr. 6, 2013).

leader Julian Bond visited the protest. Congressman Philip Burton held a Congressional hearing in the building with powerful testimony by many individuals who would later be recognized as historic disability rights leaders such as Judy Heumann and Ed Roberts.

After about two weeks, a group of leaders decided to head for Washington, D.C. Several of these individuals needed the assistance of a van with a lift to get on board otherwise inaccessible planes.

The tactics of the demonstrators in Washington were persistent and aggressive. They followed Jimmy Carter and Secretary Califano wherever they were speaking. News cameras rolling, they crawled up the steps of the inaccessible United States Capitol. Singing songs like "we shall overcome," they demonstrated outside of Carter's church and Califano's home. They met with several influential politicians, including most importantly, the Senator from California, Alan Cranston, who ultimately became one of the most influential supporters of strong Section 504 regulations.

On April 28th, ten days after the protestors had arrived in Washington, Secretary Califano endorsed the regulations and announced his intention to publish them. Building on the tactics of prior civil rights movements, the protesters had won.

The 1977 sit-ins were an important turning point for the disability rights community in the United States. It learned that visibility and activism could lead to important results.

Three years after the Section 504 regulations were issued, they received their first test in the Supreme Court in *Southeastern Community College v. Davis*, 442 U.S. 397 (1979). This case, which is excerpted in Chapter Four, Part [B][1], concerned Francis Davis, a licensed practical nurse (LPN), with "bilateral, sensori-neural hearing loss" who sought admission into a registered nursing (RN) program at Southeastern Community College in North Carolina. Even with a hearing aid, to communicate effectively with others, Davis had to rely on her lipreading skills, looking directly at whomever was speaking with her. She could not, for example, understand individuals, such as doctors in the surgical theater, who must wear surgical masks. After interviewing Davis, and consulting others, the college denied her admission on the ground that she could not safely perform some essential aspects of an RN. Davis alleged this exclusion violated Section 504.

The ultimate question in *Southeastern* was whether Davis was an "otherwise qualified individual with a disability" with regard to admission to the RN program. In exploring this question, the Court was presented with two quite different views on the scope of the protections provided under Section 504, in part, owing to the fact that the regulations implementing Section 504 came out between the time the matter was heard in the district court and the court of appeals. In the view of the district court, only those individuals with disabilities who could meet the admissions requirements of a college, *in spite of* his or her disability, were protected from disability discrimination. This interpretation of Section 504 would have protected individuals with disabilities from purposeful bias and stereotype based discrimination, but not much more. According to the appellate court, in light of administrative regulations that had been promulgated while the appeal was pending, Section 504 required Southeastern to "reconsider plaintiff's application for admission to the nursing program *without regard to her hearing ability*." This interpretation of Section 504 would have excused individuals with disabilities from having to meet many requirements that colleges considered essential. Finding for the College, Justice Powell concluded on behalf of the Court that "an otherwise qualified person is one who is able to meet all of a program's requirements in spite of his handicap." *Southeastern Community College*, 442 U.S. at 406. The Court also emphasized "Section 504 imposes no requirement upon an educational institution to lower or to effect substantial modifications of standards to accommodate a handicapped person." *Id.* at 413.

Further, the Court laid out two important principles that remain a central part of disability law. First, the Court emphasized that qualification standards that result in a denial of participation by an individual with a disability must be "necessary" or "essential." Second, the Court asked whether there is any "affirmative action" (modification, accommodations, or auxiliary aids) that the College is required by Section 504 to undertake that would enable Davis to meet these necessary requirements and become an individual with a disability otherwise qualified for admission to the RN program. Thus, although the plaintiff lost in *Southeastern*, the Supreme Court set the stage for the development of the "reasonable accommodation" doctrine that would prove to be central to the law of disability discrimination.

In addition to Section 504, other statutes preceding the ADA include the Developmental Disabilities Bill of Rights Act of 1975, as amended, 42 U.S.C. §§ 6000–6083 (1994); the Air Carrier Access Act of 1986, 49 U.S.C. § 41705 (1994) and the Voting Accessibility for the Elderly and Handicapped Act of 1984, 42 U.S.C. § 1973ee (1994).

Other than Section 504, the strongest early legislation to protect people with disabilities existed in the area of education, under the Individuals with Disabilities Education Act (IDEA), 20 U.S.C. §§ 1401–1485 (formerly known as the Education of All Handicapped Children Act). The IDEA is a process-oriented civil rights statute that guarantees that each child with disabilities will have an "individualized education program" ("IEP") so that he or she can receive a "free appropriate public education." Although not strictly an anti-discrimination statute, the IDEA was enacted in 1975 to help end the historical practice of excluding students with disabilities from school or teaching them in segregated sub-standard environments. It also sought to provide students with disabilities improved access to education.

Adverse decisions by the United States Supreme Court made it difficult to enforce some of the rights created by some of these statutes. *See, e.g.*, *Pennhurst State School & Hospital v. Halderman*, 451 U.S. 1 (1981) (no private right of action to enforce the "Bill of Rights" contained in the Developmental Disabilities Bill of Rights Act); *United States Department of Transportation v. Paralyzed Veterans of America*, 477 U.S. 597 (1986) (ruling that air carriers were not covered by Section 504). Nonetheless, the Rehabilitation Act of 1973 served as an important model for the ADA when it was enacted in 1990.

Before the passage of the Fair Housing Amendments in 1988 and ADA in 1990, there were also some important victories for the disability rights movement. One of the most important cases was *School Board of Nassau County v. Arline*, 480 U.S. 273 (1987), a case involving a school teacher who was fired after she had a relapse of tuberculosis. In this case, which will be discussed more extensively in Chapter Two, the Court found that Arline was covered by Section 504 and stated "that society's accumulated myths and fears about disability and disease are as handicapping as are the physical limitations that flow from actual impairments." *Id.* at 284.

Until 1988, nearly all the laws that prohibited disability discrimination did not cover the private sector unless the private entity accepted federal financial assistance. That fact changed in 1988 when Congress amended the Fair Housing Act to prohibit discrimination in the sale or rental of housing on the basis of disability. This amendment reflected the first time that the disability community worked with the broader civil rights community to enact legislation.

With the 1988 success in amending the Fair Housing Act, the disability community decided to seek comprehensive nondiscrimination protection in many sectors of life. It was influenced, in part, by a 1986 Louis Harris poll that provided insight into the challenges faced by individuals with disabilities. *See* http://www.harrisinteractive.com/Insights/HarrisVault.aspx (Harris surveys).

Among the findings:

- While 13% of America, as a whole, failed to finish high school, the comparable figure for individuals with disabilities was 40%.
- While 15% of American households had incomes of less than $15,000, 50% of households headed by individuals with disabilities had incomes of less than $15,000.
- 66% of individuals with disabilities between 16 & 64 years of age reported being unemployed.
- As a measure of inclusion in mainstream American social life, the poll revealed that 58% of Americans go to a restaurant at least once a week, the comparable figure for individuals with disabilities was 34%.

Looking at these and other statistics, former President George H.W. Bush noted that "disabled people are the poorest, least educated and largest minority in America."[2]

A bipartisan Congress passed the ADA with support from President George H.W. Bush. Ironically, an important jumpstart for bipartisan support came from insensitive remarks by President Ronald Reagan. During the Bush-Dukakis presidential campaign in August 1988, rumors began to circulate that Governor Michael Dukakis had undergone psychiatric treatment during two stressful periods in his life. A reporter for a publication, the *Executive Intelligence Review*, asked President Reagan at a press

---

[2] S. Rep. No. 101-116, at 9 (1989). According to the 2000 census, there are 49.7 million Americans (19%) age 5 and over in the civilian, noninstitutionalized population with at least one disability. These individuals fit in at least one of the following categories: they are (1) 5 years old or older and have a sensory, physical, mental, or self-care disability; (2) 16 years old or older and have difficulty going outside the home; or (3) 16-to-64 years old and have an employment disability. *See* http://www.census.gov/prod/2003pubs/c2kbr-17.pdf (last viewed on June 26, 2013). According to the 2010 census, those numbers increased to 56.7 million Americans (18.7 % of the population). *See* http://www.census.gov/prod/2012pubs/p70-131.pdf (last viewed on June 26, 2013).

conference what he thought about Dukakis' refusal to give the public access to his medical records. President Reagan responded: "Look, I'm not going to pick on an invalid." Reagan later said he had "attempted a joke" but "it didn't work."

While initially refusing to be drawn into the controversy, Vice-President Bush responded on August 11, 1988, by urging Congress to enact the Americans with Disabilities Act. Following his inauguration as President, Bush instructed Attorney General Richard Thornburgh to work with Congress to pass major disability discrimination legislation.[3]

Thirteen Reagan appointees who sat on the National Council on the Handicapped in 1988 proposed the first version of the ADA, which Vice-President Bush supported in principle. This first version was largely ignored before the Reagan episode and was far more sweeping in scope than the ultimately adopted bill. In the early days of the Bush administration, the 1988 bill was cut back to make it more acceptable to the business community. Some disabilities rights advocates worried that proponents of the ADA gave away too much during compromise negotiations, but the compromise bill eventually became law in the summer of 1990, creating the first legislation of its kind on the federal level.

Over time, the disability rights community became quite disappointed with the Supreme Court's interpretation of the ADA and sought to have it amended. On June 22, 1999, the Supreme Court decided three cases — *Sutton v. United Air Lines, Inc.*, 527 U.S. 471 (1999); *Murphy v. United Parcel Service, Inc.*, 527 U.S. 516 (1999); and *Albertson's, Inc. v. Kirkingburg*, 527 U.S. 555 (1999) — which resulted in pro-defendant interpretations of the statute. These pro-defendant decisions were followed on June 8, 2002 by the Court's decision in *Toyota Motor Manufacturing v. Williams*, 534 U.S. 184 (2002).

It was not until 2006 that the disability rights community was able to obtain some action from Congress to overturn these decisions. On September 29, 2006, Representatives James F. Sensenbrenner (R-WI), Steny H. Hoyer (D-MD), and John Conyers (D-MI) introduced H.R. 6258, the "Americans with Disabilities Act Restoration Act of 2006," modelled on a prior law that had been used to restore Title VI of the CRA and Title IX of the Education Amendments of 1972.

As the passage of the ADA in 1990 can be considered the result, in part, of the personal commitment to this issue by Attorney General Dick Thornburgh, who has a son who is disabled, passage of the ADA Amendment Act ("ADAAA") in 2008 can be considered the result, in part, of the personal commitment to this issue by Cheryl Sensenbrenner, the wife of Representative James Sensenbrenner. Cheryl Sensenbrenner has a sister, Tara, who was born with Down Syndrome. So, Cheryl Sensenbrenner had exposure to disability-related issues from a young age. At age 22, Cheryl Sensenbrenner was involved in a serious car accident. She was thrown from the car and suffered a spinal cord injury that paralyzed her lower extremities. She often uses a wheelchair and has been a longtime advocate for individuals with disabilities. In 2003, she joined the board of the American Association of People with Disabilities ("AAPD")

---

[3] For further discussion of the ADA's legislative history, see RUTH COLKER, THE DISABILITY PENDULUM: THE FIRST DECADE OF THE AMERICANS WITH DISABILITIES ACT (2005).

and became an active advocate for the disability community. When Congress was considering amendments to the ADA, she was the chairperson of the AAPD and one of its most tireless advocates. Because bipartisan support was necessary for these amendments to be enacted into law, the strong support by Cheryl and James Sensenbrenner, who are Republicans, was vital to its passage.

The proposed ADA Restoration Act sought to restore Congress' original intentions in passing the ADA in 1990. At hearings held on October 4, 2007, Majority Leader Hoyer testified that Congress had never anticipated or intended that the courts would interpret the definition of disability so restrictively. Hoyer stated:

> [W]e could not have fathomed that people with diabetes, epilepsy, heart conditions, cancer, mental illnesses and other disabilities would have their ADA claims denied because they would be considered too functional to meet the definition of disabled. Nor could we have fathomed a situation where the individual may be considered too disabled by an employer to get a job, but not disabled enough by the courts to be protected by the ADA from discrimination. What a contradictory position that would have been for Congress to take.[4]

Cheryl Sensenbrenner was able to offer personal testimony of negative attitudes about disability in our society. At the October 4th hearings, she testified:

> I remember once waiting for my father, then Attorney General of Wisconsin, in the lobby of a bank while he conducted some business, and I remember a bank executive staring at me and stating coldly, "People like that belong on park benches out front and not in our lobby."[5]

Cheryl Sensenbrenner was also able to generalize from her experiences to those of many others. She testified that when individuals sought redress through the court system, after being victims of discrimination that "more than 90% of the time, the courts will side with the employers rather than the individuals who faced discrimination."[6] She and others were able to persuade Congress that the courts had not honored the original intentions of the 1990 Act and that a broad-based amendment was needed to restore that original intent.

Congress began the calendar year in 2008 with a broad-reaching version of the ADA Restoration Act that would have radically redefined the term "disability" not to require an individual to have a "substantial limitation of a major life activity" to be considered disabled and protected by the statute. Negotiations occurred for four months between the United States Chamber of Commerce and other employer representatives and disability right activists in Congress. The result was a compromise bill, entitled the

---

[4] *ADA Restoration Act of 2007: Hearing on H.R. 3195 Before the Subcomm. on the Constitution, Civil Rights, and Civil Liberties of the H. Comm. on the Judiciary*, 110th Cong. 18 (2007) (oral statement of Major Leader Hoyer) (as quoted in House Judiciary Committee Report 110-730, pt. 2 — to accompany H.R. 3195 (June 23, 2008)).

[5] Testimony of Cheryl Sensenbrenner, Hearing on H.R. 3195, U.S. House of Representatives Committee on the Judiciary Subcommittee on the Constitution, Civil Rights, and Civil Liberties (Oct. 4, 2007), at 3.

[6] *Id.* at 4.

ADA Amendments Act, which sought to restore the original intentions of the ADA while also codifying a few pro-defendant rules that were important to the business community.

On July 31, 2008, Senators Tom Harkin and Orrin Hatch introduced S. 3406, the ADA Amendments Act of 2008. The Senate passed S. 3406 by voice vote on September 11, 2008. The House then cleared S. 3406 by unanimous consent and President George W. Bush signed it into law on September 25, 2008. The effective date for this overhaul of the ADA was January 1, 2009.

NOTES AND PROBLEMS FOR DISCUSSION

1. The overwhelming margin by which Congress passed the ADAAA raises interesting questions about the legislative process. If the Court's decisions were clearly inconsistent with Congress's original intent, why did it take nearly a decade for Congress to reverse those decisions through legislation? What was the precipitating factor that caused these amendments to be enacted in the fall of 2008? Some argue that the large number of returning veterans from Iraq was an impetus. Others suggest that election year politics was a factor. And others suggest that the examples of persons not covered became an affront to the will of Congress. Consider these questions as you study these amendments as part of understanding the ADA throughout this casebook.

2. The federal government currently uses the same definition of disability in the ADA, Section 504 of the Rehabilitation Act of 1973, and the Fair Housing Amendments Act of 1988. (When a change is made to one statute, Congress changes each of these statutes to be consistent.) Nonetheless, it uses a different definition of disability under the Individuals with Disabilities Education Act ("IDEA"). The IDEA definition focuses on whether an impairment has an adverse affect on educational performance. Does it make sense for different statutes to use different definitions of disability? Why or why not?

D. STATUTORY OVERVIEW

Before delving into a close examination of the ADA, it is helpful to have a broad overview of its provisions, including a description of how the ADAAA modified the statute.

The ADA begins with section 12101, entitled "Findings and Purpose." When the statute was enacted in 1990, the first finding stated that "some 43,000,000 Americans have one or more physical or mental disabilities, and this number is increasing as the population as a whole is growing older." Because the Supreme Court relied on this provision to interpret narrowly the term "individual with a disability," Congress amended that provision in 2008 to replace it with the following language: "physical or mental disabilities in no way diminish a person's right to fully participate in all aspects of society, yet many people with physical or mental disabilities have been precluded from doing so because of discrimination; others who have a record of a disability or are regarded as having a disability also have been subjected to discrimination."

In 2008, Congress also deleted paragraph (7) from the Findings and Purpose section. The language they deleted emphasized that individuals with disabilities are a "discrete and insular minority." Why would Congress consider it necessary to delete that language?

Congress also enacted a "Note" to Section 12101 in 2008 that included new Findings and Purposes. This Note (which has the force of law) emphasizes that Congress was overturning several Supreme Court cases that had narrowly interpreted the term "disability." Congress made it clear that it was "reinstating a broad scope of protection" by rejecting the Supreme Court's interpretation of the term "disability" under the ADA.

Even though the purpose of the ADAAA was to broaden the definition of disability, Congress achieved that purpose *not* by making significant changes to the basic definition of disability in the statute. The basic definition of disability (which is used for coverage throughout the entire statute) remains:

(1) a physical or mental impairment that substantially limits one or more major life activities of such individual;

(2) a record of such an impairment; or

(3) being regarded as having such an impairment.

Unlike the 1990 version, however, the statute now defines "major life activities," a subcategory called "major bodily functions," and "regarded as having such an impairment." It also has "rules of construction regarding the definition of disability." One of these rules of construction states that "the determination of whether an impairment substantially limits a major life activity shall be made without regard to the ameliorative effects of mitigating measures." The only exception to this rule is that the determination of whether someone has a visual impairment should be made *after* taking into account the ameliorate effects of ordinary eyeglasses or contact lenses.

After defining the term "disability," Congress then divided the ADA into several Titles. Each Title has a specific scope of coverage.

Title I is titled "Employment" and covers all entities that employ at least 15 persons, except the Federal Government, an Indian Tribe, or a bona fide private membership club that is exempt from federal taxation. State and local government is covered by Title I along with the private sector. The purpose of Title I is to prohibit discrimination in regard to "job application procedures, the hiring, advancement, or discharge of employees, employee compensation, job training, and other terms, conditions, and privileges of employment." 42 U.S.C. § 12112. These protections are available to a "qualified individual" which the statute defines as "an individual who, with or without reasonable accommodation, can perform the essential functions of the employment position that such individual holds or desires." 42 U.S.C. § 12111(8). In other words, an individual with a disability should be offered "reasonable accommodations" in order to perform the essential functions of the job. The defense to providing reasonable accommodations is that it would impose an "undue hardship" on the covered entity considering the cost of the accommodation and the financial resources of the covered entity. 42 U.S.C. § 12111(10). Another important defense under the statute is that the individual would pose "a direct threat to the health or safety of other individuals in the workplace." 42 U.S.C. § 12113(b).

Title II is titled "Public Services" and covers any state or local government, the National Railroad Passenger Corporation, and any commuter authority. It is modeled on Section 504 of the Rehabilitation Act and states that "no qualified individual with a disability shall, by reason of such disability, be excluded from participation in or be denied the benefits of services, programs or activities of a public entity, or be subjected to discrimination by any such entity." 42 U.S.C. § 12132. Like Title I, it defines a "qualified individual" as one who "with or without reasonable modifications to rules, policies, or practices, the removal of architectural, communication, or transportation barriers, or the provision of auxiliary aids and services, meets the essential eligibility requirements for the receipt of services or the participation in programs or activities provided by a public entity." 42 U.S.C. § 12131(2).

ADA Title II parallels the coverage already available under Section 504 of the Rehabilitation Act (which covers all entities receiving federal financial assistance). Because state and local government nearly always receives federal financial assistance for its programs and activities, few governmental entities that are covered by ADA Title II are not also covered by Section 504. Congress understood that there was broad overlap in coverage and therefore specified that the two statutes should be interpreted the same. *See* 42 U.S.C. § 12133.

The overlapping coverage between ADA Title II and Section 504 can be confusing to those who are unfamiliar with Section 504. Section 504 is a relatively brief statute that is enforced through an extensive set of regulations that have developed over the years. The statutory terms are defined in the regulations, not in the statute itself (like they are with Title I).

In addition to the relatively brief provisions banning discrimination in Part A, ADA Title II also contains a longer provision specifically on the issue of Public Transportation. Because public transportation was not previously broadly required to accommodate individuals with disabilities, these provisions are important, new material.

With respect to the accessibility rules contained in ADA Title II, there is a distinction between new construction, alterations, and structures that already existed when the ADA went into effect. These rules can be found in the regulations implementing ADA Title II. For new construction, entities should be accessible unless "a public entity can demonstrate that it is structurally impracticable to meet the requirements." 28 C.F.R. § 35.151(a)(2). "Altered" facilities are supposed to be accessible "to the maximum extent feasible." 28 C.F.R. § 35.151(b). Existing facilities are subject to a lower standard. When viewed in their entirety, programs and activities should be "accessible to and usable by individuals with disabilities" but an entity cannot be required to "fundamentally alter the service, program or activity" or incur an "undue financial and administrative burden." *See* 28 C.F.R. § 35.150.

NOTES AND PROBLEMS FOR DISCUSSION

1. Compare the definition of "qualified individual" under Title I and Title II. Notice that Title I refers to "reasonable accommodations" and Title II refers to "reasonable modifications." Title I refers to the "essential functions of the job." Title II refers to the "essential eligibility requirements." Why did Congress use different language under Title I and Title II?

2. Title I refers to "undue hardship" and Title II refers to "undue financial and administrative burden." Why do you think Congress used different language?

3. Assume that you have been hired by a major disability rights organization and asked to draft what you consider to be the ideal definition of disability under the ADA. What would be your definition of disability?

4. Assume that you have been hired by the Chamber of Commerce to propose an amendment to the ADA to narrow disability coverage. What would you recommend be the definition of disability (assuming the underlying statute is not repealed).?

5. Now assume you have been hired to reconsider the scope of coverage of entities covered by the ADA. Do you agree with the emphasis on employment, public entities and public accommodations? Are there any entities not covered by the ADA that you believe should be covered? Any covered that you think should not be covered? Professional organizations, such as the American Bar Association, are not directly covered by the ADA, but state and local prisons are covered. Does that make sense? Why or why not? Employers with fewer than 15 employees are not covered with respect to their employment policies but they are covered with respect to the accessibility of their facilities. Does that make sense? Why or why not?

6. Despite the enactment of the ADA, little progress has been made in improving the economic conditions of individuals with disabilities. The data below reflect Harris survey data from 1986, 1994 and 1998. Why do you think the ADA has not been more effective in improving the economic conditions of individuals with disabilities?

Education Survey

1986: 40% did not finish high school (norm = 13%)

1994: 25% did not finish high school (norm = 12%)

1998: 20% did not finish high school (norm = 9%)

Income Survey

1986: 50% have household incomes of less than $15,000 (norm = 15%)

1994: 59% have household incomes of less than $25,000 (norm = 37%)

Employment Survey

1986: 66% between 16 & 64 are not working.

1994: 69% between 16 & 64 are not working.

1998: 71% between 16 & 64 are not working.

Chapter 2

DEFINITION OF INDIVIDUAL WITH A DISABILITY

A. PRE-2008 DEFINITION

Individuals with "disabilities" are protected from discrimination under the ADA as well as Section 504 of the Rehabilitation Act of 1973 and the Fair Housing Act Amendments of 1988. Consequently, whether someone is such an individual is very likely the first issue addressed by any enforcement agency or judicial forum in an investigation or proceeding under these laws. If an individual cannot establish disability status, a claim of discrimination will typically not survive a motion for summary judgment by the defendant employer or entity and subsequent questions of discrimination such as bias or a failure to accommodate will not even be considered. Thus, a strong understanding of the definition of disability is crucial to the mastery of the law of disability discrimination. The definition of disability is a complex issue because the judicial, legislative, and administrative guidance used to construe the definition of disability has changed considerably over time and recently. A parallel change has also occurred with regard to how an individual documents his or her disability. In this chapter, we will explain the definition of disability, its new statutory language, along with its implementing regulations, in detail. We will also consider new guidance on the documentation of disability.

Initially, the reasoning of the Supreme Court in *School Board of Nassau County v. Arline*, 480 U.S. 273 (1987), a seminal case decided under Section 504 of the Rehabilitation Act, suggested that "disability" would not be a particularly burdensome element of proof for plaintiffs. The plaintiff in that case, Gene Arline, was discharged from her employment as a school teacher when she had a relapse of tuberculosis. In order to bring a case of unlawful discrimination under Section 504, she had to establish as a preliminary matter that she was an individual with a "disability" (or what the statute then called "handicapped"). With the AIDS epidemic in mind, the defendants had sought to argue that someone with a potentially contagious disease is not even covered by Section 504. In broad language, the Supreme Court rejected that argument. The Court said:

> Allowing discrimination based on the contagious effects of a physical impairment would be inconsistent with the basic purpose of § 504, which is to ensure that handicapped individuals are not denied jobs or other benefits because of the prejudiced attitudes or the ignorance of others . . . . Congress acknowledged that society's accumulated myths and fears about disability and disease are as handicapping as are the physical limitations that flow from actual impairment.

Arline, 480 U.S. at 284.

Similarly, in *Bragdon v. Abbott*, 524 U.S. 624 (1998), which will be discussed more significantly in this Chapter, the Court broadly interpreted the ADA to find that it covered Sidney Abbott, who had asymptomatic HIV. The Court concluded that it was sufficient to find that her HIV infection caused a significant limitation, although not utter inability, in her desire to reproduce. It stated: "When significant limitations result from the impairment, the definition is met even if the difficulties are not insurmountable." *Id.* at 641. It therefore concluded that "HIV infection, even in the so-called asymptomatic phase, is an impairment which substantially limits the major life activity of reproduction." *Id.* at 647.

Nonetheless, in four subsequent decisions, three decided at the same time, *Sutton v. United Air Lines*, 527 U.S. 471 (1999); *Murphy v. United Parcel Service*, 527 U.S. 516 (1999); *Albertson's, Inc. v. Kirkingburg*, 527 U.S. 555 (1999) ["the *Sutton* trilogy"]; and, *Toyota Motor Manufacturing v. Williams*, 534 U.S. 184 (2002), the Court made "disability" considerably more difficult to prove, to the point that the vast majority of disability discrimination claims filed in federal court failed to survive a motion for summary judgment. Although Congress would expressly reject much of the reasoning in those cases in 2008 when it amended the ADA, it is helpful to understand the narrow interpretation of the ADA crafted by the Court with that series of cases. These cases will be discussed more extensively later in this chapter.

In *Sutton*, the plaintiffs (Karen Sutton and Kimberly Hinton) were twin sisters who had uncorrected visual acuity of 20/200 in one eye and 20/400 or worse in their other eye. With the use of corrective lenses, their vision was 20/20. They sought jobs as an airline pilot and were denied employment when they could not meet the potential employer's vision standard without the assistance of corrective lenses. The Supreme Court concluded that "the ADA's coverage is restricted to only those whose impairments are not mitigated by corrective measures." *Sutton*, 527 U.S. at 487. Because their vision was corrected with lenses, they were found not to be covered by the ADA.

In *Murphy*, plaintiff Vaughn Murphy was a UPS mechanic who was dismissed from his job when his employer learned that his blood pressure was so high, measuring at 186/124, that he was not qualified for DOT health certification to drive commercial vehicles. Unlike the *Sutton* twins, he still had an impairment even after using mitigating measures (high blood pressure medication). Even so, the Supreme Court found that he was not disabled under the ADA because his physical impairment did not substantially limit him from performing any major life activities. Although UPS found him unqualified to work as a commercial mechanic, he was able to work in many other jobs that used his mechanical skills. The Court found that he was not disabled because he had "failed to show that he [was] regarded as unable to perform a class of jobs." *Murphy*, 527 U.S. at 471.

In *Albertson's*, plaintiff Hallie Kirkingburg had amblyopia, an uncorrectable condition that left him with 20/200 vision in his left eye, and thus monocular vision. He was fired from his position as a truck driver after his employer determined that he could not meet its vision standard. The Supreme Court extended the mitigating measure rule, established in *Sutton*, to include considerations of "measures undertaken, whether consciously or not, with the body's own systems." *Albertson's*, 527 U.S.

at 566. Thus, his self-learned behavior to accommodate for his monocular vision took him out of the category of being "disabled."

Finally, in *Toyota*, plaintiff Ella Williams sued Toyota under the ADA, alleging that the company had failed to provide her with a reasonable accommodation due to her carpal tunnel syndrome. The Sixth Circuit found that her carpal tunnel syndrome was a disability because it substantially limited her in the major life activity of performing manual tasks. The Supreme Court reversed, emphasizing that Congress intended the definition of disability "to be interpreted strictly to create a demanding standard for qualifying as disabled." *Toyota*, 534 U.S. at 197. It concluded that the "impairment's impact must also be permanent or long-term." *Id.* at 198. Applying those rules, the Court found she was not disabled.

As a result of the Supreme Court decisions in the *Sutton* trilogy and *Toyota*, many individuals who faced employment discrimination learned that they were not covered by the ADA. Individuals with the following kinds of impairments were found not to be covered by the ADA: intellectual disabilities ("mental retardation"), monocular vision, depression, bipolar disorder, and breast cancer. In 2008, Congress concluded that these barriers to coverage were incompatible with its objectives for the ADA, and amended the ADA through the ADA Amendments Act, Pub. L. No. 110-325, effective January 1, 2009 ("ADAAA"). This amended construction of the term "disability," as defined in 42 U.S.C. § 12102, applies to all titles of the ADA, as well as Section 504 of the Rehabilitation Act and the Fair Housing Act Amendments of 1988.

The ADAAA makes almost no change to the words used to define "disability," rather it repudiates quite significantly the principles of construction underlying *Sutton* and *Toyota*. By providing new findings, a clarified purpose, and nine new rules of construction, with particular attention to the definition of "disability," Congress sought to reinstate the reasoning of the Supreme Court in *School Board of Nassau County v. Arline*, make the burden of establishing "disability" much less demanding, and ensure that courts were much more likely to reach the question of discrimination.

NOTES AND PROBLEMS FOR DISCUSSION

1. Under the doctrine of separation of powers, under what circumstances may Congress, in effect, use legislation to modify or undo the precedential value of a decision of the Supreme Court?

2. The passage of the ADAAA required a high degree of bipartisan support. Re-read the discussion of the history of the ADA in Chapter One. How did the advocates for the ADAAA convince Congress to support the Act?

3. What strategic advantages were achieved by leaving the words used to define "disability" virtually unchanged in the ADAAA?

B. POST-2008 OVERVIEW

Although Congress amended the ADA in 2008 to broaden the definition of disability, it did not change this three-prong definition of disability except to cross-reference paragraph (3). The ADA states that:

> The term "disability" means with respect to an individual —
>
> (A) a physical or mental impairment that substantially limits one or more major life activities of such individual;
>
> (B) a record of such an impairment; or
>
> (C) being regarded as having such an impairment (as described in paragraph (3)).

42 U.S.C. § 12102(1).

The key changes in 2008 were two-fold. Congress changed the rules to be used by the courts to construe the terms "major life activities" and "substantially limits," greatly expanding the examples of such activities and making "substantial" a much less demanding standard. It also gave express authority to the Equal Employment Opportunity Commission ("EEOC") to promulgate regulations interpreting the definition of disability. *See* 42 U.S.C. § 12205a. It gave this express authority to the EEOC because the Supreme Court had concluded in *Sutton* that the EEOC did not have authority to promulgate regulations interpreting the term "disability." Because of this express power delegated to EEOC, it is therefore important to read the regulations closely to understand the meaning of the definition of disability. This guidance also applies to the other ADA Titles and Section 504

Below, we will discuss each of these three prongs in detail but it is helpful at the outset to have a general sense of what they mean. Prong one reflects an individual who is actually disabled in that the person has a physical or mental impairment that substantially limits one or more major life activities. The person has faced discrimination and seeks redress under the statute. The EEOC's Interpretive Guidance provides many examples of individuals who meet the definition under the first prong. They would include, for example, an individual with diabetes due to the substantial limitation in endocrine function. [ADA Handbook, p. 111*] Similarly, an individual would be covered by the first prong who has dyslexia or other learning disabilities because the person would "typically be substantially limited in performing activities such as learning, reading and thinking when compared to most people in the general population." [ADA Handbook, p. 107]

Prong two reflects someone who had a disability (as defined by prong one) at some time but who does not necessarily still meet the prong one definition of disability. Nonetheless, the person faces discrimination due to that past history (or record) of disability. In its Interpretive Guidance, the EEOC offers the example of "an individual who was treated for cancer ten years ago but who is now deemed by a doctor to be free

---

* Citations to the ADA Handbook refer to RUTH COLKER & PAUL GROSSMAN, THE LAW OF DISABILITY DISCRIMINATION HANDBOOK (LexisNexis 8th Ed. 2013).

from cancer" as well as the example of someone "who in the past was misdiagnosed with bipolar disorder and hospitalized as the result of a temporary reaction to medication she was taking [because she] has a record of a substantially limiting impairment, even though she did not actually have bipolar disorder." [ADA Handbook, pp. 118–19]

Prong three may include someone who is falsely regarded as being disabled or someone with an actual impairment or disability who is facing purposeful discrimination. The EEOC offers these two examples of this prong: "if an employer refused to hire an applicant because of skin graft scars, the employer had regarded the applicant as an individual with a disability. Similarly, if an employer terminates an employee because he has cancer, the employer has regarded the employee as an individual with a disability." [ADA Handbook, p. 120] In the first example, the individual could likely *only* qualify as disabled under the third prong and not the first prong because it is unlikely that the skin graft scars are actually disabling. In the second example, the individual might also be able to attain coverage under the first prong because cancer does result in an impairment of cell function. In fact, the third prong also covers nearly everyone who is covered by the first prong but, as we will see, does not provide a right to receive reasonable accommodations.

NOTES AND PROBLEMS FOR DISCUSSION

Why did Congress need to construct three different methods for qualifying as disabled? Why not have one prong — the third one? What purpose is served by having three different methods of proof?

1. Prong One: Actually Disabled

Under the first prong, an individual is considered disabled who has "a physical or mental impairment that substantially limits one or more major life activities of such individual." 42 U.S.C. § 12102(1)(A). That definition can be broken down into three separate components: (a) the person has a "physical or mental impairment," (b) the impairment limits a "major life activity" and (c) the limitation is sufficiently significant that it is considered to be "substantial." Hence, we need to understand the terms "physical or mental impairment," "major life activity" and "substantial" to interpret this prong of the definition.

a. Physical or mental impairment

i. Statutory Definition

The ADA uses the term "physical or mental impairment" but does not define it. Nonetheless, Congress did give rule-making authority to the EEOC to promulgate regulations interpreting the ADA, including the definition of disability. Thus, the EEOC regulations can be helpful in understanding the meaning of the term "physical or mental impairment."

The regulations state that physical or mental impairment means:

> (1) Any physiological disorder, or condition, cosmetic disfigurement, or anatomical loss affecting one or more body systems, such as: neurological, musculoskeletal, special sense organs, respiratory (including speech organs), cardiovascular, reproductive, digestive, genitourinary, immune, circulatory, hemic, lymphatic, skin, and endocrine; or
>
> (2) Any mental or psychological disorder, such as an intellectual disability (formerly termed "mental retardation"), organic brain syndrome, emotional or mental illness, and specific learning disabilities.

29 C.F.R. § 1630.2(h).

In its Interpretive Guidance, the EEOC also tried to clarify what would *not* be considered a physical or mental impairment. The Guidance states:

> It is important to distinguish between conditions that are impairments and physical, psychological, environmental, cultural and economic characteristics that are not impairments. The definition of the term "impairment" does not include physical characteristics such as eye color, hair color, left-handedness, or height, weight, or muscle tone that are within "normal" range and are not the result of a physiological disorder. The definition, likewise, does not include characteristic predisposition to illness or disease. Other conditions, such as pregnancy, that are not the result of a physiological disorder are also not impairments. However, a pregnancy-related impairment that substantially limits a major life activity is a disability under the first prong of the definition. . . .
>
> The definition of an impairment also does not include common personality traits such as poor judgment or a quick temper where these are not symptoms of a mental or psychological disorder. Environmental, cultural, or economic disadvantages such as poverty, lack of education, or a prison record are not impairments. Advanced age, in and of itself, is also not an impairment. However, various medical conditions commonly associated with age, such as hearing loss, osteoporosis, or arthritis would constitute impairments within the meaning of this part.

29 C.F.R. § 1630.2(h) app. [ADA Handbook pp. 99–100]

NOTES AND PROBLEMS FOR DISCUSSION

1. For individuals with disabilities, what are the advantages and disadvantages of a very inclusive definition of disability under the ADA?

2. The ADAAA repealed two findings in the ADA cited by the Supreme Court in *Sutton* to support its restrictive view of the definition of disability. These findings were that "some 43,000,000 Americans have one or more physical or mental disabilities" and that "individuals with disabilities are a discrete and insular minority." What led Congress to withdraw these findings?

3. William Jones applied for a position as a flight attendant with United Airlines. He was rejected for employment because he exceeded the maximum weight rule for someone of his height. He weighed 178 pounds and was 5 feet, 7.5 inches tall; under the rules, the maximum weight for a man of his size was 163 pounds. Jones exceeds the maximum weight for his height because he is an avid body builder; he has, in fact, a very low percentage of body fat. His physician states that it would be physically dangerous for Jones to lose 15 pounds, because his body fat is already at the low end of normal. Is Jones disabled under the ADA? *See, e.g., Tudyman v. United Airlines*, 608 F. Supp. 739 (C.D. Cal. 1984). Would the ADAAA change the results in this case?

4. Toni Cassista applied for one of three openings at Community Foods, a health food store in the City of Santa Cruz. Duties to be performed by the prospective employees included running the cash register, stocking bags of grain, carrying boxes of produce, retrieving groceries from the warehouse, changing 55-gallon drums of honey, and carrying large crates of milk. To fill the vacancies, Community Foods sought people with grocery store, retail clerk, cashier, and stocking experience. Cassista is 5 feet, 4 inches tall and weighs 305 pounds. She had previously been employed in several restaurants, managed a sandwich shop, and worked as an aide in nursing homes. When Cassista was not hired for the job at Community Foods, she was told that the company was "concerned [she] couldn't physically do the work due to [her] weight." In particular, concern was raised that she would not be able to climb ladders and stock aisles. One store manager testified that the step stools would not support her weight. There was no evidence in this case that Cassista's obesity stemmed from physiological causes. Should Cassista be considered "disabled" under the ADA? *Compare Cook v. Rhode Island Dep't of Mental Health, Retardation and Hosps.*, 10 F.3d 17 (1st Cir. 1993) (yes), *with Cassista v. Community Foods, Inc.*, 856 P.2d 1143 (Cal. 1993) (no). Would the ADAAA change the results in this case?

Can morbid obesity (527 lbs.) be a "disability," even absent evidence that the obesity is caused by a physiological condition? *E.E.O.C. v. Resources for Human Development, Inc.*, 827 F. Supp. 2d 688 (E.D. La. 2011).

5. Mary Lockhart is pregnant and experiencing quite significant nausea. Her nausea is worse when she is exposed to motion such as driving in the backseat of a car or flying. For her job, she usually flies once a week to meet with clients. She has requested that her client visits be limited to locations where she can drive to, so that she will not have to fly. Is she disabled under the ADA? What if she wanted an accommodation so as to avoid heavy lifting, but her pregnancy is "normal"? *See* Jeannette Cox, *Pregnancy as "Disability" and the Amended Americans with Disabilities Act*, 53 B.C. L. Rev. 443 (2012).

ii. Exclusions

In Title IV of the ADA, Congress provided for various exclusions from the definition of "disability." It provided that "homosexuality and bisexuality are not impairments." 42 U.S.C. § 12211(a). It also provided that "disability" shall not include:

> (1) transvestism, transsexualism, pedophilia, exhibitionism, voyeurism, gender identity disorders not resulting from physical impairments, or other sexual behavior disorders;
>
> (2) compulsive gambling, kleptomania, or pyromania; or

> (3) psychoactive substance use disorders resulting from current illegal use of drugs.

42 U.S.C. § 12211(b).

These exclusions were part of a last-minute deal to allow the ADA to pass the Senate. Senator William Armstrong came to the Senate floor and criticized the ADA's coverage of "mental impairments." See 135 CONG. REC. S10753 (Sept. 7, 1989).

Senator Orrin Hatch shared some of Armstrong's concerns and helped negotiate this list of exclusions rather than a complete exclusion of all mental impairments. Some impairments may pertain to criminal behavior but others certainly do not. The ADA also provides that the term "individual with a disability" "does not include an individual who is currently engaging in the illegal use of drugs, when the covered entity acts on the basis of such use." 42 U.S.C. § 12210(a). Nonetheless, the exclusion for current users of illegal drugs does not extend to an individual who:

> (1) has successfully completed a supervised drug rehabilitation program and is no longer engaging in the illegal use of drugs, or has otherwise been rehabilitated successfully and is no longer engaging in such use;
>
> (2) is participating in a supervised rehabilitation program and is no longer engaging in such use; or
>
> (3) is erroneously regarded as engaging in such use, but is not engaging in such use;
>
> except that it shall not be a violation . . . for a covered entity to adopt or administer reasonable policies or procedures, including but not limited to drug testing, designed to ensure that an individual described in paragraph (1) and (2) is no longer engaging in the illegal use of drugs; however, nothing in this section shall be construed to encourage, prohibit, restrict, or authorize the conducting of testing for the illegal use of drugs.

42 U.S.C. § 12210(b).

Alcoholics (both rehabilitated and non-rehabilitated) are disabled within the meaning of the Rehabilitation Act and the ADA. However, in an *employment situation*, an employer:

> (1) may prohibit the illegal use of drugs and the use of alcohol at the workplace by all employees;
>
> (2) may require that employees shall not be under the influence of alcohol or be engaging in the illegal use of drugs at the workplace;
>
> (3) may require that all employees behave in conformance with the requirements established under the Drug-Free Workplace Act of 1988 (41 U.S.C. § 701 *et seq.*);
>
> (4) may hold an employee who engages in the illegal use of drugs or who is an alcoholic to the same qualification standards for employment or job performance and behavior that such entity holds other employees, even if any

unsatisfactory performance or behavior is related to the drug use or alcoholism of such employee. . . .

42 U.S.C. § 12114(c).

Further, an employer may require that all employees comply with standards relating to alcohol and drug use established by the Department of Defense, the Nuclear Regulatory Commission and the Department of Transportation. *Id.*

NOTES AND PROBLEMS FOR DISCUSSION

1. Do you believe that some or all of the groups excluded from coverage should have been covered by the ADA? *See generally* Kevin M. Barry, *Disabilityqueer: Federal Disability Rights Protection for Transgender People*, 16 Yale Hum. Rts. & Dev. L.J. 1 (2013).

2. The ADA provides greater protection to individuals who are alcoholics than individuals who use illegal substances. Does this distinction make good sense?

In states where medical marijuana use is lawful, should employers be permitted to exclude potential employees on the basis of such use? *See James v. City of Costa Mesa*, 700 F.3d 394 (9th Cir. 2012).

3. John Quincy seeks employment at Service Truck as a service attendant. On his application form, he lists under hobbies: "attending AA meetings." In a routine check of Quincy's prior employment record, Service learns that Quincy was discharged from the military 10 years ago because of problems related to drug and alcohol use. You have been hired as a consultant to Service. The company is concerned that Quincy may still have a problem with alcohol or drug use, but is unsure as to the proper bounds of inquiry. What advice would you provide Service? Can Service ask Quincy whether he has a current alcohol or drug problem? Can it ask to speak with someone who has knowledge of Quincy's alcohol or drug use through AA?

4. Company X hires John Doe, who is a recovering cocaine addict. (John volunteers that information at the job interview and is nonetheless hired.) John has successfully completed a rehabilitation program for his drug addiction. As a condition of employment, Company X insists that John consent to daily drug testing to ensure that he is "cocaine free." John comes to you and says he is being singled out for different treatment because of his history of illegal drug use. Is such testing prohibited by the ADA? Does it matter what John's job is? What if John is a bus driver? What if he is a clerk-typist at a university?

5. John Teahan was employed by Metro-North Commuter Railroad as a telephone and telegraph maintainer. In three successive years, he had excessive absences from work and was warned that he would be discharged unless his employment record improved. He voluntarily enrolled in a substance abuse program and informed his employer about his substance abuse problem. After returning from a 30-day rehabilitation program, he once again repeated his pattern of excessive absences. His employer sent him a letter stating that he would be discharged, effective when he exhausted his internal rights to appeal the termination. Before receiving this

termination letter, Teahan had voluntarily entered an abuse rehabilitation program. Pending a review of his discharge through the employer's disciplinary procedure, Teahan returned to work for two months following his release from the substance abuse program. He had no unexcused absences during that time period. At the end of that two months, he was sent a final termination notice because his internal appeal was unsuccessful. Teahan's treating physician takes the position that Teahan is a "recovering" user of illegal drugs and has successfully undergone rehabilitation. Is Teahan's termination lawful under the ADA? *See Teahan v. Metro-North Commuter R.R. Co.*, 951 F.2d 511 (2d Cir. 1991).

6. Annie Miners worked as promotions director for a radio station. Her supervisor became suspicious that she was drinking prior to driving the company van. The company hired a private investigator to follow her. After observing Miners drinking at a local bar, the private investigator called Miners' supervisor. He demanded the keys to the van. Miners surrendered the keys and the supervisor drove away the van. The next day, Miners was informed by her supervisor that her actions the previous night were grounds for termination because they violated the unwritten company policy prohibiting drinking alcohol and driving company vehicles. The supervisor told Miners that she must either attend a chemical dependency treatment program (at no loss in pay) or be fired. After considering her options for several days, Miners rejected the offer of treatment and was fired. Does Miners have a strong cause of action under the ADA? *See Miners v. Cargill Communications, Inc.*, 113 F.3d 820 (8th Cir. 1997).

iii. Supreme Court Interpretation

The leading Supreme Court opinion interpreting "physical or mental impairment" is *Bragdon v. Abbott*, 524 U.S. 624 (1998), briefly mentioned above. Sidney Abbott, who was infected with HIV, disclosed her HIV status when she sought dental treatment. The dentist, Randon Bragdon, agreed to perform her dental work but insisted that her treatment take place at a hospital, and Abbott would be responsible for the cost of using the hospital facilities. Abbott sued Bragdon under ADA Title III, arguing that she faced disability-based discrimination at the "professional office of a health care provider." *See* 42 U.S.C. § 12181(7)(F). One issue in the case was whether the ADA covers those with infectious diseases. The Supreme Court concluded that HIV infection was a physical or mental impairment, using the following reasoning:

> In light of the immediacy with which the virus begins to damage the infected person's white blood cells and the severity of the disease, we hold it is an impairment from the moment of infection. As noted earlier, infection with HIV causes immediate abnormalities in a person's blood, and the infected person's white cell count continues to drop throughout the course of the disease, even when the attack is concentrated in the lymph nodes. In light of these facts, HIV infection must be regarded as a physiological disorder with a constant and detrimental effect on the infected person's hemic and lymphatic systems from the moment of infection. HIV infection satisfies the statutory and regulatory definition of a physical impairment during every stage of the disease.

Abbott, 524 U.S. at 637.

NOTES AND PROBLEMS FOR DISCUSSION

1. Because Congress did not amend the definition of "physical or mental impairment" when it amended the ADA in 2008, the reasoning from *Abbott v. Bragdon* is still presumably valid. Can you find any textual or regulatory support for the *Abbott* holding in the current version of the ADA?

2. The 2011 EEOC regulations have a new section entitled "Predictable assessments," discussed extensively below, in which they list impairments that "it should easily be concluded" or "nearly always" meet the actually disabled or record of prongs. On this list, they include HIV infection because it "substantially limits immune function." 29 C.F.R. § 1630.2(g)(3). Do you agree with this conclusion? Why or why not?

3. Even though the standard for demonstrating a disability is not supposed to be rigorous, the Interpretive Guidance continues to say that "Impairments that last only for a short period of time are typically not covered, although they may be covered if sufficiently severe." 29 C.F.R. § 1630, app. Applying this guidance, a court ruled that an employee who was fired for excessive absenteeism following the flu was not "disabled" for the purposes of the ADA. *See Lewis v. Florida Default Law Group*, 2011 U.S. Dist. LEXIS 105238 (M.D. Fla. Sept. 16, 2011). Should it matter whether she has Influenza A as compared with the H1N1/Swine Flu?

b. Major Life Activities

i. Statutory and Regulatory Language

The ADAAA provides extensive language about the meaning of the term "major life activities." The Amendments both expand the number of examples and create a new category of "major life activity," one that concerns the "operation of major bodily functions." The latter element is particularly likely to expand the number of individuals covered by the ADA and reduce the burden of documenting their disabilities.

The Amendments provide that major life activities "include, but are not limited to, caring for oneself, performing manual tasks, seeing, hearing, eating, sleeping, walking, standing, lifting, bending, speaking, breathing, learning, reading, concentrating, and working." 42 U.S.C. § 12102(2)(A). This statutory list is *longer* than was previously found in the EEOC regulations defining "major life activity." Until 2008 (when the statute was amended), the EEOC regulations defined "major life activities" as meaning "functions such as caring for oneself, performing manual tasks, walking, seeing, hearing, speaking, breathing, learning, and working." 29 C.F.R. § 1630.2(i) (pre-2008 language).

The current EEOC regulations broaden the list of "major life activities" beyond the ADAAA to include "eating, sleeping . . . standing, sitting, reaching, lifting, bending, speaking . . ., reading, concentrating, thinking, communicating, and interacting with others." 29 C.F.R. § 1630.2(i)(1)(i). Because Congress described the list of major life activities to be non-exhaustive, the EEOC concluded it was appropriate to lengthen the list. *See* 29 C.F.R. § 1630.2 app. [ADA Handbook, p. 100]

The ADAAA further states that: "a major life activity also includes the operation of a major bodily function, including but not limited to, functions of the immune system, normal cell growth, digestive, bowel, bladder, neurological, brain, respiratory, circulatory, endocrine, and reproductive functions." 42 U.S.C. § 12102(2)(B). The current EEOC regulations lengthened this list to include "special sense organs and skin, . . . genitourinary, . . . cardiovascular . . . hemic, lymphatic [and] musculoskeletal functions." 29 C.F.R. § 1630.2(i)(1)(ii).

Further, in its "rules of construction," Congress stated that "an impairment that substantially limits one major life activity need not limit other major life activities in order to be considered a disability." 42 U.S.C. § 12102(4)(C). As we will see below, that language was added by Congress to expressly reject the Supreme Court's reasoning in the *Toyota* case.

NOTES AND COMMENTS FOR DISCUSSION

1. Compare the ADA Amendments with the prior EEOC regulatory language. What was added? Why do you think those activities were added?

2. Do you think the courts are likely to accept the regulatory additions to the list of "major life activities"?

3. Do you think the courts are likely to accept the regulatory additions to the list of "major bodily functions"?

ii. Supreme Court Interpretation

The ADAAA with respect to "major life activities" can be understood in relationship to three Supreme Court decisions. First, in *Bragdon v. Abbott*, 524 U.S. 624 (1998), the Supreme Court had concluded that a woman who had HIV was "disabled" for the purposes of the ADA. In the discussion of "physical or mental impairment," we have already seen that the Court concluded that HIV infection is a physical or mental impairment. But the plaintiff also had to demonstrate a substantial limitation in a major life activity to be covered by the ADA. In *Bragdon*, the Supreme Court concluded that her HIV infection substantially limited her ability to have children, thereby limiting her "reproduction" system. Notice that "reproductive functions" is now listed specifically as a major life activity so, in some sense, Congress codified the decision in *Bragdon*.

Second, in *Sutton v. United Air Lines*, 527 U.S. 471 (1999), the Court questioned whether "working" should be considered a major life activity because "there may be some conceptual difficulty in defining 'major life activities' to include work, for it seems 'to argue in a circle to say that if one is excluded, for instance, by reason of [an impairment, from working with others] . . . then that exclusion is by reason of handicap.' " *Sutton*, 527 U.S. at 492 (quoting oral argument of Solicitor General in *Arline* case).

The ADAAA directly resolved that issue by including "working" in the list of major life activities.

Third, in *Toyota Motor Manufacturing v. Williams*, 534 U.S. 184 (2002), the Court found that a woman with carpal tunnel syndrome was not necessarily substantially limited in one or more major life activities. She argued that she was substantially limited in "manual tasks." In order to meet that definition, the Court said that she had to demonstrate that she was severely restricted from doing activities that are "of central importance to most people's daily lives." *Id.* at 198. The Court of Appeals had found that Williams was substantially limited in performing "repetitive work with hands and arms extended at or above shoulder levels for extended periods of time." *Id.* at 201. Because that work was "not an important part of most people's daily lives," the Supreme Court ruled those limitations should not be considered. Instead, the Supreme Court ruled that the lower courts should consider whether she was substantially limited in activities such as household chores, bathing, brushing her teeth and other activities that are of central importance to most people's daily lives. *Id.* at 202. In the Purposes section of the ADAAA, Congress rejected the language from *Toyota* requiring an individual to have "an impairment that prevents or severely restricts the individual from doing activities that are of central importance to most people's daily lives." 42 U.S.C. § 12101 note (b)(4). Congress also rejected the emphasis in *Toyota* on finding numerous activities that were substantially limited by Williams' impairment. It codified that "An impairment that substantially limits one major life activity need not limit other major life activities in order to be considered a disability." 42 U.S.C. § 12102(4)(C). Congress also codified that "performing manual tasks" is a major life activity. 42 U.S.C. § 12102(2)(A).

In its Interpretive Guidance, the EEOC explained how the ADAAA should change the outcome in *Toyota*:

> Thus, for example, lifting is a major life activity regardless of whether an individual who claims to be substantially limited in lifting actually performs activities of central importance to daily life that require lifting. Similarly, the Commission anticipates that the major life activity of performing manual tasks (which was at issue in *Toyota*) could have many different manifestations, such as performing tasks involving fine motor coordination, or performing tasks involving grasping, hand strength, or pressure. Such tasks need not constitute activities of central important to most people's daily lives, nor must an individual show that he or she is substantially limited in performing all manual tasks.

29 C.F.R. § 1630.2(i) app. [ADA Handbook, p. 102]

NOTES AND PROBLEMS FOR DISCUSSION

1. Do you think having "working" on the list of major life activities will present "conceptual difficulties" in employment discrimination cases? Why or why not?

2. In light of the ADAAA, how should a court consider a claim in the future brought by a woman who claims that her carpal tunnel syndrome caused her to avoid sweeping, to quit dancing, to occasionally seek help dressing, and to reduce how often she plays with her children, gardens, and drives long distances, as well as limits her ability to perform repetitive work with her hands and arms extended at or above her shoulders for extended periods of time?

3. David Kravits was hired as a Human Resources Specialist Intern at the Butler VA Medical Center in 2008. When he had problems completing his work adequately, he requested an ergonomic keyboard and step-by-step instructions on a checklist for his projects. He was ultimately terminated due to poor job performance and brought suit under the Rehabilitation Act (which uses the same definition of disability as the ADA). Kravits alleged that he suffers from fibromyalgia, thoracolumbar strain, irritable bowel syndrome, degenerative disc disease, sleep apnea, ulnar neuropathy at the left elbow, hypertension, depressive disorder, anxiety disorder, and post-traumatic stress disorder. Kravits argued that the Department of Veterans Affair had found that he suffered from obstructive sleep apnea that directly related to military service. He offered no other medical support to justify his disability-related assertions. The Medical Center argued he was not substantially limited in any major activities because he could engage in activities related to a home purchase and renovation; pursuing a college education; and vacationing in Thailand. The district court concluded that evidence of his physical, social and academic activities did not undermine evidence that he was substantially limited in his ability to sleep and learn, as compared to most people in the population. Denying the Medical Center's motion for summary judgment, the court concluded he was entitled to a jury trial on whether the failure to accommodate Kravits led to his discharge. *See Kravits v. Shinseki*, No. 10-861, 2012 U.S. Dist. LEXIS 24039 (W.D. Pa. Feb. 24, 2012). Should he be considered disabled under the ADA?

4. Maria Molina was a certified medical assistant formerly employed by a Texas dialysis clinic. She began working for the employer in 2003 and received accommodations over the years when her back pain restricted her ability to do heavy lifting. In 2009, she received an epidural injection and was allowed to go to a part-time schedule with lifting restrictions. Then, several months later, her employer started changing her schedule and insisted that she go on FMLA leave until she could return to work without lifting restrictions. When her FMLA leave expired, she was terminated. Subsequently, she had surgery and was cleared to return to work without restriction. Molina argued that she could perform the essential functions of the job at the time of her termination despite a lifting restriction and, if lifting were essential, she could have been provided with assistance in lifting. Molina alleged that her back condition affected her by causing significant pain. The employer alleged that she was not disabled because she continued to work even on days when she had severe pain, and she continued to do household tasks such as cooking, cleaning, and taking care of her disabled husband. The district court found that there was sufficient evidence to overcome summary judgment on the issue of whether she was disabled because a court could consider the "condition" under which she performed a major life activity (i.e., in pain), not simply whether she performed the activity. Further, the lifting restriction itself was a limitation in a major life activity (i.e., the operation of a major bodily function — musculoskeletal). *See Molina v. DSI Renal, Inc.*, 840 F. Supp. 2d 984 (W.D. Tex. 2011). Do you agree with the court's analysis?

5. Robert Lohf worked as a machinist at Great Plains Manufacturing. His lower back condition, spondylolisthesis, restricted him from lifting more than 25-30 pounds and engaging in excessive stooping and bending, prolonged sitting or standing. After many years of employment, Great Plains terminated Lohf on grounds of misconduct when he got into a conflict with another employee. Loft alleged this was a pretext for disability discrimination and that the employer no longer wished to accommodate him. While granting summary judgment for the employer on the merits, the court ruled that Lohf had established that he was an individual with a disability. "Under the ADA prior to the adoption of the ADAAA, plaintiff's lifting restrictions may not have sufficed to establish him as disabled . . . . However, under the ADAAA, the definition of disabled has been expanded. This has led several courts to conclude that lifting restrictions similar to those imposed on the plaintiff here are now adequate to constitute a disability under the ADA or sufficient to avoid summary judgment on the issue." Do you agree that the restrictions, to which Lohf had been subjected, without more, should be sufficient to establish that he was an individual with a disability? *Lohf v. Great Plains Manufacturing*, No. 10–1177–RDR, 2012 U.S. Dist. LEXIS 90935 (D. Kan. July 2, 2012).

6. A district court found that James McElwee could not demonstrate that he was disabled under the ADA. McElwee said he had Asperger's Syndrome. He worked as a volunteer at a Nursing Care and Rehabilitation facility doing janitorial and housekeeping duties for more than a decade. Several female employees complained that he acted inappropriately toward them and made them feel uncomfortable. He allegedly followed them at work and outside work or would stare at them as they went past. The defendant successfully argued he was not disabled under the ADA because his communication was merely "inappropriate, ineffective or unsuccessful." He did not lack the basic fundamental ability to communicate with others. What other functional limitations related to his disability might he have used to establish that he was an individual with a disability? Do you agree with this conclusion? *See McElwee v. County of Orange*, No. 10 Civ. 00138(KTD), 2011 U.S. Dist. LEXIS 114663 (S.D.N.Y. Sept. 29, 2011).

7. Jennifer Kellogg is a safety technician for an industrial safety company. She drives to oil fields to provide services to her clients. She was diagnosed with epilepsy in 2012 and her physician instructed her not to drive until her condition stabilized. Her employer fired her, arguing she was no longer qualified to perform her job because she could not drive. Is she disabled under the ADA? Is driving a major life activity?

8. In *Sutton*, the Supreme Court expressed some skepticism as to whether "working" was a legitimate major life activity. Prior to 2008, the EEOC regulations had special, restrictive rules for concluding that a plaintiff had a physical or mental impairment that substantially limited the major life activity of working. Congress resolved this dispute under the ADA by adding "working" to the list of major life activities. In the 2011 Regulations, the EEOC included no special regulation for the major life activity of working but also explained in its Interpretive Guidance:

> The Commission has removed from the text of the regulations a discussion of the major life activity of working. This is consistent with the fact that no other major activity requires special attention in the regulation, and with the fact that, in light of the expanded definition of disability established by the

> Amendments Act, this major life activity will be used in only very targeted situations . . . .
>
> In the rare cases where an individual has a need to demonstrate that an impairment substantially limits him or her in working, the individual can do so by showing that the impairment substantially limits his or her ability to perform a class of jobs or broad range of jobs in various classes as compared to most people having comparable training, skills, and abilities . . . . The Commission believes that the courts, in applying an overly strict standard with regard to 'substantially limits' generally, have reached conclusions with regard to what is necessary to demonstrate a substantial limitation in the major life activity of working that would be inconsistent with the changes now made by the Amendments Act . . . .
>
> Demonstrating a substantial limitation in performing the unique aspects of a single specific job is not sufficient to establish that a person is substantially limited in the major life activity of working . . . .

29 C.F.R. § 1630.2 app. [ADA Handbook, pp. 117–18]

9. In the above quoted guidance, is the EEOC really treating the major life activity of working like all other major life activities? Why would the EEOC have chosen to deal with this issue only in the regulatory guidance rather than in the body of its regulations? Is this regulatory language internally inconsistent?

10. In *Murphy v. United Parcel Service*, 527 U.S. 516, 524 (1999) (one of the *Sutton* trilogy cases involving a mechanic with high blood pressure who was terminated because he could not meet DOT medical standards for driving commercial vehicles), the Supreme Court said:

> The evidence that petitioner is regarded as unable to meet the DOT regulations is not sufficient to create a genuine issue of material fact as to whether petitioner is regarded as unable to perform a class of jobs utilizing his skills. At most, petitioner has shown that he is regarded as unable to perform the job of mechanic only when that job requires driving a commercial motor vehicle — a specific type of vehicle used on a highway in interstate commerce. 49 CFR § 390.5 (defining "commercial motor vehicle" as a vehicle weighing over 10,000 pounds, designed to carry 16 or more passengers, or used in the transportation of hazardous materials). Petitioner has put forward no evidence that he is regarded as unable to perform any mechanic job that does not call for driving a commercial motor vehicle and thus does not require DOT certification. Indeed, it is undisputed that petitioner is generally employable as a mechanic. Petitioner has "performed mechanic jobs that did not require DOT certification" for "over 22 years," and he secured another job as a mechanic shortly after leaving UPS. Moreover, respondent presented uncontroverted evidence that petitioner could perform jobs such as diesel mechanic, automotive mechanic, gas-engine repairer, and gas-welding equipment mechanic, all of which utilize petitioner's mechanical skills.
>
> Consequently, in light of petitioner's skills and the array of jobs available to petitioner utilizing those skills, petitioner has failed to show that he is

> regarded as unable to perform a class of jobs. Rather, the undisputed record evidence demonstrates that petitioner is, at most, regarded as unable to perform only a particular job. This is insufficient, as a matter of law, to prove that petitioner is regarded as substantially limited in the major life activity of working.

How would the courts resolve this case under the ADAAA and the 2011 EEOC regulations?

c. Substantial Limitation

The biggest change made by the ADAAA is the modification in the meaning of the term "substantially limits." The term "substantially limits" has raised two major interpretive questions under the ADA: (a) how significant does a limitation have to be in order to be "substantial"; and (b) does one measure the substantiality of a limitation with or without regard to the ameliorative effects of mitigating measures?

i. How Substantial?

In *Bragdon v. Abbott*, 524 U.S. 624 (1998), the Court found that the plaintiff's HIV infection substantially limited her in the major life activity of reproduction because it imposed risks on her male partner and risks to the fetus during gestation. The Court used the following language in explaining why the plaintiff could establish a "substantial limitation" in reproduction:

> The Act addresses substantial limitations on major life activities, not utter inabilities. Conception and childbirth are not impossible for an HIV victim but, without doubt, are dangerous to the public health. This meets the definition of a substantial limitation . . . . In the end, the disability definition does not turn on personal choice. When significant limitations result from the impairment, the definition is met even if the difficulties are not insurmountable.

Id. at 641.

Later, in *Toyota Motor Manufacturing v. Williams*, 534 U.S. 184 (2002), the Court applied a more stringent standard for the definition of "substantially limits." It said that a plaintiff has to demonstrate that he or she has an impairment that "*prevents or severely restricts* the individual from doing activities that are of central importance to most people's daily lives." *Id.* at 198 (emphasis added).

The EEOC regulations in force at the time, were neither consistent with nor clearly contrary to the interpretation of the Court, stating that "substantially limits" means: "(1) *unable to perform* a major life activity that the average person in the general population can perform; or (2) *significantly restricted* as to the condition, manner or duration under which an individual can perform a major life activity as compared to the condition, manner, or duration under which the average person in the general population can perform that same major life activity." 29 C.F.R. § 1630.2(j)(1) (pre-ADAAA) (emphasis added).

Lower courts had often found that plaintiffs presented insufficient evidence to meet the "substantial limitation" requirement. The Tenth Circuit found that Laura Sorenson, who was diagnosed with Multiple Sclerosis, presented insufficient evidence of a substantial limitation. *See Sorensen v. University of Utah Hospital*, 194 F.3d 1084 (10th Cir. 1999). The Eighth Circuit found that a plaintiff with a history of thyroid cancer was not disabled. *See Demming v. Housing & Redevelopment Authority*, 66 F.3d 950 (8th Cir. 1995). The Second Circuit found that Charles Ellinger, who suffered a cerebral hemorrhage, did not have sufficient limitations to qualify as disabled. *See Colwell v. Suffolk County Police Department*, 158 F.3d 635 (2d Cir. 1998). Both the Eighth and Fifth Circuits had concluded that restrictions on heavy lifting were not sufficient evidence of limitations. *See Snow v. Ridgeview Medical Center*, 128 F.3d 1201 (8th Cir. 1997); *Ray v. Glidden*, 85 F.3d 227 (5th Cir. 1996). The Eleventh Circuit found that an individual with an intellectual disability ("mental retardation"), who requested to have his job coach present for a job interview with Walmart, had presented insufficient evidence of a "substantial limitation" in learning because he was able to graduate from high school albeit with a special education diploma and attend maintenance skills classes at an community college. The court also expressed some doubt as to whether "thinking" and "communicating" were major life activities. *Littleton v. Wal-Mart*, Inc., 2007 U.S. App. LEXIS 11150 (11th Cir. May 11, 2007), *cert. denied*, 552 U.S. 944 (2007).

Congress considered these decisions to be unduly restrictive. It expressly rejected both the *Toyota* decision and the existing EEOC regulations in the Purposes section of the ADAAA when it stated that one of its purposes was:

> to convey congressional intent that the standard created by the Supreme Court in the case of *Toyota Motor Manufacturing, Kentucky, Inc. v. Williams*, 534 U.S. 184 (2002) for "substantially limits", and applied by lower courts in numerous decisions, has created an inappropriately high level of limitation necessary to obtain coverage under the ADA, to convey that it is the intent of Congress that the primary object of attention in cases brought under the ADA should be whether entities covered under the ADA have complied with their obligations, and to convey that the question of whether an individual's impairment is a disability under the ADA should not demand extensive analysis.

Pub. L. No. 110-325, § 2, 122 Stat. 3553(b)(5) (2008).

In the Findings Section, Congress also stated that the *Toyota* decision required a "greater degree of limitation than was intended by Congress" and that the EEOC regulations "defining the term 'substantially limits' as 'significantly restricted' are inconsistent with congressional intent, by expressing too high a standard." Pub. L. No. 110-325, § 2, 122 Stat. 3553(a)(7) & (8) (2008). Thus, it expressly concluded that the courts and the EEOC had misinterpreted the term "substantially limits."

Congress also created a new section of the statute entitled "Rules of Construction Regarding the Definition of Disability." In this section, the ADAAA stated:

> (B) The term "substantially limits" shall be interpreted consistently with the findings and purposes of the ADA Amendments Act of 2008.
>
> (C) An impairment that substantially limits one major life activity need not limit other major life activities in order to be considered a disability.

42 U.S.C. § 12102(4)(B) & (C).

Congress' approach in repudiating interpretations of "substantially limits" is unusual. Initially there was some discussion of substituting the term "material" for "substantial." Ultimately, rather than adopt a new term, or explicitly redefine the term itself, Congress chose to *retain* the term and set forth detailed *findings, purposes and rules of construction* concerning the meaning of the term. The EEOC took a similar approach. The EEOC explains: "Following Congress's lead . . . the Commission ultimately concluded that a new definition would inexorably lead to greater focus and intensity of attention on the threshold issue of coverage than intended by Congress. Therefore, the regulations simply provide rules of construction that must be applied in determining whether an impairment substantially limits (or substantially limited) a major life activity." 29 C.F.R. § 1630.2(j)(1) app. [ADA Handbook, p. 103]

Thus, to find the rules that the EEOC promulgated to interpret the phrase "substantially limits," one needs to look at the "Rules of Construction" rather than in a definition section. The following "Rules of Construction" are relevant to how the EEOC believes that "substantially limits" should be interpreted. Some of these rules draw on the Findings and Purpose section of the ADA; others are based on the "Rules of Construction" in the ADA.

In its Rules of Construction, the EEOC regulations state:

> i. The term "substantially limits" shall be construed broadly in favor of expansive coverage, to the maximum extent permitted by the terms of the ADA. "Substantially limits" is not meant to be a demanding standard.
>
> ii. An impairment is a disability within the meaning of this section if it substantially limits the ability of an individual to perform a major life activity as compared to most people in the general population. An impairment need not prevent, or significantly or severely restrict, the individual from performing a major life activity in order to be considered substantially limiting. Nonetheless, not every impairment will constitute a disability within the meaning of this section.
>
> iii. The primary object of attention in cases brought under the ADA should be whether covered entities have complied with their obligations and whether discrimination has occurred, not whether an individual's impairment substantially limits a major life activity. Accordingly, the threshold issue of whether an impairment "substantially limits" a major life activity should not demand extensive analysis.
>
> iv. The determination of whether an impairment substantially limits a major life activity requires an individualized assessment. However, in making this assessment, the term "substantially limits" shall be interpreted and applied to require a degree of functional limitation that is lower than the standard for "substantially limits" applied prior to the ADAAA.
>
> v. The comparison of an individual's performance of a major life activity to the performance of the same major life activity by most people in the general population usually will not require scientific, medical, or statistical analysis.

Nothing in this paragraph is intended, however, to prohibit the presentation of scientific, medical, or statistical evidence to make such a comparison where appropriate.

vi. The determination of whether an impairment substantially limits a major life activity shall be made without regard to the ameliorative effects of mitigating measures. However, the ameliorative effects of ordinary eyeglasses or contact lenses shall be considered in determining whether an impairment substantially limits a major life activity.

vii. An impairment that is episodic or in remission is a disability if it would substantially limit a major life activity when active.

viii. An impairment that substantially limits one major life activity need not substantially limit other major life activities in order to be considered a substantially limiting impairment.

ix. The six-month "transitory" part of the "transitory and minor" exception to "regarded as" coverage in § 1630.15(f) does not apply to the definition of "disability" under paragraphs (g)(1)(i) (the "actual disability" prong) or (g)(1)(ii) (the "record of" prong) of this section. The effects of an impairment lasting or expected to last fewer than six months can be substantially limiting within the meaning of this section.

29 C.F.R. § 1630.2(j)(1). [ADA Handbook, pp. 72–73]

NOTES AND COMMENTS FOR DISCUSSION

1. Compare the current EEOC regulations to the pre-2008 regulations, quoted above. Notice that the prior regulations mentioned the "average person in the general population" whereas these regulations refer to "most people in the general population." In its Interpretive Guidance, the EEOC has said that this revision "is not a substantive change" but "is intended to conform the language to the simpler and more straightforward terminology used in the legislative history to the Amendments Act." [ADA Handbook, p. 106] Do you agree that this change is not substantive but, instead, is merely simpler and more straightforward? How would one establish the capacities or performance of "most people" in the general population?

2. Read those regulations closely and try to match them to the 2008 statutory language. Do you think this language is consistent with Congress' intent in amending the ADA?

ii. Ameliorative Effects of Mitigating Measures

The most controversial decision under the ADA, and the case that largely spurred the ADAAA, was the Court's decision in *Sutton v. United Air Lines, Inc.*, 527 U.S. 471 (1999).

As mentioned above, the *Sutton* case involved twin sisters who wanted to work as commercial airline pilots. Although their vision was fully corrected with lenses, their uncorrected vision was 20/200 or worse in one eye and 20/400 or worse in the other eye. The airline had a minimum vision requirement of at least 20/100 or better in each eye without the use of corrective lenses. When they were told they could not be hired because they did not meet the vision standard, they filed suit under the ADA. Both the district court and Tenth Circuit Court of Appeals ruled that the plaintiffs could not sue under the ADA because they did not meet the definition of disability. At the time, both the EEOC and the Department of Justice had issued Interpretive Guidance stating that the issue of whether someone is disabled should be made "without regard to mitigating measures." *See* 29 C.F.R. § 1630.2(j) app. (EEOC) & 28 C.F.R. § 36.104 app. (DOJ). The lower courts disregarded those regulations in determining that the plaintiffs' disability status should be determined *after* they use mitigating measures (i.e., corrective lenses) rather than before. The Supreme Court agreed with the lower courts, concluding that "disability under the Act is to be determined with reference to corrective measures." 527 U.S. at 489.

Congress stated in the ADAAA that one of its purposes is "to reject the requirement enunciated by the Supreme Court in *Sutton v. United Air Lines, Inc.*, 527 U.S. 471 (1999) and its companion cases that whether an impairment substantially limits a major life activity is to be determined with reference to the ameliorative effects of mitigating measures."Pub. L. No. 101-325, § 2, 122 Stat. 3553(b)(2) (2008).

Congress enacted several rules to reverse the Court's decision in *Sutton* with the following statutory language in subsection (4)(E):

> (i) The determination of whether an impairment substantially limits a major life activity shall be made without regard to the ameliorative effects of mitigating measures such as —
>
> > (I) Medication, medical supplies, equipment, or appliances, low-vision devices (which do not include ordinary eyeglasses or contact lenses), prosthetics including limbs and devices, hearing aids and cochlear implants or other implantable hearing devices, mobility devices, or oxygen therapy equipment and supplies;
> >
> > (II) use of assistive technology;
> >
> > (III) reasonable accommodations or auxiliary aids or services; or
> >
> > (IV) learned behavioral or adaptive neurological modifications.
>
> (ii) The ameliorative effects of the mitigating measures of ordinary eyeglasses or contact lenses shall be considered in determining whether an impairment substantially limits a major life activity.
>
> (iii) As used in this subparagraph —
>
> > (I) the term "ordinary eyeglasses or contact lenses" means lenses that are intended to fully correct visual acuity or eliminate refractive error; and
> >
> > (II) the term "low-vision devices" means devices that magnify, enhance, or otherwise augment a visual image.

42 U.S.C. § 12102(4)(E).

Ironically, this new statutory language would not have necessarily reversed the actual holding in the *Sutton* case because the plaintiffs used ordinary eyeglasses to fully correct their visual acuity. (This issue will be discussed more fully in Chapter Three, because Congress also created a special rule to cover the situation when an employer uses selection criteria "based on an individual's uncorrected vision" *See* 42 U.S.C. § 12113(c).)

The EEOC's regulations offer further guidance with respect to the mitigating measure rule. As quoted above, the statute provides four examples of types of mitigating measures. The EEOC added a fifth category: "psychotherapy, behavioral therapy, or physical therapy." 29 C.F.R. § 1630.2(v).

In its Interpretive Guidance, the EEOC provides many examples of plaintiffs who might prevail under this new rule and who lost under the prior mitigating measures rule:

- individual with muscular dystrophy who, with the mitigating measure of "adapting" how she performed manual tasks, had successfully learned to live and work with his disability;
- individual with uncontrolled diabetes had used a careful regimen of medicine, exercise and diet;
- individual with a diagnosed learning disability had used self-accommodations that allowed him to read and achieve academic success;
- individual with clinical depression used medication to control the symptoms;
- individual with a hearing impairment used a hearing aid;
- individual with a seizure disorder used medication to reduce the frequency and intensity of the seizures

NOTES AND COMMENTS FOR DISCUSSION

1. After *Sutton* and prior to adoption of the ADAAA, the side effects of mitigating measures remained pertinent to whether an individual had a substantial impairment of a major life activity. Richard McAlindin, an individual with anxiety, panic, and somatoform disorders was successful in establishing that he was an individual with a disability, in part, because the medications he took to mitigate his psychological conditions substantially impaired the major life activities of engaging in sex and sleep. *McAlindin v. County of San Diego*, 192 F.3d 1226 (9th Cir. 1999). The ADAAA does not remove these side effects for consideration in establishing disability.

2. Would someone be considered disabled under the ADA if the person began taking medication for hypertension before experiencing substantial limitations related to the impairment if, without the medication, he or she would likely be substantially limited in functions of the cardiovascular or circulatory system? [*See* ADA Handbook, p. 108]

3. Would the use of a service animal, job coach, or personal assistant on the job be considered a type of mitigating measure? [*See* ADA Handbook, p. 108]

4. What if an individual refuses to use an available mitigating measure, such as medication for ADHD or clinical depression, to alleviate the effects of an impairment? Does that refusal preclude the individual from being considered disabled? [*See* ADA Handbook, p. 109]

5. What if an individual is using eyeglasses or contact lenses that are the wrong prescription or an outdated prescription? If a proper prescription would fully correct visual acuity, is the individual disabled under the ADA? [*See* ADA Handbook, p. 109]

iii. Predictable Assessments

In the "substantially limits" section of the regulations, the EEOC has a section entitled: "Predictable assessments." While recognizing that the ADA requires an individualized assessment, the EEOC also concludes that there are various disabilities for which one should be able to easily conclude that the individual is disabled. "[T]he necessary individualized assessment should be particularly simple and straightforward." 29 C.F.R. § 1630.2(j)(3)(ii). The EEOC then offers the following examples:

- deafness substantially limits hearing;
- blindness substantially limits seeing;
- an intellectual disability (formerly termed mental retardation) substantially limits brain function;
- partially or completely missing limbs or mobility impairments requiring the use of a wheelchair substantially limit musculoskeletal function;
- autism substantially limits brain function;
- cancer substantially limits normal cell growth;
- cerebral palsy substantially limits brain function;
- diabetes substantially limits endocrine function;
- epilepsy substantially limits neurological function;
- Human Immunodeficiency Virus (HIV) infection substantially limits immune function;
- multiple sclerosis substantially limits neurological function;
- and major depressive disorder, bipolar disorder, post-traumatic stress disorder, obsessive compulsive disorder, and schizophrenia substantially limit brain function.

29 C.F.R. § 1630.2(j)(3).

In its Interpretive Guidance, the EEOC justifies the creation of this list of "predictable assessments":

> As the regulations point out, disability is determined based on an individualized assessment. There is no "per se" disability. However, as recognized in the regulations, the individualized assessment of some kinds of impairments will virtually always result in a determination of disability . . . . Therefore, with

respect to these types of impairments, the necessary individualized assessment should be particularly simple and straightforward.

29 C.F.R. § 1630.2(j)(3) app. [ADA Handbook, p. 112]

NOTES AND PROBLEMS FOR DISCUSSION

1. What do you think of the predictable assessment approach? Are the courts likely to accept this analysis, or is it in conflict with the ADA's requirement of an individualized assessment? Will it make cases more "simple and straightforward"?

2. Michael Norton, a residence sales manager, alleged that he was terminated from employment by Assisted Living Concepts on the basis of disability when he returned to work six weeks after surgery for kidney cancer. The district court denied the employer's motion for summary judgment. It found the fact that the plaintiff might have been in remission when he returned to work was of no consequence. The court explained, "EEOC's final regulations implementing the amendments provide a list of impairments that, because they substantially limit a major life activity, will 'in virtually all cases, result in a determination of coverage under [the actual disability prong].' 29 C.F.R. § 1630.2(j)(3)(ii). One of the impairments listed is 'cancer' because it 'substantially limits the major life activity of normal cell growth. . . ." The court further noted that, "cancer at any stage 'substantially limits' the 'major life activity' of 'normal cell growth.'" *Norton v. Assisted Living Concepts, Inc.*, 786 F. Supp. 2d 1173, 1186 n.6 (E.D. Tex. 2011).

iv. Condition, Manner, or Duration

For the impairments listed in the "Predictable Assessment" regulation, the EEOC regulations state that the individualized assessment "should be particularly simple and straightforward." 29 C.F.R. § 1630.2(j)(4)(iv). But there are impairments, such as allergies, orthopedic impairments or coronary heart disease, which cannot be considered predictable because they are too variable in the degree to which they limit a major life activity. For impairments that do not fall into the predictable category, the EEOC emphasizes that it is important to apply the Rules of Construction, quoted above, but that factors such as "condition, manner, or duration" should be considered to determine whether an impairment causes a substantial limitation on a major life activity. These are the regulations governing consideration of "condition, manner, or duration":

4) *Condition, manner, or duration* —

(i) At all times taking into account the principles in paragraphs (j)(1)(i) through (ix) of this section, in determining whether an individual is substantially limited in a major life activity, it may be useful in appropriate cases to consider, as compared to most people in the general population, the condition under which the individual performs the major life activity; the manner in which the individual performs the major life activity; and/or the duration of time it takes the individual to perform the

> major life activity, or for which the individual can perform the major life activity.
>
> (ii) Consideration of facts such as condition, manner, or duration may include, among other things, consideration of the difficulty, effort, or time required to perform a major life activity; pain experienced when performing a major life activity; the length of time a major life activity can be performed; and/or the way an impairment affects the operation of a major bodily function. In addition, the non-ameliorative effects of mitigating measures, such as negative side effects of medication or burdens associated with following a particular treatment regimen, may be considered when determining whether an individual's impairment substantially limits a major life activity.
>
> (iii) In determining whether an individual has a disability under the "actual disability" or "record of" prongs of the definition of disability, the focus is on how a major life activity is substantially limited, and not on what outcomes an individual can achieve. For example, someone with a learning disability may achieve a high level of academic success, but may nevertheless be substantially limited in the major life activity of learning because of the additional time or effort he or she must spend to read, write, or learn compared to most people in the general population.
>
> (iv) Given the rules of construction set forth in paragraphs (j)(1)(i) through (ix) of this section, it may often be unnecessary to conduct an analysis involving most or all of these types of facts. This is particularly true with respect to impairments such as those described in paragraph (j)(3)(iii) of this section, which by their inherent nature should be easily found to impose a substantial limitation on a major life activity, and for which the individualized assessment should be particularly simple and straightforward.

In its Interpretive Guidance, the EEOC provides examples of impairments that may be subject to the condition, manner or duration inquiry. Note that, as the examples demonstrate, one need not consider condition, manner, *and* duration to determine that an individual is disabled; the regulations use the word "or" not "and."

- "the condition or manner under which a person with an amputated hand performs manual tasks will likely be more cumbersome than the way that someone with two hands would perform the same tasks"
- "an individual whose impairment causes pain or fatigue that most people would not experience when performing that major life activity may be substantially limited"
- "the condition or manner under which someone with coronary artery disease performs the major life activity of walking would be substantially limited if the individual experiences shortness of breath and fatigue when walking distances that most people could walk without experiencing such effects"
- "a person whose back or leg impairment precludes him or her from standing for more than two hours without significant pain would be substantially

> limited in standing, since most people can stand for more than two hours without significant pain"

29 C.F.R. 1630.2(j)(4) app. [ADA Handbook pp. 114–15]

(1) Learning disabilities

One challenging issue that these regulations seek to address is the coverage of individuals with learning disabilities, an impairment that is not listed as a "predictable impairment." Historically, a person with a learning disability has faced three barriers to establish that he or she is an individual with a disability. First, individuals with learning disabilities face many of the prejudices, myths, and stereotypes associated with "invisible disabilities," such as psychiatric disabilities. Based on ignorance of the disability, some individuals doubt the existence of the disability or associate it with assumptions of intellectual inferiority, In Chapter 4, we will explore this issue more fully in the discussion of *Guckenberger v. Boston University*, 974 F. Supp. 106, 118–19 (D. Mass. 1997), in which University President Jon Westling gave a speech in which he invented a character called "Somnolent Samantha," who was diagnosed as learning disabled and often fell asleep in her front row seat in class, to illustrate his belief "that students with learning disabilities were often fakers who undercut academic rigor."

Second, some learning disabilities, such as dyslexia, are commonly diagnosed on the basis of "intra-individual" differences. For example, dyslexia is often diagnosed on the basis of an analysis of the discrepancy between an individual's overall intelligence score and that same individual's achievement score in a particular subject area, such as reading. *See generally* SALLY SHAYWITZ, OVERCOMING DYSLEXIA 131–141 (2003). This diagnostic approach may appear contrary to the EEOC regulations that require that comparisons must be made between an individual and "most people in the general population." Nonetheless, the Rules of Construction, quoted above, while generally not requiring use of statistical measures to assess the existence of a disability, note that: "Nothing in this paragraph is intended . . . . to prohibit the presentation of scientific, medical, or statistical evidence to make such a comparison where appropriate." 29 C.F.R. § 1630.2(j)(1)(v). [ADA Handbook, p. 72] In other words, by comparing the intra-individual differences of one person between aptitude and achievement with the differences between those domains typically found in the general population, disability may be established.

The EEOC's Interpretive Guidance makes clear that it does not expect the rule about comparison to others to limit coverage of learning disabilities as a covered impairment. The Interpretive Guidance quotes from the Congressional history to make that point:

> "The Committee believes that the comparison of individuals with specific learning disabilities to 'most people' is not problematic unto itself, but requires a careful analysis of the method and manner in which an individual's impairment limits a major life activity. For the majority of the population, the basic mechanics of reading and writing do not pose extraordinary lifelong challenges; rather, recognizing and forming letters and words are effortless, unconscious, automatic processes. Because specific learning disabilities are

> neurologically-based impairments, the process of reading for an individual with a reading disability (e.g. dyslexia) is word-by-word, and otherwise cumbersome, painful, deliberate and slow — throughout life. The Committee expects that individuals with specific learning disabilities that substantially limit a major life activity will be better protected under the amended Act." 2008 House Educ. & Labor Rep. at 10–11.

29 C.F.R. § 1630.2(j)(4) app. [ADA Handbook pp. 115–16]

Third, before 2008, courts often applied a summative or "bottom-line" only analysis to the question of disability. They failed to consider how hard it was for individuals with learning disabilities to read, learn or work or how much longer it took them to read or learn with the same level of comprehension as most persons. Rather these courts simply asked whether the plaintiff read or learned well enough to get a high school or college diploma or hold a job.

Because accomplished individuals, such as medical students and law school graduates, brought many of these suits, their overall achievement was quite evidently above that of the average person in the general population. In the reasoning of these courts, this level of achievement precluded these individuals from a disability classification. *See, e.g., Price v. National Bd. of Medical Examiners*, 966 F. Supp. 419 (S.D. W. Va. 1997); *Gonzales v. National Board of Medical Examiners*, 225 F.3d 620 (6th Cir. 2000); *H.K. Wong v. University of California*, 379 F.3d 1097 (9th Cir. 2004). *Contra Bartlett v. The New York State Bd. of Law Examiners*, 970 F. Supp. 1094 (S.D.N.Y. 1997), *aff'd*, 156 F.3d 321 (2d Cir. 1998), *accord* No. 93 Civ. 4986, 2001 U.S. Dist. LEXIS 11926 (S.D.N.Y. Aug. 15, 2001). *See also* 154 Cong. Rec. H8290, 8291 (daily ed. Sept. 17, 2008) (suggesting that ADAAA would result in the coverage of individuals with learning disabilities).

The summative approach is now expressly rejected. In the definition of "Condition, manner, or duration," the EEOC regulations explicitly state that "someone with a learning disability may achieve a high level of academic success, but may nevertheless be substantially limited in the major life activity of learning because of the additional time or effort he or she must spend to read, write, or learn compared to most people in the general population." 29 C.F.R. § 1630.2(j)(4)(iii).

The EEOC Interpretive Guidance further explains:

> [S]omeone with a learning disability may achieve a high level of academic success, but may nevertheless be substantially limited in the major life activity of learning because of the additional time or effort he or she must spend to read, write, or learn compared to most people in the general population. As Congress emphasized in passing the Amendments Act, "[w]hen considering the condition, manner, or duration in which an individual with a specific learning disability performs a major life activity, it is critical to reject the assumption that an individual who has performed well academically cannot be substantially limited in activities such as learning, reading, writing, thinking, or speaking." 2008 Senate Statement of Managers at 8. Congress noted that: "In particular, some courts have found that students who have reached a high level of academic achievement are not to be considered individuals with

disabilities under the ADA, as such individuals may have difficulty demonstrating substantial limitation in the major life activities of learning or reading relative to 'most people.'" When considering the condition, manner or duration in which an individual with a specific learning disability performs a major life activity, it is critical to reject the assumption that an individual who performs well academically or otherwise cannot be substantially limited in activities such as learning, reading, writing, thinking, or speaking. As such, the Committee rejects the findings in *Price* v. *National Board of Medical Examiners, Gonzales* v. *National Board of Medical Examiners*, and *Wong* v. *Regents of University of California.*

29 C.F.R. § 1630.2(j)(4) app. [ADA Handbook p. 115]

The Department of Justice has issued a Notice of Proposed Rulemaking that would apply ADA to individuals with learning disabilities and AD/HD under Titles II and III. *See* DOJ NPRM: Department of Justice, Office of the Attorney General, 28 CFR Parts 35 and 36, CRT Docket No. 124; AG Order No., RIN 1190–AA59, Amendment of Americans with Disabilities Act Title II and Title III Regulations to Implement ADA Amendments Act of 2008 (January 22, 2014), available at http://www.ada.gov/nprm_adaaa/nprm_adaaa.htm.

NOTES AND PROBLEMS FOR DISCUSSION

1. The case of Marilyn Bartlett is one of the few exceptions to the pattern prior to 2008 of courts exclusively looking at individuals with learning disabilities through a summative lens. As such, *Bartlett* provides an example for how courts in the future should address claims by individuals with learning disabilities. *See Bartlett v. New York Board of Law Examiners*, 970 F. Supp. 1094, 1117 (S.D.N.Y. 1997), *aff'd*, 2 F. Supp. 2d (S.D.N.Y. 19979), *aff'd in part and vacated in part on other grounds* 156 F.3d 321 (2d Cir. 1998), *vacated and remanded*, 527 U.S. 1031 (1999), *aff'd in part and remanded in part*, 226 F.3d 69 (2d Cir. 2000), *aff'd in part*, 2001 U.S. Dist. Lexis 11926 (S.D. N.Y. 2001).

Bartlett earned a Ph.D. in Educational Administration and graduated from the Vermont Law College. When Bartlett registered for the New York State Bar Exam, she requested accommodations for dyslexia, including extended time, the option of recording her essays on tape, and permission to circle her multiple choice answers in the test book. Bartlett's dyslexia was documented to adversely impact her reading speed, fluency and automaticity. The experts advising the New York State Law Examiners concluded that Ms. Bartlett didn't have a disability and denied her applications for accommodations on the bar exam. Ms. Bartlett attempted the bar exam several more times, unaccommodated and without success.

In 1993, Bartlett sued the New York State Bar for disability discrimination. The *Bartlett* case wound its way through the federal courts for nine years (including a lengthy trial before then District Court Judge Sotomayor). In *Bartlett I*, 970 F. Supp. 1094 (S.D.N.Y 1997), the district court (Sotomayor) held that Bartlett was substantially limited in the major life activity of "working." The matter was appealed to the Second Circuit. After a remand trial, the district court again held that Bartlett was substantially limited in "working" in addition to finding that she was substantially limited in the major life activity of "reading," the only other major life activity addressed at the appellate level. In finding that Bartlett was substantially limited in the major life activity of reading, the court looked to the condition, manner and duration in which Bartlett read as compared to most people, finding:

> When I view the evidence as a whole, including both the positive and negative side effects of the mitigating measures plaintiff uses, I find that plaintiff is substantially limited in the major life activity of reading when compared to most people. All of plaintiff's experts agree that most people do not read with the level of difficulty experienced by plaintiff. *(internal citations omitted)* The testimony of plaintiff and her experts have convinced me that "most people" can do the following things that are extremely difficult or impossible for plaintiff: read and write quickly and automatically, recognize words and letters automatically, develop a sight vocabulary, and form letters without consciously thinking what they look like. "Most people" do not need other people to read to them, write for them, or edit their basic grammar and spelling. "Most people" are able to skim or scan text. "Most people" can read for longer than thirty minutes without experiencing fatigue. (Tr. at 163.)
>
> The effect of plaintiff's reading impairment on her life, even with all of her self-accommodations, is profound. *Cf.* 29 C.F.R. Pt. 1630, App. A § 1630.2(j) ("The determination of whether an individual has a disability is . . . based on . . . the effect of that impairment on the life of the individual."). Plaintiff has difficulty with tasks that most people perform effortlessly, including reading short e-mails, using a telephone directory or electronic database, writing a shopping list, or following a recipe. Plaintiff generally avoids reading any unnecessary material and does not read for pleasure. . . . plaintiff consistently tries to find alternative routes around reading.

Bartlett v. New York State Board of Law Examiners, 2001 U.S. Dist. Lexis 11926 (S.D.N.Y. 2001) (Sotomayor, C.J. sitting by designation).

2. If you were asked to represent a client with dyslexia, how would you use the ADA Amendments to establish that she is an individual with a disability? Would your choice of major life activities make a strategic difference? Would it be harder or easier to use the major life activities of reading, writing, thinking, learning, and/or working? Assume that beyond an intra-personal evaluation by a school psychologist, your client has no evidence to offer you. This evaluation reveals that as to some elements of reading, such as decoding, your client performs as well as most persons. In other aspects of reading, such as fluency, she performs poorly. Should it matter to a court how many or which elements of reading are impaired in order to determine if your client is an individual with a disability on the basis of impaired reading? Beyond intrapersonal discrepancies, what other kinds of comparisons might you want to provide to the court? How would you educate a judge that your client's learning disability is real?

3. If your client were an individual with the impairment of AD/HD, what evidence would you want to present that he or she was an individual with a disability?

Do you think test-taking should be a major life activity? In *Bartlett*, in 1997, then-judge Sotomayor reasoned that, of plaintiff's proposed activities, "[o]nly test-taking could arguably not be 'basic.' But in the modern era, where *test-taking begins* in the first grade, and standardized tests are a regular and often life-altering occurrence thereafter, both in school and at work, I find test-taking is within the ambit of 'major life activity.' " *Bartlett v. New York State Bd. of Law Exam'rs*, 970 F. Supp. 1094, 1117 (S.D.N.Y. 1997). *See also Doe v. Samuel Merritt University*, No. C-13-00007 JSC, 2013 U.S. Dist. LEXIS 14982, at *5 (N.D. Cal. Feb. 1, 2013) ("Since 1997, the central role of test-taking in our society has only increased.").

2. Prong Two: Record of an Impairment

The statutory language for "record of" an impairment was not changed by the ADAAA. It continues to say that an individual can be considered disabled by virtue of having "a record of such an impairment" with the word "such" referring to the first prong. In other words, an individual has a *record* of a physical or mental impairment that substantially limits one or more major life activities.

The leading case on the "record of" prong is a case under the Rehabilitation Act, *School Board of Nassau County v. Arline*, 480 U.S. 273 (1987), discussed above. In that case, the Court noted:

> This impairment [tuberculosis] was serious enough to require hospitalization, a fact more than sufficient to establish that one or more major life activities were substantially limited by her impairment. Thus, Arline's hospitalization for tuberculosis in 1957 suffices to establish that she has a "record of . . . impairment" within the meaning of 29 U.S.C. § 706(7)(B)(ii), and is therefore a handicapped individual.

Similarly, the Third Circuit has explained: "A person with a record of impairment can still qualify as a handicapped individual even if that individual's impairment does not presently limit one or more of that person's major life activities. Thus, for example, a person who has recovered from a history of mental or emotional illness, heart disease, or cancer may always be a handicapped individual under the statute. 45 C.F.R., pt. 84, App. A (1990)." *Nathanson v. Medical College of Pennsylvania*, 926 F.2d 1368 (3d Cir. 1991).

Even though Congress did not amend the definition of "record of" in the ADAAA, the EEOC promulgated new regulations to interpret this prong of the statute. These regulations state:

> (k) Has a record of such an impairment —
>
> > (1) *In general.* An individual has a record of a disability if the individual has a history of, or has been misclassified as having, a mental or physical impairment that substantially limits one or more major life activities.
> >
> > (2) *Broad construction.* Whether an individual has a record of an impairment that substantially limited a major life activity shall be construed broadly to the maximum extent permitted by the ADA and should not demand extensive analysis. An individual will be considered to

> have a record of a disability if the individual has a history of an impairment that substantially limited one or more major life activities when compared to most people in the general population, or was misclassified as having had such an impairment. In determining whether an impairment substantially limited a major life activity, the principles articulated in paragraph (j) of this section apply.
>
> (3) *Reasonable accommodation.* An individual with a record of a substantial limiting impairment may be entitled, absent undue hardship, to a reasonable accommodation if needed and related to the past disability. For example, an employee with an impairment that previously limited, but no longer substantially limits, a major life activity may need leave or a schedule change to permit him or her to attend follow-up or "monitoring" appointments with a health care provider.

29 C.F.R. § 1630.2(k).

NOTES AND PROBLEMS FOR DISCUSSION

1. Does it make sense to say that someone who is not currently "actually disabled" should be entitled to accommodations? Can you find the statutory basis for these regulations?

2. The EEOC's Interpretive Guidance provides examples of individuals who might meet this definition of disability. They include:

- an individual who was treated for cancer ten years ago but who is now deemed by a doctor to be free of cancer;
- an individual who is misclassified as having learning disabilities or intellectual disabilities;
- an individual who in the past was misdiagnosed with bipolar disorder and hospitalized as a result of a temporary reaction to medication she was taking

29 C.F.R. § 1630.2(k) app. [ADA Handbook, p. 118]

How do each of these individuals meet the "record of" definition? Do they have a history of disability? Or were they misclassified as disabled in the past? Does it make sense to say they have a history of misclassification of being disabled?

3. Does prohibiting disability discrimination in the workplace include a duty to accommodate actions that formerly disabled individuals must take to prevent the reoccurrence of a disability? For example, could an employer be required to place an individual with a record of skin cancer only in positions that did not involve direct exposure to sunlight? What if the preventive action the employee wishes to take is neither necessary nor rationale? Must an employer permit a veteran of the war in Iraq, with post-traumatic stress disorder, the opportunity to bring his bomb-sniffing dog with him to work to ensure that there are no explosive devices present in the work place?

4. Before the ADAAA, some courts construed the "record of" requirement to require that the employer acted on the basis of an inaccurate written record of plaintiff's physical condition. For example, the Eighth Circuit has said that in order for a plaintiff to have a "record of" case, an employee's "documentation must show" that he has a history of or has been subject to misclassification as disabled. *See Weber v. Strippit, Inc.*, 186 F.3d 907, 915 (8th Cir. 1999).

The EEOC's Interpretive Guidance takes a broader view of how to meet the "record of" requirement. It says: "There are many types of records that could potentially contain this information, including but not limited to, education, medical or employment records . . . . An individual may have a 'record of' a substantially limiting impairment — and thus be protected under the 'record of' prong of the statute — even if a covered entity does not specifically know about the relevant record." 29 C.F.R. § 1630.2 app. [ADA Handbook, p. 119]

Because Congress did not amend the definition of "record of" despite presumably being aware of the Eighth Circuit's interpretation of that language, should courts disregard the EEOC's interpretation of that requirement with respect to the need to have a written record?

3. Prong Three: Regarded as Having an Impairment

Congress amended the "regarded as" prong in the ADAAA to read as follows:

> (3) REGARDED AS HAVING SUCH AN IMPAIRMENT — For purposes of paragraph (1)(C):
>
> (A) An individual meets the requirement of "being regarded as having such an impairment" if the individual establishes that he or she has been subjected to an action prohibited under this Act because of an actual or perceived physical or mental impairment whether or not the impairment limits or is perceived to limit a major life activity.
>
> (B) Paragraph 1(C) shall not apply to impairments that are transitory and minor. A transitory impairment is an impairment with an actual or expected duration of 6 months or less.

42 U.S.C. § 12102(3).

In the Miscellaneous Provisions, Congress also added the following provision:

> A covered entity under subchapter I, a public entity under subchapter II, and any person who owns, leases (or leases to), or operates a place of public accommodation under subchapter III, need not provide a reasonable accommodation or a reasonable modification to policies, practices, or procedures to an individual who meets the definition of disability in section 12102(1) solely under subparagraph (C) of such section.

42 U.S.C. § 12201(h).

Read together, these statutory provisions mean that an individual is covered by the ADA if the individual has been subjected to an action prohibited by the ADA because of an actual or perceived impairment so long as the impairment is not transitory and minor. The concepts of "major life activities" and "substantial limitation" are not relevant in evaluating whether an individual is regarded as having an impairment. But an individual who qualifies as disabled under the ADA only under the "regarded as" prong *cannot* seek what Title I calls a "reasonable accommodation" or the other titles call a "reasonable modification." Hence, as the EEOC Interpretive Guidance notes in quoting a statement by the key sponsors of the ADAAA, Congress expected the first prong "of the definition to be used only by people who are affirmatively seeking reasonable accommodations or modifications. Any individual who has been discriminated against because of an impairment — short of being granted a reasonable accommodation or modification — should be bringing a claim under the third prong of the definition which will require no showing with regard to the severity of his or her impairment." 29 C.F.R. § 1630.2(l) app. [ADA Handbook, p. 122, quoting Joint Hoyer-Sensenbrenner Statement at 6]

NOTES AND PROBLEMS FOR DISCUSSION

1. Who are the individuals for whom this prong provides important protection? These are likely to be individuals who are subject to myths, stereotypes and biases about individuals with disabilities, much the same as people of color might experience discrimination on the basis of race and national origin or women on the basis of sex. In such cases, the question is likely to be whether the nondiscriminatory grounds that the employer articulated for firing an employee were a pretext for disability discrimination. Examples might include a school district that will not hire as a teacher any applicant that the district believes has a mental illness or an accounting firm that will not hire any applicant with a facial deformity because the deformity is misapprehended as evidence of an intellectual disability. The persons who experience these prejudices may be quite able to do every element of the vacancy in question, without an accommodation. They merely need a nondiscriminatory employment opportunity.

2. Does it make sense that for persons who are not seeking any form of accommodation that the threshold burden for establishing coverage under the ADA should be less than other the first two prongs? In the Purposes section of the ADAAA, Congress stated that one purpose of the Amendments was "to reject the Supreme Court's reasoning in *Sutton v. United Air Lines, Inc.*, 527 U.S. 471 (1999) with regard to coverage under the third prong of the definition of disability and to reinstate the reasoning of the Supreme Court in *School Board of Nassau County v. Arline*, 480 U.S. 273 (1987) which set forth a broad view of the third prong of the definition of handicap under the Rehabilitation Act of 1973." The language that Congress approved from *Arline* is the notion "that the negative reactions of others are just as disabling as the actual impact of an impairment." *See* 29 C.F.R. § 1630.2(l) app. [ADA Handbook, p. 120, quoting 2008 Senate Statement of Managers at 9]

How would a court apply the "regarded as" prong to the *Sutton* plaintiffs in light of the ADAAA? Would the plaintiffs even have to identify a major life activity?

3. Would Adolphus Maddox, as described below, be covered by the ADAAA?

> The City of Dallas has adopted a Driver Safety Program to reduce the risk of vehicular collisions for City employees. The City requires its "primary drivers" to have 20/40 vision (corrected) and a field of vision of at least 70 degrees in the horizontal meridian in each eye. Adolphus Maddox, a City employee, has impaired vision which can only be corrected to 20/60 in his left eye, and his horizontal field of vision in that eye is less than 70 degrees. Maddox's vision does not substantially limit any life activity, except his ability to serve as a "primary driver" for the City of Dallas. Maddox has been allowed to retain his job with the City on the condition that a co-worker drive him when he is required to work at other facilities. Does Maddox qualify as disabled under the ADA? *See Chandler v. City of Dallas*, 2 F.3d 1385 (5th Cir. 1993).

4. Individuals with mental health impairments often had difficulty meeting any prong of the prior ADA definition of disability. Consider the following two fact patterns in which the plaintiffs were found not to come within the statutory definition of disability. Would they at least qualify for prong three under the ADAAA?

> John Reeves experienced his first symptoms of severe anxiety in July 2011 when visiting Disney World. After returning home to New York, he experienced the same symptoms whenever he contemplated going to an unfamiliar place. When his employer sought to send him to a training program out of state, he was unable to fly to Virginia and instead drove there accompanied by his aunt. He was diagnosed with Panic Disorder with Agoraphobia. His condition led to pervasive avoidance of a variety of potentially panic-provoking situations including, among other things, being alone outside the home or being home alone; traveling in an automobile, bus or airplane (under certain conditions); or being on a bridge. Reeves was fully able to perform his duties at work so long he limited his overnight shifts. Reeves was discharged from his job and claimed that he was fired because of his disability. Reeves alleges that he is disabled because he is substantially limited in the major life activity of "everyday mobility."

See Reeves v. Johnson Controls World Services, Inc., 140 F.3d 144 (2d Cir. 1998).

> In early 2012, Carol Doyal began to experience significant feelings of helplessness, anxiety, excessive stress, and lack of motivation as well as difficulty thinking clearly, concentrating, learning, remembering, and interacting with others. She felt disinterested in work, life, eating, and caring for herself. She experienced insomnia, often sleeping only one to three hours a night. She saw a psychiatrist who prescribed an anti-depressant medication. The medication helped tremendously. She transferred to a new position as the Director of Human Resources. Nonetheless, she tended to forget the names of candidates that she interviewed for jobs. Like others at her workplace, she also had trouble learning the new computer system. Instead of having trouble sleeping, she now found herself sleeping for long stretches up to 14 hours. She also had obvious difficulty choosing between job candidates and appeared to have trouble making even simple decisions. Although she claimed to continue to have difficulty interacting with others after she started taking medication,

> her employer introduced evidence that she functioned normally at meetings. She was fired from her position because of her inability to make decisions and her lapses of memory, judgment, and confidentiality. Doyal brought suit under the ADA, claiming that she was discharged because of her disability. She alleges that she is disabled in the major life activities of sleeping, learning, thinking, and interacting with others.

See Doyal v. Oklahoma Heart, Inc., 213 F.3d 492 (10th Cir. 2000).

5. One of the most challenging interpretive questions under the "regarded as" definition has been the meaning of the exception for "transitory and minor" impairments. That issue recently arose in a case in the Western District of Pennsylvania. Consider the following facts from the case:

> Anthony Gaus suffered from chronic pain and took prescribed, narcotic medication to treat his condition. He was medically disqualified from his work as an electrician on January 9, 2009 and cleared to return to work in July 2010. His employer, however, refused to allow him to return to work saying his high level of narcotic medication exceeded their medical guidelines and made him unqualified to return to work. When he sought to return to work, and filed suit based on his employer's refusal to allow him to return to work, his employer argued that his impairment was "transitory and minor," that it did not "regard him" as disabled because he could not meet the "substantially limited" part of the test and that he was not "otherwise qualified" for the position because he poses a direct threat to the other individuals in the workplace.

With respect to the "transitory and minor" defense, the court found that his impairments were neither transitory nor minor because they clearly lasted more than six months. With respect to the substantial limitation issue, the court found that the ADAAA no longer require a "regarded as" plaintiff to show that his impairment substantially limits a major life activity. He need only demonstrate that he was subjected to an adverse action as a result of an actual or perceived physical or mental impairment. The district court was quite critical of the pre-2008 cases that the defendant sought to use to bolster its position. Finally, with respect to the direct threat issue, the court found that Gaus was entitled to an individualized evaluation of whether he posed a threat to the safety of others at the workplace and the defendant could not apply a blanket ban on all employees taking certain narcotic medications. Do you agree with that analysis? *See Gaus v. Norfolk Southern Railway Co.*, Civil Action No. 09 1698, 2011 U.S. Dist. LEXIS 111089 (W.D. Pa. Sept. 28, 2011).

Interpretation of the "transitory and minor" issue also arose recently in a Sixth Circuit decision. Consider the following facts:

> Joseph White returned to work with temporary lifting restrictions as a maintenance truck/trailer tech following an injury that caused him to fracture his leg. Because heavy lifting was an essential function of the position, his employer terminated his employment.

The district court found, and the Sixth Circuit agreed, that White could not meet the "regarded as" definition because the medical evidence indicated that his medical restrictions would only be in effect for a month or two, so it constituted a transitory impairment. Do you agree with that analysis? *See White v. Interstate Distributor*, 2011 U.S. App. LEXIS 17642 (6th Cir. Aug. 23, 2011). *See also LaPier v. Prince George's County, Md.*, Civil Action No. 10-CV-2851 AW, 2012 U.S. Dist. LEXIS 59496 (D. Md. Apr. 27, 2012).

It is important to remember, however, that the exception for "transitory and minor" impairments only applies to the "regarded as" prong. As recently noted by the Seventh Circuit, an impairment that is episodic or in remission is a disability if it would substantially limit a major life activity when active. *Gogos v. AMS Mechanical Systems, Inc.*, 737 F.3d 1170, 1172-73 (7th Cir. 2013). Anthimos Gogos had elevated blood pressure that caused him to experience intermittent vision loss; he was fired as a result of one episode of intermittent vision loss. The Seventh Circuit reversed the district court's dismissal of his claim, finding that he had alleged a covered disability. Similarly, as the Sixth Circuit has noted, the temporary exception does not apply to an individual who is actually impaired, even if the disability is not expected to be permanent. *See Summers v. Altarum Institute, Corp.*, 740 F.3d 325 (4th Cir. 2014) (plaintiff had a severe leg break and other injuries that precluded him from walking normally for seven months).

6. Who bears the burden of proof with regard to whether an impairment is transitory and minor? Must the Plaintiff introduce evidence of duration and severity to remove this limitation or is the burden on the employer? *Dube v. Texas Health & Human Servs. Comm'n*, Civil Action No. SA-11-CV-354-XR, 2011 U.S. Dist. LEXIS 101189 (W.D. Tex. Sept. 8, 2011). When is the question of whether an impairment is transitory and minor a matter for the court to decide in a motion for summary judgment or a question that should be left for a jury to decide? Do you agree with the following statement from a district court on that issue?

> In moving for summary judgment with respect to this element, [the employer] Valley Health contends that [the plaintiff employee] "Chamberlain was never 'regarded as' disabled because Valley Health believed her vision problem was transitory and minor." Construing all of the evidence and factual inferences in favor of Chamberlain, however, the court concludes that a reasonable jury could find to the contrary. . . . Assuming the truth of Chamberlain's assertions, the court concludes that the issue of whether Valley Health believed that Chamberlain's impairment was both transitory and minor must be decided by a jury.

Chamberlain v. Valley Health System, Inc., 781 F. Supp. 2d 305 (W.D. Va. 2011).

7. Plaintiffs seem to be increasingly using the "regarded as" prong, even when they might meet the "actually disabled" prong because that precludes them from having to demonstrate a substantial limitation of a major life activity. Consider the following case that proceeded under the "regarded as" prong:

> Elizabeth Wells experienced serious gastrointestinal problems that caused nausea, vomiting and diarrhea. She used prescription medicine to control the side effects and took intermittent FMLA leave as necessary. She worked as a nurse and had a brief period of time when her behavior was aberrant due to the side effects of one prescription drug (that she has stopped taking). When

she was cleared to return to work in July 2009, her employer refused to allow her to return to work at her original position and said her medical condition posed a direct threat to the health and safety of the patients. Nonetheless, it allowed her to work in other areas of the hospital.

The district court concluded there was sufficient evidence for a juror to conclude that she met the "regarded as" prong of the definition because her gastrointestinal problems qualified as a physiological disorder. In a confusing passage, the district court also stated: "to the extent that the side effects of Plaintiff's proper use of prescription medication adversely affected her ability to work, it would contribute to a finding that she was disabled." The confusing aspect of that passage is that a "regarded as" plaintiff need not demonstrate a substantial limitation of a major life activity. Was the court *also* finding she was "actually disabled" in the major life activity of working?

With respect to the direct threat issue, the court found that issue should go to the jury because a reasonable juror could conclude that the defendant did not consider all of the currently available information in concluding she presented a health and safety risk if she returned to work in her original position. Do you agree with that analysis? *See Wells v. Cincinnati Children's Hospital Medical Center*, 860 F. Supp. 2d 469 (S.D. Ohio 2012).

C. DOCUMENTATION

There would be no point to creating new rules of construction for the definition of disability if the various public and private entities that must decide who is an individual with a disability, such as licensing, certification, or credentialing bodies for secondary or post-secondary education, professional, or trade purposes imposed highly burdensome documentation requirements. *See* 28 C.F.R. § 36.102(a)(3).

Two of the EEOC's nine rules of construction pertain to documentation. Rule 4 states in pertinent part: "The determination of whether an impairment substantially limits a major life activity requires an individualized assessment." Rule 5 states: "The comparison of an individual's performance of a major life activity to the performance of the same major life activity by most people in the general population usually will not require scientific, medical, or statistical analysis. Nothing in this paragraph is intended, however, to prohibit the presentation of scientific, medical, or statistical evidence to make such a comparison where appropriate." 29 C.F.R. § 1630.2(j)(1)(iv) and (v), respectively.

The Department of Justice initially set out the parameters of appropriate documentation requests relating to licensing, certification, or credentialing examinations and courses in its 1991 Preamble to 28 C.F.R. part 36, stating that "requests for documentation must be reasonable and must be limited to the need for the modification or aid requested." *See* 28 C.F.R. pt. 36, app. B at 735 (2009). Since then, the Department gained administrative experience through its own enforcement efforts, research, gaining familiarity with the body of knowledge concerning testing and modifications, and by receiving extensive comments to its Notice of Proposed Rule Making (NPRM) for the current regulations.

DOJ received the most comments concerning this language from its 2008 NPRM:

> Generally, a testing entity should accept without further inquiry documentation provided by a qualified professional who has made an individualized assessment of the applicant. Appropriate documentation may include a letter from a qualified professional or evidence of a prior diagnosis, or accommodation, or classification, such as eligibility for a special education program. When an applicant's documentation is recent and demonstrates a consistent history of a diagnosis, there is no need for further inquiry into the nature of the disability. A testing entity should consider an applicant's past use of a particular auxiliary aid or service.

73 Fed. Reg. 34,508, 34,539 (June 17, 2008).

Many comments were received from testing and licensing entities, state governments, professional education organizations, and disability rights groups. Testing entities and professional organizations raised concerns about students feigning or falsely claiming disability and were apprehensive about having to rely upon cursory documentation without sufficient information to make informed decisions. Disability rights groups and other professional organizations complained of burdensome documentation requirements. They also noted that for learning disabilities in particular, personal knowledge of the test applicant was necessary to a reliable evaluation. Yet, testing entities often rejected professional evaluations submitted by students these entities had never met. These commenters further complained that some entities made it impossible to provide additional documentation in time for the next scheduled examination. One organization complained that there was no scientific basis for repeatedly assessing persons with dyslexia as at some point this impairment becomes static.

Specifically, one disability rights organization noted that:

> requiring an individual with a long and early history of disability to be assessed within three years of taking the test in question is . . . burdensome, stating that "[t]here is no scientific evidence that learning disabilities abate with time, nor that Attention Deficits abate with time * * *." This organization noted that there is no justification for repeatedly subjecting people to expensive testing regimens simply to satisfy a disbelieving industry. This is particularly true for adults with, for example, learning disabilities such as dyslexia, a persistent condition without the need for retesting once the diagnosis has been established and accepted by a standardized testing agency.

75 Fed. Reg. 56,297 (Sept. 15, 2010).

In its Section-by-Section Analysis and Response to Public Comments, DOJ responded to those concerns as follows:

> Commenters also sought clarification of the term individualized assessment. The Department's intention in using this term is to ensure that documentation provided on behalf of a testing candidate is not only provided by a qualified professional, but also reflects that the qualified professional has individually and personally evaluated the candidate as opposed to simply considering

> scores from a review of documents. This is particularly important in the learning disabilities context, where proper diagnosis requires face-to-face evaluation. Reports from experts who have personal familiarity with the candidate should take precedence over those from, for example, reviewers for testing agencies, who have never personally met the candidate or conducted the requisite assessments for diagnosis and treatment.

75 Fed. Reg. 56,297 (Sept. 15, 2010).

The potential impact of this language proposed by the DOJ was particularly important because it would create a presumption for test applicants that the conclusions reached by the qualified professionals who conduct their evaluations would be correct. This language would also accord considerable deference to a record of prior accommodations. Following the comment period, this important provision was retained. "It remains the Department's view that, when testing entities receive documentation provided by a qualified professional who has made an individualized assessment of an applicant that supports the need for the modification, accommodation, or aid requested, they shall generally accept such documentation and provide the accommodation." 75 Fed. Reg. 56,297 (Sept. 15, 2010).

On September 15, 2010, the Department of Justice published the final ADA Title III regulations, which contain the regulation governing examinations and courses. 75 Fed. Reg. 56,236 (Sept. 15, 2010). With regard to documentation, the regulations provide:

28 C.F.R. § 36.309 Examinations and courses

(a) *General.* Any private entity that offers examinations or courses related to applications, licensing, certification, or credentialing for secondary or postsecondary education, professional, or trade purposes shall offer such examinations or courses in a place and manner accessible to persons with disabilities or offer alternative accessible arrangements for such individuals.

(b) *Examinations.*

(1) Any private entity offering an examination covered by this section must assure that —

(i) The examination is selected and administered so as to best ensure that, when the examination is administered to an individual with a disability that impairs sensory, manual, or speaking skills, the examination results accurately reflect the individual's aptitude or achievement level or whatever other factor the examination purports to measure, rather than reflecting the individual's impaired sensory, manual, or speaking skills (except where those skills are the factors that the examination purports to measure);

. . . .

(iv) Any request for documentation, if such documentation is required, is reasonable and limited to the need for the modification, accommodation, or auxiliary aid or service requested.

(v) When considering requests for modifications, accommodations, or auxiliary aids or services, the entity gives considerable weight to documentation of past modifications, accommodations, or auxiliary aids or services received in similar testing situations, as well as such modifications, accommodations, or related aids and services provided in response to an Individualized Education Program (IEP) provided under the Individuals with Disabilities Education Act or a plan describing services provided pursuant to section 504 of the Rehabilitation Act of 1973, as amended (often referred as a Section 504 Plan).

(vi) The entity responds in a timely manner to requests for modifications, accommodations, or aids to ensure equal opportunity for individuals with disabilities.

NOTES AND PROBLEMS FOR DISCUSSION

1. According to the Department of Justice, its authority to issue the testing documentation regulations, quoted above, are based on language in ADA Title III governing "Examinations and Courses." This statutory provision, which will be more fully discussed in Chapter Five, states:

> Any person that offers examinations or courses related to applications, licensing, certification, or credentialing for secondary or postsecondary education, professional, or trade purposes shall offer such examinations or courses in a place and manner accessible to persons with disabilities or offer alternative accessible arrangements for such individuals.

42 U.S.C. § 12189.

Do you think that this brief legislative passage is sufficient authority for the Department of Justice to issue the extensive guidance on examination and courses found in 28 C.F.R. § 36.309, above? *See Enyart v. National Conference of Bar Examiners*, 630 F.3d 1153 (9th Cir.), *cert. denied*, 132 S. Ct. 366 (2011).

2. A number of organizations that commented on the Title III regulation, quoted above, questioned why a similar regulation was not issued for Title II, particularly as many licensing entities are elements of state governments. The Justice Department responded to this concern in its Section-by-Section Analysis and Response to Public Comments for the ADA Title II regulations:

> . . . Because section 309 of the ADA 42 U.S.C. 12189, reaches "[a]ny person that offers examinations or courses related to applications, licensing, certification, or credentialing for secondary or post secondary education, professional, or trade purposes," public entities also are covered by this section of the ADA. Indeed, the requirements contained in title II (including the general prohibitions against discrimination, the program access requirements, the reasonable modifications requirements, and the communications

> requirements) apply to courses and examinations administered by public entities that meet the requirements of section 309. While the Department considers these requirements to be sufficient to ensure that examinations and courses administered by public entities meet the section 309 requirements, the Department acknowledges that the title III regulation, because it addresses examinations in some detail, is useful as a guide for determining what constitutes discriminatory conduct by a public entity in testing situations. *See* 28 C.F.R. 36.309.

75 Fed. Reg. 56,236 (Sept. 15, 2010).

3. Why didn't the Justice Department simply use its authority under Title II to create rules that parallel the Title III regulations on documentation? What does it mean when one regulation is intended as a "guide" in interpreting another regulation? Was the term "guide" used to recognize that there may be some important differences between public and private entities? What might those differences be? Does the term "guide" render 28 C.F.R. § 36.309 advisory at best for public entities facing documentation questions?

4. In a routine post-secondary setting, do these Title III regulation rules, which are largely about licensing and certification exams, make sense? Should a college officer, who is responsible for providing a student with many accommodations over a number of years, be expected to know more about a student than a standardized testing entity that will be providing accommodations only once or twice? *See* Association on Higher Education and Disability (AHEAD), *Supporting Accommodation Requests: Guidance On Documentation Practices* (Apr. 2012), available at http://www.ahead.org/resources/documentation_guidance (last viewed on Apr. 28, 2013).

Chapter 3

EMPLOYMENT DISCRIMINATION

A. GENERAL INFORMATION

ADA Title I prohibits a covered entity from discriminating against a qualified individual with a disability because of the disability of such individual in regard to most aspects of the employment relationship. 42 U.S.C. § 12112. A "covered entity" means an "employer, employment agency, labor organization, or joint labor-management committee." 42 U.S.C. § 12111(2). ADA Title II, which only covers public entities, also protects qualified individuals with disabilities from discrimination, including employment discrimination. *See* 42 U.S.C. § 12132. Thus, employment discrimination against individuals with disabilities is prohibited under the ADA by both Title I (employment title) and Title II (public entities title). To create uniformity in the standards applied to public and private entities, the Equal Employment Opportunity Commission (EEOC) has specified that the rules and regulations promulgated under Title I are equally applicable to Title II. *See* 28 C.F.R. § 35.140(b)(1). Thus, the rules and standards of ADA Title I are incorporated into the case law involving public entities under ADA Title II. Also, to create uniformity, the Rehabilitation Act Amendments of 1992, 138 Cong. Rec. H10735-36 (daily ed. Oct. 2, 1992), provide that ADA Title I standards apply to employment discrimination actions arising under Sections 504 and 501 of the Rehabilitation Act. Accordingly, this chapter will discuss employment discrimination claims brought against both private and public entities, with the emphasis being on ADA Title I standards.

The general rule of nondiscrimination set forth in ADA Title I provides that:

> No covered entity shall discriminate against a qualified individual on the basis of disability in regard to job application procedures, the hiring, advancement or discharge of employees, employee compensation, job training, and other terms, conditions, and privileges of employment.

42 U.S.C. § 12112(a).

When Congress amended the ADA in 2008, it added a provision in the Miscellaneous Section (Title V) to clarify that "reverse discrimination" claims are not permissible under the ADA. Section 12201(g) states: "Nothing in this Act shall provide the basis for a claim by a person without a disability that he or she was subject to discrimination because of his or her lack of disability." This language arguably became necessary because the amended ADA did not require that an individual be an "individual with a disability" to bring suit under Title I. Instead, one has to establish only that one is a qualified individual who has faced discrimination on the "basis of disability." In the absence of the language in Section 12201(g), a court could have interpreted Section

12112(a) to permit reverse discrimination suits on the basis of a lack of disability.

Although ADA Title I prohibits many forms of discrimination, EEOC statistics indicate that an unlawful discharge is the most frequently cited ADA violation. In 2009, the EEOC reported that unlawful discharge has been cited in 54.2% of cases. The second most cited violation, at 40.3%, is failure to provide reasonable accommodation. Failure to hire was cited in 26.4% of cases.[1] Thus, "discharge" is the most frequently cited violation rather than "failure to hire."

B. QUALIFIED INDIVIDUAL WITH A DISABILITY

1. General Requirements

In the 1990 version of the ADA, the statute referred to a "qualified individual with a disability" in section 12111(8). The 2008 Amendments deleted the phrase "with a disability" in that provision. Similarly, look at the redlined version of section 12112 [ADA Handbook, p. 17*] to see how Congress made minor changes in how it used the phrase "a qualified individual on the basis of disability."

The EEOC has explained in its Interpretive Guidance that the purpose of those changes is to "signal to both lawyers and courts to spend less time and energy on the minutia of an individual's impairment, and more time and energy on the merits of the case — including whether discrimination occurred because of the disability, whether an individual was qualified for a job or eligible for a service, and whether a reasonable accommodation or modification was called for under the law." 29 C.F.R. § 1630.4 app. [ADA Handbook, pp. 131–32] (quoting Joint Hoyer-Sensenbrenner Statement at 4).

Each title of the ADA contains its own definition of a "qualified individual" although these definitions do contain many basic similarities. The Title I definition (which is relevant in the employment context) states that the term "qualified individual":

> means an individual who, with or without reasonable accommodation, can perform the essential functions of the employment position that such individual holds or desires. For the purposes of this subchapter, consideration shall be given to the employer's judgment as to what functions of a job are essential, and if an employer has prepared a written description before advertising or interviewing applicants for the job, this description shall be considered evidence of the essential functions of the job.

42 U.S.C. § 12111(8).

The term "qualified individual" contains other important statutory phrases such as "reasonable accommodation" and "essential functions of the employment position." In this Part of the chapter, we will consider the term "qualified individual" in relation to the "essential functions" requirement. In Part C(1) of this chapter, we will consider the

---

[1] *See* http://www.eeoc.gov/eeoc/litigation/reports/09annrpt.cfm#3.

* Citations to the ADA Handbook refer to Ruth Colker & Paul Grossman, The Law of Disability Discrimination Handbook (LexisNexis 8th Ed. 2013).

meaning of the term "reasonable accommodation" in relation to the requirement that an entity provide a reasonable accommodation to an individual with a disability. When you get to Part C(1), you should return to the definition of "qualified individual" to help you understand the interrelationship between the "qualified individual" and "reasonable accommodation" requirements of the statute.

The concept of a "qualified individual" was first interpreted by the United States Supreme Court in a Section 504 case, *Southeastern Community College v. Davis*, 442 U.S. 397 (1979), which was mentioned in Chapter One and will be discussed extensively in Chapter Four. In that case, involving Section 504, the Court said: "An otherwise qualified person is one who is able to meet all of a program's requirements in spite of his handicap." *Davis*, 442 U.S. at 406.

ADA Title I's definition of a "qualified individual" is derived from the Section 504 definition. Unlike the *Davis* definition, however, the ADA Title I definition does not refer to an individual's ability to meet "all" of a program's requirements and does not include the adjective "otherwise" before "qualified." Instead, it refers to an individual's ability to meet the "essential" functions of the employment position with or without reasonable accommodations. *See* 42 U.S.C. § 12111(8). Finally, it is important to note that ADA Title I states that a court should give "consideration" to the employer's judgment as to what functions of a job are essential without specifying how strong that consideration should be. *See* 42 U.S.C. § 12111(8). In *Albertson's v. Kirkingburg*, 527 U.S. 555 (1999), the Supreme Court provided some guidance on how much weight should be given to the employer's judgment. In the notes that follow this excerpt of the *Alberston's* decision, we shall consider in more detail the issues that are confronting the courts in defining the term "qualified individual" with respect to the requirement that an individual be able to perform the "essential functions of the job."

ALBERTSON'S, INC. v. KIRKINGBURG
527 U.S. 555 (1999)

Justice Souter delivered the opinion for a unanimous Court with respect to Part III of the opinion.

[Hallie Kirkingburg was discharged from his position as a truck driver when Albertson's determined that he could not meet its vision standards due to his monocular vision. In Parts I and II, the Court concluded that the Ninth Circuit used the wrong analysis in determining that he met the definition of disability. That part of the Court's analysis is largely overruled by the 2008 Amendments and is discussed in Chapter Two.]

III

Petitioner's primary contention is that even if Kirkingburg was disabled, he was not a "qualified" individual with a disability, *see* 42 U.S.C. § 12112(a), because Albertson's merely insisted on the minimum level of visual acuity set forth in the DOT's Motor Carrier Safety Regulations, 49 CFR § 391.41(b)(10) (1998). If Albertson's was entitled to enforce that standard as defining an "essential job functio[n] of the employment position," *see* 42 U.S.C. § 12111(8), that is the end of the case, for Kirkingburg concededly could not satisfy it.[13]

Under Title I of the ADA, employers may justify their use of "qualification standards . . . that screen out or tend to screen out or otherwise deny a job or benefit to an individual with a disability," so long as such standards are "job-related and consistent with business necessity, and . . . performance cannot be accomplished by reasonable accommodation. . . ."

Kirkingburg and the Government argue that these provisions do not authorize an employer to follow even a facially applicable regulatory standard subject to waiver without making some enquiry beyond determining whether the applicant or employee meets that standard, yes or no . . .

The Government extends this argument by reference to a further section of the statute, which at first blush appears to be a permissive provision for the employer's and the public's benefit. An employer may impose as a qualification standard "a requirement that an individual shall not pose a direct threat to the health or safety of other individuals in the workplace," § 12113(b), with "direct threat" being defined by the Act as "a significant risk to the health or safety of others, that cannot be eliminated by reasonable accommodation," § 12111(3); *see also* 29 C.F.R. § 1630.2(r) (1998). The Government urges us to read subsections (a) and (b) together to mean that when an employer would impose any safety qualification standard, however specific, tending to screen out individuals with disabilities, the application of the requirement must satisfy the ADA's "direct threat" criterion . . . .[15]

The Court of Appeals majority concluded that the waiver program "precludes [employers] from declaring that persons determined by DOT to be capable of performing the job of commercial truck driver are incapable of performing that job by virtue of their disability," and that in the face of a waiver an employer "will not be able to avoid the [ADA's] strictures by showing that its standards are necessary to prevent a direct safety threat." The Court of Appeals thus assumed that the regulatory provisions for the waiver program had to be treated as being on par with the basic visual acuity regulation, as if the general rule had been modified by some different safety standard made applicable by grant of a waiver. *Cf. Conroy v. Aniskoff*, 507 U.S. 511, 515 (1993) (noting the "cardinal rule that a statute is to be read as a whole" (quoting *King v. St. Vincent's Hospital*, 502 U.S. 215, 221 (1991))). On this reading, an

---

[13] Kirkingburg asserts that in showing that Albertson's initially allowed him to drive with a DOT certification, despite the fact that he did not meet the DOT's minimum visual acuity requirement, he produced evidence from which a reasonable juror could find that he satisfied the legitimate prerequisites of the job. But Petitioner's argument is a legal, not a factual, one. In any event, the ample evidence in the record on Petitioner's policy of requiring adherence to minimum DOT vision standards for its truckdrivers would bar any inference that Petitioner's failure to detect the discrepancy between the level of visual acuity Kirkingburg was determined to have had during his first two certifications and the DOT's minimum visual acuity requirement raised a genuine factual dispute on this issue.

[15] This appears to be the position taken by the EEOC in the Interpretive Guidance promulgated under its authority to issue regulations to carry out Title I of the ADA . . . . Although it might be questioned whether the Government's interpretation, which might impose a higher burden on employers to justify safety-related qualification standards than other job requirements, is a sound one, we have no need to confront the validity of the reading in this case.

individualized determination under a different substantive safety rule was an element of the regulatory regime, which would easily fit with any requirement of 42 U.S.C. §§ 12113(a) and (b) to consider reasonable accommodation. An employer resting solely on the federal standard for its visual acuity qualification would be required to accept a waiver once obtained, and probably to provide an applicant some opportunity to obtain a waiver whenever that was reasonably possible. If this was sound analysis, the District Court's summary judgment for Albertson's was error.

But the reasoning underlying the Court of Appeals's decision was unsound, for we think it was error to read the regulations establishing the waiver program as modifying the content of the basic visual acuity standard in a way that disentitled an employer like Albertson's to insist on it. To be sure, this is not immediately apparent. If one starts with the statutory provisions authorizing regulations by the DOT as they stood at the time the DOT began the waiver program, one would reasonably presume that the general regulatory standard and the regulatory waiver standard ought to be accorded equal substantive significance, so that the content of any general regulation would as a matter of law be deemed modified by the terms of any waiver standard thus applied to it.[16] Safe operation is supposed to be the touchstone of regulation in each instance.

As to the general visual acuity regulations in force under the former provision, affirmative determinations that the selected standards were needed for safe operation were indeed the predicates of the DOT action. Starting in 1937, the federal agencies authorized to regulate commercial motor vehicle safety set increasingly rigorous visual acuity standards, culminating in the current one, which has remained unchanged since it became effective in 1971.[20] When the FHWA proposed it, the agency found that "[a]ccident experience in recent years has demonstrated that reduction of the effects of organic and physical disorders, emotional impairments, and other limitations of the good health of drivers are increasingly important factors in accident prevention," 34 Fed. Reg. 9080, 9081 (1969) (Notice of Proposed Rule Making); the current standard was adopted to reflect the agency's conclusion that "drivers of modern, more complex vehicles" must be able to "withstand the increased physical and mental demands that their occupation now imposes." 35 Fed. Reg. 6458 (1970). Given these findings and "in the light of discussions with the Administration's medical advisers," *id.* at 6459, the FHWA made a considered determination about the level of visual acuity needed for safe operation of commercial motor vehicles in interstate commerce, an "area [in

---

[16] Congress recently amended the waiver provision in the Transportation Equity Act for the 21st Century, Pub. L. 105-178, 112 Stat. 107. It now provides that the Secretary of Transportation may issue a 2-year renewable "exemption" if "such exemption would likely achieve a level of safety that is equivalent to, or greater than, the level that would be achieved absent such exemption." *See* § 4007, 112 Stat. 401, 49 U.S.C.A. § 31315(b) (Supp. 1999).

[20] The Interstate Commerce Commission promulgated the first visual acuity regulations for interstate commercial drivers in 1937, requiring "[g]ood eyesight in both eyes (either with or without glasses, or by correction with glasses), including adequate perception of red and green colors." 2 Fed. Reg. 113120 (1937). In 1939, the vision standard was changed to require "visual acuity (either without glasses or by correction with glasses) of not less than 20/40 (Snellen) in one eye, and 20/100 (Snellen) in the other eye; form field of not less than 45 degrees in all meridians from the point of fixation; ability to distinguish red, green, and yellow." 57 Fed. Reg. 6793–6794 (1992) (internal quotation marks omitted). In 1952, the visual acuity standard was strengthened to require at least 20/40 (Snellen) in each eye. *Id.* at 6794.

which] the risks involved are so well known and so serious as to dictate the utmost caution." *Id.* at 17419.

For several reasons, one would expect any regulation governing a waiver program to establish a comparable substantive standard (albeit for exceptional cases), grounded on known facts indicating at least that safe operation would not be jeopardized . . . .And yet, despite this background, the regulations establishing the waiver program did not modify the general visual acuity standards. It is not that the waiver regulations failed to do so in a merely formal sense, as by turning waiver decisions on driving records, not sight requirements. The FHWA in fact made it clear that it had no evidentiary basis for concluding that the pre-existing standards could be lowered consistently with public safety. When, in 1992, the FHWA published an "[a]dvance notice of proposed rulemaking" requesting comments "on the need, if any, to amend its driver qualification requirements relating to the vision standard," *id.* at 6793, it candidly proposed its waiver scheme as simply a means of obtaining information bearing on the justifiability of revising the binding standards already in place, *see id.* at 10295. The agency explained that the "object of the waiver program is to provide objective data to be considered in relation to a rulemaking exploring the feasibility of relaxing the current absolute vision standards in 49 CFR part 391 in favor of a more individualized standard." *Ibid.* As proposed, therefore, there was not only no change in the unconditional acuity standards, but no indication even that the FHWA then had a basis in fact to believe anything more lenient would be consistent with public safety as a general matter. After a bumpy stretch of administrative procedure, *see Advocates for Highway and Auto Safety v. FHWA*, 28 F.3d 1288, 1290 (D.C. Cir. 1994), the FHWA's final disposition explained again that the waivers were proposed as a way to gather facts going to the wisdom of changing the existing law. The waiver program "will enable the FHWA to conduct a study comparing a group of experienced, visually deficient drivers with a control group of experienced drivers who meet the current Federal vision requirements. This study will provide the empirical data necessary to evaluate the relationships between specific visual deficiencies and the operation of [commercial motor vehicles]. The data will permit the FHWA to properly evaluate its current vision requirement in the context of actual driver performance, and, if necessary, establish a new vision requirement which is safe, fair, and rationally related to the latest medical knowledge and highway technology." 57 Fed. Reg. 31458 (1992). And if all this were not enough to show that the FHWA was planning to give waivers solely to collect information, it acknowledged that a study it had commissioned had done no more than " 'illuminat[e] the lack of empirical data to establish a link between vision disorders and commercial motor vehicle safety,' " and " 'failed to provide a sufficient foundation on which to propose a satisfactory vision standard for drivers of [commercial motor vehicles] in interstate commerce,' " *Advocates for Highway and Safety, supra*, at 1293 (quoting 57 Fed. Reg. at 31458).

In sum, the regulatory record made it plain that the waiver regulation did not rest on any final, factual conclusion that the waiver scheme would be conducive to public safety in the manner of the general acuity standards and did not purport to modify the substantive content of the general acuity regulation in any way. The waiver program was simply an experiment with safety, however well intended, resting on a hypothesis whose confirmation or refutation in practice would provide a factual basis for reconsidering the existing standards.

Nothing in the waiver regulation, of course, required an employer of commercial drivers to accept the hypothesis and participate in the Government's experiment. The only question, then, is whether the ADA should be read to require such an employer to defend a decision to decline the experiment. Is it reasonable, that is, to read the ADA as requiring an employer like Albertson's to shoulder the general statutory burden to justify a job qualification that would tend to exclude the disabled, whenever the employer chooses to abide by the otherwise clearly applicable, unamended substantive regulatory standard despite the Government's willingness to waive it experimentally and without any finding of its being inappropriate? If the answer were yes, an employer would in fact have an obligation of which we can think of no comparable example in our law. The employer would be required in effect to justify *de novo* an existing and otherwise applicable safety regulation issued by the Government itself. The employer would be required on a case-by-case basis to reinvent the Government's own wheel when the Government had merely begun an experiment to provide data to consider changing the underlying specifications. And what is even more, the employer would be required to do so when the Government had made an affirmative record indicating that contemporary empirical evidence was hard to come by. It is simply not credible that Congress enacted the ADA (before there was any waiver program) with the understanding that employers choosing to respect the Government's sole substantive visual acuity regulation in the face of an experimental waiver might be burdened with an obligation to defend the regulation's application according to its own terms.

The judgment of the Ninth Circuit is accordingly reversed.

NOTES AND PROBLEMS FOR DISCUSSION

1. In *School Board of Nassau County v. Arline*, 480 U.S. 273 (1987) (discussed in Chapter Two), the Supreme Court said that the determination of whether an individual is qualified should, "in most cases," be based on an "individualized inquiry." Is that the rule followed by the Supreme Court in *Albertson's*? Why or why not?

2. The ADA specifies that "consideration shall be given to the employer's judgment as to what functions of a job are essential, and if an employer has prepared a written description before advertising or interviewing applicants for the job, this description shall be considered evidence of the essential functions of the job." Does this "consideration" mean that the court should defer to an employer's written job description? Should this consideration take the form of a rebuttable presumption? *See Jones v. Walgreen Co.*, 679 F.3d 9, 14 (1st Cir. 2012) (taking the employer's written job description "as our starting point, mindful, however, that an employer's good-faith view of what a job entails, though important, is not dispositive").

3. Fred Haven is visually impaired and recently received training in typing from dictation from a local rehabilitation organization. His training program was excellent, and he can type very accurately and quickly from dictation. Fred responded to an advertisement for a typist having the ability to type 70 words per minute with fewer than two errors. When Fred went for his typing test, he was handed handwritten copy and asked to type a letter. He said that he would like to take the typing test from dictation, and was confident that he could score 100 words per minute with less than two errors under such conditions. The employer refused, stating that none of its employees dictate. The employer said that everyone would understand implicitly that a typist would be required to type from copy; the company had not considered it necessary to put such an obvious requirement into the job description. Does Fred have a strong case under the ADA? What arguments would you make on his behalf? How do you believe the employer would respond? How will the rule about written job descriptions in 42 U.S.C. § 12111(8) affect Fred's case?

4. Maria Tuck is a registered nurse. After working for a hospital for 10 years, she injured her back at work. Following two surgeries on her back, and a several-month recovery period, she returned to work with instructions that she not engage in extensive labor, such as pushing, bending, heavy lifting, or pulling. She was assigned to a position with a 12-hour shift. She was relieved of heavy lifting work; in exchange, she agreed to perform some of the less strenuous tasks for the other nurses. The other nurses on the ward complained that Tuck was not fulfilling her part of the bargain by helping them with their light tasks, in exchange for their helping her with her lifting. Tuck requested that she be reassigned to a position with eight-hour shifts because the 12-hour shift caused her to suffer back pain. Claiming that no suitable positions existed for Tuck, the hospital terminated her employment. Tuck brought suit under the ADA, claiming that she was qualified for one of the eight-hour positions for which the hospital was advertising at the time of her discharge. Although the hospital had several positions advertised as available, including some eight-hour shifts, the personnel director testified at a deposition that these positions were not genuinely open. It was common practice for the hospital to run advertisements, regardless of whether the positions were open. Based on this evidence, the hospital moved for summary judgment at trial. Should a court grant summary judgment? *See Tuck v. HCA Health Servs. of Tennessee, Inc.*, 7 F.3d 465 (6th Cir. 1993). Is an individual not otherwise qualified if co-employees refuse to cooperate to make a requested accommodation effective? What if Tuck's co-employees complained that the accommodation provided to Tuck caused stress on *their* backs by greatly increasing the amount of lifting they were required to perform on the job? Does the fact that an employer frequently delegates or reassigns tasks that it labels as essential functions inform the inquiry as to whether those functions are truly essential? *See Jones v. Walgreen Co.*, 679 F.3d 9, 17 (1st Cir. 2012) (such evidence may "inform our inquiry" but "by no means ends it").

5. Geneva Johnston was hired as a food server in Morrison's L&N Seafood restaurant. Ms. Johnston suffers from "panic attack disorder" that makes it difficult for her to work effectively in crowded and busy situations. When she told her employer of this condition, the employer assigned her to the least busy work station in the restaurant where she was responsible for the fewest number of customers. Nonetheless, on New Year's Eve, six months after she commenced work, the restaurant became very crowded even in Ms. Johnston's section. Ms. Johnston suffered a "panic attack" and was not able to perform her job. The employer discharged her, stating that it was essential for a food server to be able to work in crowded conditions. Until this incident, however, it had been easy to accommodate Ms. Johnston because the other food

servers were happy to be moved out of the slowest sections of the restaurant since compensation is tied to tips. Is Ms. Johnston an otherwise qualified individual under the ADA? *See Johnston v. Morrison, Inc.*, 849 F. Supp. 777 (N.D. Ala. 1994).

6. Suppose an employer requires all secretaries to type 75 words per minute and an applicant, due to a disability, can type only 65 words per minute. Assume that use of a typewriter or computer is an essential function of the job, and that no reasonable accommodation will allow the applicant to reach that speed. Should the employer be required to reduce the requisite typing speed to accommodate that applicant? *See* 29 C.F.R. pt. 1630, app. § 1630.2(n). [ADA Handbook, p. 124]

7. The courts are divided over the question of whether there should be a presumption that uninterrupted attendance is an essential job requirement *See Dutton v. Johnson County Bd. of County Comm'rs*, 859 F. Supp. 498, 507 (D. Kan. 1994) (collecting cases under Section 504, which support the position that an essential part of any job is the requirement of reasonably regular and predictable attendance). The Eleventh Circuit has found that an employer can specify that an employee's "presence" is an essential function of the job and can therefore be terminated once his attendance on the job is "sporadic" and "unpredictable" even if he has not exceeded the number of absences permitted by the employer. *See Jackson v. Veterans Admin.*, 22 F.3d 277 (11th Cir. 1994). Several courts have recently disagreed with the Eleventh Circuit's approach in *Jackson*, holding that an employer should not benefit from a presumption that uninterrupted attendance is an essential function of the job. *See Ward v. Massachusetts Health Research Inst., Inc.*, 209 F.3d 29 (1st Cir. 2000) (genuine fact issues existed as to whether regular and predictable schedule was essential function of arthritic employee's data entry clerk position); *Cehrs v. Northeast Ohio Alzheimer' s Research Ctr.*, 155 F.3d 775, 782 (6th Cir. 1998) (stating that "[t]he presumption that uninterrupted attendance is an essential job requirement improperly dispenses with the burden-shifting analysis [required by the ADA]. In addition, the presumption eviscerates the individualized attention that the Supreme Court has deemed 'essential' in each disability claim. . . . We therefore conclude that no presumption should exist that uninterrupted attendance is an essential job requirement, and find that a medical leave of absence can constitute a reasonable accommodation under appropriate circumstances."); *Criado v. IBM Corp.*, 145 F.3d 437 (1st Cir. 1998) (finding that IBM had violated the ADA by firing an employee who requested temporary leave to receive treatment for depression); *Norris v. Allied-Sysco Food Servs., Inc.*, 948 F. Supp. 1418, 1439 (N.D. Cal. 1996), *aff'd*, 191 F.3d 1043 (9th Cir. 1999) (stating that "[u]pon reflection, we are not sure that there should be a *per se* rule that an unpaid leave of indefinite duration (or a very lengthy period, such as one year) could never constitute a 'reasonable accommodation' under the ADA. It is not clear why unpaid leave should be analyzed differently from any other proposed accommodation under the ADA."). Which view do you consider to be more well-reasoned — that a presumption should exist, or that attendance should be considered under the same framework as all other alleged job requirements?

Another permutation of the attendance issue is whether an employee should be permitted to telework as a reasonable accommodation. The Sixth Circuit has recently said that while attendance may be an essential requirement of most jobs, technology has advanced such that attendance at the workplace no longer is assumed to mean attendance at the employer's physical location. *See EEOC v. Ford Motor Co.*, 2014 U.S. App. LEXIS 7502 (6th Cir. 2014).

8. Consider the application of the *Albertson's* holding to the following fact pattern:

An individual who wishes to become a UPS package-car driver (in the familiar brown UPS trucks) must be an employee of UPS in a qualifying position and must "bid" on a package-car driving position. One requirement for being selected is that an individual pass the physical exam the DOT requires drivers of commercial vehicles to pass. The DOT rules require that individuals be able to pass a "forced whisper" standard under which they can hear and understand words within a five-foot range. *See* 49 C.F.R. § 391.41(b)(11). The DOT rule technically only applies to commercial vehicles that are larger than the UPS "brown trucks." Nonetheless, UPS contends that it is entitled to maintain a higher standard than the DOT standard and that drivers with hearing impairments, on average, are worse drivers than drivers without hearing impairments. UPS introduced empirical and anecdotal evidence in support of this claim. The most well-accepted empirical study demonstrated that deaf males had 1.8 times the number of accidents as hearing males but that there was no significant difference between deaf and hearing females. A class action was brought by male and female employees at UPS who had hearing impairments and who, by virtue of this rule, could not attain driver positions. The plaintiffs argued that it violated the ADA for them to be categorically denied a position by operation of this rule and that, at a minimum, they should be allowed to make an individualized showing that they were safe drivers. How should a court rule? *See Bates v. UPS*, 465 F.3d 1069 (9th Cir. 2006).

9. Nicholas Keith has been deaf since birth in 1980. He communicates using American Sign Language and has a cochlear impact, which allows him to hear alarms, whistles and people calling him. He successfully completed a course to qualify as a lifeguard. Keith was offered a job as a lifeguard with the County of Oakland conditioned upon him passing a physical. The examining physician failed to certify Keith as medically qualified solely because of his deafness. If you were working for the County of Oakland, what steps would you recommend they take to determine whether to offer the position to Keith? Should they rely on the doctor's opinion? *See Keith v. County of Oakland*, 703 F.3d 918 (6th Cir. 2013).

2. Judicial Estoppel

Many individuals who file claims of discrimination under Section 504 or the ADA have also filed claims for compensation under the workers' compensation laws or Social Security Disability Insurance. Should an individual be permitted to claim under Section 504 and the ADA that he or she is a qualified individual with a disability, yet claim to be totally disabled for the purposes of those other statues? Consider the following case:

CLEVELAND v. POLICY MANAGEMENT SYSTEMS CORPORATION

526 U.S. 795 (1999)

JUSTICE BREYER delivered the opinion of the Court.

The Social Security Disability Insurance (SSDI) program provides benefits to a person with a disability so severe that she is "unable to do [her] previous work" and "cannot . . . engage in any other kind of substantial gainful work which exists in the national economy." § 223(a) of the Social Security Act, as set forth in 42 U.S.C. § 423(d)(2)(A). This case asks whether the law erects a special presumption that would significantly inhibit an SSDI recipient from simultaneously pursuing an action for disability discrimination under the Americans with Disabilities Act of 1990 (ADA), claiming that "with . . . reasonable accommodation" she could "perform the essential functions" of her job. 42 U.S.C. § 12111(8).

We believe that, in context, these two seemingly divergent statutory contentions are often consistent, each with the other. Thus pursuit, and receipt, of SSDI benefits does not automatically estop the recipient from pursuing an ADA claim. Nor does the law erect a strong presumption against the recipient's success under the ADA. Nonetheless, an ADA plaintiff cannot simply ignore her SSDI contention that she was too disabled to work. To survive a defendant's motion for summary judgment, she must explain why that SSDI contention is consistent with her ADA claim that she could "perform the essential functions" of her previous job, at least with "reasonable accommodation."

I

After suffering a disabling stroke and losing her job, Carolyn Cleveland sought and obtained SSDI benefits from the Social Security Administration (SSA). She has also brought this ADA suit in which she claims that her former employer, Policy Management Systems Corporation, discriminated against her on account of her disability.

On September 22, 1995, the week before her SSDI award, Cleveland brought this ADA lawsuit. She contended that Policy Management Systems had "terminat[ed]" her employment without reasonably "accommodat[ing] her disability." She alleged that she requested, but was denied, accommodations such as training and additional time to complete her work. And she submitted a supporting affidavit from her treating physician. The District Court did not evaluate her reasonable accommodation claim on the merits, but granted summary judgment to the defendant because, in that court's view, Cleveland, by applying for and receiving SSDI benefits, had conceded that she was totally disabled. And that fact, the court concluded, now estopped Cleveland from proving an essential element of her ADA claim, namely that she could "perform the essential functions" of her job, at least with "reasonable accommodation." 42 U.S.C. § 12111(8). The Fifth Circuit affirmed the District Court's grant of summary judgment. . . .

We granted certiorari in light of disagreement among the Circuits about the legal effect upon an ADA suit of the application for, or receipt of, disability benefits. . . .

II

> The Social Security Act and the ADA both help individuals with disabilities, but in different ways. The Social Security Act provides monetary benefits to every insured individual who "is under a disability"

42 U.S.C. § 423(a)(1).

> The Act defines "disability" as an: inability to engage in any substantial gainful activity by reason of any . . . physical or mental impairment which can be expected to result in death or which has lasted or can be expected to last for a continuous period of not less than 12 months.

§ 423(d)(1)(A).

> The individual's impairment, as we have said, must be of such severity that [she] is not only unable to do [her] previous work but cannot, considering [her] age, education, and work experience, engage in any other kind of substantial gainful work which exists in the national economy. . . .

§ 423(d)(2)(A).

The ADA seeks to eliminate unwarranted discrimination against disabled individuals in order both to guarantee those individuals equal opportunity and to provide the Nation with the benefit of their consequently increased productivity. *See, e.g.*, 42 U.S.C. §§ 12101(a)(8), (9). The Act prohibits covered employers from discriminating "against a qualified individual with a disability because of the disability of such individual." § 12112(a). The Act defines a "qualified individual with a disability" as a disabled person "who . . . can perform the essential functions" of her job, including those who can do so only "with . . . reasonable accommodation." § 12111(8).

The case before us concerns an ADA plaintiff who both applied for, and received, SSDI benefits. It requires us to review a Court of Appeals decision upholding the grant of summary judgment on the ground that an ADA plaintiff's "represent[ation] to the SSA that she was totally disabled" created a "rebuttable presumption" sufficient to "judicially esto[p]" her later representation that, "for the time in question," with reasonable accommodation, she could perform the essential functions of her job. The Court of Appeals thought, in essence, that claims under both Acts would incorporate two directly conflicting propositions, namely "I am too disabled to work" and "I am not too disabled to work." And in an effort to prevent two claims that would embody that kind of factual conflict, the court used a special judicial presumption, which it believed would ordinarily prevent a plaintiff like Cleveland from successfully asserting an ADA claim.

In our view, however, despite the appearance of conflict that arises from the language of the two statutes, the two claims do not inherently conflict to the point where courts should apply a special negative presumption like the one applied by the Court of Appeals here. That is because there are too many situations in which an SSDI claim and an ADA claim can comfortably exist side by side.

For one thing, as we have noted, the ADA defines a "qualified individual" to include a disabled person "who . . . can perform the essential functions" of her job "*with reasonable accommodation.*"

By way of contrast, when the SSA determines whether an individual is disabled for SSDI purposes, it does *not* take the possibility of "reasonable accommodation" into account, nor need an applicant refer to the possibility of reasonable accommodation when she applies for SSDI. The omission reflects the facts that the SSA receives more than 2.5 million claims for disability benefits each year; its administrative resources are limited; the matter of "reasonable accommodation" may turn on highly disputed workplace-specific matters; and an SSA misjudgment about that detailed, and often fact-specific matter would deprive a seriously disabled person of the critical financial support the statute seeks to provide. The result is that an ADA suit claiming that the plaintiff can perform her job *with* reasonable accommodation may well prove consistent with an SSDI claim that the plaintiff could not perform her own job (or other jobs) *without* it.

For another thing, in order to process the large number of SSDI claims, the SSA administers SSDI with the help of a five-step procedure that embodies a set of presumptions about disabilities, job availability, and their interrelation. The SSA asks:

> *Step One*: Are you presently working? (If so, you are ineligible.) *See* 20 CFR § 404.1520(b) (1998).
>
> *Step Two*: Do you have a "severe impairment," *i.e.*, one that "significantly limits" your ability to do basic work activities? (If not, you are ineligible.) *See* § 404.1520(c).
>
> *Step Three*: Does your impairment "mee[t] or equa[l]" an impairment on a specific (and fairly lengthy) SSA list? (If so, you are eligible *without more.*) *See* §§ 404.1520(d), 404.1525, 404.1526.
>
> *Step Four*: If your impairment does not meet or equal a listed impairment, can you perform your "past relevant work?" (If so, you are ineligible.) *See* § 404.1520(e).
>
> *Step Five*: If your impairment does not meet or equal a listed impairment and you cannot perform your "past relevant work," then can you perform other jobs that exist in significant numbers in the national economy? (If not, you are eligible.) *See* §§ 404.1520(f), 404.1560(c).

The presumptions embodied in these questions — particularly those necessary to produce Step Three's list, which, the Government tells us, accounts for approximately 60 percent of all awards, grow out of the need to administer a large benefits system efficiently. But they inevitably simplify, eliminating consideration of many differences potentially relevant to an individual's ability to perform a particular job. Hence, an individual might qualify for SSDI under the SSA's administrative rules and yet, due to special individual circumstances, remain capable of "perform[ing] the essential functions" of her job.

Further, the SSA sometimes grants SSDI benefits to individuals who not only can work, but are working. . . .

Finally, if an individual has merely applied for, but has not been awarded, SSDI benefits, any inconsistency in the theory of the claims is of the sort normally tolerated by our legal system. . . .

In light of these examples, we would not apply a special legal presumption permitting someone who has applied for, or received, SSDI benefits to bring an ADA suit only in "some limited and highly unusual set of circumstances." 120 F.3d at 517.

Nonetheless, in some cases an earlier SSDI claim may turn out genuinely to conflict with an ADA claim. Summary judgment for a defendant is appropriate when the plaintiff "fails to make a showing sufficient to establish the existence of an element essential to [her] case, and on which [she] will bear the burden of proof at trial." *Celotex Corp. v. Catrett*, 477 U.S. 317, 322 (1986). An ADA plaintiff bears the burden of proving that she is a "qualified individual with a disability" — that is, a person "who, with or without reasonable accommodation, can perform the essential functions" of her job. 42 U.S.C. § 12111(8). And a plaintiff's sworn assertion in an application for disability benefits that she is, for example, "unable to work" will appear to negate an essential element of her ADA case — at least if she does not offer a sufficient explanation. For that reason, we hold that an ADA plaintiff cannot simply ignore the apparent contradiction that arises out of the earlier SSDI total disability claim. Rather, she must proffer a sufficient explanation.

The lower courts, in somewhat comparable circumstances, have found a similar need for explanation. They have held with virtual unanimity that a party cannot create a genuine issue of fact sufficient to survive summary judgment simply by contradicting his or her own previous sworn statement (by, say, filing a later affidavit that flatly contradicts that party's earlier sworn deposition) without explaining the contradiction or attempting to resolve the disparity. Although these cases for the most part involve purely factual contradictions (as to which we do not necessarily endorse these cases, but leave the law as we found it), we believe that a similar insistence upon explanation is warranted here, where the conflict involves a legal conclusion. When faced with a plaintiff's previous sworn statement asserting "total disability" or the like, the court should require an explanation of any apparent inconsistency with the necessary elements of an ADA claim. To defeat summary judgment, that explanation must be sufficient to warrant a reasonable juror's concluding that, assuming the truth of, or the plaintiff's good faith belief in, the earlier statement, the plaintiff could nonetheless "perform the essential functions" of her job, with or without "reasonable accommodation."

III

In her brief in this Court, Cleveland explains the discrepancy between her SSDI statements that she was "totally disabled" and her ADA claim that she could "perform the essential functions" of her job. The first statements, she says, "were made in a forum which does not consider the effect that reasonable workplace accommodations would have on the ability to work." Moreover, she claims the SSDI statements were "accurate statements" if examined "in the time period in which they were made." *Ibid.* The parties should have the opportunity in the trial court to present, or to contest, these explanations, in sworn form where appropriate. Accordingly, we vacate the judgment of the Court of Appeals and remand the case for further proceedings consistent with this opinion.

NOTES AND PROBLEMS FOR DISCUSSION

1. It is important to recognize that whether a court applies the judicial estoppel doctrine may not be determinative of the question of whether the individual is considered to be a qualified individual with a disability. For example, in *Dush v. Appleton Elec. Co.*, 124 F.3d 957 (8th Cir. 1997), the Eighth Circuit affirmed the trial court's decision that summary judgment should be granted because plaintiff failed to present a triable issue of fact concerning whether she was a qualified individual with a disability. Although the court did not apply the estoppel theory, the plaintiff's statements before the Social Security Administration virtually precluded plaintiff from demonstrating that she was a qualified individual with a disability. The court said:

> Where, as here, the party opposing the motion has made sworn statements attesting to her total disability and has actually received payments as a result of her condition, the courts should carefully scrutinize the evidence that she marshals in an attempt to show she is covered by the ADA. The burden faced by ADA claimants in this position is, by their own making, particularly cumbersome, for summary judgment should issue unless there is "strong countervailing evidence that the employee . . . is, in fact, qualified."

Id. at 963.

2. Douglas Parker was the executive director of Film and Tape Operations. He injured his back while working at the facility on March 16, 1995. After undergoing back surgery, he was on medical leave for several months to recuperate from the back surgery. When he sought to return to work on September 13, 1995, he was informed that he had exhausted the company's six-month limit on paid leave and that his employment would be terminated. Parker sought long-term disability benefits and SSDI benefits while also pursuing an ADA lawsuit against the company. In his September 13, 1995 application for long-term disability benefits, Parker responded to the question, "Why are you unable to work?" by stating that he was "completely incapacitated — disabled — treatment daily." Later that month, he stated in his SSDI application that he "had problems sitting, standing, and walking for sustained periods; had constant pain, and problems in his legs." He also asserted in his SSDI application that he "became unable to work" on March 16, 1995, and that he was "still disabled."

On the basis of those statements, the employer moved for summary judgment on the grounds that Parker was not a qualified individual with a disability at the time of his termination. Should a court grant the motion? *See Parker v. Columbia Pictures Industries*, 204 F.3d 326 (2d Cir. 2000).

3. Lawrence Mitchell was the head custodian at the Washingtonville High School. His right leg was amputated above the knee following an automobile accident in 1977

and he wears a prosthesis. In 1995, he experienced swelling and pain in his right leg, which prevented him from wearing his prosthesis, and at times from coming to work. Beginning in 1999, he suffered approximately three skin "breakdowns" on his leg each year, lasting for three to four days each time. When this happened, he was required to limit his use of his prosthesis and take occasional sick leave. Following a particularly strenuous day of work on November 5, 1999, his leg began to "drain," causing him considerable discomfort. He thereafter stopped reporting to work and notified the School District that he had been injured on the job. He then filed a worker's compensation claim in which he alleged that he had been injured at work as a result of "strenuous walking." At a hearing, his treating physician testified that Mitchell had to limit his walking and standing and be able to sit down immediately if he experienced pain. Mitchell also applied for SSDI, asserting, "I am totally disabled and unable to engage in any type of gainful employment due to being on my feet for long periods of time which resulted in a cyst." Later, he stated in an SSDI application, "I am totally disabled and unable to engage in gainful employment due to being an amputee, my right leg from the knee down. This disability prevents me from any type of prolonged standing or ambulation."

Mitchell also sought to return to work at Washingtonville in more sedentary employment. He argued that the School District should have accommodated his disability by restructuring his duties and reassigning the physical duties of the work to other custodians, transferring him to a smaller school within the district, or retraining him for a more sedentary job such as courier or bus dispatcher. The school district denied his requests, terminating his employment.

Mitchell filed suit under the ADA, arguing that he was unlawfully discharged. The School District moved for summary judgment, arguing that his statements before the Workers' Compensation Board and the Social Security Administration judicially estopped Mitchell from arguing for the purposes of the ADA that he was capable of doing work in other than a sedentary position. How should a court rule on that motion? In *Cleveland*, the Court noted that the case before it did not "involve directly conflicting statements about purely factual matters, such as . . . 'I can/cannot raise my arm above my head[,]' " and that the decision "leaves the law related to . . . purely factual . . . conflict[s] where [the Court] found it." *Cleveland*, 526 U.S. at 802. Would it therefore be inconsistent with *Cleveland* to apply judicial estoppel to Mitchell's case in order to preclude him from arguing, as a factual matter, that he could stand and walk at work? *See Mitchell v. Washingtonville Cent. Sch. Dist.*, 190 F.3d 1 (2d Cir. 1999).

C. NONDISCRIMINATION REQUIREMENTS

42 U.S.C. § 12112(a) provides the general rule against discrimination. It states:

> No covered entity shall discriminate against a qualified individual on the basis of disability in regard to job application procedures, the hiring, advancement, or discharge of employees, employee compensation, job training, and other terms, conditions, and privileges of employment.

Section 12112(b) lists seven types of discrimination covered by Title I. (We will see examples of nearly all these nondiscrimination requirements in this chapter.) In this Part, we will focus on two nondiscrimination requirements that are relatively unique to the ADA: the requirement to provide reasonable accommodation and the requirement to offer medical examinations in a nondiscriminatory manner.

1. Reasonable Accommodations and Undue Hardship

a. Statutory and Regulatory Language

Section 12112(b) provides that the term "discriminate" includes:

> (5)(A) not making reasonable accommodations to the known physical or mental limitations of an otherwise qualified individual with a disability who is an applicant or employee, unless such covered entity can demonstrate that the accommodation would impose an undue hardship on the operation of the business of such covered entity; or
>
> (B) denying employment opportunities to a job applicant or employee who is an otherwise qualified individual with a disability, if such denial is based on the need of such covered entity to make reasonable accommodation to the physical or mental impairments of the employee or applicant. . . .

Section 12111(9) (which is in the definitions section of Title I) further states that the term reasonable accommodation may include:

> (A) making existing facilities used by employees readily accessible to and usable by individuals with disabilities;
>
> (B) job restructuring, part-time or modified work schedules, reassignment to a vacant position, acquisition or modification of equipment or devices, appropriate adjustment or modifications of examinations, training materials or policies, the provision of qualified readers or interpreters, and other similar accommodations for individuals with disabilities.

Section 12111(10) defines undue hardship. It states:

> (A) In general
>
> The term "undue hardship" means an action requiring significant difficulty or expense, when considered in light of the factors set forth in subparagraph (B).
>
> (B) Factors to be considered
>
> In determining whether an accommodation would impose an undue hardship on a covered entity, factors to be considered include —
>
> (i) the nature and cost of the accommodation needed under this chapter;
>
> (ii) the overall financial resources of the facility or facilities involved in the provision of the reasonable accommodation; the number of persons employed at such facility; the effect on expenses and resources; or the impact otherwise of such accommodation upon the operation of the facility;

> (iii) the overall financial resources of the covered entity; the overall size of the business of a covered entity with respect to the number of its employees; the number, type, and location of its facilities; and
>
> (iv) the type of operation or operations of the covered entity, including the composition, structure, and functions of the workforce of such entity; the geographic separateness, administrative, or fiscal relationship of the facility or facilities in question to the covered entity.

Finally, ADA Title IV, 42 U.S.C. § 12201(d) provides:

> Nothing in this chapter shall be construed to require an individual with a disability to accept an accommodation, aid, service, opportunity, or benefit which such individual chooses not to accept.

Other than clarifying that "regarded as" plaintiffs are not entitled to reasonable accommodations, the EEOC regulations and interpretive guidance remained largely unchanged after the 2008 Amendments were implemented. Nonetheless, the EEOC added the following clarifying language in its Interpretive Guidance:

> In general, an accommodation is any change in the work environment or in the way things are customarily done that enables an individual with a disability to enjoy equal employment opportunities. There are three categories of reasonable accommodation. These are (1) accommodations that are required to ensure equal opportunity in the application process; (2) accommodations that enable the employer's employees with disabilities to perform the essential functions of the position held or desired; and (3) accommodations that enable the employer's employees with disabilities to enjoy equal benefits and privileges of employment as are enjoyed by employees without disabilities. It should be noted that nothing in this part prohibits employers or other covered entities from providing accommodations beyond those required by this part.

29 C.F.R. § 1630.2(o) app. [ADA Handbook, p. 125]

NOTES AND PROBLEMS FOR DISCUSSION

1. Chai Feldblum suggests that the ADA and Section 504 embody two different anti-discrimination concepts. The first concept is a traditional one — it assumes that characteristics such as disability are always, or often, irrelevant to competent performance of a job or enjoyment of a business good or service. This concept forbids an institution or individual from taking disability into account when making employment decisions or in serving customers. The second concept is relatively unique to disability law. It presumes that a person's disability is often *very relevant* to the person's ability, or inability, to adequately perform a job or to enjoy a particular good or service. The concept further presumes, however, that such inability may not be viewed in a vacuum. Rather, the inability must be viewed in the context of the *interaction* between societal realities and choices and the individual's disability, and not in the context of the individual's disability *per se.* Under the second concept, the role that various *societal decisions* play in determining the real-life ramifications of a person's disability is scrutinized and, in a sense, "called to account." That is, the law requires employers and businesses to take affirmative steps that will "undo" the barriers that have been set up by society, often unintentionally, to keep people with disabilities unemployed or underemployed and unable to enjoy goods and services. These requirements are termed "reasonable accommodations" in the employment area, and are termed "modifying policies, practices, and procedures," providing "auxiliary aids and services," and making physical access changes in the goods and services area. For further discussion of these two concepts of anti-discrimination under the ADA, see Chai R. Feldblum, *Antidiscrimination Requirements of the ADA, in* IMPLEMENTING THE AMERICANS WITH DISABILITIES ACT: RIGHTS AND RESPONSIBILITIES OF ALL AMERICANS 35, 35–36 (Lawrence O. Gostin & Henry A. Beyer eds., 1993).

2. Because courts are no longer likely to conclude that a plaintiff fails to demonstrate that he or she is disabled, more cases are likely to reach the question of whether the plaintiff was unlawfully denied a request for a reasonable accommodation. The following cases reflect some recent cases in which plaintiffs (who might have not been found to be disabled in the pre-2008 Amendment era) brought claims of denial of reasonable accommodation.

> Martin Jakubowski was a medical resident at a hospital who had Asperger's Syndrome. He was terminated from his position. He acknowledged that he had communication problems with patients, staff and others but proposed that he could be accommodated by making other physicians and nurses aware of his condition and symptoms. The hospital argued that his suggested accommodation would be extremely time consuming and expensive and would not solve their concerns with patient care and safety. The Sixth Circuit found that the hospital had acted in good faith in terms of having an interactive discussion with Jakubowski about possible accommodations but the suggested accommodations would still not enable him to do every essential function of the job. *See Jakubowski v. The Christ Hospital*, 627 F.3d 195 (6th Cir. 2010).
>
> Mauricio Centeno has been deaf since birth; his primary language is ASL. He brought suit against UPS alleging that it did not provide him with a sign language interpreter for certain staff meetings, disciplinary sessions and training. The district court judge granted summary judgment for the employer, but the Ninth Circuit reversed and remanded, finding that there were genuine issues of fact that should be decided by the jury. The employer had insisted on having someone provide Centeno with notes summarizing meetings; Centeno found meetings quite boring and was sometimes reprimanded for falling asleep during them. He was also reprimanded for insubordination if he refused to attend a meeting when there was no interpreter present. Centeno also said he often did not understand the words used in the written communications, including a communication that involved a reprimand. In granting summary judgment, the district court found that providing "note-writing, agendas, and summaries in connection with the weekly meetings discharged UPS's duty under the ADA as a matter of law." Further, the district court found that there was no evidence that Centeno "tried to use the dictionary but it was ineffective." The Ninth Circuit reversed, finding that UPS was aware of Centeno's limited proficiency in written English and there was a genuine issue of fact regarding when UPS should have been aware that

its accommodations were ineffective. *See EEOC v. UPS Supply Chain*, 620 F.3d 1103 (9th Cir. 2010).

Jeanne Gratzl suffers from incontinence. She obtained a job an as electronic court reporter at the DuPage County courthouse. She was able to manage her incontinence problem so well that no one was aware of it. The job description, however, was changed so that she would have to work in a court room for a significant part of her courtload. The employer offered her various accommodations that would have allowed her to take a break whenever she raised her hand but she did not believe that these accommodations would work due to the large number of people who would have to be notified about her medical condition on an ongoing basis. She requested permission to continue to work in the control room but her employer concluded that such an arrangement was not reasonable. The district court concluded, and the Seventh Circuit affirmed, that the court had fulfilled its obligation of offering a reasonable accommodation, and that she was therefore not a qualified individual to continue in her position. *See Gratzl v. Office of the Chief Judges*, 601 F.3d 674 (7th Cir. 2010).

3. Sometimes, reasonable accommodation claims are coupled with retaliation claims. Consider these facts: Maritza Valle-Arce made repeated requests for reasonable accommodations for her chronic fatigue syndrome. After two years of ignored accommodation requests and the prospect of termination, she filed charges with the EEOC. The very next day, many of her accommodation requests were granted. But she soon received a second letter of intent to terminate for using an agency computer and agency supplies during working hours to write a letter to colleagues who had offered to donate to her a day of their accrued vacation to cover a garnishment of her wages to pay a debt she owed to the agency. She was also notified she would be terminated for using another employee's personnel file as evidence in an administrative appeal of what the agency had contended was her mishandling of a matter. The ADA prohibits retaliation against "any individual because such individual has opposed any act or practice made unlawful" by the ADA. 42 U.S.C. § 12203(a). A plaintiff's retaliation claim may succeed even where her disability claim fails. Reversing the district court's dismissal of the case, the First Circuit found that a jury could conclude that Valle's termination was an act of retaliation because (1) she was singled out for different treatment than other employees who used agency resources and (2) the timing of events supported an inference of retaliation. *See Valle-Arce v. Puerto Rico Ports Authority*, 651 F.3d 190 (1st Cir. 2011). Proving retaliation, however, can be difficult. In *EEOC v. Picture People, Inc.*, 684 F.3d 981 (10th Cir. 2012), another case involving an allegation of retaliation for seeking accommodations, the Tenth Circuit affirmed summary judgment for the defendant even though the plaintiff's performance evaluation criticized him for "becom[ing] angry and threaten[ing] to bring a grievance against the Picture People when you didn't get your hours increased." *Id.* at 992. The dissent criticized the majority in quite strong language: "The majority's startling holding here that direct evidence of retaliatory motive is insufficient to create a genuine issue of material fact is directly contrary to [Tenth Circuit] precedents." *Id.* at 1001.

b. Interpretive Questions

This myriad of rules creates many interpretive questions. Who has the burden of proof for establishing that an accommodation is reasonable? Does the concept of reasonable accommodation permit or require a cost-benefit analysis? The following opinion by Judge Posner is cited frequently with respect to the answer to these questions.

VANDE ZANDE v. STATE OF WISCONSIN DEPARTMENT OF ADMINISTRATION
44 F.3d 538 (7th Cir. 1995)

Posner, Chief Judge.

In 1990, Congress passed the Americans with Disabilities Act, 42 U.S.C. §§ 12101 *et seq.* The stated purpose is "to provide a clear and comprehensive national mandate for the elimination of discrimination against individuals with disabilities" said by Congress to be 43 million in number and growing. §§ 12101(a), (b)(1). "Disability" is broadly defined. It includes not only "a physical or mental impairment that substantially limits one or more of the major life activities of [the disabled] individual," but also the state of "being regarded as having such an impairment." §§ 12102(2)(A), (C). The latter definition, although at first glance peculiar, actually makes a better fit with the elaborate preamble to the Act, in which people who have physical or mental impairments are compared to victims of racial and other invidious discrimination. Many such impairments are not in fact disabling but are believed to be so, and the people having them may be denied employment or otherwise shunned as a consequence. Such people, objectively capable of performing as well as the unimpaired, are analogous to capable workers discriminated against because of their skin color or some other vocationally irrelevant characteristic. (The Act is not limited to employment discrimination, but such discrimination, addressed by Subchapter I of the Act, is the only kind at issue in this case and we limit our discussion accordingly.)

The more problematic case is that of an individual who has a vocationally relevant disability — an impairment such as blindness or paralysis that limits a major human capability, such as seeing or walking. In the common case in which such an impairment interferes with the individual's ability to perform up to the standards of the workplace, or increases the cost of employing him, hiring and firing decisions based on the impairment are not "discriminatory" in a sense closely analogous to employment discrimination on racial grounds. The draftsmen of the Act knew this. But they were unwilling to confine the concept of disability discrimination to cases in which the disability is irrelevant to the performance of the disabled person's job. Instead, they defined "discrimination" to include an employer's "not making reasonable accommodations to the known physical or mental limitations of an otherwise qualified individual with a disability who is an applicant or employee, unless . . . [the employer] can demonstrate that the accommodation would impose an undue hardship on the operation of the . . . [employer's] business." § 12112(b)(5)(A).

The term "reasonable accommodations" is not a legal novelty, even if we ignore its use (arguably with a different meaning, however, *Prewitt v. United States Postal Service*, 662 F.2d 292, 308 n.22 (5th Cir. 1981); H.R. Rep. No. 485, 101st Cong., 1st Sess. 68 (1990)) in the provision of Title VII forbidding religious discrimination in employment. 42 U.S.C. § 2000e(j); *see Trans World Airlines, Inc. v. Hardison*, 432 U.S. 63 (1977). It is one of a number of provisions in the employment subchapter that were borrowed from regulations issued by the Equal Employment Opportunity Commission in implementation of the Rehabilitation Act of 1973, 29 U.S.C. §§ 701 *et seq. See* 29 C.F.R. § 1613.704; S. Rep. No. 116, 101st Cong., 2d Sess. 31 (1989). Indeed, to a great extent the employment provisions of the new Act merely generalize to the economy as a whole the duties, including that of reasonable accommodation, that the regulations under the Rehabilitation Act imposed on federal agencies and federal contractors. We can therefore look to the decisions interpreting those regulations for clues to the meaning of the same terms in the new law.

It is plain enough what "accommodation" means. The employer must be willing to consider making changes in its ordinary work rules, facilities, terms, and conditions in order to enable a disabled individual to work. The difficult term is "reasonable." The plaintiff in our case, a paraplegic, argues in effect that the term just means apt or efficacious. An accommodation is reasonable, she believes, when it is tailored to the particular individual's disability. A ramp or lift is thus a reasonable accommodation for a person who like this plaintiff is confined to a wheelchair. Considerations of cost do not enter into the term as the plaintiff would have us construe it. Cost is, she argues, the domain of "undue hardship" (another term borrowed from the regulations under the Rehabilitation Act, *see* S. Rep. No. 116, *supra*, at 36) — a safe harbor for an employer that can show that it would go broke or suffer other excruciating financial distress were it compelled to make a reasonable accommodation in the sense of one effective in enabling the disabled person to overcome the vocational effects of the disability.

These are questionable interpretations both of "reasonable" and of "undue hardship." To "accommodate" a disability is to make some change that will enable the disabled person to work. An unrelated, inefficacious change would not be an accommodation of the disability at all. So "reasonable" may be intended to qualify (in the sense of weaken) "accommodation," in just the same way that if one requires a "reasonable effort" of someone this means less than the maximum possible effort, or in law that the duty of "reasonable care," the cornerstone of the law of negligence, requires something less than the maximum possible care. It is understood in that law that in deciding what care is reasonable the court considers the cost of increased care. (This is explicit in Judge Learned Hand's famous formula for negligence. *United States v. Carroll Towing Co.*, 159 F.2d 169, 173 (2d Cir. 1947).) Similar reasoning could be used to flesh out the meaning of the word "reasonable" in the term "reasonable accommodations." It would not follow that the costs and benefits of altering a workplace to enable a disabled person to work would always have to be quantified, or even that an accommodation would have to be deemed unreasonable if the cost exceeded the benefit however slightly. But, at the very least, the cost could not be disproportionate to the benefit. Even if an employer is so large or wealthy — or, like the principal defendant in this case, is a state, which can raise taxes in order to finance any accommodations that it must make to disabled employees — that it may not be able to plead "undue *hardship*," it would not be required to expend enormous sums in order to bring about a trivial improvement in the life of a disabled employee. If the nation's employers have potentially unlimited financial obligations to 43 million disabled persons, the Americans with Disabilities Act will have imposed an indirect tax potentially greater than the national debt. We do not find an intention to bring about such a radical result in either the language of the Act or its history. The preamble actually "markets" the Act as a cost saver, pointing to "billions of dollars in unnecessary expenses resulting from dependency and nonproductivity." § 12101(a)(9). The savings will be illusory if employers are required to expend many more billions in accommodation than will be saved by enabling disabled people to work.

The concept of reasonable accommodation is at the heart of this case. The plaintiff sought a number of accommodations to her paraplegia that were turned down. The principal defendant as we have said is a state, which does not argue that the plaintiff's proposals were rejected because accepting them would have imposed undue hardship on the state or because they would not have done her any good. The district judge nevertheless granted summary judgment for the defendants on the ground that the evidence obtained in discovery, construed as favorably to the plaintiff as the record permitted, showed that they had gone as far to accommodate the plaintiff's demands as reasonableness, in a sense distinct from either aptness or hardship — a sense based, rather, on considerations of cost and proportionality — required. 851 F. Supp. 353. On this analysis, the function of the "undue hardship" safe harbor, like the "failing company" defense to antitrust liability (on which see *International Shoe Co. v. FTC*, 280 U.S. 291, 302 (1930); *United States v. Greater Buffalo Press, Inc.*, 402 U.S. 549, 555 (1971); 4 Phillip Areeda & Donald F. Turner, *Antitrust Law* 924-31 (1980)), is to excuse compliance by a firm that is financially distressed, even though the cost of the accommodation to the firm might be less than the benefit to disabled employees.

This interpretation of "undue hardship" is not inevitable — in fact probably is incorrect. It is a defined term in the Americans with Disabilities Act, and the definition is "an action requiring significant difficulty or expense," 42 U.S.C. § 12111(10)(A). The financial condition of the employer is only one consideration in determining whether an accommodation otherwise reasonable would impose an undue hardship. *See* 42 U.S.C. §§ 12111(10)(B)(ii), (iii). The legislative history equates "undue hardship" to "unduly costly." S. Rep. No. 116, *supra*, at 35. These are terms of relation. We must ask, "undue" in relation to what? Presumably (given the statutory definition and the legislative history) in relation to the benefits of the accommodation to the disabled worker as well as to the employer's resources.

So it seems that costs enter at two points in the analysis of claims to an accommodation to a disability. The employee must show that the accommodation is reasonable in the sense both of efficacious and of proportional to costs. Even if this prima facie showing is made, the employer has an opportunity to prove that upon more careful consideration the costs are excessive in relation either to the benefits of the accommodation or to the employer's financial survival or health. In a classic negligence case, the idiosyncrasies of the particular employer are irrelevant. Having above-average costs, or being in a precarious financial situation, is not a defense to negligence. *Vaughan v. Menlove*, 3 Bing. (N.C.) 468, 132 Eng. Rep. 490 (Comm. Pl. 1837). One interpretation of "undue hardship" is that it permits an employer to escape liability if he can carry the burden of proving that a disability accommodation reasonable for a normal employer would break him. *Barth v. Gelb*, 2 F.3d 1180, 1187 (D.C. Cir. 1993).

Lori Vande Zande, aged 35, is paralyzed from the waist down as a result of a tumor of the spinal cord. . . . We hold that Vande Zande's pressure ulcers are a part of her disability, and therefore a part of what the State of Wisconsin had a duty to accommodate — reasonably.

Vande Zande worked for the housing division of the state's department of administration for three years, beginning in January 1990. The housing division supervises the state's public housing programs. Her job was that of a program assistant, and involved preparing public information materials, planning meetings, interpreting regulations, typing, mailing, filing, and copying. In short, her tasks were of a clerical, secretarial, and administrative-assistant character. In order to enable her to do this work, the defendants, as she acknowledges, "made numerous accommodations relating to the plaintiff's disability." As examples, in her words, "they paid the landlord to have bathrooms modified and to have a step ramped; they bought special adjustable furniture for the plaintiff; they ordered and paid for one-half of the cost of a cot that the plaintiff needed for daily personal care at work; they sometimes adjusted the plaintiff's schedule to perform backup telephone duties to accommodate the plaintiff's medical appointments; they made changes to the plans for a locker room in the new state office building; and they agreed to provide some of the specific accommodations the plaintiff requested in her October 5, 1992 Reasonable Accommodation Request."

But she complains that the defendants did not go far enough in two principal respects. One concerns a period of eight weeks when a bout of pressure ulcers forced her to stay home. She wanted to work full time at home and believed that she would be able to do so if the division would provide her with a desktop computer at home (though she already had a laptop). Her supervisor refused, and told her that he probably would have only 15 to 20 hours of work for her to do at home per week and that she would have to make up the difference between that and a full work week out of her sick leave or vacation leave. In the event, she was able to work all but 16.5 hours in the eight-week period. She took 16.5 hours of sick leave to make up the difference. As a result, she incurred no loss of income, but did lose sick leave that she could have carried forward indefinitely. She now works for another agency of the State of Wisconsin, but any unused sick leave in her employment by the housing division would have accompanied her to her new job. Restoration of the 16.5 hours of lost sick leave is one form of relief that she seeks in this suit.

She argues that a jury might have found that a reasonable accommodation required the housing division either to give her the desktop computer or to excuse her from having to dig into her sick leave to get paid for the hours in which, in the absence of the computer, she was unable to do her work at home. No jury, however, could in our view be permitted to stretch the concept of "reasonable accommodation" so far. Most jobs in organizations public or private involve team work under supervision rather than solitary unsupervised work, and team work under supervision generally cannot be performed at home without a substantial reduction in the quality of the employee's performance. This will no doubt change as communications technology advances, but is the situation today. Generally, therefore, an employer is not required to accommodate a disability by allowing the disabled worker to work, by himself, without supervision, at home. This is the majority view, illustrated by *Tyndall v. National Education Centers, Inc.*, 31 F.3d 209, 213–14 (4th Cir. 1994), and *Law v. United States Postal Service*, 852 F.2d 1278 (Fed. Cir. 1988) (per curiam). The District of Columbia Circuit disagrees. *Langon v. Dept. of Health & Human Services*, 959 F.2d 1053, 1060–61 (D.C. Cir. 1992); *Carr v. Reno*, 23 F.3d 525, 530 (D.C. Cir. 1994). But we think the majority view is correct. An employer is not required to allow disabled workers to work at home, where their productivity inevitably would be greatly reduced. No doubt to this as to any generalization about so complex and varied an activity as employment there are exceptions, but it would take a very extraordinary case for the employee to be able to create a triable issue of the employer's failure to allow the employee to work at home.

And if the employer, because it is a government agency and therefore is not under intense competitive pressure to minimize its labor costs or maximize the value of its output, or for some other reason, bends over backwards to accommodate a disabled worker — goes further than the law requires — by allowing the worker to work at home, it must not be punished for its generosity by being deemed to have conceded the reasonableness of so far-reaching an accommodation. That would hurt rather than help disabled workers. Wisconsin's housing division was not required by the Americans with Disabilities Act to allow Vande Zande to work at home; even more clearly it was not required to install a computer in her home so that she could avoid using up 16.5 hours of sick leave. It is conjectural that she will ever need those 16.5 hours; the expected cost of the loss must, therefore, surely be slight. An accommodation that allows a disabled worker to work at home, at full pay, subject only to a slight loss of sick leave that may never be needed, hence never missed, is, we hold, reasonable as a matter of law. *See* 29 C.F.R. pt. 1630 app., § 1630.2(o); *Guice-Mills v. Derwinski*, 967 F.2d 794, 798 (2d Cir. 1992); *cf. Alexander v. Choate*, 469 U.S. 287, 302 (1985).

Vande Zande complains that she was reclassified as a part-time worker while she was at home, and that this was gratuitous. She was not reclassified. She received her full pay (albeit with a little help from her entitlement to sick leave), and full benefits, throughout the period. It is true that at first her supervisor did not think he would have full-time work for her to do at home. Had that turned out to be true, we do not see on what basis she could complain about being reclassified; she would be working on a part-time basis. It did not turn out to be true, so she was not reclassified, and we therefore do not understand what she is complaining about.

Her second complaint has to do with the kitchenettes in the housing division's building, which are for the use of employees during lunch and coffee breaks. Both the sink and the counter in each of the kitchenettes were 36 inches high, which is too high for a person in a wheelchair. The building was under construction, and the kitchenettes not yet built, when the plaintiff complained about this feature of the design. But the defendants refused to alter the design to lower the sink and counter to 34 inches, the height convenient for a person in a wheelchair. Construction of the building had begun before the effective date of the Americans with Disabilities Act, and Vande Zande does not argue that the failure to include 34-inch sinks and counters in the design of the building violated the Act. She could not argue that; the Act is not retroactive. *Raya v.*

Maryatt Industries, 829 F. Supp. 1169, 1172–75 (N.D. Cal. 1993); Mark Daniels, *Employment Law Guide to the Americans with Disabilities Act* § 1.3 (1992); *cf. Landgraf v. USI Film Products*, 114 S. Ct. 1483 (1994); *Rivers v. Roadway Express, Inc.*, 114 S. Ct. 1510 (1994). But she argues that once she brought the problem to the attention of her supervisors, they were obliged to lower the sink and counter, at least on the floor on which her office was located but possibly on the other floors in the building as well, since she might be moved to another floor. All that the defendants were willing to do was to install a shelf 34 inches high in the kitchenette area on Vande Zande's floor. That took care of the counter problem. As for the sink, the defendants took the position that since the plumbing was already in place it would be too costly to lower the sink and that the plaintiff could use the bathroom sink, which is 34 inches high.

Apparently it would have cost only about $150 to lower the sink on Vande Zande's floor; to lower it on all the floors might have cost as much as $2,000, though possibly less. Given the proximity of the bathroom sink, Vande Zande can hardly complain that the inaccessibility of the kitchenette sink interfered with her ability to work or with her physical comfort. Her argument rather is that forcing her to use the bathroom sink for activities (such as washing out her coffee cup) for which the other employees could use the kitchenette sink stigmatized her as different and inferior; she seeks an award of compensatory damages for the resulting emotional distress. We may assume without having to decide that emotional as well as physical barriers to the integration of disabled persons into the workforce are relevant in determining the reasonableness of an accommodation. But we do not think an employer has a duty to expend even modest amounts of money to bring about an absolute identity in working conditions between disabled and nondisabled workers. The creation of such a duty would be the inevitable consequence of deeming a failure to achieve identical conditions "stigmatizing." That is merely an epithet. We conclude that access to a particular sink, when access to an equivalent sink, conveniently located, is provided, is not a legal duty of an employer. The duty of reasonable accommodation is satisfied when the employer does what is necessary to enable the disabled worker to work in reasonable comfort.

In addition to making these specific complaints of failure of reasonable accommodation, Vande Zande argues that the defendants displayed a "pattern of insensitivity or discrimination." She relies on a number of minor incidents, such as her supervisor's response, "Cut me some slack," to her complaint on the first day on which the housing division moved into the new building that the bathrooms lacked adequate supplies. He meant that it would take a few days to iron out the bugs inevitable in any major move. It was clearly a reasonable request in the circumstances; and given all the accommodations that Vande Zande acknowledges the defendants made to her disability, a "pattern of insensitivity or discrimination" is hard to discern. But the more fundamental point is that there is no separate offense under the Americans with Disabilities Act called engaging in a pattern of insensitivity or discrimination. The word "pattern" does not appear in the employment subchapter, and the Act is not modeled on RICO. As in other cases of discrimination, a plaintiff can ask the trier of fact to draw an inference of discrimination from a pattern of behavior when each individual act making up that pattern might have an innocent explanation. The whole can be greater than the sum of the parts. But in this case all we have in the way of a pattern is that the employer made a number of reasonable and some more than reasonable — unnecessary — accommodations, and turned down only requests for unreasonable accommodations. From such a pattern no inference of unlawful discrimination can be drawn.

AFFIRMED.

NOTES AND PROBLEMS FOR DISCUSSION

1. In *Vande Zande*, the Seventh Circuit ruled that the employer was not required to lower the sink on plaintiff's floor, although the cost was estimated to be only $150. Do you agree with the court's analysis of that issue? What other factors, in addition to cost, should play a part in the reasonable accommodation/undue hardship analysis? How should these factors interrelate with one another?

2. Joseph Myers, who is employed by defendant as a bus driver, suffers from chronic heart disease and hypertension. He has been hospitalized for congestive heart failure and unstable angina. He has phlebitis, which has twice required hospitalization. He also has diabetes, which is not currently under control. He has recently been unable to pass medical exams for bus drivers because of his various disabilities. His doctor says that if Myers were granted a leave of absence, he might be able to stabilize his diet and medication at appropriate levels so he could pass the medical exams and work as a bus driver. Assume that the employer has a rule providing for unpaid leaves of absence at the discretion of the employer. Is Myers' leave request reasonable? Would it help if the physician could be more specific with respect to the length of the proposed leave of absence? *See Myers v. Hose*, 50 F.3d 278 (4th Cir. 1995) (emphasizing that the regulations require a protected individual to be presently qualified rather than qualified at some indefinite future time).

3. Should an employer have to engage in a reasonable accommodation inquiry if the employee's disability causes him to be a threat to the well-being of other employees? In *Palmer v. Circuit Court of Cook County*, 117 F.3d 351 (7th Cir. 1997), the court concluded that a reasonable accommodation inquiry was not required when the employee had verbally threatened other employees. The court stated:

> It is true that an employer has a statutory duty to make a "reasonable accommodation" to an employee's disability, that is, an adjustment in working conditions to enable the employee to overcome his disability, if the employer can do this without "undue hardship." But we cannot believe that this duty runs in favor of employees who commit or threaten to commit violent acts. The retention of such an employee would cause justifiable anxiety to coworkers and supervisors. It would be unreasonable to demand of the employer either that it force its employees to put up with this or that it station guards to prevent the mentally disturbed employee from getting out of hand.

Id. at 353. Do you agree with the court's analysis? Should the court lump together individuals who threaten violence and individuals who have already committed violence? (In the *Palmer* case, there is no evidence that plaintiff ever carried through with the threats toward her supervisor.)

4. Suppose an employee who is a quadriplegic requires the assistance of another person to help him or her with personal needs at work — such as eating and toileting. Must the employer provide such personal assistance if the undue hardship test is not satisfied?

The Interpretive Guidelines to the EEOC's ADA Title I regulations state that "[p]roviding personal assistants, such as a page turner for an employee with no hands or a travel attendant to act as a sighted guide to assist a blind employee on occasional business trips, may also be a reasonable accommodation." 29 C.F.R. pt. 1630, app. § 1630.2(o). [ADA Handbook, pp. 125–26] The explanatory section to the regulations notes that the interpretive guidelines "make clear that it may be a reasonable accommodation to provide personal assistants to help with specified duties related to the job." Are eating and toileting "specified duties related to the job?" If this phrase were interpreted literally, could it defeat a purpose of ADA Title I?

5. James Nelson works for a social service agency. He used a guide dog to travel to the homes of his social service clients until the dog died. When Nelson obtained a new guide dog, he used holiday and vacation time to attend training sessions. Unfortunately, the dog did not prove satisfactory. When another dog became available, Nelson asked for 14 days of paid leave to train with the new dog. The employer approved an advance leave, but would not allow special paid leave that would not be charged against Nelson's regular leave allowances. Does Nelson have a valid claim under the ADA against the employer for failure to provide him with a reasonable accommodation? Assume that Nelson used a cane and taxi cabs when he did not have the services of a guide dog, but found those modes of travel to be less safe and efficient than using a guide dog. Also assume that Nelson uses the guide dog for personal needs at home, as well as at work. *See Nelson v. Ryan*, 860 F. Supp. 76 (W.D.N.Y. 1994).

6. To what extent must an employer provide readers or interpreters for employees who are blind or deaf? Suppose the cost of the interpreter or reader is half the amount of the salary of a disabled employee? Suppose that cost equaled the salary of a disabled employee? At what point would it be fair to say that the interpreter or reader was actually performing the job?

7. What role should cost play in the reasonable accommodation/undue hardship analysis? When should an accommodation be held "too costly" to be reasonable? *Compare, e.g., Lyons v. Legal Aid Soc'y*, 68 F.3d 1512, 1517 (2d Cir. 1995) (the request of an employee with a disability for an accommodation of employer-paid parking space at a cost of up to 26% of her total salary could be reasonable; the court stated that "an accommodation may not be considered unreasonable merely because it requires the employer 'to assume more than a *de minimis* cost' or because it will cost the employer more overall to obtain the same level of performance from the disabled employee"), *with Williams v. Avnet, Inc.*, 910 F. Supp. 1124 (E.D.N.C. 1995), *aff'd sub nom. Williams v. Channel Master Satellite Sys.*, 101 F.3d 346 (4th Cir. 1996) (disagreeing with *Lyons* and holding that cost alone, regardless of the employer's financial ability, was the deciding factor in determining whether an accommodation was reasonable).

8. What should be the impact on the undue hardship analysis if other individuals, in addition to the particular individual with a disability seeking an accommodation, will benefit from that accommodation? Is the undue hardship test satisfied if it is shown

that provision of the required accommodation has a negative impact on the morale of other employees?

9. Note that only the employer's *net* costs are to be considered when determining whether provision of an accommodation is reasonable. 29 C.F.R. § 1630.2(p)(2)(i). Government and other benefits, such as tax credits and rehabilitation agency grants, must be subtracted before the employer's costs are calculated. Further, an employer must pay for that portion of an accommodation that would not cause an undue hardship if other funding sources are available to pay for the remainder. *See* 29 C.F.R. pt. 1630, app. § 1630.2(p). [ADA Handbook, p. 128]

10. Generally, the undue hardship test looks to the employer's business as a whole, rather than to just one aspect or facility of that business. The House Report, however, notes one situation when it might be appropriate to look only to the effect of the accommodation on a single facility of the employer's business. H.R. Rep. No. 101-485, pt. 3 (1990), *reprinted in* 1990 U.S.C.C.A.N. 445 (1990). The Report cites a situation where a department store chain is operating a store in a rural area at a loss. If the result of the required accommodation would be closure of the store or the reduction of overall employment at the store, thereby depriving the community of the benefit of the store, the Report concludes that the undue hardship test would be satisfied. Could similar reasoning apply in other situations?

11. One issue that is confronting the courts is what are the consequences for an employer of failing to engage in an interactive process in good faith with an employee when a reasonable accommodation is requested. The EEOC interpretive guidance states:

> [T]he employer must make a reasonable effort to determine the appropriate accommodation. The appropriate reasonable accommodation is best determined through a flexible, interactive process that involves both the employer and the [employee] with a disability.

29 C.F.R. pt. 1630, app. § 1630.9. [ADA Handbook, p. 137]

Is an employee entitled to a remedy merely because the employer failed to engage in an interactive process? *See Taylor v. Phoenixville Sch. Dist.*, 184 F.3d 296, 317–18 (3d Cir. 1999).

12. Should the courts require a nexus between the claimed disability and the requested accommodation? Consider that question in light of the following fact pattern:

> Daniel Didier injured his right wrist and arm during an accident at work. Following surgery, a functional capacity evaluation was conducted, and it was determined that he needed to be restricted to carrying 10 pounds or less. Specifically, he could not drive a truck route by himself because he could not open the truck doors due to their weight. Didier was a manager who occasionally had to drive trucks. He requested, as an accommodation, that another employee always accompany him when he needed to drive a truck. Further, Didier argued that he was an individual with a disability because he had difficulty shaving, brushing his teeth, grooming, cleaning himself, wiping

after going to the bathroom, feeding himself with a spoon, and dressing himself. He learned to do many of those activities left-handed but asserted that it takes him longer to do those tasks than the typical person. In analyzing this fact pattern, the Eighth Circuit stated: "[W]e note that even if we were to find that Didier is disabled within the meaning of the ADA, the accommodation he requested — having another employee drive open routes or handle the truck doors — is not related to his claimed disability of being substantially limited in the life activity of caring for himself." *Didier v. Schwan Food Company*, 465 F.3d 838, 842–843 (8th Cir. 2006). Do you agree with the Eighth Circuit that that issue is a proper part of the legal analysis?

13. After the 2008 ADA amendments, establishing that a plaintiff is an individual with a disability has become much easier. That fact, in turn, has put pressure on other parts of the legal analysis, such as whether the plaintiff has requested an accommodation that is reasonable. For example, employers have tried to argue that an accommodation is only reasonable if it makes it possible for an employee to perform an essential function of the job. In *Feist v. Louisiana, Department of Justice*, 730 F.3d 450 (5th Cir. 2013), an attorney with osteoarthritis of the knee requested a free on-site parking space to accommodate her disability. The district court granted summary judgment for the employer, saying that the plaintiff failed to demonstrate a need for an accommodation to perform her essential functions. The Fifth Circuit reversed, saying that a request for a reasonable accommodation does not have to be connected to an essential job function. Look at the statutory language, and relevant regulations. What is the basis for the Fifth Circuit's opinion?

c. Reassignment to a Vacant Position as a Reasonable Accommodation

In the list of what "may" constitute a reasonable accommodation, ADA Title I lists "reassignment to a vacant position." This rule only applies to incumbent employees who become disabled and unable to perform their current position with reasonable accommodation. This rule did not exist explicitly under Section 504 and has created many interpretive questions under the ADA. Does the position have to be vacant at the time that the individual becomes disabled? Should the individual receive priority over incumbent employees? Can this rule be combined with the "job restructuring" reasonable accommodation requirement? Consider these questions in reference to the following case and notes that follow.

US AIRWAYS, INC. v. BARNETT*
535 U.S. 391 (2002)

Justice BREYER delivered the opinion of the Court.

The Americans with Disabilities Act of 1990 (ADA or Act), 42 U.S.C. § 12101 *et seq.*, prohibits an employer from discriminating against an "individual with a disability" who, with "reasonable accommodation," can perform the essential functions of the job. §§ 12112(a) and (b). This case, arising in the context of summary judgment, asks us how the Act resolves a potential conflict between: (1) the interests of a disabled worker who seeks assignment to a particular position as a "reasonable accommodation," and (2) the interests of other workers with superior rights to bid for the job under an employer's seniority system. In such a case, does the accommodation demand trump the seniority system?

In our view, the seniority system will prevail in the run of cases. As we interpret the statute, to show that a requested accommodation conflicts with the rules of a seniority system is ordinarily to show that the accommodation is not "reasonable." Hence such a showing will entitle an employer/defendant to summary judgment on the question — unless there is more. The plaintiff remains free to present evidence of special circumstances that make "reasonable" a seniority rule exception in the particular case. And such a showing will defeat the employer's demand for summary judgment. Fed. Rule Civ. Proc. 56(e).

I

In 1990, Robert Barnett, the plaintiff and respondent here, injured his back while working in a cargo-handling position at petitioner US Airways, Inc. He invoked seniority rights and transferred to a less physically demanding mailroom position. Under US Airways' seniority system, that position, like others, periodically became open to seniority-based employee bidding. In 1992, Barnett learned that at least two employees senior to him intended to bid for the mailroom job. He asked US Airways to accommodate his disability-imposed limitations by making an exception that would allow him to remain in the mailroom. After permitting Barnett to continue his mailroom work for five months while it considered the matter, US Airways eventually decided not to make an exception. And Barnett lost his job.

Barnett then brought this ADA suit claiming, among other things, that he was an "individual with a disability" capable of performing the essential functions of the mailroom job, that the mailroom job amounted to a "reasonable accommodation" of his disability, and that US Airways, in refusing to assign him the job, unlawfully discriminated against him. US Airways moved for summary judgment. It supported its motion with appropriate affidavits, Fed. Rule Civ. Proc. 56, contending that its

---

* The caption of the case gives the company's name as "US Airways, Inc." That is also the spelling used on the company's website. Within the published opinion, however, the Court often refers to it as "U.S. Airways." We have changed these references to reflect the correct spelling.

"well-established" seniority system granted other employees the right to obtain the mailroom position.

The District Court found that the undisputed facts about seniority warranted summary judgment in US Airways' favor. The Act says that an employer who fails to make "reasonable accommodations to the known physical or mental limitations of an [employee] with a disability" discriminates "*unless*" the employer "can demonstrate that the accommodation would impose an *undue hardship* on the operation of [its] business." 42 U.S.C. § 12112(b)(5)(A) (emphasis added). The court said:

> "[T]he uncontroverted evidence shows that the USAir seniority system has been in place for 'decades' and governs over 14,000 USAir Agents. Moreover, seniority policies such as the one at issue in this case are common to the airline industry. Given this context, it seems clear that the USAir employees were justified in relying upon the policy. As such, any significant alteration of that policy would result in undue hardship to both the company and its non-disabled employees."

An en banc panel of the United States Court of Appeals for the Ninth Circuit reversed. It said that the presence of a seniority system is merely "a factor in the undue hardship analysis." 228 F.3d 1105, 1120 (9th Cir. 2000). And it held that "[a] case-by-case fact intensive analysis is required to determine whether any particular reassignment would constitute an undue hardship to the employer." *Ibid.*

US Airways petitioned for certiorari, asking us to decide whether

> "the [ADA] requires an employer to reassign a disabled employee to a position as a 'reasonable accommodation' even though another employee is entitled to hold the position under the employer's bona fide and established seniority system."

The Circuits have reached different conclusions about the legal significance of a seniority system. *Compare* 228 F.3d at 1120, *with EEOC v. Sara Lee Corp.*, 237 F.3d 349, 354 (4th Cir. 2001). We agreed to answer US Airways' question.

II

In answering the question presented, we must consider the following statutory provisions. First, the ADA says that an employer may not "discriminate against a qualified individual with a disability." 42 U.S.C. § 12112(a). Second, the ADA says that a "qualified" individual includes "an individual with a disability who, *with* or without *reasonable accommodation*, can perform the essential functions of" the relevant "employment position." § 12111(8) (emphasis added). Third, the ADA says that "discrimination" includes an employer's "*not making reasonable accommodations* to the known physical or mental limitations of an otherwise qualified . . . employee, *unless* [the employer] can demonstrate that the accommodation would impose an *undue hardship* on the operation of [its] business." § 12112(b)(5)(A) (emphasis added). Fourth, the ADA says that the term " 'reasonable accommodation' may include . . . reassignment to a vacant position." § 12111(9)(B).

The parties interpret this statutory language as applied to seniority systems in radically different ways. In US Airways' view, the fact that an accommodation would violate the rules of a seniority system always shows that the accommodation is not a "reasonable" one. In Barnett's polar opposite view, a seniority system violation never shows that an accommodation sought is not a "reasonable" one. Barnett concedes that a violation of seniority rules might help to show that the accommodation will work "undue" employer "hardship," but that is a matter for an employer to demonstrate case by case. We shall initially consider the parties' main legal arguments in support of these conflicting positions.

A

US Airways' claim that a seniority system virtually always trumps a conflicting accommodation demand rests primarily upon its view of how the Act treats workplace "preferences." Insofar as a requested accommodation violates a disability-neutral workplace rule, such as a seniority rule, it grants the employee with a disability treatment that other workers could not receive. Yet the Act, US Airways says, seeks only "equal" treatment for those with disabilities. *See, e.g.*, 42 U.S.C. § 12101(a)(9). It does not, it contends, require an employer to grant preferential treatment. *Cf.* H.R. Rep. No. 101-485, pt. 2, p. 66 (1990), U.S. Code Cong. & Admin. News 1990, pp. 303, 348–349; S. Rep. No. 101-116, pp. 26–27 (1989) (employer has no "obligation to prefer *applicants* with disabilities over other *applicants*" (emphasis added)). Hence it does not require the employer to grant a request that, in violating a disability-neutral rule, would provide a preference.

While linguistically logical, this argument fails to recognize what the Act specifies, namely, that preferences will sometimes prove necessary to achieve the Act's basic equal opportunity goal. The Act requires preferences in the form of "reasonable accommodations" that are needed for those with disabilities to obtain the *same* workplace opportunities that those without disabilities automatically enjoy. By definition any special "accommodation" requires the employer to treat an employee with a disability differently, *i.e.*, preferentially. And the fact that the difference in treatment violates an employer's disability-neutral rule cannot by itself place the accommodation beyond the Act's potential reach.

Were that not so, the "reasonable accommodation" provision could not accomplish its intended objective. Neutral office assignment rules would automatically prevent the accommodation of an employee whose disability-imposed limitations require him to work on the ground floor. Neutral "break-from-work" rules would automatically prevent the accommodation of an individual who needs additional breaks from work, perhaps to permit medical visits. Neutral furniture budget rules would automatically prevent the accommodation of an individual who needs a different kind of chair or desk. Many employers will have neutral rules governing the kinds of actions most needed to reasonably accommodate a worker with a disability. *See* 42 U.S.C. § 12111(9)(b) (setting forth examples such as "job restructuring," "part-time or modified work schedules," "acquisition or modification of equipment or devices," "and other similar accommodations"). Yet Congress, while providing such examples, said nothing suggesting that the presence of such neutral rules would create an automatic exemption. Nor have the lower courts made any such suggestion. *Cf. Garcia Ayala v.*

Lederle Parenterals, Inc., 212 F.3d 638, 648 (1st Cir. 2000) (requiring leave beyond that allowed under the company's own leave policy); *Hendricks-Robinson v. Excel Corp.*, 154 F.3d 685, 699 (7th Cir. 1998) (requiring exception to employer's neutral "physical fitness" job requirement).

In sum, the nature of the "reasonable accommodation" requirement, the statutory examples, and the Act's silence about the exempting effect of neutral rules together convince us that the Act does not create any such automatic exemption. The simple fact that an accommodation would provide a "preference" — in the sense that it would permit the worker with a disability to violate a rule that others must obey — cannot, *in and of itself*, automatically show that the accommodation is not "reasonable." As a result, we reject the position taken by US Airways and Justice SCALIA to the contrary.

US Airways also points to the ADA provisions stating that a "'reasonable accommodation' may include . . . reassignment to a *vacant* position." § 12111(9)(B) (emphasis added). And it claims that the fact that an established seniority system would assign that position to another worker automatically and always means that the position is not a "vacant" one. Nothing in the Act, however, suggests that Congress intended the word "vacant" to have a specialized meaning. And in ordinary English, a seniority system can give employees seniority rights allowing them to bid for a "vacant" position. The position in this case was held, at the time of suit, by Barnett, not by some other worker; and that position, under the US Airways seniority system, became an "open" one. Moreover, US Airways has said that it "reserves the right to change any and all" portions of the seniority system at will. Consequently, we cannot agree with US Airways about the position's vacancy; nor do we agree that the Act would automatically deny Barnett's accommodation request for that reason.

B

Barnett argues that the statutory words "reasonable accommodation" mean only "effective accommodation," authorizing a court to consider the requested accommodation's ability to meet an individual's disability-related needs, and nothing more. On this view, a seniority rule violation, having nothing to do with the accommodation's effectiveness, has nothing to do with its "reasonableness." It might, at most, help to prove an "undue hardship on the operation of the business." But, he adds, that is a matter that the statute requires the employer to demonstrate, case by case.

In support of this interpretation Barnett points to Equal Employment Opportunity Commission (EEOC) regulations stating that "reasonable accommodation means . . . [m]odifications or adjustments . . . that *enable* a qualified individual with a disability to perform the essential functions of [a] position." 29 CFR § 1630(o)(ii) (2001) (emphasis added). *See also* H.R. Rep. No. 101-485, pt. 2, at 66, U.S. Code Cong. & Admin. News 1990, pp. 303, 348–349; S. Rep. No. 101-116, at 35 (discussing reasonable accommodations in terms of "effectiveness," while discussing costs in terms of "undue hardship"). Barnett adds that any other view would make the words "reasonable accommodation" and "undue hardship" virtual mirror images — creating redundancy in the statute. And he says that any such other view would create a practical burden of proof dilemma.

The practical burden of proof dilemma arises, Barnett argues, because the statute imposes the burden of demonstrating an "undue hardship" upon the employer, while the burden of proving "reasonable accommodation" remains with the plaintiff, here the employee. This allocation seems sensible in that an employer can more frequently and easily prove the presence of business hardship than an employee can prove its absence. But suppose that an employee must counter a claim of "seniority rule violation" in order to prove that an "accommodation" request is "reasonable." Would that not force the employee to prove what is in effect an absence, *i.e.*, an absence of hardship, despite the statute's insistence that the employer "demonstrate" hardship's presence?

These arguments do not persuade us that Barnett's legal interpretation of "reasonable" is correct. For one thing, in ordinary English the word "reasonable" does not mean "effective." It is the word "accommodation," not the word "reasonable," that conveys the need for effectiveness. An *ineffective* "modification" or "adjustment" will not *accommodate* a disabled individual's limitations. Nor does an ordinary English meaning of the term "reasonable accommodation" make of it a simple, redundant mirror image of the term "undue hardship." The statute refers to an "undue hardship on the operation of the business." 42 U.S.C. § 12112(b)(5)(A). Yet a demand for an effective accommodation could prove unreasonable because of its impact, not on business operations, but on fellow employees — say because it will lead to dismissals, relocations, or modification of employee benefits to which an employer, looking at the matter from the perspective of the business itself, may be relatively indifferent.

Neither does the statute's primary purpose require Barnett's special reading. The statute seeks to diminish or to eliminate the stereotypical thought processes, the thoughtless actions, and the hostile reactions that far too often bar those with disabilities from participating fully in the Nation's life, including the workplace. *See generally* §§ 12101(a) and (b). These objectives demand unprejudiced thought and reasonable responsive reaction on the part of employers and fellow workers alike. They will sometimes require affirmative conduct to promote entry of disabled people into the workforce. *See supra*, at 1521. They do not, however, demand action beyond the realm of the reasonable.

Neither has Congress indicated in the statute, or elsewhere, that the word "reasonable" means no more than "effective." The EEOC regulations do say that reasonable accommodations "enable" a person with a disability to perform the essential functions of a task. But that phrasing simply emphasizes the statutory provision's basic objective. The regulations do not say that "enable" and "reasonable" mean the same thing. And as discussed below, no circuit court has so read them. *But see* 228 F.3d, at 1122–1123 (Gould, J., concurring).

Finally, an ordinary language interpretation of the word "reasonable" does not create the "burden of proof" dilemma to which Barnett points. Many of the lower courts, while rejecting both US Airways' and Barnett's more absolute views, have reconciled the phrases "reasonable accommodation" and "undue hardship" in a practical way.

They have held that a plaintiff/employee (to defeat a defendant/employer's motion for summary judgment) need only show that an "accommodation" seems reasonable on its face, *i.e.*, ordinarily or in the run of cases. *See, e.g., Reed v. LePage Bakeries, Inc.*,

244 F.3d 254, 259 (1st Cir. 2001) (plaintiff meets burden on reasonableness by showing that, "at least on the face of things," the accommodation will be feasible for the employer); *Borkowski v. Valley Central School Dist.*, 63 F.3d 131, 138 (2d Cir. 1995) (plaintiff satisfies "burden of production" by showing "plausible accommodation"); *Barth v. Gelb*, 2 F.3d 1180, 1187 (D.C. Cir. 1993) (interpreting parallel language in Rehabilitation Act, stating that plaintiff need only show he seeks a "*method of accommodation* that is reasonable in the run of cases" (emphasis in original)).

Once the plaintiff has made this showing, the defendant/employer then must show special (typically case-specific) circumstances that demonstrate undue hardship in the particular circumstances. *See Reed, supra*, at 258–259 ("'undue hardship inquiry focuses on the hardships imposed . . . in the context of the particular [employer's] operations'") (quoting *Barth, supra*, at 1187); *Borkowski, supra*, at 138 (after plaintiff makes initial showing, burden falls on employer to show that particular accommodation "would cause it to suffer an undue hardship"); *Barth, supra*, at 1187 ("undue hardship inquiry focuses on the hardships imposed . . . in the context of the particular agency's operations").

Not every court has used the same language, but their results are functionally similar. In our opinion, that practical view of the statute, applied consistently with ordinary summary judgment principles, *see* Fed. Rule Civ. Proc. 56, avoids Barnett's burden of proof dilemma, while reconciling the two statutory phrases ("reasonable accommodation" and "undue hardship").

III

The question in the present case focuses on the relationship between seniority systems and the plaintiff's need to show that an "accommodation" seems reasonable on its face, *i.e.*, ordinarily or in the run of cases. We must assume that the plaintiff, an employee, is an "individual with a disability." He has requested assignment to a mailroom position as a "reasonable accommodation." We also assume that normally such a request would be reasonable within the meaning of the statute, were it not for one circumstance, namely, that the assignment would violate the rules of a seniority system. *See* § 12111(9) ("reasonable accommodation" may include "reassignment to a vacant position"). Does that circumstance mean that the proposed accommodation is not a "reasonable" one?

In our view, the answer to this question ordinarily is "yes." The statute does not require proof on a case-by-case basis that a seniority system should prevail. That is because it would not be reasonable in the run of cases that the assignment in question trump the rules of a seniority system. To the contrary, it will ordinarily be unreasonable for the assignment to prevail.

A

Several factors support our conclusion that a proposed accommodation will not be reasonable in the run of cases. Analogous case law supports this conclusion, for it has recognized the importance of seniority to employee-management relations. This Court has held that, in the context of a Title VII religious discrimination case, an employer need not adapt to an employee's special worship schedule as a "reasonable accommodation" where doing so would conflict with the seniority rights of other employees. *Trans World Airlines, Inc. v. Hardison*, 432 U.S. 63, 79-80 (1977). The lower courts have unanimously found that collectively bargained seniority trumps the need for reasonable accommodation in the context of the linguistically similar Rehabilitation Act. *See Eckles v. Consolidated Rail Corp.*, 94 F.3d 1041, 1047–1048 (7th Cir. 1996) (collecting cases). . . . And several Circuits, though differing in their reasoning, have reached a similar conclusion in the context of seniority and the ADA. . . . All these cases discuss *collectively bargained* seniority systems, not systems (like the present system) which are unilaterally imposed by management. But the relevant seniority system advantages, and related difficulties that result from violations of seniority rules, are not limited to collectively bargained systems.

For one thing, the typical seniority system provides important employee benefits by creating, and fulfilling, employee expectations of fair, uniform treatment. These benefits include "job security and an opportunity for steady and predictable advancement based on objective standards." Brief for Petitioner 32 (citing Fallon & Weiler, Firefighters v. Stotts: *Conflicting Models of Racial Justice*, 1984 S. Ct. Rev. 1, 57–58). *See also* 1 B. Lindemann & P. Grossman, Employment Discrimination Law 72 (3d ed. 1996) ("One of the most important aspects of competitive seniority is its use in determining who will be laid off during a reduction in force"). They include "an element of due process," limiting "unfairness in personnel decisions." Gersuny, *Origins of Seniority Provisions in Collective Bargaining*, 33 Lab. L.J. 518, 519 (1982). And they consequently encourage employees to invest in the employing company, accepting "less than their value to the firm early in their careers" in return for greater benefits in later years. J. Baron & D. Kreps, Strategic Human Resources: Frameworks For General Managers 288 (1999).

Most important for present purposes, to require the typical employer to show more than the existence of a seniority system might well undermine the employees' expectations of consistent, uniform treatment — expectations upon which the seniority system's benefits depend. That is because such a rule would substitute a complex case-specific "accommodation" decision made by management for the more uniform, impersonal operation of seniority rules. Such management decisionmaking, with its inevitable discretionary elements, would involve a matter of the greatest importance to employees, namely, layoffs; it would take place outside, as well as inside, the confines of a court case; and it might well take place fairly often. *Cf.* ADA, 42 U.S.C. § 12101(a)(1) (estimating that some 43 million Americans suffer from physical or mental disabilities). We can find nothing in the statute that suggests Congress intended to undermine seniority systems in this way. And we consequently conclude that the employer's showing of violation of the rules of a seniority system is by itself ordinarily sufficient.

B

The plaintiff (here the employee) nonetheless remains free to show that special circumstances warrant a finding that, despite the presence of a seniority system (which the ADA may not trump in the run of cases), the requested "accommodation" is "reasonable" on the particular facts. That is because special circumstances might alter the important expectations described above. *Cf. Borkowski*, 63 F.3d at 137 ("[A]n accommodation that imposed burdens that would be unreasonable for most members of an industry might nevertheless be required of an individual defendant in light of that employer's particular circumstances"). *See also Woodman v. Runyon*, 132 F.3d 1330, 1343–1344 (10th Cir. 1997). The plaintiff might show, for example, that the employer, having retained the right to change the seniority system unilaterally, exercises that right fairly frequently, reducing employee expectations that the system will be followed — to the point where one more departure, needed to accommodate an individual with a disability, will not likely make a difference. The plaintiff might show that the system already contains exceptions such that, in the circumstances, one further exception is unlikely to matter. We do not mean these examples to exhaust the kinds of showings that a plaintiff might make. But we do mean to say that the plaintiff must bear the burden of showing special circumstances that make an exception from the seniority system reasonable in the particular case. And to do so, the plaintiff must explain why, in the particular case, an exception to the employer's seniority policy can constitute a "reasonable accommodation" even though in the ordinary case it cannot.

IV

In its question presented, US Airways asked us whether the ADA requires an employer to assign a disabled employee to a particular position even though another employee is entitled to that position under the employer's "established seniority system." We answer that *ordinarily* the ADA does not require that assignment. Hence, a showing that the assignment would violate the rules of a seniority system warrants summary judgment for the employer — unless there is more. The plaintiff must present evidence of that "more," namely, special circumstances surrounding the particular case that demonstrate the assignment is nonetheless reasonable.

Because the lower courts took a different view of the matter, and because neither party has had an opportunity to seek summary judgment in accordance with the principles we set forth here, we vacate the Court of Appeals' judgment and remand the case for further proceedings consistent with this opinion.

Justice Stevens, concurring.

While I join the Court's opinion, my colleagues' separate writings prompt these additional comments.

A possible conflict with an employer's seniority system is relevant to the question whether a disabled employee's requested accommodation is "reasonable" within the meaning of the Americans With Disabilities Act of 1990. For that reason, to the extent that the Court of Appeals concluded that a seniority system is only relevant to the question whether a given accommodation would impose an "undue hardship" on an employer, or determined that such a system has only a minor bearing on the reasonableness inquiry, it misread the statute. [Rest of opinion omitted]

Justice O'CONNOR, concurring. [Editor's note: Justice O'Connor joined the Court's opinion, providing the fifth vote]

I agree with portions of the opinion of the Court, but I find problematic the Court's test for determining whether the fact that a job reassignment violates a seniority system makes the reassignment an unreasonable accommodation under the Americans with Disabilities Act of 1990 (ADA or Act), 42 U.S.C. § 12101 *et seq.* Although a seniority system plays an important role in the workplace, for the reasons I explain below, I would prefer to say that the effect of a seniority system on the reasonableness of a reassignment as an accommodation for purposes of the ADA depends on whether the seniority system is legally enforceable. "Were it possible for me to adhere to [this belief] in my vote, and for the Court at the same time to [adopt a majority rule]," I would do so. *Screws v. United States*, 325 U.S. 91, 134 (1945) (Rutledge, J., concurring in result). "The Court, however, is divided in opinion," *ibid.*, and if each member voted consistently with his or her beliefs, we would not agree on a resolution of the question presented in this case. Yet "[s]talemate should not prevail," *ibid.*, particularly in a case in which we are merely interpreting a statute. Accordingly, in order that the Court may adopt a rule, and because I believe the Court's rule will often lead to the same outcome as the one I would have adopted, I join the Court's opinion despite my concerns. *Cf. Bragdon v. Abbott*, 524 U.S. 624, 655-656 (1998) (STEVENS, J., joined by BREYER, J., concurring); *Olmstead v. L.C.*, 527 U.S. 581 (1999) (STEVENS, J., concurring in part and concurring in judgment).

The ADA specifically lists "reassignment to a vacant position" as one example of a "reasonable accommodation." 42 U.S.C. § 12111(9)(B). In deciding whether an otherwise reasonable accommodation involving a reassignment is unreasonable because it would require an exception to a seniority system, I think the relevant issue is whether the seniority system prevents the position in question from being vacant. The word "vacant" means "not filled or occupied by an incumbent [or] possessor." WEBSTER'S THIRD NEW INTERNATIONAL DICTIONARY 2527 (1976). In the context of a workplace, a vacant position is a position in which no employee currently works and to which no individual has a legal entitlement. For example, in a workplace without a seniority system, when an employee ceases working for the employer, the employee's former position is vacant until a replacement is hired. Even if the replacement does not start work immediately, once the replacement enters into a contractual agreement with the employer, the position is no longer vacant because it has a "possessor." In contrast, when an employee ceases working in a workplace with a legally enforceable seniority system, the employee's former position does not become vacant if the seniority system entitles another employee to it. Instead, the employee entitled to the position under the seniority system immediately becomes the new "possessor" of that position. In a workplace with an unenforceable seniority policy, however, an employee expecting assignment to a position under the seniority policy would not have any type of contractual right to the position and so could not be said to be its "possessor." The position therefore would become vacant.

Given this understanding of when a position can properly be considered vacant, if a seniority system, in the absence of the ADA, would give someone other than the individual seeking the accommodation a legal entitlement or contractual right to the position to which reassignment is sought, the seniority system prevents the position from being vacant. If a position is not vacant, then reassignment to it is not a reasonable accommodation. The Act specifically says that "reassignment to a *vacant* position" is a type of "reasonable accommodation." § 12111(9)(B) (emphasis added). Indeed, the legislative history of the Act confirms that Congress did not intend reasonable accommodation to require bumping other employees. H.R. Rep. No. 101-485, pt. 2, p. 63 (1990), U.S. Code Cong. & Admin. News 1990, pp. 303, 345 ("The Committee also wishes to make clear that reassignment need only be to a vacant position — 'bumping' another employee out of a position to create a vacancy is not required"); S. Rep. No. 101-116, p. 32 (1989) (same).

Petitioner's Personnel Policy Guide for Agents, which contains its seniority policy, specifically states that it is "*not* intended to be a contract (express or implied) or otherwise to create legally enforceable obligations," and that petitioner "reserves the right to change any and all of the stated policies and procedures in [the] Guide at any time, without advanc[e] notice." Lodging of Respondent 2 (emphasis in original). Petitioner conceded at oral argument that its seniority policy does not give employees any legally enforceable rights. Tr. of Oral Arg. 16. Because the policy did not give any other employee a right to the position respondent sought, the position could be said to have been vacant when it became open for bidding, making the requested accommodation reasonable.

In Part II of its opinion, the Court correctly explains that "a plaintiff/employee (to defeat a defendant/employer's motion for summary judgment) need only show that an 'accommodation' seems reasonable on its face, *i.e.*, ordinarily or in the run of cases." *Ante*, at 1523. In other words, the plaintiff must show that the method of accommodation the employee seeks is reasonable in the run of cases. *See ante*, at 1523 (quoting *Barth v. Gelb*, 2 F.3d 1180, 1187 (D.C. Cir. 1993)). As the Court also correctly explains, "[o]nce the plaintiff has made this showing, the defendant/employer then must show special . . . circumstances that demonstrate undue hardship" in the context of the particular employer's operations. *Ante*, at 1523. These interpretations give appropriate meaning to both the term "reasonable," 42 U.S.C. § 12112(b)(5)(A), and the term "undue hardship," *ibid.*, preventing the concepts from overlapping by making reasonableness a general inquiry and undue hardship a specific inquiry. When the Court turns to applying its interpretation of the Act to seniority systems, however, it seems to blend the two inquiries by suggesting that the plaintiff should have the opportunity to prove that there are special circumstances in the context of that particular seniority system that would cause an exception to the system to be reasonable despite the fact that such exceptions are unreasonable in the run of cases.

Although I am troubled by the Court's reasoning, I believe the Court's approach for evaluating seniority systems will often lead to the same outcome as the test I would have adopted. Unenforceable seniority systems are likely to involve policies in which employers "retai[n] the right to change the system," *ante*, at 1525, and will often "permi[t] exceptions," *ante*, at 1525. They will also often contain disclaimers that "reduc[e] employee expectations that the system will be followed." *Ibid.* Thus, under the Court's test, disabled employees seeking accommodations that would require exceptions to unenforceable seniority systems may be able to show circumstances that make the accommodation "reasonable in the[ir] particular case." *Ibid.* Because I think the Court's test will often lead to the correct outcome, and because I think it important that a majority of the Court agree on a rule when interpreting statutes, I join the Court's opinion.

Justice SCALIA with whom Justice THOMAS joins, dissenting [omitted].

Justice SOUTER, with whom Justice GINSBURG joins, dissenting.

"[R]eassignment to a vacant position," 42 U.S.C. § 12111(9), is one way an employer may "reasonabl[y] accommodat[e]" disabled employees under the Americans with Disabilities Act of 1990, 42 U.S.C. § 12101 *et seq.* The Court today holds that a request for reassignment will nonetheless most likely be unreasonable when it would violate the terms of a seniority system imposed by an employer. Although I concur in the Court's appreciation of the value and importance of seniority systems, I do not believe my hand is free to accept the majority's result and therefore respectfully dissent.

Nothing in the ADA insulates seniority rules from the "reasonable accommodation" requirement, in marked contrast to Title VII of the Civil Rights Act of 1964 and the Age Discrimination in Employment Act of 1967, each of which has an explicit protection for seniority. *See* 42 U.S.C. § 2000e-2(h) ("Notwithstanding any other provision of this subchapter, it shall not be an unlawful employment practice for an employer to [provide different benefits to employees] pursuant to a bona fide seniority . . . system. . . ."); 29 U.S.C. § 623(f) ("It shall not be unlawful for an employer . . . to take any action otherwise prohibited [under previous sections] . . . to observe the terms of a bona fide seniority system [except for involuntary retirement] . . ."). Because Congress modeled several of the ADA's provisions on Title VII, its failure to replicate Title VII's exemption for seniority systems leaves the statute ambiguous, albeit with more than a hint that seniority rules do not inevitably carry the day.

In any event, the statute's legislative history resolves the ambiguity. The Committee Reports from both the House of Representatives and the Senate explain that seniority protections contained in a collective-bargaining agreement should not amount to more than "a factor" when it comes to deciding whether some accommodation at odds with the seniority rules is "reasonable" nevertheless. H.R. Rep. No. 101-485, pt. 2, p. 63 (1990), U.S. Code Cong. & Admin. News 1990, pp. 303, 345, (existence of collectively bargained protections for seniority "would not be determinative" on the issue whether an accommodation was reasonable); S. Rep. No. 101-116, p. 32 (1989) (a collective-bargaining agreement assigning jobs based on seniority "may be considered as a factor in determining" whether an accommodation is reasonable). Here, of course, it does not matter whether the congressional committees were right or wrong in thinking that views of sound ADA application could reduce a collectively bargained seniority policy to the level of "a factor," in the absence of a specific statutory provision to that effect. In fact, I doubt that any interpretive clue in legislative history could trump settled law specifically making collective bargaining agreements enforceable. *See, e.g.*, § 301(a), Labor Management Relations Act, 1947, 29 U.S.C. § 185(a) (permitting suit in federal court to enforce collective bargaining agreements); *Textile Workers v. Lincoln Mills of Ala.*, 353 U.S. 448 (1957) (holding that § 301(a) expresses a federal policy in favor of the enforceability of labor contracts); *Charles Dowd Box Co. v. Courtney*, 368 U.S. 502, 509 (1962) ("Section 301(a) reflects congressional recognition of the vital importance of assuring the enforceability of [collective-bargaining] agreements"). The point in this case, however, is simply to recognize that if Congress considered that sort of agreement no more than a factor in the analysis, surely no greater weight was meant for a seniority scheme like the one before us, unilaterally imposed by the employer, and, unlike collective bargaining agreements, not singled out for protection by any positive federal statute.

This legislative history also specifically rules out the majority's reliance on *Trans World Airlines, Inc. v. Hardison*, 432 U.S. 63 (1977), *ante*, at 1524, a case involving a request for a religious accommodation under Title VII that would have broken the seniority rules of a collective-bargaining agreement. We held that such an accommodation would not be "reasonable," and said that our conclusion was "supported" by Title VII's explicit exemption for seniority systems. 432 U.S. at 79–82. The committees of both Houses of Congress dealing with the ADA were aware of this case and expressed a choice against treating it as authority under the ADA, with its lack of any provision for maintaining seniority rules. *E.g.*, H.R. Rep. No. 101-485, pt. 2, at 68, U.S. Code Cong. & Admin. News 1990, pp. 303, 350 ("The Committee wishes to make it clear that the principles enunciated by the Supreme Court in *TWA v. Hardison* . . . are not applicable to this legislation."); S. Rep. No. 101-116, at 36 (same).

Because a unilaterally-imposed seniority system enjoys no special protection under the ADA, a consideration of facts peculiar to this very case is needed to gauge whether Barnett has carried the burden of showing his proposed accommodation to be a "reasonable" one despite the policy in force at US Airways. The majority describes this as a burden to show the accommodation is "plausible" or "feasible," *ante*, at 1523, and I believe Barnett has met it.

He held the mailroom job for two years before learning that employees with greater seniority planned to bid for the position, given US Airways's decision to declare the job "vacant." Thus, perhaps unlike ADA claimants who request accommodation through reassignment, Barnett was seeking not a change but a continuation of the status quo. All he asked was that US Airways refrain from declaring the position "vacant"; he did not ask to bump any other employee and no one would have lost a job on his account. There was no evidence in the District Court of any unmanageable ripple effects from Barnett's request, or showing that he would have overstepped an inordinate number of seniority levels by remaining where he was.

In fact, it is hard to see the seniority scheme here as any match for Barnett's ADA requests, since US Airways apparently took pains to ensure that its seniority rules raised no great expectations. In its policy statement, US Airways said that "[t]he Agent Personnel Policy Guide is *not* intended to be a contract" and that "USAir reserves the right to change any and all of the stated policies and procedures in this Guide at any time, without advanced notice." Lodging of Respondent 2 (emphasis in original). While I will skip any state-by-state analysis of the legal treatment of employee handbooks (a source of many lawyers' fees) it is safe to say that the contract law of a number of jurisdictions would treat this disclaimer as fatal to any claim an employee might make to enforce the seniority policy over an employer's contrary decision.

With US Airways itself insisting that its seniority system was noncontractual and modifiable at will, there is no reason to think that Barnett's accommodation would have resulted in anything more than minimal disruption to US Airways's operations, if that. Barnett has shown his requested accommodation to be "reasonable," and the burden ought to shift to US Airways if it wishes to claim that, in spite of surface appearances, violation of the seniority scheme would have worked an undue hardship. I would therefore affirm the Ninth Circuit.

NOTES AND PROBLEMS FOR DISCUSSION

1. The *Barnett* decision is a splintered decision by the Court. The majority consists of five members of the Court, including Justice O'Connor who concurred separately in an opinion in which she makes clear that she would have preferred a somewhat more lenient rule in which the reasonableness of reassignment as a reasonable accommodation depends on whether the seniority system is legally enforceable. The seniority system at issue in the *Barnett* case was not the result of a legally enforceable collective bargaining agreement. Nonetheless, the majority opinion states that "the typical seniority system provides important employee benefits by creating, and fulfilling, employee expectations of fair, uniform treatment." In fact, most seniority systems that are found in personnel manuals rather than in collective bargaining agreements are not legally enforceable. Personnel manuals often have boilerplate language stating that the rules listed therein are not legally enforceable. US Airways had such a statement in its personnel manual. As noted by the dissenters, the personnel manual stated that it was "*not* intended to be a contract" and that the company "reserves the right to change any and all of the stated policies and procedures in this Guide at any time." The majority opinion seems to skirt the question of whether seniority systems are legally enforceable when only found in personnel manuals. It states that these rules include "an element of due process" but never goes so far as to say they are legally enforceable. In stating what kind of special circumstance the plaintiff could demonstrate in order to acquire a modification in the seniority system as a reasonable accommodation, the majority cites as nonexhaustive examples that:

> [T]he employer, having retained the right to change the seniority system unilaterally, exercises that right fairly frequently, reducing employee expectations that the system will be followed — to the point where one more departure, needed to accommodate an individual with a disability, will not likely make a difference. The plaintiff might show that the system already contains exceptions such that, in the circumstances, one further exception is unlikely to matter.

Under the majority rule, it is not enough that the seniority system is not legally enforceable. The plaintiff needs to show that the seniority system is often not followed by the employer.

The Supreme Court remanded this case to the lower courts to consider the fact pattern in a framework consistent with its opinion. There are no facts in the original decision about whether US Airways rigorously followed its seniority system. How much deviation from the seniority system will have to be found in order for the lower court to conclude that a reassignment accommodation is reasonable? Do the deviations have to be pervasive or are isolated incidents sufficient for plaintiff to meet her burden of proof?

2. The EEOC's ADA Title I regulations explicitly define an employer's obligation to consider "reassignment to a vacant position" as part of its obligation to provide reasonable accommodations for an incumbent employee. 29 C.F.R. § 1630.2(o)(2)(ii). The Interpretive Guidelines to the regulations explain that request more fully. The guidelines state that reassignment is not available to applicants, but suggest that an incumbent employee should be reassigned when accommodation within the individual's current position would pose an undue hardship. Does that rule mean that an employer needs to combine two part-time positions into one full-time position to accommodate an incumbent employee? *See Fedro v. Reno*, 21 F.3d 1391 (7th Cir. 1994).

3. Carl Daugherty was a part-time city bus driver who was diagnosed as an insulin-dependent diabetic. That diagnosis precluded him from meeting the Federal Department of Transportation's requirements for driving a bus. After being relieved of his job, he argued that the city should have reassigned him to another position for which he was qualified. The city argued that movement from a part-time position to a full-time position is based on city seniority. Because Daugherty had less than one year's experience at the time of his diagnosis and discharge, under city policy, he was not eligible for transfer to a full-time position. Daugherty and the city agreed that no suitable part-time positions existed for which Daugherty was interested or qualified. Has the city violated the ADA's reasonable accommodation rule by failing to provide Daugherty with a full-time position that was comparable in pay and responsibility to the bus driver position for which he was no longer qualified? *See Daugherty v. City of El Paso*, 56 F.3d 695 (5th Cir. 1995).

4. In December, Mari Kennedy was diagnosed with attention deficit disorder (ADD), which made it difficult for her to concentrate on problems at her job as a secretary when her work was interrupted by another project. She asked her employer to restructure her job in the following ways so that her ADD would not interfere with her work performance:

a. play "white noise" to cover distracting conversations,

b. move her desk away from high-traffic areas such as copy machines, and

c. have employees give her instructions in writing rather than verbally.

The employer refused to make these accommodations. The employer opined that ADD is not a covered disability under the ADA, and that the requested accommodations were not reasonable because a secretary must be able to work effectively despite interruptions. The employer said Ms. Kennedy could remain in her current position but would have to fulfill all aspects of her job description. If she could not, she would be subject to corrective action. Alternatively, the employer offered Ms. Kennedy three weeks' severance pay if she desired to resign.

Ms. Kennedy comes to you for legal advice. She "voluntarily quit" her job to begin her own medical transcription business which is quite successful. Nonetheless, she seeks compensation for what she considers a constructive discharge and failure to provide reasonable accommodations. Does she have a strong case under the ADA?

5. Police Officer Smith has worked in the narcotics division of the city police department for 22 years. Following a very violent altercation with some suspects, he experienced acute depression and anxiety and was no longer able to perform his job. He took work-related medical leave and began receiving intensive psychiatric treatment. Initially, he could not leave his home, but after a while he began functioning normally in nonwork-related situations. He has been on medical leave for two years and is anxious to return to the police department because he needs to put in 25 years in order to receive a full pension. The employer is also anxious to have Smith either return to work or be discharged because it cannot afford to continue to compensate him on medical leave. Moreover, the employer does not feel that an employee should be able to earn a pension while on leave. Smith and the city therefore mutually agree that he should try to return to work. Upon consultation with his psychiatrist, Smith says that he requires a position that involves no stress. The only position he knows of that fits that description is janitorial. The Department frequently has janitorial openings, so Smith requests the next opening. The city responds that it is only required under the ADA to allow Smith to work in a position comparable to the one that he previously had, such as desk job rather than a patrol job, or a position in the training academy rather than on the street. The city says it is willing to restructure any other officer position through part-time work or other reasonable modifications but that Smith can only return to work if he can work at some officer position. Is the city's position supportable under the ADA? Is the city's concern about its pension plan cognizable under the ADA?

6. As an Englewood police officer, Thomas Conklin injured his ankle while pursuing a suspect in December 1991. His ankle injury worsened and he was placed on light-duty status in September 1992. He received full compensation and benefits through April 1993 in that capacity. At that time, he was told there was no more light-duty work for him to perform. After consultation with his doctor, Conklin said that he would be able to perform the job of dispatcher despite his disability but that he wanted to receive police officer pay in that position. (Police officers were paid almost twice as much as dispatchers.) Did Conklin request a reasonable accommodation under the ADA? *See Conklin v. City of Englewood*, 98 F.3d 1341 (6th Cir. 1996) (unpublished table decision).

7. Although the plaintiff in *Barnett* did not obtain relief, the Supreme Court's analysis reinvigorated the reassignment rule in the Seventh Circuit, which had interpreted it narrowly. The Seventh Circuit had previously ruled that an employer could treat a disabled employee seeking reassignment on a competitive basis with all other employees seeking an opening. In other words, there would be no preference for the disabled employee. In *EEOC v. United Airlines, Inc.*, 693 F.3d 760 (7th Cir. 2012), the Seventh Circuit reconsidered its prior decision in light of *Barnett* and ruled that the reassignment rule does require preferential treatment of an employee with a disability. It set forth the appropriate test as follows:

> In this case, the district court must first consider (under *Barnett* step one) if mandatory reassignment is ordinarily, in the run of cases, a reasonable accommodation. Assuming that the district court finds that mandatory

> reassignment is ordinarily reasonable, the district [court] must then determine (under *Barnett* step two) if there are fact-specific considerations particular to United's employment system that would create an undue hardship and render mandatory reassignment unreasonable.

United Airlines, 693 F.3d at 764.

The Tenth and D.C. Circuits have taken similar positions. *See Smith v. Midland Brake, Inc.*, 180 F.3d 1154 (10th Cir. 1999); *Aka v. Washington Hospital Center*, 156 F.3d 1284 (D.C. Cir. 1998). *But see Huber v. Wal-Mart*, 486 F.3d 480 (8th Cir. 2007).

2. Medical Examinations and Inquiries

Some individuals with disabilities have hidden disabilities that are discoverable based on the results of medical examinations or inquiries. In order to protect these individuals from discrimination based on myths and stereotypes about their condition, the ADA has developed a complex system of rules governing medical examinations and inquiries. Read these rules and try to figure out how they might help prevent some categories of employment discrimination.

> ADA Title I § 12112 Discrimination
>
> (d) Medical examinations and inquiries
>
> (1) In general
>
> The prohibition against discrimination as referred to in subsection (a) of this section shall include medical examinations and inquiries.
>
> (2) Preemployment
>
> (A) Prohibited examination or inquiry
>
> Except as provided in paragraph (3), a covered entity shall not conduct a medical examination or make inquiries of a job applicant as to whether such applicant is an individual with a disability or as to the nature or severity of such disability.
>
> (B) Acceptable inquiry
>
> A covered entity may make preemployment inquiries into the ability of an applicant to perform job-related functions.
>
> (3) Employment entrance examination
>
> A covered entity may require a medical examination after an offer of employment has been made to a job applicant and prior to the commencement of the employment duties of such applicant, and may condition an offer of employment on the results of such examination, if —
>
> (A) all entering employees are subjected to such an examination regardless of disability;

(B) information obtained regarding the medical condition or history of the applicant is collected and maintained on separate forms and in separate medical files and is treated as a confidential medical record, except that —

(i) supervisors and managers may be informed regarding necessary restrictions on the work or duties of the employee and necessary accommodations;

(ii) first aid and safety personnel may be informed, when appropriate, if the disability might require emergency treatment; and

(iii) government officials investigating compliance with this chapter shall be provided relevant information on request; and

(C) the results of such examination are used only in accordance with this subchapter.

(4) Examination and inquiry

(A) Prohibited examinations and inquiries

A covered entity shall not require a medical examination and shall not make inquiries of an employee as to whether such employee is an individual with a disability or as to the nature or severity of the disability, unless such examination or inquiry is shown to be job-related and consistent with business necessity.

(B) Acceptable examinations and inquiries

A covered entity may conduct voluntary medical examinations, including voluntary medical histories, which are part of an employee health program available to employees at that work site. A covered entity may make inquiries into the ability of an employee to perform job-related functions.

(C) Requirement

Information obtained under subparagraph (B) regarding the medical condition or history of any employee are subject to the requirements of subparagraphs (B) and (C) of paragraph (3).

The EEOC defines a "pre-employment examination or inquiry" as one that seeks to determine "whether an applicant is an individual with a disability or as to the nature or severity of such disability." 29 C.F.R. § 1630.13(a). Nonetheless, a covered entity "may make pre-employment inquiries into the ability of an applicant to perform job-related functions, and/or may ask an applicant to describe or to demonstrate how, with or without reasonable accommodation, the applicant will be able to perform job-related functions." 29 C.F.R. § 1630.14(a).

In understanding these rules, it is helpful to break them down into subparts. The following Notes and Comments seek to assist in that exercise.

NOTES AND PROBLEMS FOR DISCUSSION

1. Do you have to be an "individual with a disability" to proceed under this section? Notice that section 12112(d)(2)(A) refers to a "job applicant," not a job applicant with a disability. Similarly, section 12112(d)(4)(A) refers to an "employee," not an employee with a disability. Nonetheless, the statute is entitled the "Americans with Disabilities Act." Should the statutory title be used to make the policy argument that Congress intended only individuals with disabilities to be able to have a cause of action? *Compare Griffin v. Steeltek, Inc.*, 160 F.3d 591 (10th Cir. 1998), *with Krocka v. Bransfield*, 969 F. Supp. 1073 (N.D. Ill. 1997). Joining the other circuits that have considered the issue, the Eleventh Circuit has recently ruled that the language of the ADA does not predicate suit under the statute on an applicant's disability status. *See Harrison v. Benchmark Electronics*, 593 F.3d 1206 (11th Cir. 2010). Like the other circuits, the Eleventh Circuit also required evidence of damages sufficient to overcome summary judgment to bring a claim under section 12112(d) but found that the plaintiff in this case did have sufficient evidence to overcome summary judgment. A reasonable jury could infer that the defendant based its decision not to hire the plaintiff on information gleaned from an improper medical inquiry.

2. For pre-employment inquiries, one issue is what is the scope of a "medical examination" or "inquiry"? Is it illegal to ask a job applicant who is deaf how that person would communicate in offices where no one knew sign language? *See Adeyemi v. District of Columbia*, 525 F.3d 1222 (D.C. Cir. 2008). Is it illegal to ask if a job applicant has a driver's license, if driving is a job function? *See* 29 C.F.R. § 1630.13(a) app. [ADA Handbook, p. 143]

3. The medical examination rule has stringent confidentiality requirements with only three exceptions. Consider the following hypothetical in light of those rules:

> Guillermo Blanco applied for a position with Bath Iron Works Corporation in January 2008. In February, 2008, he was offered a job subject to satisfactory completion of a pre-placement medical screening, called the "Medical Surveillance History Questionnaire." He sought to answer the questions truthfully based on his understanding of the questions. In March, 2008, he began working for Bath Iron Works as a designer. His job performance was satisfactory until September 2008 when he was transferred to a new team where His work required more multitasking. Blanco has ADHD and, in September 2008, he sought accommodations at work due to his ADHD. He provided medical documentation of his ADHD as part of this request. Upon receiving his request for accommodation, Bath Iron Works requested that Blanco meet with its in-house salaried medical provider, Dr. Maria Mazorra. Dr. Mazorra discussed Blanco's answers on the Medical Surveillance Questionnaire with him at this meeting and accused him of lying on that questionnaire to hide his ADHD. She then informed his supervisors that, in her opinion, Blanco had lied on the Questionnaire. Blanco was terminated for lying on the Questionnaire. Did Dr. Mazorra violate the ADA's confidentiality provisions? Would it make a difference if Blanco had failed to disclose a condition that might pose a health or safety risk to himself or others?

See Blanco v. Bath Iron Works Corp., 802 F. Supp. 2d 215 (D. Me. 2011).

4. For pre-employment medical exams, there is no statutory limit on the scope of the exam. *See Norman-Bloodsaw v. Lawrence Berkeley Laboratory*, 135 F.3d 1260 (9th Cir. 1998) (no cause of action for being tested, without the applicant's knowledge, for private and sensitive information such as syphilis, sickle cell trait, and pregnancy). For incumbent employees, the exam or inquiries must be "job-related and consistent with business necessity." Why do you think Congress only imposed that restriction on exams of incumbent employees?

5. Courts have struggled to determine what is a "medical exam" that is "job-related and consistent with business necessity," especially for employees who are seeking to return to work after a medical leave. Consider that issue in light of the following facts:

> Kris Indergard work at Georgia-Pacific's Wauna mill facility from December 27, 1984 until February 8, 2006. On December 9, 2003, she took medical leave to undergo surgery for work-related and non-work related injuries to her knees. She remained on medical leave until March 21, 2005, when her orthopedic surgeon authorized her to return to work, but with permanent restrictions. GP policy required employees to participate in a physical capacity evaluation before returning to work from medical leave, and GP so informed Indergard. On October 11, 2005, Indergard provided GP with a note from her doctor removing the permanent restrictions he had previously identified.
>
> GP required Indergard to undergo an evaluation conducted by a licensed occupational therapist. The occupational therapist administered various tests, evaluated her performance and made a recommendation based on those tests as to whether she could return to work. In addition to testing whether Indergard could perform discrete job-related tasks, the exam also included subjective reports of her pain level, use of medication and assistive devices, and communication, cognitive ability, attitude and behavior. The occupational therapist recorded Indergard's heart rate and breathing pattern after a treadmill test as well as her muscle pain and stiffness. Nonetheless, no blood was drawn, no urine samples collected, no lab-work performed, and no x-rays or scans taken. No doctor or nurse examined, diagnosed, or treated her.

See Indergard v. Georgia-Pacific Corp., 582 F.3d 1049 (9th Cir. 2009) (2-1 decision).

6. When may an employer require an employee to take a psychiatric fitness-for-duty exam? Consider these facts:

> During a meeting with management, an employee banged his hand on the table, after describing what he considered to be harassing treatment on the basis of his national origin, and said that someone was "going to pay for this." His employer referred him to a psychiatric fitness-for-duty exam, where he was given the Minnesota Multiphasic Personality Inventory. The plaintiff's job was a quality assurance specialist; he typically worked from home but was required to report to the call center for certain meetings. Was the employer legally permitted to require him to take that psychiatric exam?

See Owusu-Ansah v. Coca-Cola Co., 715 F.3d 1306 (11th Cir. 2013) (yes).

How do these rules apply to former employees who seek to become re-employed? Consider the following case:

GRENIER v. CYANAMID PLASTICS, INC.

70 F.3d 667 (1st Cir. 1995)

SARIS, District Judge.

Appellant Andre Grenier ("Grenier") was employed as an electrician for Cyanamid Plastics, Inc., d/b/a Cyro Industries ("Cyro"), for several years before he was placed on disability leave due to psychological problems. After his employment had officially terminated by automatic operation of the company disability policy, but while still receiving disability benefits, Grenier notified Cyro that he was an individual with a disability who needed reasonable accommodation to return to work and applied to be re-hired into his previous position. Before making him a job offer, Cyro requested Grenier to provide certification from his physician stating that he was prepared to return to work without restrictions or identifying the reasonable accommodations necessary for him to return to work. When Grenier failed to do so, his application was rejected.

The difficult issue on appeal is whether Cyro violated the Americans with Disabilities Act ("ADA"), 42 U.S.C. § 12112(d), which prohibits certain preemployment medical examinations and inquiries of a job applicant. Concluding that Cyro did not violate this provision of the ADA, we affirm the district court's entry of summary judgment for Cyro.

I. *STATEMENT OF THE CASE*

A. Facts

Reviewing the factual record in the light most favorable to the nonmoving party, as we must at summary judgment. We treat the following facts as undisputed.

1. The Disability Leave

Andre Grenier worked as a shift electrician for Cyro at its plant in Sanford, Maine, from 1980 to 1989. Grenier's technical skill as an electrician was good. In 1989, Grenier and several other employees were questioned about vandalism of plant machinery that had occurred during their shift. Grenier responded to the questioning "in a highly emotional and irrational manner" and failed to report to his next scheduled shift. He informed his supervisor, William Kennedy, that he was afraid to be on a shift without an alibi, and that he was "losing it." Stating that Grenier's behavior was "very disruptive and potentially dangerous," Kennedy placed Grenier on medical leave in November 1989. This leave was explicitly "until such a time when you can be cleared by our medical department to return to work." Kennedy informed Grenier in writing that in order to return he would have to go through the standard reentry screening process, including permitting his doctors to discuss the specifics of his case with the company doctor.

In August 1990, Grenier mailed the first of a series of letters to Cyro, including a one-page letter received September 27, 1990, and a six-page "statement" of April 11, 1991. In these letters, Grenier criticized the plant manager Skip Brogli and complained that company actions in investigating vandalism at the plant and placing him on medical leave had caused him to suffer increased anxiety. . . .

Grenier informed Cyro in his letters that his analyst Dr. Stewart "describes me as being Narcissistic," but noted that "I prefer the word 'proud.' " . . . He stated repeatedly, however, that he refused to quit his job.

Grenier would not voluntarily terminate his employment. He remained on indefinite disability leave until May 12, 1991, when his employment at Cyro terminated automatically as a result of the expiration of his continuous service credits. Cyro informed Grenier of his termination by letter May 15, 1991.

Grenier received disability benefits from Cyro for a two-year period ending December 31, 1992. Under the company's plan, benefits were payable for up to two years if Grenier was under the regular care of a licensed physician and unable to perform the duties of his specific job, but benefits would have continued beyond this period only if the Disability Department determined that his medical condition prevented him "from working at any job for which [he was] reasonably qualified to perform." On December 4, 1992, the Cyro disability department wrote Grenier that based on information received from an independent medical examination of July 30, 1992, he was not disabled to this extent and, therefore, no benefits were payable after January 1, 1993.

2. Application for Re-Employment

In a letter dated December 18, 1992, and addressed to Robert Lysaght, the Personnel Operations Manager at the Sanford plant, Grenier asked to be considered an applicant for the job of shift electrician, his former position. Grenier was still receiving disability benefits at this time. In this letter, which was under the heading "request for employment accommodation," Grenier stated:

> I qualify as an individual with a disability as defined by Federal and State Civil Rights laws.
>
> I understand that CYRO Industries is conducting interviews for the position of shift mechanic in the electrical department. The purpose of this letter is to request accommodation to return to work in the same capacity as I had been working since September of 1980.
>
> I believe that I should be afforded the opportunity to be accommodated to return to my job, at the very least, for a trial period, to prove that I am able to perform my job.

> I believe that, under reasonable circumstances, I should be able to perform in a safe and reliable manner.

In response, Lysaght told Grenier in a January 5, 1993, letter that "CYRO is not currently accepting applications" but that the Maine unemployment office would be notified when Cyro was soliciting applications. In reality, a job notice was posted on January 4, 1993 — subsequent to Grenier's request for consideration as an applicant, but prior to the date of Lysaght's response. Lysaght requested in his letter:

> Since your termination of employment came as a result of the expiration of Continuous Service Credits while you were on an extended medical leave, CYRO would reasonably request that you provide us with certification from a physician that you are prepared to return to work without restrictions or identifying any accommodations that are required for you to return to work at the Sanford location. Of course, any requests for employment accommodation will be considered with regard to the reasonableness at the time of the employment interview process.
>
> Therefore, in order to return to work with CYRO Industries you need 1) keep in touch with the Maine Unemployment office in Sanford to learn when CYRO is accepting employment applications; 2) complete an employment application for a position for which you are qualified; and 3) provide CYRO with notice from your physician that you are prepared to return to work without restrictions or identifying those reasonable accommodations that may be necessary.

By letter of January 15, 1993, Grenier forwarded his therapist's certification that he was disabled and requested to discuss accommodation with Cyro Vice President William Loman. He also maintained that his employment had never terminated, and argued that the May 15, 1991, letter that informed him of the termination "simply implies that my employment is terminated."

Cyro's New Jersey-based Personnel Director Thomas Ayres responded by letter of January 25th by informing Grenier that he must follow the steps outlined in Lysaght's January 5th letter in order to be considered for employment.

Additional correspondence ensued. Grenier asserted that he was "capable of performing the essential functions of the job with or without accommodation" but failed to describe how he would perform and refused to provide medical documentation. Cyro continued to request the documentation.

On February 22, 1993, Cyro mailed Grenier an employment application, which Grenier promptly returned. By letter of March 15, 1993, Cyro rejected Grenier's application for employment, stating that, "[a]fter careful review of all relevant information, your request for employment consideration is denied."

B. Proceedings Below

[The] District Court entered summary judgment for Cyro. Grenier argues on appeal that Cyro's pre-offer inquiry violated the ADA and that there are genuine issues of material fact with respect to his claim that Cyro's failure to hire him constituted intentional discrimination.

II. *ANALYSIS*

A. Standard of Review

This court reviews the district court's grant of summary judgment *de novo*. . . .

B. Statutory Framework

A close analysis of the statutory and regulatory framework is essential to determine the employer's obligations under the ADA when dealing with the known disability of a job applicant.

1. The Statute

[The court quotes the ADA statutory requirements for pre-employment examinations and inquiries of current employees.]

2. The Regulations

The regulations adopted under the ADA by the Equal Employment Opportunity Commission ("EEOC") provide that an employer may make "pre-employment inquiries into the ability of an applicant to perform job-related functions, and/or may ask an applicant to describe or to demonstrate how, with or without reasonable accommodation, the applicant will be able to perform job-related functions." 29 C.F.R. § 1630.14(a). The EEOC crafted § 1630.14(a) in response to comments on the proposed regulation from employers asking "whether an employer may ask how an individual will perform a job function when the individual's known disability appears to interfere with or prevent performance of job-related functions." 56 Fed. Reg. 35725, 35732 (1991).

The EEOC published as an appendix to the regulations a section-by-section "Interpretive Guidance on Title I of the Americans with Disabilities Act." 29 C.F.R. Pt. 1630, App. We have looked to this source in interpreting the ADA. *See Carparts Distrib. Ctr., Inc. v. Automotive Wholesaler's Ass'n*, 37 F.3d 12, 16 (1st Cir. 1994). Such administrative interpretations of the Act by the enforcing agency, "while not controlling upon the courts by reason of their authority, do constitute a body of experience and informed judgment to which courts and litigants may properly resort for guidance." *Meritor Sav. Bank, FSB v. Vinson*, 477 U.S. 57, 65 (1986).

3. The Guidance

An EEOC Enforcement Guidance, dated May 19, 1994, further aids our interpretation of the rules concerning pre-offer inquiries of applicants with known disabilities. *See* Equal Employment Opportunity Comm'n, *Enforcement Guidance: Preemployment Disability-Related Inquiries and Medical Examinations Under the Americans with Disabilities Act of 1990* (EEOC Notice 915.002) (May 19, 1994) [hereinafter *Guidance*]. The Guidance was designed "for interim use by EEOC investigators, pending coordination with other federal agencies." *Id.*, Exec. Summ. It is not binding law, but as a detailed analysis of the relevant ADA provisions, it aids our interpretation of the statute.

The EEOC explains that allowing an employer to ask an applicant with a known disability to describe or demonstrate how he would perform a job-related function "is in the interest of both applicants and employers." *Id.* at n.23. Employers are entitled to know whether an applicant with an apparently interfering disability can perform job-related functions, with or without reasonable accommodation. It is in the interest of an applicant with such a disability to describe or demonstrate performance in order to dispel notions that s/he is unable to perform the job because of the disability. *Id.*

In a section entitled "Inquiries Concerning Need for Accommodation and Requests for Documentation if Applicant Asks for Accommodation," the Guidance permits an employer during the hiring process to require an applicant "to inform the employer of any reasonable accommodation needed" to take an "interview" or perform a "job demonstration." *Id.* § IV.B.6.a. . . .

When an applicant requests reasonable accommodation, an employer may request "documentation from an appropriate professional (e.g., a doctor, rehabilitation counselor, etc.), stating that s/he has a disability." *Id.* § IV.B.6.b. An employer may also require documentation as to an applicant's functional limitations "for which reasonable accommodation is requested (and which flow from the disability.)" *Id.* The EEOC reasoned that such requests are not prohibited pre-offer inquiries because:

> Requesting such documentation is consistent with the ADA's legislative history. For example, Congress specifically anticipated that when an applicant requests reasonable accommodation for the application process (or when an employee requests reasonable accommodation for the job), *the employer should engage in an interactive process with the individual to determine an effective reasonable accommodation.*

Id. (emphasis added). As an example, the EEOC stated that an employer may at the pre-offer stage require an applicant to obtain documentation from a professional stating she cannot lift a certain amount and needs reasonable accommodation. *Id.*

C. The Pre-Offer Inquiry

With this statutory and regulatory framework in mind, we turn to Grenier's claim that Cyro's requirement of a medical certification violates ADA § 12112(d).

1. Getting Along

First, Grenier argues that Cyro's letter requiring a medical certification constituted an impermissible inquiry because the request was not for information about how he would perform the job-related functions. Rather than ask "whether he possessed the requisite skills to perform the electrical and electronic tasks called for in the job description," Grenier complains, "Cyro assumed that his ability to perform job related functions was called into question by his history of mental illness." Grenier argues that Cyro already had knowledge that he was able to do the essential job-related functions because he had worked there for nine years and was "technically qualified."

Grenier incorrectly assumes that the essential functions of the job of shift electrician require only technical ability and experience as an electrician. "The term essential functions means the fundamental job duties of the employment position the individual with a disability holds or desires." 29 C.F.R. § 1630.2(n)(1). Technical skills and experience are not the only essential requirements of a job.

More specifically, an employer may reasonably believe that an employee known to have a paranoia about the plant manager is not able to perform his job.

The ADA does not require an employer to wear blinders to a known disability at the pre-offer stage, but permits an "interactive process" beneficial to both the employer and applicant. The EEOC regulations recognize this by providing that an employer can ask an applicant with a known disability to describe or demonstrate how "with or without reasonable accommodation" the applicant will be able to do the job. 29 C.F.R. § 1630.14(a). Here, Cyro knew that the applicant had just recently been unable to perform his specific job at Cyro as a result of a mental disability for which he was still receiving benefits from Cyro and undergoing psychiatric treatment. Indeed, Grenier himself had claimed he was totally disabled from performing any work, not just his specific job at Cyro. *Cf. August v. Offices Unlimited, Inc.*, 981 F.2d 576, 581–82 (1st Cir. 1992) (man who had asserted on insurance forms that he was "totally disabled" and had presented no contrary evidence could not be found to be "qualified handicapped person" under Massachusetts anti-discrimination statute, Mass. Gen. L. ch. 151B); *Reigel v. Kaiser Found. Health Plan*, 859 F. Supp. 963, 969 (E.D.N.C. 1994) (woman who certified to her disability insurer that she could not perform her job was estopped from asserting that during the same time period she had been qualified to perform for purposes of the ADA). We hold that this employer did not violate the prohibition in § 12112(d) by inquiring into Grenier's ability to function effectively in the workplace and to get along with his co-workers and supervisor, rather than just his technical qualifications as an electrician.[4]

[4] We note that the inquiry made by Cyro would not necessarily be permissible under different circumstances, such as where the employer was less familiar with the nature or extent of the applicant's disability, or with the effect of the disability on job performance. As the EEOC recognized when preparing the Guidance, "there are sometimes subtle distinctions between a permissible and a prohibited pre-offer inquiry." *Guidance* § IV.B.6.b. *See generally* Paul F. Mickey, Jr. & Maryelena Pardo, *Dealing with Mental Disabilities Under the ADA*, 9 Lab. Law. 531 (1993); Janet L. Hamilton, *New Protections for Persons with Mental Illness in the Workplace under the Americans with Disabilities Act of 1990*, 40 Clev. St. L. Rev. 63, 92 (1992).

2. The Medical Certification

Next Grenier argues that Cyro's pre-offer requirement of a medical certification is an illegal pre-offer inquiry under the ADA because the regulations "do not by their terms permit a request to someone other than the applicant at the pre-offer stage."

As a preliminary matter, we address whether a request for medical certification constitutes a "medical examination" or whether it is instead an "inquiry." The ADA prohibits an employer from conducting any pre-offer "medical examination" of a job applicant. § 12112(d)(2). This prohibition applies to psychological examinations. *See Guidance* at n.47 (citing H.R. Rep. No. 485 (Pt. 3), 101st Cong., 2d Sess. 46 (1990), *reprinted in* 1990 U.S.C.C.A.N. vol. 4, Legis. Hist., 445, 469). The EEOC defined "medical examination" as follows:

> Medical examinations are procedures or tests that seek information about the existence, nature, or severity of an individual's physical or mental impairment, or that seek information regarding an individual's physical or psychological health.

Guidance § V.A. We conclude that a certification from a treating psychiatrist that does not necessitate new tests or procedures is best analyzed as an "inquiry" rather than as a "medical examination."

Also, contrary to Grenier's assertion, the EEOC interprets the ADA to allow certain inquiries of third parties at the pre-offer stage. With respect to "inquiries to third parties regarding an applicant's medical condition," the Guidance provides that "[a]t the pre-offer stage", an employer can "ask a third party (*e.g.*, a reference) anything that it could ask the applicant directly." *Guidance* § IV.B.15. Further, the EEOC finds that requests for documentation from health care providers to confirm the existence of a disability are permissible where, as here, requests for reasonable accommodation are made in connection with the hiring process or job. *See Guidance* § IV.B.6.b. We conclude that an employer may request that an applicant provide medical certification from doctors of ability to perform so long as the inquiry does not otherwise run afoul of § 12112(d)(2)(A).

The primary thrust of Grenier's appeal is that this inquiry — the requirement of medical certification of ability to perform from a former disabled employee applying to return to work with the same employer — violates § 12112(d)(2)(A) in that it constitutes an inquiry of a "job applicant as to whether such applicant is an individual with a disability or as to the nature or severity of such disability."

[T]his Court faces the quandary of determining the appropriate parameters of a pre-offer inquiry of a former employee who is the recipient of disability benefits and now seeks re-employment. Cyro argues that an employer should not be forced to have "amnesia" with respect to a former employee where it is well aware of the nature and severity of that employee's disability because it had previously received medical information that formed the basis for its determination of eligibility for disability benefits. Rather, it urges, Grenier should be treated as an existing employee returning from disability leave, in which case the employer would be able to demand medical certification of ability to return to work. . . . We agree that this case is similar to that of an employee returning from disability leave. It appears that neither Congress nor the EEOC took into account the case of a returning employee when formulating the restrictions on pre-offer inquiries. Here, as in the case of the returning employee, the employer must be able to assess the extent of the applicant's recovery from inability to perform. Further, if accommodations are necessary to enable job performance, the employer, who is already familiar with the disability, must learn of those accommodations in order to have any realistic chance of assessing ability to perform.

Grenier contends that the ADA as interpreted in the Guidance prohibits an employer's requirement that a physician identify the *type of* reasonable accommodations required for an employee to return to work. The Guidance states: "If an applicant has voluntarily disclosed that s/he would need a reasonable accommodation to perform the job, the employer still may not make inquiries at the pre-offer stage about the *type* of required reasonable accommodation." *Guidance* § IV.B.6.a.

We conclude that the ADA does not preclude an employer from asking an applicant with a *known* disability who seeks a reasonable accommodation to specify the type of accommodation he seeks. As the District Court pointed out, the Guidance prohibits pre-offer inquiry into the type of accommodation because it is "likely to elicit information about the nature and severity of a disability." *Guidance* § IV.B.6.a. The central purpose of the prohibition on pre-offer inquiries generally is to ensure that an applicant's hidden disability remains hidden. *See* H.R. Rep. No. 485 (Pt. 2), 101st Cong., 2d Sess., at 73, *reprinted in* 1990 U.S.C.C.A.N. vol. 4, Legis. Hist., 303, 355 ("The legislation prohibits any identification of a disability by inquiry or examination at the preoffer stage."); *Guidance* § IV.A ("This prohibition is to ensure that an applicant's possible hidden disability (including prior history of a disability) is not considered by the employer prior to the assessment of the applicant's non-medical qualifications.").

With respect to known disabilities, however, the emphasis is on encouraging the employer to "engage in an interactive process with the individual to determine an effective reasonable accommodation." *Guidance* § IV.B.6.b (citing H.R. Rep. No. 485 (Pt. 2), *supra*, at 65–66, U.S.C.C.A.N. at 347–48). That is why the EEOC allows an employer to ask an applicant with known claustrophobia to describe pre-offer how she would perform the job, with or without reasonable accommodation. There could be no meaningful interaction if this court would accept the strict interpretation Grenier presses on us that an employer who knows the precise nature of a disability that interferes with essential job functions cannot, on being informed pre-offer that accommodation will be necessary, follow up with the logical question "what kind?"[6]

---

[6] On October 10, 1995, subsequent to oral argument, the EEOC issued a new Guidance. Although neither party has argued that we ought to consider this newest guidance, we note that the EEOC has revised its interpretation of the ADA and now reaches the same conclusion. Under a section headed "The Pre-Offer Stage," the EEOC now explains:

> However, when an employer could reasonably believe that an applicant will need reasonable accommodation to perform the functions of the job, the employer may ask that applicant certain limited questions. Specifically, the employer may ask *whether s/he needs reasonable accommodation* and *what type of reasonable accommodation* would be needed to perform the functions of the job.

In sum, an employer does not violate § 12112(d)(2) of the ADA by requiring a former employee with a recent known disability applying for re-employment to provide medical certification as to ability to return to work with or without reasonable accommodation, and as to the type of any reasonable accommodation necessary, as long as it is relevant to the assessment of ability to perform essential job functions.

III. CONCLUSION

For the foregoing reasons, the District Court's grant of summary judgment is AFFIRMED.

NOTES AND PROBLEMS FOR DISCUSSION

1. Do you think the First Circuit's decision was affected by the category of disability — psychiatric? Would the same kind of inquiry have been permitted in the context of a physical or medical condition?

2. Jane Roe is an accounts manager for the Cheyenne Mountain Conference Resort ("CMCR"). CMCR employees were given copies of a new drug and alcohol testing policy which stated:

> a. Employees are strictly prohibited from possessing, consuming, or being under the influence of alcohol during work hours or on company property.
>
> b. Employees are strictly prohibited from possessing, consuming, or being under the influence of any illegal drugs, controlled substance, any prescribed or over the counter drug or medication that has been illegally obtained or is being used in an improper manner.
>
> c. Employees must report without qualification, all drugs present within their body system [sic]. Further, they must remain free of drugs while on the job. They must not use, possess, conceal, manufacture, distribute, dispense, transport, or sell drugs while on the job, in CMCR vehicles or on CMCR property or to the property to which they have been assigned in the course of their employment. Additionally, prescribed drugs may be used only to the extent that they have been reported and approved by an employee supervisor and that they can be taken by the employee without risk of sensory impairment and/or injury to any person or employee.

Jane Roe takes a prescription medication to alleviate her symptoms of depression. This medication is fully effective, so that she does not consider her medical condition to limit her in any major life activities. For privacy reasons, Roe objects to this medical inquiry. Does she have standing to challenge these testing requirements under the ADA? If so, should she prevail on her ADA claim? *See Roe v. Cheyenne Mountain Conference Resort, Inc.*, 124 F.3d 1221 (10th Cir. 1997).

3. Steven Sharp worked at Prevo's Family Market as a part-time produce clerk.

Enforcement Guidance: Pre-Employment Disability-Related Questions and Medical Examinations (Oct. 10, 1995) (emphasis in original).

He informed his employer that he had recently tested positive for HIV infection because he would be doing some public speaking on the subject and did not want the employer to hear about his HIV status from someone else. The owner of the supermarket was concerned that Steven handled sharp knives as part of his duties, and that cuts and nicks were commonplace. He asked Sharp to provide verification of his HIV condition from a physician. Sharp was placed on paid leave pending receipt of this information. Sharp chose not to provide this information to his employer and his employment was subsequently terminated. Has his employer violated the ADA? *See EEOC v. Prevo' s Family Market, Inc.*, 135 F.3d 1089 (6th Cir. 1998).

D. SPECIAL ISSUES RELATING TO CATEGORIES OF PLAINTIFFS

1. "Regarded as" Disabled

Individuals who are "regarded as" disabled are not entitled to reasonable accommodations. The ADA states in Section 12201:

> (h) Reasonable accommodations and modifications. A covered entity under title I, a public entity under title II, and any person who owns, leases, or operates a place of public accommodation under title III, need not provide a reasonable accommodation or a reasonable modification to policies, practices, or procedures to an individual who meets the definition of disability in section 3(1) solely under subparagraph (C) of such section.

The EEOC's Interpretive Guidance further explains the meaning of this provision:

> An individual with a disability is considered "qualified" if the individual can perform the essential functions of the position held or desired with or without reasonable accommodation. A covered entity is required, absent undue hardship, to provide reasonable accommodation to an otherwise qualified individual with a substantially limiting impairment or a "record of" such an impairment. However, a covered entity is not required to provide an accommodation to an individual who meets the definition of disability solely under the "regarded as" prong.
>
> The legislative history of the ADAA makes clear that Congress included this provision in response to various court decisions that had held (pre-Amendments Act) that individuals who were covered solely under the "regarded as" prong were eligible for reasonable accommodations. In those cases, the plaintiffs had been found not to be covered under the first prong of the definition of disability "because of the overly stringent manner in which the courts had been interpreting that prong." 2008 Senate Statement of Managers at 11. The legislative history goes on to explain that "[b]ecause of [Congress's] strong belief that accommodating individuals with disabilities is a key goal of the ADA, some members [of Congress] continue to have reservations about this provision." *Id.* However, Congress ultimately concluded that clarifying that individuals covered solely under the "regarded as"

> prong are not entitled to reasonable accommodations "is an acceptable compromise given our strong expectation that such individuals would now be covered under the first prong of the definition [of disability], properly applied." Further, individuals covered under the third prong still may bring discrimination claims (other than failure-to-accommodate claims) under title I of the ADA. 2008 Senate Statement of Managers at 9-10.

29 C.F.R. § 1630.2(o) app. [ADA Handbook, p. 125]

NOTES AND PROBLEMS FOR DISCUSSION

1. Examine this rule in light of the language of Title I. Does it also mean that individuals who seek to sue under the "association" rule (Section 12112(b)(4)) also cannot seek reasonable accommodations?

2. What about plaintiffs who sue under the "record of" disability rule? Can they seek reasonable accommodations?

3. And what about individuals who are covered by Title I when they challenge a rule requiring them to be evaluated without use of corrective lenses? Can they request reasonable accommodations?

2. Individuals Who Engage in the Illegal Use of Drugs and Use of Alcohol

As mentioned in Chapter Two, individuals who engage in the illegal use of drugs and alcohol do not receive the same range of protection under ADA Title I as other individuals. Section 12114(c) states that a covered entity:

> may hold an employee who engages in the illegal use of drugs or who is an alcoholic to the same qualification standards for employment or job performance and behavior that such entity holds other employees, even if any unsatisfactory performance or behavior is related to the drug use or alcoholism of such employee.

Consider how this rule would affect an individual with alcoholism who requested a reasonable accommodation at the workplace. Could the individual request a restructured workday to facilitate his or her attendance at AA meetings? Could the individual request some changes in job duties to lessen his or her stress at the workplace?

Further, Section 12114(a) specifies that the term "qualified individual with a disability" does not include "any employee or applicant who is currently engaging in the illegal use of drugs, when the covered entity acts on the basis of such use." (Note that this rule does not apply to alcoholics, since the use of alcohol is typically not illegal for adults.) This rule raises the question of what it means to be a "current" user of drugs. What if the individual used drugs during the weeks and months prior to discharge but was participating in a drug rehabilitation program and is drug-free on the day he or she was fired? [For further discussion of these issues, review the Notes and Discussion in [B][1][a][ii] Chapter Two.]

Does Section 12114(a) preclude employers from considering prior drug use when they are being asked to re-hire someone they previously discharged?

RAYTHEON COMPANY v. HERNANDEZ
540 U.S. 44 (2003)

Justice THOMAS delivered the opinion of the Court.

The Americans with Disabilities Act of 1990 (ADA), 104 Stat. 327, as amended, 42 U.S.C. § 12101 *et seq.*, makes it unlawful for an employer, with respect to hiring, to "discriminate against a qualified individual with a disability because of the disability of such individual." § 12112(a). We are asked to decide in this case whether the ADA confers preferential rehire rights on disabled employees lawfully terminated for violating workplace conduct rules. The United States Court of Appeals for the Ninth Circuit held that an employer's unwritten policy not to rehire employees who left the company for violating personal conduct rules contravenes the ADA, at least as applied to employees who were lawfully forced to resign for illegal drug use but have since been rehabilitated. Because the Ninth Circuit improperly applied a disparate-impact analysis in a disparate-treatment case in order to reach this holding, we vacate its judgment and remand the case for further proceedings consistent with this opinion. We do not, however, reach the question on which we granted certiorari. 537 U.S. 1187 (2003).

I

Respondent, Joel Hernandez, worked for Hughes Missile Systems for 25 years.[1] On July 11, 1991, respondent's appearance and behavior at work suggested that he might be under the influence of drugs or alcohol. Pursuant to company policy, respondent took a drug test, which came back positive for cocaine. Respondent subsequently admitted that he had been up late drinking beer and using cocaine the night before the test. Because respondent's behavior violated petitioner's workplace conduct rules, respondent was forced to resign. Respondent's "Employee Separation Summary" indicated as the reason for separation: "discharge for personal conduct (quit in lieu of discharge)." App. 12a.

More than two years later, on January 24, 1994, respondent applied to be rehired by petitioner. Respondent stated on his application that he had previously been employed by petitioner. He also attached two reference letters to the application, one from his pastor, stating that respondent was a "faithful and active member" of the church, and the other from an Alcoholics Anonymous counselor, stating that respondent attends Alcoholics Anonymous meetings regularly and is in recovery. *Id.*, at 13a-15a.

Joanne Bockmiller, an employee in the company's Labor Relations Department, reviewed respondent's application. Bockmiller testified in her deposition that since

---

[1] Hughes has since been acquired by petitioner, Raytheon Company. For the sake of clarity, we refer to Hughes and Raytheon collectively as petitioner or the company.

respondent's application disclosed his prior employment with the company, she pulled his personnel file and reviewed his employee separation summary. She then rejected respondent's application. Bockmiller insisted that the company had a policy against rehiring employees who were terminated for workplace misconduct. *Id.*, at 62a. Thus, when she reviewed the employment separation summary and found that respondent had been discharged for violating workplace conduct rules, she rejected respondent's application. She testified, in particular, that she did not know that respondent was a former drug addict when she made the employment decision and did not see anything that would constitute a "record of" addiction. *Id.*, at 63a-64a.

Respondent subsequently filed a charge with the Equal Employment Opportunity Commission (EEOC). Respondent's charge of discrimination indicated that petitioner did not give him a reason for his nonselection, but that respondent believed he had been discriminated against in violation of the ADA.

Petitioner responded to the charge by submitting a letter to the EEOC, in which George M. Medina, Sr., Manager of Diversity Development, wrote:

> "The ADA specifically exempts from protection individuals currently engaging in the illegal use of drugs when the covered entity acts on the basis of that use. Contrary to Complainant's unfounded allegation, his non-selection for rehire is not based on any legitimate disability. Rather, Complainant's application was rejected based on his demonstrated drug use while previously employed and the complete lack of evidence indicating successful drug rehabilitation.
>
> "The Company maintains it's [*sic*] right to deny re-employment to employees terminated for violation of Company rules and regulations. . . . Complainant has provided no evidence to alter the Company's position that Complainant's conduct while employed by [petitioner] makes him ineligible for rehire." *Id.*, at 19a-20a.

This response, together with evidence that the letters submitted with respondent's employment application may have alerted Bockmiller to the reason for respondent's prior termination, led the EEOC to conclude that petitioner may have "rejected [respondent's] application based on his record of past alcohol and drug use." *Id.*, at 94a EEOC Determination Letter, Nov. 20, 1997. The EEOC thus found that there was "reasonable cause to believe that [respondent] was denied hire to the position of Product Test Specialist because of his disability." *Id.*, at 95a. The EEOC issued a right-to-sue letter, and respondent subsequently filed this action alleging a violation of the ADA.

Respondent proceeded through discovery on the theory that the company rejected his application because of his record of drug addiction and/or because he was regarded as being a drug addict. *See* 42 U.S.C. §§ 12102(2)(B)-(C).[2] In response to petitioner's

[2] The ADA defines the term "disability" as:

"(A) a physical or mental impairment that substantially limits one or more of the major life activities of such individual;

"(B) a record of such an impairment; or

motion for summary judgment, respondent for the first time argued in the alternative that if the company really did apply a neutral no rehire policy in his case, petitioner still violated the ADA because such a policy has a disparate impact. The District Court granted petitioner's motion for summary judgment with respect to respondent's disparate-treatment claim. However, the District Court refused to consider respondent's disparate-impact claim because respondent had failed to plead or raise the theory in a timely manner.

The Court of Appeals agreed with the District Court that respondent had failed timely to raise his disparate-impact claim. *Hernandez v. Hughes Missile Systems Co.*, 298 F.3d 1030, 1037, n. 20 (9th Cir. 2002). In addressing respondent's disparate-treatment claim, the Court of Appeals proceeded under the familiar burden-shifting approach first adopted by this Court in *McDonnell Douglas Corp. v. Green*, 411 U.S. 792 (1973).[3] First, the Ninth Circuit found that with respect to respondent's prima facie case of discrimination, there were genuine issues of material fact regarding whether respondent was qualified for the position for which he sought to be rehired, and whether the reason for petitioner's refusal to rehire him was his past record of drug addiction.[4] 298 F.3d, at 1034–1035. The Court of Appeals thus held that with respect to respondent's prima facie case of discrimination, respondent had proffered sufficient evidence to preclude a grant of summary judgment. *Id.*, at 1035. Because petitioner does not challenge this aspect of the Ninth Circuit's decision, we do not address it here.

The parties are also not disputing in this Court whether respondent was qualified for the position for which he applied.

The Court of Appeals then moved to the next step of *McDonnell Douglas*, where the burden shifts to the defendant to provide a legitimate, nondiscriminatory reason for its employment action. 411 U.S., at 802. Here, petitioner contends that Bockmiller applied the neutral policy against rehiring employees previously terminated for violating workplace conduct rules and that this neutral company policy constituted a legitimate and nondiscriminatory reason for its decision not to rehire respondent. The Court of Appeals, although admitting that petitioner's no-rehire rule was lawful on its face, held

---

"(C) being regarded as having such an impairment." 42 U.S.C. § 12102(2).

[3] The Court in *McDonnell Douglas* set forth a burden-shifting scheme for discriminatory-treatment cases. Under *McDonnell Douglas*, a plaintiff must first establish a prima facie case of discrimination. The burden then shifts to the employer to articulate a legitimate, nondiscriminatory reason for its employment action. 411 U.S., at 802. If the employer meets this burden, the presumption of intentional discrimination disappears, but the plaintiff can still prove disparate treatment by, for instance, offering evidence demonstrating that the employer's explanation is pretextual. *See Reeves v. Sanderson Plumbing Products, Inc.*, 530 U.S. 133, 143 (2000). The Courts of Appeals have consistently utilized this burden-shifting approach when reviewing motions for summary judgment in disparate-treatment cases. *See, e.g., Pugh v. Attica*, 259 F.3d 619, 626 (7th Cir. 2001) (applying burden-shifting approach to an ADA disparate-treatment claim).

[4] The Court of Appeals noted that "it is possible that a drug *user* may not be 'disabled' under the ADA if his drug use does not rise to the level of an addiction which substantially limits one or more of his major life activities." 298 F.3d, at 1033–1034, n. 9. The parties do not dispute that respondent was "disabled" at the time he quit in lieu of discharge and thus a record of the disability exists. We therefore need not decide in this case whether respondent's employment record constitutes a "record of addiction," which triggers the protections of the ADA.

the policy to be unlawful "as applied to former drug addicts whose only work-related offense was testing positive because of their addiction." 298 F.3d, at 1036. The Court of Appeals concluded that petitioner's application of a neutral no-rehire policy was not a legitimate, nondiscriminatory reason for rejecting respondent's application:

> "Maintaining a blanket policy against rehire of *all* former employees who violated company policy not only screens out persons with a record of addiction who have been successfully rehabilitated, but may well result, as [petitioner] contends it did here, in the staff member who makes the employment decision remaining unaware of the 'disability' and thus of the fact that she is committing an unlawful act. . . . Additionally, we hold that a policy that serves to bar the reemployment of a drug addict despite his successful rehabilitation violates the ADA." *Id.*, at 1036–1037.

In other words, while ostensibly evaluating whether petitioner had proffered a legitimate, nondiscriminatory reason for failing to rehire respondent sufficient to rebut respondent's prima facie showing of disparate treatment, the Court of Appeals held that a neutral no-rehire policy could never suffice in a case where the employee was terminated for illegal drug use, because such a policy has a disparate impact on recovering drug addicts. In so holding, the Court of Appeals erred by conflating the analytical framework for disparate-impact and disparate-treatment claims. Had the Court of Appeals correctly applied the disparate-treatment framework, it would have been obliged to conclude that a neutral no-rehire policy is, by definition, a legitimate, nondiscriminatory reason under the ADA.[5] And thus the only remaining question would be whether respondent could produce sufficient evidence from which a jury could conclude that "petitioner's stated reason for respondent's rejection was in fact pretext." *McDonnell Douglas, supra*, at 804.

II

This Court has consistently recognized a distinction between claims of discrimination based on disparate treatment and claims of discrimination based on disparate impact. The Court has said that " '[d]isparate treatment' . . . is the most easily understood type of discrimination. The employer simply treats some people less favorably than others because of their race, color, religion, sex, or [other protected characteristic]." *Teamsters v. United States*, 431 U.S. 324, 335, n. 15 (1977). *See also Hazen Paper Co. v. Biggins*, 507 U.S. 604, 609 (1993) (discussing disparate-treatment claims in the context of the Age Discrimination in Employment Act of 1967). Liability in a disparate-treatment case "depends on whether the protected trait . . . actually motivated the employer's decision." *Id.*, at 610. By contrast, disparate-impact claims "involve employment practices that are facially neutral in their treatment of different groups but that in fact fall more harshly on one group than another and cannot be

[5] This would not, of course, resolve the dispute over whether petitioner did in fact apply such a policy in this case. Indeed, the Court of Appeals expressed some confusion on this point, as the court first held that respondent "raise[d] a genuine issue of material fact as to whether he was denied re-employment because of his past record of drug addiction," *id.*, at 1034, but then later stated that there was "no question that [petitioner] applied this [no-rehire] policy in rejecting [respondent's] application." *Id.*, at 1036, n. 17.

justified by business necessity." *Teamsters, supra*, at 335–336, n. 15. Under a disparate-impact theory of discrimination, "a facially neutral employment practice may be deemed [illegally discriminatory] without evidence of the employer's subjective intent to discriminate that is required in a 'disparate-treatment' case." *Wards Cove Packing Co. v. Atonio*, 490 U.S. 642, 645–646 (1989), *superseded by statute on other grounds*, Civil Rights Act of 1991, § 105, 105 Stat. 1074–1075, 42 U.S.C. § 2000e-2(k) (1994 ed.).

Both disparate-treatment and disparate-impact claims are cognizable under the ADA. *See* 42 U.S.C. § 12112(b) (defining "discriminate" to include "utilizing standards, criteria, or methods of administration . . . that have the effect of discrimination on the basis of disability" and "using qualification standards, employment tests or other selection criteria that screen out or tend to screen out an individual with a disability"). Because "the factual issues, and therefore the character of the evidence presented, differ when the plaintiff claims that a facially neutral employment policy has a discriminatory impact on protected classes," *Texas Dep't of Community Affairs v. Burdine*, 450 U.S. 248, 252, n. 5 (1981), courts must be careful to distinguish between these theories. Here, respondent did not timely pursue a disparate-impact claim. Rather, the District Court concluded, and the Court of Appeals agreed, that respondent's case was limited to a disparate-treatment theory, that the company refused to rehire respondent because it regarded respondent as being disabled and/or because of respondent's record of a disability. 298 F.3d, at 1037, n. 20.

Petitioner's proffer of its neutral no-rehire policy plainly satisfied its obligation under *McDonnell Douglas* to provide a legitimate, nondiscriminatory reason for refusing to rehire respondent. Thus, the only relevant question before the Court of Appeals, after petitioner presented a neutral explanation for its decision not to rehire respondent, was whether there was sufficient evidence from which a jury could conclude that petitioner did make its employment decision based on respondent's status as disabled despite petitioner's proffered explanation. Instead, the Court of Appeals concluded that, as a matter of law, a neutral no-rehire policy was not a legitimate, nondiscriminatory reason sufficient to defeat a prima facie case of discrimination. The Court of Appeals did not even attempt, in the remainder of its opinion, to treat this claim as one involving only disparate treatment. Instead, the Court of Appeals observed that petitioner's policy "screens out persons with a record of addiction," and further noted that the company had not raised a business necessity defense, 298 F.3d, at 1036–1037, and n. 19, factors that pertain to disparate-impact claims but not disparate-treatment claims. *See, e.g., Grano v. Department of Development of Columbus*, 637 F.2d 1073, 1081 (6th Cir. 1980) ("In a disparate impact situation . . . the issue is whether a neutral selection device . . . screens out disproportionate numbers of [the protected class]").[7] By improperly focusing on these factors, the Court

[7] Indeed, despite the fact that the Nation's antidiscrimination laws are undoubtedly aimed at "the problem of inaccurate and stigmatizing stereotypes," *ibid.*, the Court of Appeals held that the unfortunate result of petitioner's application of its neutral policy was that Bockmiller may have made the employment decision in this case "remaining unaware of [respondent's] 'disability.' " 298 F.3d, at 1036. The Court of Appeals did not explain, however, how it could be said that Bockmiller was motivated to reject respondent's application because of his disability if Bockmiller was entirely unaware that such a disability existed. If Bockmiller were truly unaware that such a disability existed, it would be impossible for her hiring decision

of Appeals ignored the fact that petitioner's no rehire policy is a quintessential legitimate, nondiscriminatory reason for refusing to rehire an employee who was terminated for violating workplace conduct rules. If petitioner did indeed apply a neutral, generally applicable no-rehire policy in rejecting respondent's application, petitioner's decision not to rehire respondent can, in no way, be said to have been motivated by respondent's disability.

The Court of Appeals rejected petitioner's legitimate, nondiscriminatory reason for refusing to rehire respondent because it "serves to bar the re-employment of a drug addict despite his successful rehabilitation." 298 F.3d, at 1036–1037. We hold that such an analysis is inapplicable to a disparate-treatment claim. Once respondent had made a prima facie showing of discrimination, the next question for the Court of Appeals was whether petitioner offered a legitimate, nondiscriminatory reason for its actions so as to demonstrate that its actions were not motivated by respondent's disability. To the extent that the Court of Appeals strayed from this task by considering not only discriminatory intent but also discriminatory impact, we vacate its judgment and remand the case for further proceedings consistent with this opinion.

It is so ordered.

Justice Souter took no part in the decision of this case. Justice Breyer took no part in the consideration or decision of this case.

NOTES AND PROBLEMS FOR DISCUSSION

1. The case was remanded to the Ninth Circuit under a disparate treatment standard. On remand, the Ninth Circuit found there was sufficient basis to deny summary judgment to the employer and sent the case back to the trial court for a jury trial to determine whether Raytheon refused to re-hire Hernandez because of his past record of addiction rather than because of a no-rehire rule. *See Hernandez v. Hughes Missile Systems*, 362 F.3d 564 (9th Cir. 2004).

2. What if the plaintiff had proceeded on a disparate impact theory? What could be the basis of a disparate impact argument? Would such a policy have a disparate impact on rehabilitated drug or alcohol users who are otherwise qualified to work? *See* Christine Neylon O'Brien & Jonathan J. Darrow, *The Question Remains After* Raytheon Co. v. Hernandez*: Whether No-Rehire Rules Disparately Impact Alcoholics and Former Drug Abusers?*, 7 U. Pa. J. Lab. & Emp. L. 157 (2004).

3. Associational Discrimination

In general, individuals are covered by the ADA if they are disabled, are regarded as disabled, or have a record of disability. ADA Title I, however, adds another category of covered individuals — individuals who "associate" with individuals with disabilities. This rule is set forth in 42 U.S.C. § 12112(b)(4): "The term 'discriminate'

---

to have been based, even in part, on respondent's disability. And, if no part of the hiring decision turned on respondent's status as disabled, he cannot, ipso facto, have been subject to disparate treatment.

includes . . . excluding or otherwise denying equal jobs or benefits to a qualified individual because of the known disability of an individual with whom the qualified individual is known to have a relationship or association." It is applied in the following case.

DEN HARTOG v. WASATCH ACADEMY

129 F.3d 1076 (10th Cir. 1997)

Ebel, Circuit Judge.

Defendant Wasatch is a private boarding school for students in the ninth through twelfth grades, located in Mt. Pleasant, Utah. In recent years, its student body has numbered approximately 160 students, and it has employed about 45 full-time staff and faculty members. Mt. Pleasant is a small town, consisting of less than 2 1/2 square miles and approximately 2,000 residents. Co-defendant Joseph Loftin ("Loftin") has served as headmaster for Wasatch from 1988 to the present. During the times at issue, Loftin lived on campus with his wife and three children.

Except for two years during which he taught elsewhere, plaintiff Howard Den Hartog was employed by Wasatch Academy from 1964 until July 1994, pursuant to a series of one-year contracts. During that period, Den Hartog worked as a teacher, in the buildings and grounds department, and as a school historian. In accordance with Wasatch's general policy requiring full-time faculty to live on campus, Den Hartog lived on the Wasatch campus with his wife and four children every year that he taught there.

Den Hartog's youngest child, Nathaniel Den Hartog ("Nathaniel"), was born in December 1971. Nathaniel lived with his parents until he graduated from Wasatch in June 1990. During the 1990-91 school year, Nathaniel went away to college. However, Nathaniel did not return to college the next year, but instead lived on the Wasatch campus with his parents.

In July 1992, Den Hartog took Nathaniel to Dr. John Merriweather, a psychologist in private practice in Mt. Pleasant. Dr. Merriweather tentatively diagnosed Nathaniel as having "bipolar affective disorder" (formerly called "manic depressive psychosis"), and recommended that Nathaniel be hospitalized and treated. Accordingly, Nathaniel was admitted to the Western Institute of Neuropsychiatry in Salt Lake City on July 20, 1992, where Dr. Merriweather's diagnosis was confirmed and Nathaniel was treated with lithium. Nathaniel was discharged on July 30, 1992, and returned to his parents' home on the Wasatch campus. At that time, Loftin was aware of Nathaniel's diagnosis and at some point became aware of Nathaniel's lithium treatment. Upon Nathaniel's return, Loftin hired him to do part-time work on campus including yard work, painting, and assisting in the day care center.

Around November, 1992, Nathaniel moved to California. However, after two months there, he stopped taking his lithium and as a result suffered a manic episode. In January, 1993, the police found Nathaniel selling his possessions in a grocery store parking lot. Following that incident, his mother flew to California and brought him back to Wasatch, where Loftin once again hired him to do part-time work on campus.

During early 1993, when Nathaniel was twenty-one years old, he developed "close ties" with Loftin's sixteen-year-old son Travis. On March 12, 1993, Nathaniel took Travis to Provo, Utah, without the Loftins' knowledge, and attempted to have Travis admitted to Charter Canyon Hospital, a psychiatric hospital there. When a hospital employee called Joseph Loftin, Loftin went to Provo to pick up Travis. Before Loftin arrived, Nathaniel left the hospital without Travis.

Two days later, Nathaniel telephoned the Loftin home several times, looking for Travis. Nathaniel told Loftin that he would slit his own wrists if Loftin did not put Travis on the phone. Loftin, in response, called both the police and Nathaniel's counselor Brian Whipple. That same evening, Nathaniel visited his treating psychiatrist, Dr. J. Bruce Harless, to discuss these phone calls. At this visit, Nathaniel told Dr. Harless that he really had no intention of harming himself, but was merely attempting to coerce the Loftins into disclosing Travis's location.

On March 18, 1993, the Loftins found a number of messages from Nathaniel on their answering machine. In one of these messages, while speaking in a tone of voice which scared Loftin and which Dr. Harless "readily perceived as being threatening," Nathaniel stated that the Loftins should keep a very close eye out on their four-year-old daughter, Allison. In another message, Nathaniel said that he had drained quarts of blood from his body recently, and offered to show this blood to Loftin to prove he was "serious."

After listening to the recorded messages, Loftin called the police, who listened to the messages and told Loftin to take the threats seriously. The police also called Dr. Harless. Nathaniel's parents were then contacted. Although the Den Hartogs agreed to take Nathaniel to a hospital, they were unable to coax or coerce Nathaniel out of their house. Consequently, they called the police, who transported Nathaniel to the Utah Valley Regional Medical Center, where Nathaniel was temporarily admitted. The next day, at the request of Dr. Harless, Loftin applied for Nathaniel to be involuntarily committed to an institution.

On March 31, 1993, a Utah state judge determined that Nathaniel posed "an immediate danger of physical injury" to himself or others, and ordered his commitment to the custody of the Utah State Division of Mental Health for six months.

The next day, April 1, 1993, Den Hartog and his wife Esther met with Loftin and others to discuss the situation. The Den Hartogs recorded the meeting. At the meeting, Loftin repeatedly told the Den Hartogs that he did not want Nathaniel on campus because of his threatening behavior. Loftin also said that if Nathaniel's condition resulted in the Den Hartogs being unable to live at Wasatch, then Den Hartog might be terminated. Esther Den Hartog responded that "if we lived here [on campus] and we were having a Christmas celebration with our family we would not say, Nathaniel, you cannot come home because Joe Loftin says you cannot here." Den Hartog did not object to this statement.

On April 16, 1993, the Wasatch Board of Trustees met and voted unanimously to:

> endorse the action of the Headmaster, President of the Board, and the Executive Committee in this matter: essentially

1. Restraining order on Nathaniel Den Hartog

2. Apartment in [Salt Lake City] for Esther and Nathaniel for an undetermined period

3. If necessary, pay out their contract if they must leave the community.

Pursuant to this vote, Wasatch rented an apartment in Salt Lake City for Nathaniel and his mother to live in after Nathaniel was released. Two Wasatch Trustees visited the Den Hartogs in their home the next day, to inform them of the Board's decision. No restraining order was ever obtained against Nathaniel.

Despite having been remanded to state custody for six months on March 31, Nathaniel was released from the Utah Valley Regional Medical Center on April 19, 1993. Within a week of his release, Nathaniel visited Mt. Pleasant, where he came onto the Wasatch campus. Several Wasatch Trustees received calls from staff and faculty who were concerned about Nathaniel's presence. Loftin became concerned that as long as Den Hartog worked and lived on campus Nathaniel would continue visiting. As a result, on May 14, 1993, Wasatch assigned Den Hartog to spend the 1993-94 school year writing a school history from Wasatch's development office in Salt Lake City. Den Hartog was to receive his full salary plus a living allowance to pay for a home, utilities, and food.

In August, 1993, Nathaniel enrolled in Snow College and moved to Ephraim, Utah, twenty miles from Mt. Pleasant. Den Hartog provided Nathaniel with a car and placed no restrictions on where Nathaniel could go. On one occasion Nathaniel drove to the Wasatch campus to attend a basketball game which his father was attending. Then, on Christmas Eve, 1993, and on another occasion the following week, Nathaniel went to the Loftin home in an attempt to see Travis Loftin. By that time, Nathaniel had dropped out of Snow College.

On January 24, 1994, Nathaniel and an accomplice battered Byron Bond, a former schoolmate of Nathaniel's, in Bond's home in Mt. Pleasant. Bond sustained several broken ribs and was treated in the hospital. After Bond was released from the hospital, he informed Loftin of the battery and warned him that during the attack Nathaniel had stated that he planned to "get" Loftin next. Nathaniel was arrested for aggravated assault, booked into Sanpete County Jail, and then sent to the Utah State Hospital in Provo for a competency evaluation.

In February, 1994, while Nathaniel was hospitalized, Loftin decided not to renew Den Hartog's contract for the next year. On March 4, 1994, Loftin met with Den Hartog and told him that his contract would not be renewed because the school historian position, which Den Hartog then held, was being eliminated. Although Loftin told Den Hartog that the reason for non-renewal was the elimination of his position, Loftin testified in his deposition that absent Nathaniel's behavior Den Hartog "[v]ery possibly" would still be employed by Wasatch.

Den Hartog filled out an intake form with the Utah Anti-Discrimination Division on April 4, 1994. Then, on April 11, 1994, Den Hartog filed a complaint of discrimination with both the Utah Anti-Discrimination Division and the federal Equal Employment Opportunity Commission ("EEOC").

On May 16, 1994, after being found competent to stand trial, Nathaniel was discharged from the Utah State Hospital. He eventually pled guilty to assault and was sentenced to one year of probation. Loftin was unsuccessful in having Nathaniel prohibited from going on the Wasatch Academy campus as a condition of his probation. From his May 16, 1994 release through August, 1995, Nathaniel lived with his parents in Salt Lake City.

On November 10, 1994, Den Hartog sued Wasatch and Loftin in federal district court, alleging violations of Title I of the Americans with Disabilities Act ("ADA"). . . . In their answer, the defendants raised as affirmative defenses that they had properly terminated Den Hartog's employment because he and/or Nathaniel were "direct threats" under ADA Section 12113(b). . . .

The district court, which exercised jurisdiction pursuant to 28 U.S.C. §§ 1331, 1367(a) (1994), granted summary judgment in favor of Wasatch and Loftin on the ADA claim. . . .

DISCUSSION

I. *BIPOLAR DISORDER AS A DISABILITY UNDER THE ADA*

[The Court concludes that bipolar affective disorder is a disability under the ADA.]

II. *THE ASSOCIATION PROVISION OF THE ADA*

A. *General Discussion*

As the district court noted, "Den Hartog's ADA claim is unique in that it is based on the rather new and undeveloped 'association discrimination' provision of the ADA." . . .

The association provision has been the subject of very little litigation, and none in this court prior to the present case. It was apparently inspired in part by testimony before House and Senate Subcommittees pertaining to a woman who was fired from her long-held job because her employer found out that the woman's son, who had become ill with AIDS, had moved into her house so she could care for him. *See* H.R. Rep. No. 101-485, pt. 2, at 30 (1990), *reprinted in* 1990 U.S.C.C.A.N. 303, 312 (citing this testimony as evidence of the need for the association provision).

By the time the ADA was enacted, two separate House Committees had reported favorably on the bill (H.R. 2273), and had issued Committee Reports describing certain intended applications (and unintended misapplications) of the association provision. The House Committee on Education and Labor posed the following pair of hypotheticals to illustrate the association provision's parameters:

> [A]ssume, for example that an applicant applies for a job and discloses to the employer that his or her spouse has a disability. The employer believes the applicant is qualified for the job. The employer, however, assuming without

> foundation that the applicant will have to miss work or frequently leave work early or both, in order to care for his or her spouse, declines to hire the individual for such reasons. Such a refusal is prohibited by this subparagraph.
>
> In contrast, assume that the employer hires the applicant. If he or she violates a neutral employer policy concerning attendance or tardiness, he or she may be dismissed even if the reason for the absence or tardiness is to care for the spouse. The employer need not provide any accommodation to the nondisabled employee. The individuals covered under this section are any individuals who are discriminated against because of their known association with an individual with a disability.

H.R. Rep. No. 101-485, pt. 2, at 61–62 (1990), *reprinted in* 1990 U.S.C.C.A.N. 303, 343–44.

The House Judiciary Committee sought to clarify the "intent" element which a plaintiff must prove to prevail on a claim brought under the association provision. As that Committee explained:

> This provision applies only when the employer knows of the association with the other person and knows of that other person's disability. The burden of proof is on the individual claiming discrimination to prove that the discrimination was motivated by that individual's relationship or association with a person with a disability.
>
> For example, it would be discriminatory for an employer to discriminate against a qualified employee who did volunteer work for people with AIDS, if the employer knew of the employee's relationship or association with the people with AIDS, and if the employment action was motivated by that relationship or association.
>
> Similarly, it would be illegal for an employer to discriminate against a qualified employee because that employee had a family member or a friend who had a disability, if the employer knew about the relationship or association, knew that the friend or family member has a disability, and acted on that basis. Thus, if an employee had a spouse with a disability, and the employer took an adverse action against the employee based on the spouse's disability, this would then constitute discrimination.
>
> This section would not apply if the employer did not know of the relationship or association, or if the employer did not know of the disability of the other person. Thus, if an employer fired an employee, and did not know of a relationship or association of the employee with a person with a disability, the employee could not claim discrimination under this section.

H.R. Rep. No. 101-485, pt. 3, at 38–39 (1990), *reprinted in* 1990 U.S.C.C.A.N. 445, 461–62.

In a floor debate held subsequent to the publication of these two reports, Congressman Bartlett, a sponsor of the bill, sought to answer what he characterized as some "frequent questions raised by business persons" about the ADA. *See* 136 Cong. Rec. H9072 (1990) (statement of Rep. Bartlett).

One such question was the following: "If an able-bodied employee who is about to be terminated for cause, claims a relationship with a disabled individual, can he or she claim discrimination by association and be protected by the ADA?" *Id.* Congressman Bartlett answered that "[g]iven the hypothetical posed, the terminating employee would have to prove that the employer knew of the association and was terminating the employee because of that association, and not because he or she was otherwise [un]qualified." *Id.*

In the present case, Wasatch does not claim that Den Hartog's performance as a schoolteacher was in any way deficient, except inasmuch as his presence on the campus may have attracted Nathaniel to the campus. Thus, the primary question presented in the present case — whether the association provision of the ADA protects a qualified employee from adverse employment action based on his disabled associate's misconduct, where the associate's misconduct does not impair the employee's job performance — is different from those presented in [other cases]. . . . This question also appears not to have been con-fronted by the authors of the above-quoted House Reports, nor to have been addressed during Congressional floor debate on the ADA.

B. *Reasonable Accommodation*

The ADA states that no covered employer "shall discriminate against a qualified individual with a disability because of the disability of such individual. . . ." 42 U.S.C. § 12112(a). In the context of this general prohibition, the word "discriminate" is a term of art which includes "not making reasonable accommodations." *See* 42 U.S.C. § 12112(b)(5) (1994); 29 C.F.R. § 1630.9(a) (1996). By the plain terms of § 12112(b)(5), however, the ADA does not require an employer to make any "reasonable accommodation" to the disabilities of relatives or associates of an employee who is not himself disabled.

Specifically, 42 U.S.C. § 12112(b)(5)(A) (1994) defines the term "discriminate" to include "not making reasonable accommodations to the known physical or mental limitations of an otherwise qualified individual with a disability *who is an applicant or employee*. . . ." (emphasis added). Further, 42 U.S.C. § 12112(b)(5)(B) (1994) defines "discriminate" to include "denying employment opportunities to *a job applicant or employee* who is an otherwise qualified individual with a disability, if such denial is based on the need of such covered entity to make reasonable accommodation to the physical or mental impairments *of the employee or applicant.*" (emphasis added). Thus, the plain language of both these provisions — the only two provisions requiring "reasonable accommodation" in Title I of the ADA — suggests that only job applicants or employees, but not their relatives or associates, need be reasonably accommodated.

We are confident that the lack of any reference to the associates or relatives of the employee or applicant in Section 12112(b)(5)'s articulation of the ADA's "reasonable accommodation" requirement is not due to any inadvertent omission. In its Report, the House Education and Labor Committee clearly expressed its intention that under the association provision, "[t]he employer need not provide any accommodation to the nondisabled employee." H.R. Rep. No. 101-485, pt. 2, at 61–62 (1990), *reprinted in* 1990 U.S.C.C.A.N. 303, 344. *See* Subpart A, *supra.*

Our conclusion in this regard has also been reached by the EEOC, which, pursuant to 42 U.S.C. § 12116 (1994), has issued regulations and Interpretive Guidance on the ADA. The Interpretive Guidance notes that where an associate or relative of the employee is disabled, but the employee himself is not disabled:

> an employer need not provide the applicant or employee without a disability with a reasonable accommodation because that duty only applies to qualified applicants or employees with disabilities. Thus, for example, an employee would not be entitled to a modified work schedule as an accommodation to enable the employee to care for a spouse with a disability.

29 C.F.R. Pt. 1630.8 app. at 349 (1996) (citing legislative history materials). Thus, Wasatch was not required under the ADA to provide Den Hartog with any "reasonable accommodation" of *Nathaniel's* disability.

III. *DISABILITY-CAUSED MISCONDUCT UNDER THE ADA*

Both the district court and the appellees on appeal have attempted to draw a bright line between discrimination based on a disability (which they concede is generally prohibited by the ADA) and discrimination based on *misconduct* by the disabled person (which they agree is not prohibited by the ADA). In evaluating that proffered dichotomy, we look to the general provisions of the ADA. However, in looking to the general provisions of the ADA for guidance in this case where the misconduct comes not from the employee but rather from an associated person, we must keep in mind that 1) summary judgment in this case could not be predicated upon misconduct by Den Hartog and 2) Wasatch had no duty to reasonably accommodate Nathaniel's disability.

The text of the ADA makes only one specific reference to "disability-caused misconduct," where an employer is authorized to disregard the fact that the misconduct or prior performance may be caused by a disability and where the employer can hold the disabled person to exactly the same conduct as a non-disabled person. It provides that an employer:

> may hold an employee who engages in the illegal use of drugs or who is an alcoholic to the same qualification standards for employment or job performance and behavior that such entity holds other employees, even if any unsatisfactory performance or behavior is related to the alcoholism or drug use of such employee.

42 U.S.C. § 12114(c)(4) (1994); *see also* 42 U.S.C. § 12114(a) (1994) (providing that the term "qualified individual with a disability" under the ADA shall not include illegal drug users when the covered entity acts on that basis). Den Hartog claims that because Congress only expressly permitted employers to hold illegal drug users and alcoholics to the same objective standards of conduct as other employees even though their disability *causes* misconduct or poor performance, Congress implicitly did not intend to extend the same employer prerogative to employees with *other* disabilities. *See Andrus v. Glover Constr. Co.*, 446 U.S. 608, 616–17 (1980) ("Where Congress explicitly enumerates certain exceptions to a general prohibition, additional exceptions are not to be implied, in the absence of evidence of a contrary legislative intent."). He

thus claims that the district court erred by importing the "disability v. disability-caused misconduct" dichotomy into a case in which neither drugs nor alcohol were involved. We agree.

As a general rule, an employer may *not* hold a disabled employee to precisely the same standards of conduct as a non-disabled employee unless such standards are job-related and consistent with business necessity. *See, e.g., EEOC Enforcement Guidance: Psychiatric Disabilities and the Americans With Disabilities Act,* 2 EEOC Compl. Man. (BNA), filed after Section 902, at 28 ¶ 30 (Mar. 25, 1997) (stating by way of example that an employer must make some reasonable exception to a general policy requiring employees to be neat and courteous in order to accommodate a mentally disabled employee whose disability led to a deterioration of neatness and courtesy where neatness and courtesy are not essential to that employee's job because it does not involve interaction with customers or co-workers).

Pursuant to 42 U.S.C. § 12114(c)(4), employers need not make any reasonable accommodations for employees who are illegal drug users and alcoholics. However, that is in marked contrast to all other disabilities, where the ADA does require that the employer extend reasonable accommodations. Thus, the disability v. disability-caused conduct dichotomy seems to be unique to alcoholism and drugs.

Further, any such sharp dichotomy would make no sense when considering other provisions of the ADA. For example, an employer need not make any accommodation that would constitute an "undue hardship." 42 U.S.C. § 12112(b)(5)(A) (1994); *see also* 42 U.S.C. § 12111(10) (1994) (defining "undue hardship" and delineating factors to be considered in determining what constitutes an undue hardship). In addition, an employer may take action against an employee who poses a "direct threat" to the health or safety of other individuals in the workplace. 42 U.S.C. § 12113(b) (1994). The availability of these affirmative defenses establish that there are certain levels of disability-caused conduct that need not be tolerated or accommodated by employers. However, the necessary corollary is that there must be certain levels of disability-caused conduct that have to be tolerated or accommodated. Thus, appellees' effort to put all disability-caused conduct beyond the pale of ADA protection cannot be correct.

Mental illness is manifested by abnormal behavior, and is in fact normally diagnosed on the basis of abnormal behavior. *See Diagnostic and Statistical Manual of Mental Disorders* 350 (4th ed. 1994) (stating that bipolar disorder may be diagnosed "by the occurrence of one or more Manic Episodes or Mixed Episodes"). To permit employers carte blanche to terminate employees with mental disabilities on the basis of any abnormal behavior would largely nullify the ADA's protection of the mentally disabled.

The district court misinterpreted the holdings of our sister circuits when it stated that "the majority of Circuit Courts of Appeal interpreting [42 U.S.C. § 12112(a) — the basic ADA provision prohibiting discrimination because of disability] have concluded that the 'because of the disability' language requires some discrimination caused by the disability itself and not on misconduct which may be caused by the disability." *Den Hartog,* 909 F. Supp. at 1401 (citing cases). In fact, all three cases cited by the district court in direct support of this proposition involved either illegal drug using or alcoholic employees, expressly unprotected under 42 U.S.C. § 12114(c)(4) (1994). *See Collings v.*

Longview Fibre Co., 63 F.3d 828, 832 (9th Cir. 1995), *cert. denied*, 516 U.S. 1048 (1996) (employees discharged for drug-related misconduct at the workplace); *Despears v. Milwaukee County*, 63 F.3d 635, 637 (7th Cir. 1995) (alcoholic plaintiff demoted because he lost his driver's license as a result of driving drunk); *Maddox v. University of Tenn.*, 62 F.3d 843, 848 (6th Cir. 1995) (alcoholic plaintiff discharged following arrest for drunk driving). Unlike the three cases cited by the district court, the present case does not involve an application of 42 U.S.C. § 12114(c)(4). For this reason, these cases have only limited relevance to cases, including the present case, in which the plaintiff is *not* an illegal drug user or alcoholic.

We therefore disagree with the district court's conclusion that the ADA's general anti-discrimination provision, 42 U.S.C. § 12112(a), contemplates a stark dichotomy between "disability" and "disability-caused misconduct." Rather, the language of the ADA, its statutory structure, and the pertinent case law, suggest that an employer should normally consider whether a mentally disabled employee's purported misconduct could be remedied through a reasonable accommodation. If so, then the employer should attempt the accommodation. If not, the employer may discipline the disabled employee only if one of the affirmative defenses articulated in 42 U.S.C. §§ 12113, 12114 (1994) applies. Otherwise, the employer must tolerate eccentric or unusual conduct caused by the employee's mental disability, so long as the employee can satisfactorily perform the essential functions of his job. *See, e.g., EEOC Enforcement Guidance: Psychiatric Disabilities and the Americans With Disabilities Act*, 2 EEOC Compl. Man. (BNA), filed after Section 902, at 28 ¶ 30 (Mar. 25, 1997) (stating by way of example that an employer must make an exception to a general policy requiring employees to be neat and courteous in order to accommodate a mentally disabled employee whose job does not involve interaction with customers or co-workers).

We thus proceed to determine whether any such affirmative defenses apply to the present case.

IV. "*DIRECT THREAT*" *DEFENSE*

A. *Factual Record of Direct Threat by Den Hartog and Nathaniel*

The "direct threat" defense is codified at 42 U.S.C. §§ 12111(3), 12113(b) (1994). Under the ADA, the term "direct threat" means "a significant risk to the health or safety of others that cannot be eliminated by reasonable accommodation." 42 U.S.C. § 12111(3) (1994). Without running afoul of the ADA, an employer may define as a qualification for any job that "an individual shall not pose a direct threat to the health or safety of [the individual himself or] other individuals in the workplace." 42 U.S.C. § 12113(b) (1994); *see also* 29 C.F.R. § 1630.15(b)(2) (1996) (including "the individual" himself in the definition). The C.F.R. provides several criteria for determining whether an individual poses a "direct threat." These factors include:

(1) The duration of the risk;

(2) The nature and severity of the potential harm;

(3) The likelihood that the potential harm will occur; and

(4) The imminence of the potential harm.

29 C.F.R. § 1630.2(r) (1996). These factors are to be evaluated "based on an individualized assessment of the individual's present ability to safely perform the essential functions of the job." *Id.* Further, they are to be evaluated "based on a reasonable medical judgment that relies on the most current medical knowledge and/or on the best available objective evidence." *Id.*

In the present case, Wasatch and Loftin have alleged that both Den Hartog and Nathaniel were "direct threats" under 42 U.S.C. §§ 12111(3), 12113(b) (1994). In particular, they have alleged that Nathaniel was a "direct threat" in the literal sense, while Den Hartog was a direct threat "insofar as he was unwilling to cooperate in keeping his son Nathaniel off campus and away from Mt. Pleasant."

Given the presence in the record of Loftin and Loughlin's testimony stating that Den Hartog did not pose a direct threat to Wasatch, Den Hartog has created at least a genuine issue of material fact as to whether he did pose such a threat. Indeed, the gravamen of the defendants' argument on this issue seems to accuse Den Hartog of being an "indirect threat," rather than a "direct threat." Thus, the defendants are not entitled to summary judgment on the ground that Den Hartog posed a direct threat to Wasatch.

Alternatively, the defendants seek summary judgment on the ground that Nathaniel posed a "direct threat" to Wasatch or Loftin. Den Hartog responds, as a threshold matter, that the evidence in the record supporting the defendants' claim does not meet the evidentiary level established by 29 C.F.R. § 1630.2(r) (1996). Den Hartog predicates this response solely on Loftin's failure to obtain medical evidence prior to deciding that Nathaniel's presence on the Wasatch campus posed a risk to the safety of the members of the Wasatch community. Den Hartog's argument lacks merit.

We hold on this record that there is no genuine issue of material fact as to whether Nathaniel posed a significant risk to the safety of members of the Wasatch community.

B. *Does the "Direct Threat" Defense Apply to Associates or Relatives?*

The legal issue remaining is whether the ADA permits an employer to discipline or discharge a non-disabled employee whose disabled relative or associate, because of his or her disability, poses a direct threat to the employer's workplace. This issue appears to be one of first impression.

As Den Hartog notes, the language of the ADA might be read to suggest that the "direct threat" affirmative defense applies only where the *employee* poses the direct threat to the workplace, because the defense arises in the context of elaborating upon the permissible "qualification standards" for a job. *See* 42 U.S.C. § 12113(b) (1994). Job qualifications are expressed in 42 U.S.C. § 12113(a), which clearly refers to employees or job applicants. Job qualifications obviously do not apply directly to associates or relatives of an employee because they are not the ones being employed. However, although the pertinent EEOC regulations and interpretive guidance discuss the "direct threat" defense in terms of a threat to individuals in the workplace, they do not *require* that the threat come only from the employee, as opposed to the associate or relative of the employee. *See* 29 C.F.R. §§ 1630.2(r), 1630.15(b)(2) (1996); 29 C.F.R. Pt. 1630 app. at 346–47 (1996).

Although the language of 42 U.S.C. §§ 12111(3), 12113(b) does not expressly cover the present situation, it would be odd that the ADA would permit an employer to take steps to protect its workplace from "direct threats" posed by mentally disabled *employees*, 42 U.S.C. §§ 12111(3), 12113(b), and also from "direct threats" posed by mentally disabled *customers*, 42 U.S.C. § 12182(b)(3), but not allow the employer to protect its workplace from "direct threats" posed by mentally disabled *associates or relatives* of non-disabled employees. Because of the apparent oddness of a statutory scheme which would provide an employer with no recourse against "direct threats" posed by this one small group of individuals, but does provide recourse in all other "direct threat" situations, we feel compelled to search for evidence that Congress intended such a result before holding that result to obtain. *See Public Citizen v. United States Dep't of Justice*, 491 U.S. 440, 454 (1989) ("Where the literal reading of a statutory term would 'compel an odd result,' we must search for other evidence of congressional intent to lend the term its proper scope.") (internal citation omitted).

In its Committee Report on the ADA, the House Judiciary Committee expressed its intention that the "direct threat" standard should codify the standard applied under the Rehabilitation Act by the Supreme Court in *School Bd. of Nassau County v. Arline*, 480 U.S. 273, 287–88 (1987). H.R. Rep. No. 101-485, pt. 3, at 34, 45 (1990), *reprinted in* 1990 U.S.C.C.A.N. 445, 457, 468. In *Arline*, the Court remanded for further findings of the contagiousness of a school teacher who had contracted tuberculosis to determine whether she posed a significant risk of communicating her disease to others in the workplace and whether reasonable accommodation could eliminate that risk. *Arline*, 480 U.S. at 288–89. Although the schoolteacher there was an employee, the thrust of the case was not whether the threat came from an employee or a relative or associate of an employee, but rather whether the employer was acting upon actual objective evidence of a threat, or upon stereotypical assumptions of the threat. *See* H.R. Rep. No. 101-485, pt. 3, at 45 (1990), *reprinted in* 1990 U.S.C.C.A.N. 445, 468.

> [A]n employer may not assume that a person with a mental disability . . . poses a direct threat to others. This would be an assumption based on fear and stereotype. The purpose of creating the "direct threat" standard is to eliminate exclusions which are not based on objective evidence about the individual involved. Thus, in the case of a person with mental illness there must be objective evidence from the person's behavior that the person has a recent history of committing overt acts or making threats which caused harm or which directly threatened harm.

Id. at 45–46, 1990 U.S.C.C.A.N. at 468–69.

Elsewhere in the Report, the Committee also expressed its intention that the "direct threat" defense should extend to permit an entity to deny a disabled individual from participating in or benefiting from the goods, services, facilities, privileges, advantages and accommodations of the entity, where the disabled individual poses a direct threat to the health or safety of others. *See id.* at 62, 1990 U.S.C.C.A.N. at 485. The Committee intended that "[t]his provision [be] identical to one added in the employment section," and advised that "the discussion of this issue there applies here as well." *Id. See also* 42 U.S.C. § 12182(b)(3) (1994) (codifying this application of the "direct threat" defense).

The legislative history of the association provision, discussed in Part IIA, *supra*, does not discuss any affirmative defenses to claims brought under that provision. In our view, this lack of discussion is most likely due to the Committee's presumption that the affirmative defenses available to employers defending association discrimination claims — including the "direct threat" defense — would be identical to those available in other ADA contexts. This presumption would logically follow from the association provision's location in the ADA, as part of the statutory definition of "discriminate," which appears in the basic anti-discrimination provisions of 42 U.S.C. § 12112(a). *See* 42 U.S.C. § 12112(b)(4).

Our conclusion in this regard is bolstered by the fact that the association provision does not require any "reasonable accommodation," *see* Part IIB, *supra*, and therefore provides *less* protection against discrimination to employees than does the ADA's basic provision, 42 U.S.C. § 12112(a). We see nothing in the legislative history indicating that Congress intended to provide *less* protection to non-disabled employees with disabled relatives or associates than to disabled employees and job applicants with respect to ADA's central "reasonable accommodation" requirement, yet simultaneously to provide, *sub silentio, more* protection to non-disabled employees whose disabled relatives or associates posed direct threats to the employees' workplace than to disabled employees and job applicants who posed identical direct threats to the same workplace. We think it far more likely that Congress assumed that 42 U.S.C. § 12113(b)'s "direct threat" defense would apply to cases where the direct threat came from relatives or associates of the employee as well as to those cases where the direct threat came from the employee himself or herself. *Cf. Moragne v. States Marine Lines, Inc.*, 398 U.S. 375, 392 (1970) ("By the terms of a statute, [the legislature] also indicates its conception of the sphere within which the policy is to have effect.").

As with the maritime statutes at issue in *Moragne*, we think that the language of the association provision of the ADA reflects the dimensions of the particular problem that came to the attention of the legislature and that provision invites "the conclusion that the legislative policy is equally applicable to other situations in which the mischief is identical." *Id.* at 392. Because the legislative policy underlying the availability of the "direct threat" defense under the primary provisions of the ADA is equally applicable to the association provision, we hold that the ADA permits an employer to discipline or discharge a non-disabled employee whose disabled relative or associate, because of his or her disability, poses a direct threat to the employer's workplace.

Accordingly, the district court's grant of summary judgment in favor of the defendants with respect to Den Hartog's ADA claim is affirmed. Because we hold that the defendant's motive for terminating Den Hartog was lawful, we need not reach Den Hartog's claim pertaining to the defendants' alleged "mixed motives." Similarly, because we affirm the district court's grant of summary judgment in favor of Wasatch and Loftin for the reasons discussed above, we need not consider Wasatch and Loftin's claim that Den Hartog's "wrongful transfer" claim is time-barred under ADA's statute of limitations.

NOTES AND PROBLEMS FOR DISCUSSION

1. This case was decided before the 2008 Amendments to the ADA were adopted. 42 U.S.C. § 12201(h) provides that a covered entity need not provide a reasonable accommodation to "an individual who meets the definition of disability in section 3(1) solely under subparagraph (C) of such section." How does that language affect the outcome of this case?

2. In October 1992, Joan Ennis adopted a son who was HIV-positive. She enrolled him in her company's health insurance plan. She communicated that information to many people at her office, including her supervisor. In December 1992, her employer sent a memo to all employees describing their insurance policy. The memo noted that if the number of individuals electing coverage went beyond 50, premium increases would be based on the participant's actual expenses, rather than the current "pool" coverage. In addition, the memo stated that "if we have a couple of very expensive cases, our rates could be more dramatically affected than they currently are." Six months later, Joan Ennis was notified that her employment would be terminated because of substandard work performance. She had made three serious errors in the last several months in her work as a data entry operator. These errors, her supervisor stated, demonstrated that she had an unacceptable level of performance. Joan's son was asymptomatic and she had submitted only standard, modest medical claims on his behalf. Does Joan have a strong claim under the ADA for associational discrimination? *See Ennis v. National Ass'n of Bus. and Educ. Radio, Inc.*, 53 F.3d 55 (4th Cir. 1995).

3. Wayne Micek is an employee of the City of Chicago. He obtains medical insurance through his employer. The insurance policy does not provide coverage for hearing aids or long-term speech therapy. His son is deaf and requires both a hearing aid and long-term speech therapy. Under the terms of the policy, Wayne may obtain benefits for his son with regard to any other health problems that his son may experience, at the same levels as other people. However, he may not obtain benefits for the two medical needs that Wayne can anticipate he will need on an ongoing basis — hearing aids and speech therapy. Can Wayne bring a case of "associational discrimination" under these facts? *See Micek v. City of Chicago*, 1999 U.S. Dist. LEXIS 16263, 16 Nat'l Disab. L. Rep. (LRP Publications) ¶ 226 (N.D. Ill. Sept. 30, 1999) (no).

E. DEFENSES

ADA Title I § 12113 Defenses

(a) In general

It may be a defense to a charge of discrimination under this chapter that an alleged application of qualification standards, tests, or selection criteria that screen out or tend to screen out or otherwise deny a job or benefit to an individual with a disability has been shown to be job-related and consistent with business necessity, and such performance cannot be accomplished by reasonable accommodation, as required under this subchapter.

(b) Qualification standards

The term "qualification standards" may include a requirement that an individual shall not pose a direct threat to the health or safety of other individuals in the workplace.

ADA Title I § 12111 Definitions

(3) Direct Threat

The term "direct threat" means a significant risk to the health or safety of others that cannot be eliminated by reasonable accommodation.

ADA Title I EEOC Regulations: 29 CFR § 1630.2(r)

Direct threat means a significant risk of substantial harm to the health or safety of the individual or others that cannot be eliminated or reduced by reasonable accommodation. . . .

CHEVRON U.S.A. INC. v. ECHAZABAL

536 U.S. 73 (2002)

SOUTER, J., delivered the opinion for a unanimous Court.

A regulation of the Equal Employment Opportunity Commission authorizes refusal to hire an individual because his performance on the job would endanger his own health, owing to a disability. The question in this case is whether the Americans with Disabilities Act of 1990, 42 U.S.C. § 12101 *et seq.*, permits the regulation. We hold that it does.

I

Beginning in 1972, respondent Mario Echazabal worked for independent contractors at an oil refinery owned by petitioner Chevron U.S.A. Inc. Twice he applied for a job directly with Chevron, which offered to hire him if he could pass the company's physical examination. *See* 42 U.S.C. § 12112(d)(3). Each time, the exam showed liver abnormality or damage, the cause eventually being identified as Hepatitis C, which Chevron's doctors said would be aggravated by continued exposure to toxins at Chevron's refinery. In each instance, the company withdrew the offer, and the second time it asked the contractor employing Echazabal either to reassign him to a job without exposure to harmful chemicals or to remove him from the refinery altogether. The contractor laid him off in early 1996.

Echazabal filed suit, ultimately removed to federal court, claiming, among other things, that Chevron violated the Americans With Disabilities Act in refusing to hire him, or even to let him continue working in the plant, because of a disability, his liver condition. Chevron defended under a regulation of the Equal Employment Opportunity Commission permitting the defense that a worker's disability on the job would pose a "direct threat" to his health, *see* 29 CFR § 1630.15(b)(2) (2001). Although two medical witnesses disputed Chevron's judgment that Echazabal's liver function was impaired and subject to further damage under the job conditions in the refinery, the District Court granted summary judgment for Chevron. It held that Echazabal raised no genuine issue of material fact as to whether the company acted reasonably in relying on its own doctors' medical advice, regardless of its accuracy.

On appeal, the Ninth Circuit asked for briefs on a threshold question not raised before, whether the EEOC's regulation recognizing a threat-to-self defense, *ibid.*, exceeded the scope of permissible rulemaking under the ADA. 226 F.3d 1063, 1066, n.3 (9th Cir. 2000). The Circuit held that it did and reversed the summary judgment. The court rested its position on the text of the ADA itself in explicitly recognizing an employer's right to adopt an employment qualification barring anyone whose disability would place others in the workplace at risk, while saying nothing about threats to the disabled employee himself. The majority opinion reasoned that "by specifying only threats to 'other individuals in the workplace,' the statute makes it clear that threats to other persons — including the disabled individual himself — are not included within the scope of the [direct threat] defense," *id.* at 1066–1067, and it indicated that any such regulation would unreasonably conflict with congressional policy against paternalism in the workplace, *id.* at 1067–1070. The court went on to reject Chevron's further argument that Echazabal was not " 'otherwise qualified' " to perform the job, holding that the ability to perform a job without risk to one's health or safety is not an " 'essential function' " of the job. *Id.* at 1070.

The decision conflicted with one from the Eleventh Circuit, *Moses v. American Nonwovens, Inc.*, 97 F.3d 446, 447 (1996), and raised tension with the Seventh Circuit case of *Koshinski v. Decatur Foundry, Inc.*, 177 F.3d 599, 603 (1999). We granted certiorari, 534 U.S. 991 (2001), and now reverse.

II

Section 102 of the Americans with Disabilities Act of 1990, 42 U.S.C. § 12101 *et seq.*, prohibits "discriminat[ion] against a qualified individual with a disability because of the disability . . . in regard to" a number of actions by an employer, including "hiring." 42 U.S.C. § 12112(a). The statutory definition of "discriminat[ion]" covers a number of things an employer might do to block a disabled person from advancing in the workplace, such as "using qualification standards . . . that screen out or tend to screen out an individual with a disability." § 12112(b)(6). By that same definition, *ibid.*, as well as by separate provision, § 12113(a), the Act creates an affirmative defense for action under a qualification standard "shown to be job-related for the position in question and . . . consistent with business necessity." Such a standard may include "a requirement that an individual shall not pose a direct threat to the health or safety of other individuals in the workplace," § 12113(b), if the individual cannot perform the job safely with reasonable accommodation, § 12113(a). By regulation, the EEOC carries the defense one step further, in allowing an employer to screen out a potential worker with a disability not only for risks that he would pose to others in the workplace but for risks on the job to his own health or safety as well: "The term 'qualification standard' may include a requirement that an individual shall not pose a direct threat to the health or safety of the individual or others in the workplace." 29 CFR § 1630.15(b)(2) (2001).

Chevron relies on the regulation here, since it says a job in the refinery would pose a "direct threat" to Echazabal's health. In seeking deference to the agency, it argues that nothing in the statute unambiguously precludes such a defense, while the regulation was adopted under authority explicitly delegated by Congress, 42 U.S.C. § 12116, and after notice-and-comment rulemaking. *See United States v. Mead Corp.*, 533 U.S. 218, 227 (2001); *Chevron U.S.A. Inc. v. Natural Resources Defense Council, Inc.*, 467 U.S. 837, 842–844 (1984). Echazabal, on the contrary, argues that as a matter of law the statute precludes the regulation, which he claims would be an unreasonable interpretation even if the agency had leeway to go beyond the literal text.

A

As for the textual bar to any agency action as a matter of law, Echazabal says that Chevron loses on the threshold question whether the statute leaves a gap for the EEOC to fill. *See id.* at 843–844. Echazabal recognizes the generality of the language providing for a defense when a plaintiff is screened out by "qualification standards" that are "job-related and consistent with business necessity" (and reasonable accommodation would not cure the difficulty posed by employment). 42 U.S.C. § 12113(a). Without more, those provisions would allow an employer to turn away someone whose work would pose a serious risk to himself. That possibility is said to be eliminated, however, by the further specification that " 'qualification standards' may include a requirement that an individual shall not pose a direct threat to the health or safety of other individuals in the workplace." § 12113(b); *see also* § 12111(3) (defining "direct threat" in terms of risk to others). Echazabal contrasts this provision with an EEOC regulation under the Rehabilitation Act of 1973, 87 Stat. 357, as amended, 29 U.S.C. § 701 *et seq.*, antedating the ADA, which recognized an employer's right to consider threats both to other workers and to the threatening employee himself. Because the ADA defense provision recognizes threats only if they extend to another, Echazabal reads the statute to imply as a matter of law that threats to the worker himself cannot count.

The argument follows the reliance of the Ninth Circuit majority on the interpretive canon, *expressio unius exclusio alterius*, "expressing one item of [an] associated group or series excludes another left unmentioned." *United States v. Vonn*, 535 U.S. 55, 65 (2002). The rule is fine when it applies, but this case joins some others in showing when it does not. . . .

The first strike against the expression-exclusion rule here is right in the text that Echazabal quotes. Congress included the harm-to-others provision as an example of legitimate qualifications that are "job-related and consistent with business necessity." These are spacious defensive categories, which seem to give an agency (or in the absence of agency action, a court) a good deal of discretion in setting the limits of permissible qualification standards. That discretion is confirmed, if not magnified, by the provision that "qualification standards" falling within the limits of job relation and business necessity "may include" a veto on those who would directly threaten others in the workplace. Far from supporting Echazabal's position, the expansive phrasing of "may include" points directly away from the sort of exclusive specification he claims. *United States v. New York Telephone Co.*, 434 U.S. 159, 169 (1977); *Federal Land Bank of St. Paul v. Bismarck Lumber Co.*, 314 U.S. 95, 100 (1941).[3]

Just as statutory language suggesting exclusiveness is missing, so is that essential extrastatutory ingredient of an expression-exclusion demonstration, the series of terms from which an omission bespeaks a negative implication. The canon depends on identifying a series of two or more terms or things that should be understood to go hand in hand, which are abridged in circumstances supporting a sensible inference that the term left out must have been meant to be excluded. E. Crawford, *Construction of Statutes* 337 (1940) (*expressio unius* " 'properly applies only when in the natural association of ideas in the mind of the reader that which is expressed is so set over by way of strong contrast to that which is omitted that the contrast enforces the affirmative inference' ") (quoting *State ex rel. Curtis v. De Corps*, 16 N.E.2d 459, 462 (1938)); *United States v. Vonn, supra.*

Strike two in this case is the failure to identify any such established series, including both threats to others and threats to self, from which Congress appears to have made a deliberate choice to omit the latter item as a signal of the affirmative defense's scope. The closest Echazabal comes is the EEOC's rule interpreting the Rehabilitation Act of 1973, 87 Stat. 357, as amended, 29 U.S.C. § 701 *et seq.*, a precursor of the ADA. That statute excepts from the definition of a protected "qualified individual with a handicap" anyone who would pose a "direct threat to the health or safety of other individuals," but, like the later ADA, the Rehabilitation Act says nothing about threats to self that particular employment might pose. 42 U.S.C. § 12113(b). The EEOC nonetheless extended the exception to cover threat-to-self employment, 29 CFR § 1613.702(f) (1990), and Echazabal argues that Congress's adoption only of the threat-to-others exception in the ADA must have been a deliberate omission of the Rehabilitation Act regulation's tandem term of threat-to-self, with intent to exclude it.

But two reasons stand in the way of treating the omission as an unequivocal implication of congressional intent. The first is that the EEOC was not the only agency interpreting the Rehabilitation Act, with the consequence that its regulation did not establish a clear, standard pairing of threats to self and others. While the EEOC did amplify upon the text of the Rehabilitation Act exclusion by recognizing threats to self along with threats to others, three other agencies adopting regulations under the Rehabilitation Act did not. *See* 28 CFR § 42.540(*l*)(1) (1990) (Department of Justice), 29 CFR § 32.3 (1990) (Department of Labor), and 45 CFR § 84.3(k)(1) (1990) (Department of Health and Human Services).[4] It would be a stretch, then, to say that

[3] In saying that the expansive textual phrases point in the direction of agency leeway we do not mean that the defense provisions place no limit on agency rulemaking. Without deciding whether all safety-related qualification standards must satisfy the ADA's direct-threat standard, *see Albertson's, Inc. v. Kirkingburg*, 527 U.S. 555, 569–570, n.15 (1999), we assume that some such regulations are implicitly precluded by the Act's specification of a direct-threat defense, such as those allowing "indirect" threats of "insignificant" harm. This is so because the definitional and defense provisions describing the defense in terms of "direct" threats of "significant" harm, 42 U.S.C. §§ 12113(b), 12111(3), are obviously intended to forbid qualifications that screen out by reference to general categories pretextually applied. *See infra*, at 2052–2053, and n.5. Recognizing the "indirect" and "insignificant" would simply reopen the door to pretext by way of defense.

[4] In fact, we have said that the regulations issued by the Department of Health and Human Services, which had previously been the regulations of the Department of Health, Education, and Welfare, are of "particular significance" in interpreting the Rehabilitation Act because "HEW was the agency responsible

there was a standard usage, with its source in agency practice or elsewhere, that connected threats to others so closely to threats to self that leaving out one was like ignoring a twin.

Even if we put aside this variety of administrative experience, however, and look no further than the EEOC's Rehabilitation Act regulation pairing self and others, the congressional choice to speak only of threats to others would still be equivocal. Consider what the ADA reference to threats to others might have meant on somewhat different facts. If the Rehabilitation Act had spoken only of "threats to health" and the EEOC regulation had read that to mean threats to self or others, a congressional choice to be more specific in the ADA by listing threats to others but not threats to self would have carried a message. The most probable reading would have been that Congress understood what a failure to specify could lead to and had made a choice to limit the possibilities. The statutory basis for any agency rulemaking under the ADA would have been different from its basis under the Rehabilitation Act and would have indicated a difference in the agency's rulemaking discretion. But these are not the circumstances here. Instead of making the ADA different from the Rehabilitation Act on the point at issue, Congress used identical language, knowing full well what the EEOC had made of that language under the earlier statute. Did Congress mean to imply that the agency had been wrong in reading the earlier language to allow it to recognize threats to self, or did Congress just assume that the agency was free to do under the ADA what it had already done under the earlier Act's identical language? There is no way to tell. Omitting the EEOC's reference to self-harm while using the very language that the EEOC had read as consistent with recognizing self-harm is equivocal at best. No negative inference is possible.

There is even a third strike against applying the expression-exclusion rule here. It is simply that there is no apparent stopping point to the argument that by specifying a threat-to-others defense Congress intended a negative implication about those whose safety could be considered. When Congress specified threats to others in the workplace, for example, could it possibly have meant that an employer could not defend a refusal to hire when a worker's disability would threaten others outside the workplace? If Typhoid Mary had come under the ADA, would a meat packer have been defenseless if Mary had sued after being turned away? *See* 42 U.S.C. § 12113(d). *Expressio unius* just fails to work here.

B

Since Congress has not spoken exhaustively on threats to a worker's own health, the agency regulation can claim adherence under the rule in *Chevron*, 467 U.S. at 843, so long as it makes sense of the statutory defense for qualification standards that are "job-related and consistent with business necessity." 42 U.S.C. § 12113(a). Chevron's reasons for calling the regulation reasonable are unsurprising: moral concerns aside, it wishes to avoid time lost to sickness, excessive turnover from medical retirement or

---

for coordinating the implementation and enforcement of § 504 of the Rehabilitation Act, 29 U.S.C. § 794," prohibiting discrimination against individuals with disabilities by recipients of federal funds. *Toyota Motor Mfg., Ky., Inc. v. Williams*, 534 U.S. 184 (2002). Unfortunately for Echazabal's argument, the congruence of the ADA with the HEW regulations does not produce an unequivocal statement of congressional intent.

death, litigation under state tort law, and the risk of violating the national Occupational Safety and Health Act of 1970, 84 Stat. 1590, as amended, 29 U.S.C. § 651 *et seq.* Although Echazabal claims that none of these reasons is legitimate, focusing on the concern with OSHA will be enough to show that the regulation is entitled to survive.

Echazabal points out that there is no known instance of OSHA enforcement, or even threatened enforcement, against an employer who relied on the ADA to hire a worker willing to accept a risk to himself from his disability on the job. In Echazabal's mind, this shows that invoking OSHA policy and possible OSHA liability is just a red herring to excuse covert discrimination. But there is another side to this. The text of OSHA itself says its point is "to assure so far as possible every working man and woman in the Nation safe and healthful working conditions," § 651(b), and Congress specifically obligated an employer to "furnish to each of his employees employment and a place of employment which are free from recognized hazards that are causing or are likely to cause death or serious physical harm to his employees," § 654(a)(1). Although there may be an open question whether an employer would actually be liable under OSHA for hiring an individual who knowingly consented to the particular dangers the job would pose to him, *see* Brief for United States et al. as *Amici Curiae* 19, n.7, there is no denying that the employer would be asking for trouble: his decision to hire would put Congress's policy in the ADA, a disabled individual's right to operate on equal terms within the workplace, at loggerheads with the competing policy of OSHA, to ensure the safety of "each" and "every" worker. Courts would, of course, resolve the tension if there were no agency action, but the EEOC's resolution exemplifies the substantive choices that agencies are expected to make when Congress leaves the intersection of competing objectives both imprecisely marked but subject to the administrative leeway found in 42 U.S.C. § 12113(a).

Nor can the EEOC's resolution be fairly called unreasonable as allowing the kind of workplace paternalism the ADA was meant to outlaw. It is true that Congress had paternalism in its sights when it passed the ADA, *see* § 12101(a)(5) (recognizing "overprotective rules and policies" as a form of discrimination). But the EEOC has taken this to mean that Congress was not aiming at an employer's refusal to place disabled workers at a specifically demonstrated risk, but was trying to get at refusals to give an even break to classes of disabled people, while claiming to act for their own good in reliance on untested and pretextual stereotypes.[5] Its regulation disallows just this sort of sham protection, through demands for a particularized enquiry into the

[5] Echazabal's contention that the Act's legislative history is to the contrary is unpersuasive. Although some of the comments within the legislative history decry paternalism in general terms, *see, e.g.*, H.R. Rep. No. 101-485, pt. 2, p. 72 (1990), U.S. Code Cong. & Admin. News 1990, pp. 303, 354 ("It is critical that paternalistic concerns for the disabled person's own safety not be used to disqualify an otherwise qualified applicant"); ADA Conf. Rep., 136 Cong. Rec. 17377 (1990) (statement of Sen. Kennedy) ("[A]n employer could not use as an excuse for not hiring a person with HIV disease the claim that the employer was simply 'protecting the individual' from opportunistic diseases to which the individual might be exposed"), those comments that elaborate actually express the more pointed concern that such justifications are usually pretextual, rooted in generalities and misperceptions about disabilities. *See, e.g.*, H.R. Rep. No. 101-485, at 74, U.S. Code Cong. & Admin. News 1990, pp. 303, 356 ("Generalized fear about risk from the employment environment, such as exacerbation of the disability caused by stress, cannot be used by an employer to disqualify a person with a disability"); S. Rep. No. 101-116, p. 28 (1989) ("It would also be a violation to deny employment to an applicant based on generalized fears about the safety of the applicant. . . . By definition,

harms the employee would probably face. The direct threat defense must be "based on a reasonable medical judgment that relies on the most current medical knowledge and/or the best available objective evidence," and upon an expressly "individualized assessment of the individual's present ability to safely perform the essential functions of the job," reached after considering, among other things, the imminence of the risk and the severity of the harm portended. 29 CFR § 1630.2(r) (2001). The EEOC was certainly acting within the reasonable zone when it saw a difference between rejecting workplace paternalism and ignoring specific and documented risks to the employee himself, even if the employee would take his chances for the sake of getting a job.[6]

Finally, our conclusions that some regulation is permissible and this one is reasonable are not open to Echazabal's objection that they reduce the direct threat provision to "surplusage," *see Babbitt v. Sweet Home Chapter of Communities for Great Ore.*, 515 U.S. 687, 698 (1995). The mere fact that a threat-to-self defense reasonably falls within the general "job related" and "business necessity" standard does not mean that Congress accomplished nothing with its explicit provision for a defense based on threats to others. The provision made a conclusion clear that might otherwise have been fought over in litigation or administrative rulemaking. It did not lack a job to do merely because the EEOC might have adopted the same rule later in applying the general defense provisions, nor was its job any less responsible simply because the agency was left with the option to go a step further. A provision can be useful even without congressional attention being indispensable.

Accordingly, we reverse the judgment of the Court of Appeals and remand the case for proceedings consistent with this opinion.

NOTES AND PROBLEMS FOR DISCUSSION

1. What language in the ADA was the Court interpreting? The "direct threat" defense? The "business necessity" defense? The definition of "qualified employee"?

2. On remand, the Ninth Circuit considered whether Chevron had met the requirements for assertion of the direct threat defense. Chevron had offered medical

---

such fears are based on averages and group-based predictions. This legislation requires individualized assessments").

Similarly, Echazabal points to several of our decisions expressing concern under Title VII, which like the ADA allows employers to defend otherwise discriminatory practices that are "consistent with business necessity," 42 U.S.C. § 2000e-2(k), with employers adopting rules that exclude women from jobs that are seen as too risky. *See, e.g., Dothard v. Rawlinson*, 433 U.S. 321, 335 (1977); *Automobile Workers v. Johnson Controls, Inc.*, 499 U.S. 187, 202 (1991). Those cases, however, are beside the point, as they, like Title VII generally, were concerned with paternalistic judgments based on the broad category of gender, while the EEOC has required that judgments based on the direct threat provision be made on the basis of individualized risk assessments.

[6] Respect for this distinction does not entail the requirement, as Echazabal claims, that qualification standards be "neutral," stating what the job requires, as distinct from a worker's disqualifying characteristics. Brief for Respondent 26. It is just as much business necessity for skyscraper contractors to have steelworkers without vertigo as to have well-balanced ones. *See* 226 F.3d at 1074 (Trott, J., dissenting). Reasonableness does not turn on formalism. We have no occasion, however, to try to describe how acutely an employee must exhibit a disqualifying condition before an employer may exclude him from the class of the generally qualified. *See* Brief for Respondent 31. This is a job for the trial courts in the first instance.

evidence that Echazabal had an abnormally high level of certain enzymes in his bloodstream, and therefore, should not be exposed to chemicals that could be toxic to his liver. Echazabal countered with his own medical evidence which suggested that enzyme tests do not properly measure liver function, and that the proper tests demonstrated that his liver was functioning properly. The Ninth Circuit concluded that this evidence was sufficient to preclude a grant of summary judgment to the defendant on the issue of direct threat because there was sufficiently conflicting evidence for the case to go to the jury. *See Echazabal v. Chevron USA, Inc.*, 336 F.3d 1023 (9th Cir. 2003). In a sharp dissent, Judge Trott argues that the majority should not have considered the testimony of Echazabal's doctors, which were not produced until the filing of the lawsuit. He argued that Chevron should be shielded from liability because it acted on the basis of two contemporary medical opinions and that Echazabal offered no contradicting medical reports at the time of its action. Judge Trott said: "[T]his case stands for the proposition that securing the opinion of a health-compromised job applicant's own treating doctor is not enough to protect an employer from costly litigation, litigation that comes complete with a prayer for punitive damages." *Id.* at 1036 (Trott, J., dissenting). Do you agree with the dissent?

3. In footnote 5, the Court discusses the relevant legislative history to the ADA. Could you construct an argument that the legislative history demonstrates that the EEOC regulation is not a plausible or reasonable interpretation of the statute?

Does this statement from Senator Edward Kennedy, one of the co-sponsors of the ADA, provide any guidance?

> The ADA provides that a valid qualification standard is that a person not pose a direct threat to the health or safety of other individuals in the workplace — *that is, to other coworkers or customers*. A specific decision was made to state clearly in the statute that, as a defense, an employer could prove that an applicant or employee posed a significant risk to the health or safety of others, which could not be eliminated by reasonable accommodation. This is a restatement of the standard set forth by the Supreme Court in *School Board of Nassau County versus Arline*. It is important, however, that *the ADA specifically refers to health and safety threats to others. Under the ADA, employers may not deny a person an employment opportunity based on paternalistic concerns regarding the person's health.* For example, an employer could not use as an excuse for not hiring a person with HIV disease the claim that the employer was simply "protecting the individual" from opportunistic diseases to which the individual might be exposed. That is a concern that should rightfully be dealt with by the individual, in consultation with his or her private physician.

136 Cong. Rec. S9,684-03, S9,697 (July 13, 1990) (statement of Sen. Kennedy) (emphasis added).

4. The Court said in *Arline* that an employer may legitimately consider factors such as the need to avoid exposing others to significant health and safety risks as part of its determination whether an individual is "otherwise qualified." The Court emphasized that this assessment should be individualized, and approved of the guidelines suggested by the American Medical Association. The ADA partially codified

the *Arline* holding. It permits an employer to include a qualification standard that an "individual shall not pose a direct threat to the health or safety of other individuals in the workplace." 42 U.S.C. § 12113(b). Is this the same standard as set forth in *Arline*? Should a court use the *Arline* four-part AMA test when the drafters of the ADA did not choose to use the exact language from *Arline* in the ADA?

5. There have been a number of cases under Section 504 and the ADA involving HIV-positive health care workers. The question in these cases has been whether the workers' HIV status posed a direct threat to the health or safety of others. *See, e.g.*, *Estate of Mauro v. Borgess Med. Ctr.*, 137 F.3d 398 (6th Cir. 1998); *Doe v. University of Maryland Med. Sys. Corp.*, 50 F.3d 1261 (4th Cir. 1995); *Bradley v. University of Texas M.D. Anderson Cancer Ctr.*, 3 F.3d 922 (5th Cir. 1993); *Leckelt v. Board of Comm'rs of Hosp. Dist. No. 1*, 909 F.2d 820 (5th Cir. 1990).

The cases involving health care workers tend to rely on guidelines prepared by the Centers for Disease Control (CDC) to assess whether a health care worker who is HIV- or HBV-positive poses a risk to the health and safety of others. The CDC's July 1991 guidelines state that mandatory HIV testing of health care workers is not recommended. *See* Centers for Disease Control, U.S. Dept. of Health and Human Servs., Recommendations for Preventing Transmission of Human Immunodeficiency Virus and Hepatitis B Virus to Patients During Exposure Prone Activities in 40 Morbidity & Mortality Weekly Report at RR-08 (1991). However, health care workers who perform exposure-prone invasive procedures should determine their HIV and hepatitis B surface antigen status. Workers who are infected with HIV or HBV antigen should not perform exposure-prone procedures unless they have sought counsel from an expert review panel and been advised under what circumstances, if any, they may continue to perform those procedures. Such circumstances would include informing patients of the worker's infection before exposure-prone procedures are performed.

The 1991 guidelines state that exposure-prone procedures are defined as including "digital palpation of a needle tip in a body cavity, or the simultaneous presence of the health care worker's fingers and a needle or other sharp instrument or object in a poorly visualized or highly confined anatomic site." Examples of exposure-prone procedures include certain oral, cardiothoracic, colorectal, and obstetric and gynecologic procedures.

In the July 1991 guidelines, the CDC authorized medical, surgical, and dental organizations and institutions at which the procedures are performed to develop a list of exposure-prone procedures. At a November 1991 meeting, CDC officials proposed a list of categories of procedures that may and may not be considered exposure-prone, and requested input on those categories from medical and dental associations. Those professional organizations told the CDC that it was not possible for them to create lists of exposure-prone procedures because there was not enough scientific data to determine which procedures posed a risk to patients. The groups also said that a determination of the potential for exposure of a patient to an infected health care worker's blood should include consideration of the worker's technique, skill, and medical status.

Following the November meeting, the CDC announced that it had revised its July 1991 guidelines and was seeking comments on the revision within the U.S. Public

Health Service. The revised guidelines had to be approved by HHS Secretary Louis W. Sullivan, MD, before being released for public comment. In the draft, the agency did not advise health organizations and facilities to develop lists of exposure-prone procedures. Instead, the agency recommended that infected workers who perform surgical or obstetric procedures that involve surgical entry into tissues, cavities, or organs, and dental workers who perform procedures involving manipulation, cutting, or removal of oral or perioral tissues — including teeth structure — know their HIV status and seek counsel from an expert review panel before continuing to perform those procedures. Technique, skill, experience, and infection control compliance were among the factors to be considered when evaluating the worker.

After spending nearly a year considering various revisions to the July 1991 guidelines on HIV-infected health care providers, the federal Centers for Disease Control in Atlanta surprised the medical community by deciding not to publish revised guidelines. In a letter sent to each state health officer on June 18, 1992, the CDC stated that it would not be modifying the July 12, 1991 guidelines and was not developing a national list of exposure-prone procedures, as stated in those guidelines. Instead, state health departments may decide on a case-by-case basis which, if any, procedures are exposure-prone, taking into consideration the specific procedure as well as the skill, technique, and possible impairment of the infected health care worker.

In recent years, the CDC has emphasized the importance of using exposure management to avoid the transmission of HIV from patient to health care worker. These guidelines were most recently updated in 2005. *See* http://www.aidsinfo.nih.gov/contentfiles/HealthCareOccupExpoGL.pdf. Although the principles of exposure management have remained unchanged, the CDC now recommends post-exposure prophylaxis regimens for health care workers who may have been exposed to HIV.

6. The City of Z has recently learned that one of its paramedics, Suzie Q, is HIV-positive. Paramedics perform a wide variety of medical tasks, depending on the kind of emergency involved. Their job is to perform first aid at the site and transport the patient to the hospital as quickly as possible. Their tasks can include delivering a baby, pulling someone out of a car containing a broken windshield and other sharp objects, or performing mouth-to-mouth resuscitation on a drowning victim. Paramedics travel in two-person crews and perform first aid as a team. Most calls are not emergency in nature and basically involve transporting an individual to the hospital with little or no first aid performed on site. City Z has two concerns. First, it is concerned that Suzie Q poses a health risk to herself or others. Second, it is concerned that individuals being treated by Suzie Q have not given "informed consent" if they do not know of her HIV status. The City therefore reassigns Suzie to a desk job in which she answers emergency first aid calls over the telephone (the "911" line). Suzie, however, would like to get back in the field. She says that in the 12 years she served as a paramedic, she never had an incident where she could have transmitted blood from herself to others and that, in fact, she has known of her HIV status for over two years and has been especially careful to comply with all universal barrier precautions. The City has reassigned Suzie based on its guidelines, which provide:

> When Emergency response personnel become aware of infection with a bloodborne pathogen, he/she shall "immediately refrain from performing/

> assisting in exposure-prone procedures." An "exposure-prone procedure" is defined as "procedures or situations which present a risk of transmitting bloodborne pathogens from one person to another by the potential for contact of blood or body fluids of the infected individual with an open wound or mucous membrane of a non-infected individual."

Is City Z complying with the ADA? Are its actions consistent with the CDC guidelines? What if Suzie were a firefighter? Would the legal analysis be the same? *See Doe v. District of Columbia*, 796 F. Supp. 559 (D.D.C. 1992). *See also Bradley v. University of Texas M.D. Anderson Cancer Ctr.*, 3 F.3d 922 (5th Cir. 1993) (surgical assistant); *Doe v. University of Maryland Med. Sys. Corp.*, 50 F.3d 1261 (4th Cir. 1995).

7. Michael Breece is a person with a hearing impairment. He would like to be admitted to the tractor-trailer school operated by Alliance, a private corporation. Breece communicates through a sign language interpreter. At the time of his application to the tractor-trailer program, he requested that Alliance provide him with an interpreter during all aspects of the training program, including the on-the-road segment. Breece stated that he could "glance around" during his driving sessions to communicate with his instructor. Alliance rejected Breece's application, finding that it could not safely accommodate Breece's hearing impairment during the public road segment of the course. At trial, Dr. Robinson, an expert in education courses on automobile, motorcycle, and truck driving, testified that Breece could be safely accommodated with an earphone amplification device, a truck driving simulator, and expanded in-class training, although Dr. Robinson had never used any of those techniques with a student with a hearing impairment. Mr. Hoback, a driver with Alliance for more than 20 years and a certified tractor-trailer teacher, testified that Dr. Robinson's suggested tactics would not provide Breece with sufficient on-road training for him to become a competent driver. Mr. Hoback questioned Dr. Robinson's expertise because Dr. Robinson had far less experience than Mr. Hoback in driving tractor-trailers. Dr. Robinson, by contrast, questioned Mr. Hoback's expertise, suggesting that Mr. Hoback had no scientific training in this field and was only saying what his employer wanted to hear. Does Breece have a valid claim of discrimination under the ADA? How should a court evaluate this conflicting testimony? *See Breece v. Alliance Tractor-Trailer Training II*, 824 F. Supp. 576 (E.D. Va. 1993).

8. Prior to the final passage of the ADA, an attempt was made to add an amendment to the Act that would have permitted employers to discriminate at will against persons with infectious diseases (such as AIDS) with respect to jobs involving the handling of food. After much controversy, that amendment was deleted from the final version. The ADA is premised on the philosophy that absent an *actual* (rather than imagined) threat, an employer cannot fire or refuse to hire a person with a disability based on fears relating to safety.

The ADA requires the Secretary of the Department of Health and Human Services to:

> (A) review all infectious and communicable diseases which may be transmitted through handling the food supply;

(B) publish a list of infectious and communicable diseases which are transmitted through handling the food supply;

(C) publish the methods by which such diseases are transmitted; and

(D) widely disseminate such information regarding the list of diseases and their modes of transmissibility to the general public.

Such list must be updated annually.

42 U.S.C. § 12113(d)(1).

If an individual has an infectious or communicable disease that can be transmitted through the handling of food — *as included on the DHHS list* — and the risk of transmission cannot be eliminated by the provision of reasonable accommodation(s), "a covered entity may refuse to assign or continue to assign such individual to a job involving food handling." 42 U.S.C. § 12113(d)(2). DHHS has never included AIDS or HIV on that list.

9. It is not always easy to determine whether a case belongs under the direct threat defense or the business necessity defense. For example, consider the following fact pattern:

> Exxon developed a substance abuse policy in response to the 1989 Exxon Valdez incident, in which one of its tankers ran aground, causing environmental injury and resulting in billions of dollars of liability for Exxon. The policy permanently removes any employee who has undergone treatment for substance abuse from certain safety-sensitive, little-supervised positions. The policy affects about 10% of Exxon's positions at the workplace. The EEOC brought suit on behalf of certain Exxon employees, alleging that Exxon's substance abuse policy violates the ADA. The EEOC argued that Exxon must defend this rule under the direct threat test because it is a safety-based requirement. In support of this position, it cites its Interpretive Guidance which states:
>
> With regard to safety requirements that screen out or tend to screen out an individual with a disability or a class of individuals with disabilities, an employer must demonstrate that the requirement, as applied to the individual, satisfies the "direct threat" standard in § 1630.2(r) in order to show that the requirement is job-related and consistent with business necessity.

29 C.F.R. pt. 1630, app. § 1630.15(b) and (c).

Exxon contends that because the statute does not explicitly mandate the direct threat test for every safety-based qualification, it may defend its policy under the business necessity or direct threat standard. *See EEOC v. Exxon Corp.*, 203 F.3d 871 (5th Cir. 2000). In support of its argument, the EEOC notes that Justice Souter questioned the soundness of the EEOC's position in note 15 in *Albertson's v. Kirkingburg* (discussed at the beginning of this chapter) that the defendant must show a "direct threat" to justify a safety-related qualification standard.

Who has the stronger argument in the *Exxon* case — the employer or the EEOC? Should Exxon be required to justify its safety-based qualification standard under the business necessity rule rather than the direct threat rule? Do you believe that the choice of legal standard would make a significant difference in this fact pattern? Why or why not?

10. The ADA is not entirely clear as to which party should bear the burden of proof in a case in which the defendant alleges that the plaintiff is not qualified for the position in question because she poses a direct threat to others. Most courts have concluded that the defendant should bear the burden of proof on this issue because "direct threat" is considered to be an affirmative defense under the statute. Typically, defendants have the burden of proof on affirmative defenses. Three dissenting judges in the *en banc* decision in *Rizzo v. Children's World Learning Centers, Inc.*, 213 F.3d 209, 217–18 (5th Cir. 2000) (Judges Jones, Smith, and Wiener, dissenting), however, have taken issue with this prevailing assumption. In a case involving whether an individual with a hearing impairment was qualified to drive the van at a preschool, the dissenting judges stated:

> Under the proper rule, the employee, not the employer, has the burden to prove that he can perform essential job functions safely notwithstanding his disability and does not thereby pose a direct threat to the health or safety of others in the workplace.
>
> Unfortunately, we cannot rely on the text of the ADA to tell us how to assign the burden of proof, because different provisions conflict, and analogies to other federal employment discrimination laws are of limited utility. . . .
>
> To sustain an action under the ADA, an employee first must prove, as part of his prima facie case, that he is a "qualified individual with a disability." 42 U.S.C. § 12112(a). In other words, he has the burden to prove that he is "an individual with a disability who, with or without reasonable accommodation, can perform the essential functions of the employment position that such individual holds or desires." § 12111(8) In the context of the ADA, ability to perform an essential function means, inter alia, doing so without constituting a direct threat.
>
> Plainly then, when discharging his burden of establishing the second element of a prima facie ADA case — qualification for the job — the plaintiff must show that, in performing each essential function, he does not pose such a threat. Where, as here, the function is (1) driving (2) a van (3) full of pre-school-age children (4) on public streets in a high-traffic urban area, an employee with a disability that has an obvious nexus to performing that job function in a safe manner must negate the threat.
>
> True, the ADA also provides employers with the affirmative defense of showing a direct threat. [Court quotes § 12113(b).]
>
> In other words, it is the employee's burden to prove that he is a qualified individual with a disability (which includes, in some cases, negating direct threat), and it is the employer's burden to establish that an employee poses a direct threat to the health or safety of other individuals in the workplace. These provisions, however, leave a troubling gap, one that is exposed by the facts of this case: Whose burden is it if, according to the employer, an

employee is not a qualified individual because, as a result of his disability, his unsafe performance of an essential job function renders him a direct threat to others in the workplace?

On the one hand, imposing the burden on the employee requires him to prove that he is not a direct threat — a rule that appears to conflict with § 12113(b), which assigns the burden, completely and without exception, to the employer to prove direct threat, and not to the employee to disprove such a threat. On the other hand, placing the burden on the employer requires it to show that the employee cannot perform an essential job function safely — a rule that conflicts with provisions of the ADA that expressly assign the burden to the employee to prove that, as a qualified individual, he can perform all essential job functions.

To place the burden on the employer is to hold — absurdly, in our view — that unsafe execution of job duties nevertheless constitutes adequate performance. This approach effectively rewrites the ADA to require an employee merely to prove his ability to "perform the essential functions of the employment position," § 12111(8), without regard "to the health or safety of other individuals in the workplace," § 12113(b). As a matter of statutory construction if nothing else, such a rule is untenable.

213 F.3d at 217–18 (Judges Jones, Smith, and Wiener, dissenting) (footnotes omitted).

Do you agree with the dissenters? In strong language, the dissenters also asserted:

The result in this case is facially absurd: An employee whose numerous duties as assistant teacher and administrative aid include driving small children in the school van is asked temporarily not to drive until she can show that her poor hearing does not endanger her young passengers. For this purportedly reprehensible deed, done in the interest of child safety, the school must pay the impaired employee $100,000 plus attorney's fees.

213 F.3d at 215. Is that result facially absurd?

The Tenth Circuit has allocated the burden of proof on the direct threat issue depending on how it is raised in a case. The court said:

We hold that, in a Title I ADA case, it is the plaintiff's burden to show that he or she can perform *the essential functions of the job*, and is therefore "qualified." Where those essential job functions necessarily implicate the safety of others, plaintiff must demonstrate that she can perform those functions in a way that does not endanger others. There may be other cases under Title I where the issue of direct threat is not tied to the issue of essential job functions but is purely a matter of defense, on which the defendant would bear the burden.

Borgialli v. Thunder Basin Coal Co., 235 F.3d 1284, 1292 (10th Cir. 2000).

How could the direct threat issue arise out of the "essential functions of the job" context? Has the Tenth Circuit made the direct threat issue not a defense?

11. The courts continue to wrestle with application of the direct threat defense. Consider the following fact patterns:

> Nurse Evelyn Burner reported to her supervisor that employee Richard Pence had stated: "when he leaves here that he will be taking a bunch of people with him" and, in response to further questioning from her, allegedly stated that "he has AK's and more ammo than Rockingham County." After placing Pence on paid disability leave and referring him to a psychologist who was "unable to provide an opinion one way or another" on whether Pence had a mental health disorder, the employer terminated Pence on the formal ground that his threatening statements violated workplace rules that prohibited "threatening, intimidating, coercing, or harassing co-workers." Pence brought a wrongful termination claim under the ADA. The district court granted summary judgment for the employer. The district court ruled that the ADA is not violated even if an employer discharges an employee because of a mistaken perception of misconduct and the misconduct was disability-related so long as the employer treats disabled and nondisabled employees alike. The employee appealed.

See Pence v. Tenneco Automotive Operating Company, 2006 U.S. App. LEXIS 5734 (4th Cir. Mar. 7, 2006).

> Sidney Justice sought to return to his work as an electrician at the Crown Cork plant following a stroke. Upon returning to work, his doctor indicated that he could not work at unprotected heights and could not work around hazardous or moving machinery or equipment. Initially, Justice returned to work without any difficulty. He was scheduled alongside other electricians who could perform any tasks that he could not perform due to his restrictions (which occurred infrequently). After working for a year, his physician relaxed his restrictions somewhat, saying he could not work on a ladder above six feet (but could work on shorter ladders and platform lifts). He continued to work without incident for two years. Following a strike, he was rescheduled to night duty and with a supervisor who had not previously worked with him. Following an observation of Justice having difficulty performing a task outside his restrictions, he initiated an investigation of Justice's ability to do his job. A company physical therapist examined Justice and then visited the plant site. She observed various potential hazards at the workplace for someone with balance difficulties such as slippery surfaces, multiple level changes, frequent tight turns and the need to crouch in some areas. Upon receiving her report, the company concluded that Justice could no longer work as an electrician and offered him a position as a janitor (the lowest paid position at the company). Does Justice have a strong ADA claim?

See Justice v. Crown Cork and Seal Co., 527 F.3d 1080 (10th Cir. 2008).

F. RELATIONSHIP BETWEEN ADA TITLE I AND THE FAMILY AND MEDICAL LEAVE ACT

The Family and Medical Leave Act of 1993 (FMLA), 29 U.S.C. §§ 2601–2654, requires employers having 50 or more employees to grant up to 12 weeks of unpaid medical leave per year to employees with one year of service (*i.e.*, who have worked 1,250 hours during the year) and who have a serious health condition. 29 U.S.C. § 2612(a)(1)(D). The term "serious health condition" means, *inter alia,* an illness, injury, impairment, or physical or mental condition that involves: (1) a period of incapacity connected with inpatient care (*i.e.*, an overnight stay) at a hospital or medical care facility; (2) continuing treatment by a health care provider for more than three consecutive calendar days, which also involves treatment two or more times by a health care provider or treatment on one occasion which results in a regimen of continuing treatment; (3) any period of incapacity due to pregnancy; (4) any period of incapacity due to a chronic serious health condition; (5) a period of incapacity that is permanent or long-term due to a condition for which treatment may not be effective; or (6) any period of absence to receive multiple treatments by a health care provider for restorative surgery or for a condition that would likely result in a period of incapacity of more than three consecutive calendar days in the absence of medical intervention or treatment. *See* 29 C.F.R. § 825.800 (definition of "serious health condition entitling an employee to FMLA leave"). During the period of unpaid leave which may be taken on a part-time basis when medically necessary or when employer and employee agree, the employer is required to maintain the employee's group health insurance. 29 U.S.C. §§ 2612(b)(1) and 2614(c)(1). Upon return to work, the employee is entitled *either* to the job he or she previously held *or* an equivalent job with equivalent benefits, pay, and other terms of employment. 29 U.S.C. § 2614(a). (There are certain exceptions to this provision for "highly compensated employees." 29 U.S.C. § 2614(b).)

An individual may be both "disabled" within the meaning of ADA Title I and have a "serious health condition" within the meaning of the FMLA. In such cases, it is important to understand the relationship — and interplay — between ADA Title I and the FMLA. Portions of the Department of Labor's (DOL) FMLA regulations clarify the interplay between the FMLA and ADA Title I:

> Nothing in [the] FMLA modifies any Federal or State law prohibiting discrimination on the basis of . . . disability. [The] FMLA's legislative history explains that [the] FMLA is "not intended to modify or affect the Rehabilitation Act of 1973, as amended, the regulations concerning employment which have been promulgated pursuant to the statute, or the Americans with Disabilities Act of 1990, or the regulations issued under that [A]ct. Thus, the leave provisions of the [FMLA] are wholly distinct from the reasonable accommodation obligations of employers covered under the [ADA], employers who receive Federal financial assistance, employers who contract with the Federal government, or the Federal government itself. The purpose of the FMLA is to make leave available to eligible employees and employers within its coverage, and not to limit already existing rights and protection." S. Rep. No. 3, 103d Cong., 1st Sess. 38 (1993). An employer must therefore provide

> leave under whichever statutory provision provides the greater rights to employees. When an employer violates both FMLA and a discrimination law, an employee may be able to recover under either or both statutes [double relief may not be awarded for the same loss]; when remedies coincide a claimant may be allowed to utilize whichever avenue of relief is desired.

29 C.F.R. § 825.702(a).

The FMLA regulations further note that when an employee is a qualified individual with a disability under ADA Title I, the employer must make reasonable accommodations for the employee, while at the same time affording the employee his or her rights under the FMLA. The regulations note several differences between the obligations and rights of employers and employees under the two Acts:

> [The] FMLA entitles eligible employees to 12 weeks of leave in any 12-month period, whereas the ADA allows an indeterminate amount of leave, barring undue hardship, as a reasonable accommodation. [The] FMLA requires employers to maintain employees' group health plan coverage during FMLA leave on the same conditions as coverage would have been provided if the employee had been continuously employed during the leave period, whereas ADA does not require maintenance of health insurance unless other employees receive health insurance during leave under the same circumstances.

29 C.F.R. § 825.702(b).

The regulations explain that under ADA Title I, a covered employee may be reasonably accommodated by the provision of a part-time job with no health benefits (if the employer did not provide health benefits for other part-time employees). Under the FMLA, however, an employee could work "a reduced leave schedule until the equivalent of 12 workweeks of leave were used, with group health benefits maintained during the period." 29 C.F.R. § 825.702(c)(1).

Further, the regulations explain that under the FMLA, an employer may permissibly transfer "an employee who is taking leave intermittently or on a reduced schedule to an alternative position," while under ADA Title I, reassignment to a vacant position is only permitted if the employee cannot perform the essential functions of his or her current position with or without the provision of reasonable accommodations. *Id.*

Because an employer must comply with both ADA Title I and the FMLA when an employee is covered under both Acts, the EEOC has noted that an employee with a disability who has used his or her 12 weeks of FMLA medical leave is entitled to additional unpaid leave under the ADA unless the undue hardship defense is satisfied. The EEOC has further noted that when determining whether this additional leave would be an undue hardship, the employer may consider the impact of having already provided 12 weeks of FMLA medical leave. But the EEOC opines that the "FMLA does *not* mean that more than 12 weeks of unpaid leave automatically imposes an undue hardship on employers for purposes of the ADA." The DOL concurs with that analysis. 60 Fed. Reg. 2,232 (1995).

The DOL's FMLA regulations provide several examples demonstrating the interaction between ADA Title I and the FMLA, as follows:

> [A] qualified individual with a disability who is also an "eligible employee" entitled to FMLA leave requests 10 weeks of medical leave as a reasonable accommodation, which the employer grants because it is not an undue hardship. The employer advises the employee that the 10 weeks of leave is also being designated as FMLA leave and will count towards the employee's FMLA leave entitlement. This designation does not prevent the parties from also treating the leave as a reasonable accommodation and reinstating the employee into the *same* job, as required by the ADA, rather than an equivalent position under FMLA, if that is the greater right available to the employee. At the same time, the employee would be entitled under FMLA to have the employer maintain group health plan coverage during the leave, as that requirement provides the greater right to the employee.
>
> [If] the same employee needed to work part-time (a reduced leave schedule) after returning to his or her same job, the employee would still be entitled under [the] FMLA to have group health plan coverage maintained for the remainder of the two-week equivalent of FMLA leave entitlement, notwithstanding an employer policy that part-time employees do not receive health insurance. This employee would be entitled under the ADA to reasonable accommodations to enable the employee to perform the essential functions of the part-time position. In addition, because the employee is working a part-time schedule as a reasonable accommodation, the employee would be shielded from [the] FMLA's provision for temporary assignment to a different alternative position. Once the employee has exhausted his or her remaining FMLA leave entitlement while working the reduced (part-time) schedule, if the employee is a qualified individual with a disability, and if the employee is unable to return to the same full-time position at that time, the employee might continue to work part-time as a reasonable accommodation, barring undue hardship; the employee would then be entitled to only those employment benefits ordinarily provided by the employer to part-time employees.
>
> [At] the end of the FMLA leave entitlement, an employer is required under [the] FMLA to reinstate the employee in the same or an equivalent position, with equivalent pay and benefits, to that which the employee held when leave commenced. The employer's FMLA obligations would be satisfied if the employer offered the employee an equivalent full-time position. If the employee were unable to perform the essential functions of that equivalent position even with reasonable accommodation, because of a disability, the ADA may require the employer to make a reasonable accommodation at that time by allowing the employee to work part-time or by reassigning the employee to a vacant position, barring undue hardship.

29 C.F.R. § 825.702(c)(2)–(4).

The FMLA regulations further provide that if an employee is entitled to leave under the FMLA, an employer may not *require* an employee to take another job as a reasonable accommodation in lieu of FMLA leave. 29 C.F.R. § 825.702(d). The regulations note, however, that under the ADA, the employer may be required to *offer* the employee such a position, and provide that "[a]n employer may not change the essential functions of the job in order to deny FMLA leave . . . ." In addition, the regulations address the interplay between workers' compensation absence and FMLA leave, and note that "[i]f the employee returning from the workers' compensation injury is a qualified individual with a disability, he or she will have rights under the ADA." *Id.*

The regulations explain that the FMLA permits an employer to implement a uniform policy regulating certification of employees' fitness for duty to return to work after taking leave, but the employer must comply with the requirements under ADA Title I "that a fitness for duty physical be job-related and consistent with business necessity." 29 C.F.R. § 825.702(e).

The regulations further provide that all medical records created for purposes of the FMLA must comply with ADA Title I confidentiality requirements when an employee is covered by both Acts. 29 C.F.R. § 825.500(g).

G. REMEDIES

1. General Principles of Enforcement

The EEOC is responsible for overseeing and enforcing the employment discrimination provisions (Title I) of the ADA. The EEOC is obligated to work in conjunction with the offices of Civil Rights of all agencies having enforcement authority under the Rehabilitation Act (primarily Section 504) to ensure that administrative complaints are "dealt with in a manner that avoids duplication of effort and prevents imposition of inconsistent or conflicting standards for the same requirements [under the two Acts]." 42 U.S.C. § 12117(b).

Title I provides that the powers, remedies, and procedures of Title VII of the Civil Rights Act are available to the EEOC, to the Attorney General, and to "any person alleging discrimination" in violation of the employment provisions of the ADA or regulations promulgated thereunder. 42 U.S.C. § 12117(o). Thus, the Act contemplates both governmental and individual enforcement of the employment provisions. Before an individual may take judicial action against a covered entity under this section, however, administrative remedies must be pursued just as they must be pursued under Title VII. (Note, however, that courts have held that employees alleging employment discrimination by an entity covered under ADA Title II do not have to exhaust administrative remedies under Title I.)

An individual may file both a state workers' compensation claim and a charge under the ADA (including filing an action in court after completing administrative prerequisites). "Exclusivity" clauses in state workers' compensation laws do not bar actions under the ADA.

The Supreme Court has held that state and federal courts have concurrent jurisdiction over matters arising under Title VII. *See Yellow Freight System, Inc. v.*

Donnelly, 494 U.S. 820 (1990). Because the ADA's Title I enforcement provisions follow those under Title VII, this same rule applies under Title I.

NOTES AND PROBLEMS FOR DISCUSSION

1. Another issue that often arises under the ADA is whether courts should enforce a requirement in a collective bargaining agreement that an employment discrimination suit be subjected to mandatory arbitration. Supreme Court doctrine on this issue is confusing, leading to conflicting results in the lower courts. In 1974, the Supreme Court held in *Alexander v. Gardner-Denver Co.*, 415 U.S. 36 (1974), that an arbitration provision in a collective bargaining agreement could not preclude a Title VII lawsuit. In reaching that conclusion, the Supreme Court determined that in enacting Title VII, Congress endowed individual employees with a statutory right to equal employment opportunities that is not susceptible to prospective waiver by the "majoritarian process" of collective bargaining. *Id.* at 51–52. Seventeen years later, however, in *Gilmer v. Interstate/Johnson Lane Corp.*, 500 U.S. 20 (1991), the Supreme Court ruled that a mandatory arbitration clause was enforceable where the employee had personally agreed to arbitration as his exclusive remedy for any controversy arising out of his employment or the termination of that employment. (The agreement was not part of a collective bargaining agreement.) *Gilmer* did not explicitly overrule *Alexander*; instead, the Court distinguished the two cases. *See* 500 U.S. at 33–35. Nonetheless, some courts have interpreted *Gilmer* as implicitly overruling *Alexander*. *Compare Austin v. Owens-Brockway Glass Container, Inc.*, 78 F.3d 875 (4th Cir. 1996) (enforcing arbitration agreement to bar employee's access to federal court), *with Brisentine v. Stone & Webster Eng'g Corp.*, 117 F.3d 519 (11th Cir. 1997) (not enforcing arbitration agreement).

The United States Supreme Court considered this issue in *Wright v. Universal Maritime Serv. Corp.*, 525 U.S. 70 (1998). In that case, a longshoreman had filed suit under the ADA despite the existence of a general arbitration clause in the collective bargaining agreement. Justice Scalia delivered the opinion for a unanimous Court in which it found that the general arbitration clause did not require the longshoreman to use arbitration for his ADA claim. But the Court did not resolve the arguable conflict between *Gardner-Denver* and *Gilmer*, finding that no waiver occurred on the specific facts of the collective bargaining agreement at issue. It did find that a plaintiff's statutory claim is not subject to the ordinary presumption of arbitrability that applies in the collective bargaining context. Instead, it found that any collective bargaining requirement to arbitrate must be particularly clear. The arbitration clause at issue merely provided for arbitration of "matters under dispute," which the Court found was not a "clear and unmistakable waiver of the covered employees' rights to a judicial forum for federal claims of employment discrimination." The Court therefore did not reach the question of whether a proper waiver would be enforceable.

2. Title I creates a limited exemption for religious entities. 42 U.S.C. § 12113(c) provides that religious entities, although covered by Title I, are nonetheless allowed to give preference in employment to individuals of their stated religion. In addition, a religious organization may require that all applicants and employees conform to the religious tenets of such organization. Consider the reasons for, and practical ramifi-

cations of, these exceptions. Could a religious entity refrain from hiring, or firing, a person with AIDS without violating the ADA if that person had acquired AIDS as a result of non-marital sexual relations or homosexual activity, based on the theory that such sexual activity contravenes the religious tenets of the entity?

Note that Title III, which prohibits public accommodations from discriminating on the basis of disability in their programs or activities, has an even broader exemption for religious entities. 42 U.S.C. § 12187 exempts private clubs or establishments, as well as religious organizations or entities controlled by religious organizations, including places of worship.

3. The Supreme Court had to determine whether an agreement between an employer and an employee to arbitrate employment-related disputes bars the Equal Employment Opportunity Commission (EEOC) from pursuing victim-specific judicial relief, such as backpay, reinstatement, and damages, in an enforcement action alleging that the employer has violated Title I of the ADA. In a 6-3 decision, it concluded that the arbitration agreement did not preclude EEOC enforcement. *EEOC v. Waffle House, Inc.*, 534 U.S. 279 (2002).

4. Like Title VII, the ADA provides for attorney's fees to the prevailing party. *See* 42 U.S.C. § 12205. These principles apply to all lawsuits brought under the ADA, not simply employment discrimination cases. In *Buckhannon Board and Care Home, Inc v. West Virginia Dep't of Health and Human Resources*, 532 U.S. 598 (2001), the Supreme Court offered guidance on what it meant to be the "prevailing party" for these purposes. The Supreme Court held that the ADA requires a party to secure either a judgment on the merits or a court-ordered consent decree in order to qualify as "prevailing party." The question in *Buckhannon* was whether a court could award attorney's fees to a party if the action of bringing a lawsuit brought about a voluntary change in the defendant's conduct without formal judicial sanction. The Court held (in a 5-4 opinion) that it did not. The United States Department of Justice had urged the Court to accept a limited form of the "catalyst" theory under which a plaintiff could recover attorney's fees if he or she established that the "complaint had sufficient merit to withstand a motion to dismiss for lack of jurisdiction or failure to state a claim on which relief may be granted." But the Supreme Court rejected even this limited version of the catalyst theory. Prior to 1994, every Federal Court of Appeals (except the Fourth Circuit, which had not addressed the issue) had concluded that plaintiffs could obtain a fee award if their suit acted as a "catalyst" for the change they sought, even if they did not obtain a judgment or consent decree. How may litigation behavior be modified in the future to take into account the decision in *Buckhannon*?

5. In *Clackamas Gastroenterology Associates v. Wells*, 538 U.S. 440 (2003), the Supreme Court clarified the meaning of the word "employees" under ADA Title I. Like Title VII, ADA Title I only covers employers that have "15 or more employees for each working day in each of 20 or more calendar weeks in the current or preceding calendar year." 42 U.S.C. § 1211(5). The question in the case was whether four physicians actively engaged in medical practice as shareholders and directors of a professional corporation should be counted as "employees." The court of appeals had concluded that the physicians should be counted as employees. The Supreme Court reversed and remanded the case, concluding that, on remand, the court should apply the common

law's definition of the master-servant relationship.

2. Damages

Pursuant to the Rehabilitation Act Amendments of 1992, the standards used to determine whether an employer has impermissibly discriminated against an individual on the basis of disability are to be the same under Sections 501, 503, and 504 of the Rehabilitation Act and Title I of the ADA. 29 U.S.C. §§ 791(g), 793(d), and 794(d). Thus, to the extent that an employer is found to have intentionally discriminated against an applicant or employee with a disability under ADA Title I, the employer will also be found to have intentionally discriminated against such an individual under the Rehabilitation Act — assuming, of course, that the employer is a covered entity under any section of the Rehabilitation Act. Interestingly, however, while an employer who is a recipient of federal financial assistance may be subject to the same *liability* under the ADA, Section 501 and Section 504, the employee may be subject to greater *damages* under Section 504 than under ADA Title I or Section 501.

As initially enacted, Title I of the ADA provided only for equitable remedies. Under the Civil Rights Act of 1991 (*see* 137 Cong. Rec. S15503-04 (daily ed. Oct. 30, 1991)), however, Congress provided for compensatory and punitive damages to be awarded under ADA Title I — and under Section 501 — against an employer who engages in unlawful intentional discrimination. Under that Act, where an employer is found liable for intentional discrimination, a plaintiff whose suit was filed under ADA Title I or Section 501 may recover — in addition to equitable remedies — compensatory damages ("for future pecuniary losses, emotional pain, suffering, inconvenience, mental anguish, loss of enjoyment of life, and other nonpecuniary losses") and punitive damages *not to exceed a combined total* of: (a) $50,000 when the defendant employer has between 15 and 100 employees (including temporary and part-time employees according to the EEOC) in each of 20 or more calendar weeks in the current or preceding calendar year; (b) $100,000 when the defendant employer has between 101 and 200 employees during that period; (c) $200,000 when the defendant employer has between 201 and 500 employees during that period; or (d) $300,000 when the defendant employer has more than 500 employees during that period. *Id.* at § 15504.

In no event, therefore, may an individual plaintiff recover more than $300,000 in combined compensatory and punitive damages against an employer who has intentionally discriminated on the basis of disability in violation of ADA Title I or Section 501. (The EEOC takes the position, however, that when a claim is filed against a single employer on behalf of more than one individual, each individual may claim the maximum damages. *See* EEOC ENFORCEMENT GUIDANCE: COMPENSATORY AND PUNITIVE DAMAGES AVAILABLE UNDER § 102 OF THE CIVIL RIGHTS ACT OF 1991, No. 915.002, at 6 (1992).)

Further, the Civil Rights Act expressly provides that where a discriminatory practice involves the provision of reasonable accommodation pursuant to the ADA, damages may not be awarded where the employer

> demonstrates good faith efforts, in consultation with the person with the disability who has informed the covered entity that accommodation is needed, to identify and make a reasonable accommodation that would provide such individual with an equally effective opportunity and would not cause an undue hardship on the operation of the business.

137 Cong. Rec. S15504 (daily ed. Oct. 30, 1991).

While the damage provisions of the Civil Rights Act of 1991 apply to Section 501 and Title I of the ADA, they do not apply to Section 504, presumably because the purpose of the Civil Rights Act of 1991 was to modify Title VII of that Act upon which Title I of the ADA and Section 501 were premised. Section 504, unlike Section 501 and ADA Title I, was not premised on Title VII of the Civil Rights Act, but upon Title VI of that Act. Thus, the Civil Rights Act of 1991 does not govern Section 504. The extent to which damages are available against employers who have intentionally discriminated on the basis of disability in violation of Section 504, therefore, must be decided by looking to relevant case law, wholly apart from the issue of the extent to which damages are available for such discrimination under ADA Title I or Section 501.

The Supreme Court's decision in *Franklin v. Gwinnett County Public Schools*, 503 U.S. 60 (1992), effectively resolves the issue of whether damages are available for intentional discrimination in violation of Section 504. In *Franklin*, the Supreme Court held that monetary damages are available in actions brought under Title IX of the 1972 Educational Amendments, 20 U.S.C. §§ 1681–1688, which prohibits discrimination on the basis of sex in any educational program or activity receiving federal financial assistance.

The circuit courts have unanimously recognized the availability of monetary damage claims in suits under Section 504 against private entities and state and local governments, but have limited them to cases involving *intentional* discrimination. *See, e.g.*, *Ferguson v. City of Phoenix*, 157 F.3d 668, 674 (9th Cir. 1998). Moreover, the Supreme Court recently confirmed in *Alexander v. Sandoval*, 532 U.S. 275, 282–83 (2001), that "private individuals c[an] not recover compensatory damages under Title VI except for intentional discrimination."

The *Sandoval* decision may have an impact on Section 504 claims for *unintentional* discrimination. In *Sandoval*, the Court held that plaintiffs could not pursue a private right of action for *disparate impact* claims under Title VI because that cause of action is not recognized by language of Title VI; it is only recognized in the regulations promulgated to enforce Title VI. This decision was grounded on the conclusion that Title VI only bars intentional discrimination, and disparate impact claims do not constitute intentional discrimination. 532 U.S. at 292–93. The Court suggested that the general principle of there not being a cause of action to enforce regulations that go beyond the statutory language also applies to Section 504.

Lower courts interpreting the *Sandoval* decision, however, have distinguished Title VI from Section 504 and held that disparate impact claims are still viable under Section 504. They acknowledge that Congress modeled Section 504 on Title VI, but note that in *Alexander v. Choate*, 469 U.S. 287 (1985), the Court rejected the argument that Section 504 only barred intentional discrimination. Courts distinguishing *San-*

doval also note, as did the *Choate* Court that, by the time Congress enacted Section 504, model enforcement regulations for Title VI had incorporated a disparate-impact standard, and every Cabinet Department and about 40 federal agencies had adopted standards in which Title VI was interpreted to bar programs with a discriminatory impact. "Thus, while the conduct regulated by section 601 of Title VI is limited to intentional discrimination . . . the same cannot be said for section 504. With section 504, Congress clearly sought to remedy a problem of a different, and for these purposes broader, nature." *Frederick L. v. Department of Public Welfare*, 157 F. Supp. 2d 509, 537 (E.D. Pa. 2001); *see also Robinson v. Unified School District No. 443*, 295 F.3d 1183, 1187 (10th Cir. 2002) ("While the language of the relevant sections of the Rehabilitation Act and Title VI are essentially identical, . . . the Court's decision in *Choate* laid out the different aim of the Rehabilitation Act as well as the different context in which the Act was passed. . . . Therefore, [an earlier decision recognizing cause of action under section 504 based on claims of disparate impact] continues to control[].").

In *Barnes v. Gorman*, 536 U.S. 181 (2002), the Court held that punitive damages are not available under Section 504. The Court noted that it had often characterized statutes involving the provision of federal funding to be "much in the nature of a *contract*: in return for federal funds, the [recipients] agree to comply with federally imposed conditions." *Id.* at 185. Punitive damages, unlike compensatory damages and injunction, are generally not available for breach of contract, and the Court reasoned they should also not be available to enforce Section 504 and other federal funding statutes.

In sum, under Section 501 of the Rehabilitation Act and Title I of the ADA, Congress has placed strict limitations on the amount of compensatory and punitive damages available to disabled victims of intentional employment discrimination. Under the Court's decision in *Franklin*, however, no such limitation is imposed under Section 504. Despite the fact that Title I of the ADA and Sections 501 and 504 are to be interpreted in the same manner where employment discrimination is at issue, the remedies available for intentional discrimination are actually much more liberal under Section 504 than under ADA Title I or Section 501. Moreover, in jurisdictions in which courts would permit damages for unintentional employment discrimination under Section 504, a plaintiff would again have greater remedies under that section because under the Civil Rights Act of 1991, damages for disparate impact employment discrimination are not available under ADA Title I or Section 501.

A plaintiff whose employer is a recipient of federal financial assistance covered under both ADA Title I and Section 504, and who seeks damages for intentional discrimination, would be wiser to sue under Section 504 to take advantage of the unlimited damages available under that section. A plaintiff whose employer is a federal agency covered by both Sections 501 and 504 may also be wiser to sue under Section 504, as well as under Section 501, *if* the court permits the plaintiff to do so. (The courts are in some disagreement as to whether an individual may sue a federal agency for employment discrimination under both Sections 501 and 504. Some courts have allowed individuals to file suit under both sections, while other courts have held that such suits must be filed only under Section 501. For a discussion of this issue, see Bonnie P. Tucker & Bruce A. Goldstein, Legal Rights of Persons with Disabilities:

An Analysis of Federal Law (1st ed. 1990 & Supps. 1991–1998, at chapter 9).) In addition to the larger *amount* of damages that may be available under Section 504, the Civil Rights Act of 1991 provides that punitive damages are not available against government employers, which covers all employers governed by Section 501.

Further, under Title II of the ADA, state and local government employers having the requisite number of employees to otherwise fall within the coverage of Title I (15 or more employees) must comply with the mandates of Title I — and the EEOC's regulations promulgated thereunder — with respect to employment discrimination. *See* 28 C.F.R. § 35.140. Yet, Title II itself provides that the remedies for violations of the ADA by state and local government entities are those available under Section 505 of the Rehabilitation Act, 29 U.S.C. § 794a. Section 505 of the Rehabilitation Act provides that the remedies under Section 504 are those available under Title VI of the Civil Rights Act (*see* 29 U.S.C. § 794a(a)(1)). Where those remedies are different, as they appear to be with respect to the damages available for employment discrimination, it is unclear which provision should govern. Presumably, the remedies consistent with Title I will govern when a state or local government entity would be subject to Title I. When a state or local government entity would not be subject to Title I because the entity has less than 15 employees, the Title II regulations provide that the entity is subject to Section 504 principles with respect to employment discrimination. *See* 28 C.F.R. § 35.140. In such a case, therefore, the Section 504 remedies would presumably govern. The curious result under this interpretation is that state and local government entities having a smaller number of employees could be subject to larger damages for intentional discrimination on the basis of disability.

NOTES AND PROBLEMS FOR DISCUSSION

1. Consider the remedies available under ADA Title I, in conjunction with the relevant portions of the Civil Rights Act of 1991.

2. Compensatory relief is quite complicated in employment cases in which the allegation of discrimination involves a failure to provide reasonable accommodations. As previously noted, the Civil Rights Act of 1991 provides that compensatory and punitive damages are *not* available in cases involving the provision of a reasonable accommodation when the covered entity "demonstrates good faith efforts, in consultation with the person with the disability who has informed the covered entity that accommodation is needed." Although there are very few cases interpreting that provision, it appears that it would only insulate an employer from compensatory and punitive damages where the employer had actively engaged in the interactive reasonable accommodation process that is recommended in the Interpretive Guidance. *See* 29 C.F.R. pt. 1630, app. § 1630.9 ("Reasonable Accommodation Process Illustrated"). The good faith defense, however, is explicitly not available in *all* ADA employment cases. The Civil Rights Act of 1991 only refers to cases brought under 42 U.S.C. § 12112(b)(5). Thus, it will be advantageous to plaintiffs to bring cases under the theories of discrimination other than Section 12112(b)(5) to avoid the applicability of the good faith defense. Consider the following example to understand that strategy:

a. Are the remedies adequate?

b. How do these remedies work?

c. Are the damage limitations reasonable?

d. Should the damage limitations be interpreted as applying to a plaintiff's entire case, or to each cause of action alleged?

e. Is the governmental exclusion from punitive damages warranted?

f. Why was Section 504 excluded from the Civil Rights Act's imposition of damage awards?

Company Z is seeking to hire individuals for a typing position where the typist will always be asked to type from a handwritten or typed manuscript. In order to conduct an initial screening for that position, Company Z decides to engage in 20-minute telephone interviews. Jimmy X, who is hearing impaired, is an applicant for that position. He informs Company Z of his hearing impairment and requests a face-to-face interview, at which the employer would provide a sign language interpreter. The company says that it will grant him a face-to-face interview, but will not provide an interpreter. Jimmy attends the interview without an interpreter and is not hired for the position. He decides to sue under the ADA. How could he construct his case so as to avoid the good faith defense? How would the employer construct its case to try to preserve the good faith defense?

3. Another type of relief often awarded in ADA cases is reinstatement or front pay. Reinstatement is the presumptive relief, but front pay is awarded when reinstatement does not seem practical. For example, someone else may now be performing plaintiff's job and it would be unfair to fire that individual so that plaintiff could be re-hired. Alternatively, there may have been so much workplace disruption over plaintiff's case that it is impractical to believe that plaintiff could be successfully reinstated. Plaintiffs themselves often are reluctant to return to their former places of work after winning their lawsuits, and defendants are often reluctant to reinstate plaintiffs whom they had previously unlawfully fired. A court then may award "front pay" as a legal substitute for reinstatement. The scope of front pay, however, is difficult to ascertain. Plaintiffs will often have experts testify as to the proper scope of front pay. How long can one reasonably expect it to take plaintiff to find a job of comparable pay and stature? When there is a jury trial, some judges will refer the question of the scope of front pay to the jury because it is a subjective factual question.

When courts awarded front pay, they had to determine whether the front pay award was subject to the limitation on damages award provided in the Civil Rights Act of 1991. In *Pollard v. E.I. du Pont de Nemours*, 532 U.S. 843 (2001), however, the Supreme Court held that front pay was not an element of compensatory damages within the meaning of the Civil Rights Act of 1991, and, therefore, was not subject to the Act's statutory cap.

4. Courts must also determine whether the circumstances require reduction of an award. Reductions may occur with respect to unemployment compensation, worker's compensation, disability benefits, periods of disability, actual interim earnings, potential interim earnings, unconditional offers of reinstatement, and self-employment. Each of these potential areas for reduction of award require discretionary judgments by the court. For example, if an individual is self-employed, how does one determine earnings — by gross receipts, gross receipts minus all business-related expenses, or via some middle ground?

5. Plaintiffs have a responsibility to mitigate their damages by seeking employment elsewhere. Whether mitigation has taken place is a subjective question, particularly in view of the fact that individuals are not expected to take demeaning work in order to mitigate. What if a woman decides to become pregnant while she is unemployed and her lawsuit is pending? Is she mitigating during her pregnancy? After the child is born? What if she testifies that she would not have tried to get pregnant but for the involuntary unemployment brought upon her by defendant's illegal action of firing her?

6. The Civil Rights Act of 1991 created a two-tiered system of remedies for violations of ADA Title I: compensatory damages for intentional disparate treatment; and punitive damages for intentional discrimination "with malice or with reckless indifference to the federally protected rights of an aggrieved individual." 42 U.S.C. § 1981a(b)(1). However, as discussed above, such damages are not available in some cases involving the provision of reasonable accommodation.

The Supreme Court considered two questions under the Civil Rights Act of 1991 in a case involving Title VII: (1) whether an employer's conduct must satisfy an "egregious" misconduct standard in order for the jury to be instructed on punitive damages, and (2) whether an employer can be found to be vicariously liable for the discriminatory employment decisions of managerial agents, where those decisions are contrary to the employer's good faith efforts to comply with Title VII.

In *Kolstad v. American Dental Association*, 527 U.S. 526 (1999), the Supreme Court ruled (in Part IIA of its opinion, written by Justice O'Connor and joined by Justices Stevens, Scalia, Kennedy, Souter, Ginsburg, and Breyer) that employers need not engage in conduct having some independent, "egregious" quality before being subject to a punitive damage award. The Court ruled that eligibility for punitive damages should be determined by reference to a defendant's motive or intent rather than the seriousness of his misconduct. The Court also noted, however, that "egregious or outrageous acts may serve as evidence supporting an inference of the requisite 'evil motive' " *Id.* at 538.

In Part IIB of the Court's opinion, written by Justice O'Connor and joined by Chief Justice Rehnquist and Justices Scalia, Kennedy, and Thomas, the Court ruled that agency principles should limit the circumstances in which an agent's misconduct may be imputed to the principal for purposes of awarding punitive damages. The Court suggested that an employer that has made "every effort" to comply with Title VII should not be held liable for the discriminatory acts of agents acting in a managerial capacity. In reaching this conclusion, the Court "modified" standard agency principles under which an employer is ordinarily liable for the acts of an agent who "was employed in a managerial capacity and was acting in the scope of employment." *See* RESTATEMENT (SECOND) OF AGENCY, § 217C (1958). The Court justified that decision as follows:

> Applying the Restatement of Agency's "scope of employment" rule in the Title VII punitive damages context . . . would reduce the incentive for employers to implement antidiscrimination programs. In fact, such a rule would likely exacerbate concerns among employers that § 1981a's "malice" and "reckless indifference" standard penalizes those employers who educate themselves and their employees on Title VII's prohibitions.

Id. at 544.

Do you agree with the Court's resolution of this issue? (Justice Stevens' dissent on this issue, which was joined by Justices Souter, Ginsburg, and Breyer, criticized the Court for resolving an issue in the absence of briefing or meaningful argument. His dissent did not discuss the merits.)

7. Are compensatory and punitive damages available for a retaliation claim under ADA Title I? Does the availability of compensatory and punitive damages under the Civil Rights Act of 1991 extend this remedy to retaliation claims? The courts are split on this issue. Some courts have closely parsed the language of the Civil Rights Act of 1991, 42 U.S.C. § 1981a(a)(2), to conclude that Congress did not express an intent to include retaliation claims in this provision. Others rely on the general anti-retaliation language in the ADA to conclude that Congress intended to allow the jury to decide what compensation is appropriate. How do you think the courts will ultimately resolve this issue?

8. On May 1, 2013, a jury awarded the EEOC damages totalling $240 million — the largest verdict in the federal agency's history — for disability discrimination and severe abuse. The jury awarded each plaintiff $2 million in punitive damages and $5.5 million in compensatory damages. The judge had previously awarded them an additional $1.3 million for unlawful disability-based wage discrimination. The plaintiffs were 32 men with intellectual disabilities who worked for twenty years at an Iowa turkey processing plant. The EEOC describes the work conditions in its press release:

> EEOC presented evidence to the jury that Henry's Turkey exploited these workers, whose jobs involved eviscerating turkeys, because their intellectual disabilities made them particularly vulnerable and unaware of the extent to which their legal rights were being denied. The affected men lived in Muscatine County, Iowa, where they worked for 20 years as part of a contract between Henry's Turkey and West Liberty Foods, an Iowa turkey processing plant.
>
> . . . .
>
> Specifically, the EEOC presented evidence that for years and years the owners and staffers of Henry's Turkey subjected the workers to abusive verbal and physical harassment; restricted their freedom of movement; and imposed other harsh terms and conditions of employment such as requiring them to live in deplorable and sub-standard living conditions, and failing to provide adequate medical care when needed.
>
> Verbal abuses included frequently referring to the workers as "retarded," "dumb ass" and "stupid." Class members reported acts of physical abuse

including hitting, kicking, at least one case of handcuffing, and forcing the disabled workers to carry heavy weights as punishment. The Henry's Turkey supervisors, also the workers' purported caretakers, were often dismissive of complaints of injuries or pain.

. . . .

In addition to the EEOC's disability-based harassment and discrimination verdict, the EEOC earlier won a $1.3 million wage discrimination judgment when Senior U.S. District Court Judge Charles R. Wolle found that, rather than the total of $65 dollars per month Henry's Turkey paid to the disabled workers while contracted to work on an evisceration line at the plant, the employees should have been compensated at the average wage of $11-12 per hour, reflecting pay typically earned by workers without intellectual disabilities who performed the same or similar work. The EEOC's wage claims for each worker ranged from $28,000 to $45,000 in lost income over the course of their last two years before the Henry's Turkey Service operation was shut down in February 2009.

See http://www.eeoc.gov/eeoc/newsroom/release/5-1-13b.cfm (last viewed on May 7, 2013).

Chapter 4

HIGHER EDUCATION

A. INTRODUCTION AND OVERVIEW

Historically, many public and private colleges and universities in America were segregated by race, color, national origin, sex or religion. Others had exclusionary quotas. Many colleges, particularly those with health care and trade programs, maintained preadmission standards, such as physical, mental health and similar criteria, that tended to screen out individuals with disabilities. Most institutions simply assumed that few individuals with disabilities were "college material." With the implementation of the duty to provide a free and appropriate public education under the IDEA and Section 504, this stereotype became harder to maintain. With stronger preparation in primary and secondary school, more students with disabilities were able to do college level work and sought access to higher education. The United States Department of Education reports that eleven percent of undergraduates indicate that they have a disability, with the overwhelming majority of them indicating they have a learning disability.[1]

Individuals with disabilities have long valued higher education as a vehicle to independence and success in life. The leadership of the Section 504 sit-in in San Francisco, discussed in Chapter 1, was predominantly composed of undergraduate and graduate students from the University of California at Berkeley. Most recently, colleges and universities are learning to adapt to the surge of veterans and "wounded warriors" returning from Iraq and Afghanistan. Colleges are also coming to realize that individuals with autism, Asperger's Syndrome, and intellectual disabilities can benefit from higher education and be life-long learners. These newer populations of individuals with disabilities are likely to have profound effects on the mission and nature of post-secondary institutions.

Both Section 504 and the ADA prohibit postsecondary educational institutions from discriminating on the basis of disability. Section 504 governs all such institutions that receive federal financial assistance, nearly every college and university in America. ADA Title II governs all state funded or supported institutions. ADA Title III governs all private institutions, with the exception of private postsecondary educational institutions that are controlled by religious entities, which, nonetheless, in most respects, remain subject to the jurisdiction of Section 504.

---

[1] *See* http://nces.ed.gov/fastfacts/display.asp?id=60 (last viewed on Apr. 25, 2013) (National Center of Education Statistics). *See also* GAO Report, Higher Education and Disability: Education Needs a Coordinated Approach to Improve Its Assistance to Schools in Supporting Students (Oct. 2009), available at http://www.gao.gov/new.items/d1033.pdf#page13 (last viewed on Apr. 26, 2013).

Generally, the same principles will apply under all three statutes. However, the regulations implementing Section 504 are the only ones with provisions and requirements that expressly apply to post-secondary institutions. *See* 34 C.F.R. pt. 104, Subpart E. At the same time, for persons with sensory impairments (individuals who are deaf or hard of hearing, individuals who are blind or have low vision) attending public institutions, the provisions of Title II pertaining to equal communication may exceed, or at least more specifically articulate, the duty to provide such persons with auxiliary aids such as sign language interpreting, computer-assisted real time captioning (CART) and similar accommodations. *See* 28 C.F.R. pt. 35, Subpart E.

Except for provisions pertaining to retaliation, Section 504 protects only otherwise qualified individuals with a disability. With respect to postsecondary and vocational education services, an otherwise qualified handicapped person is one "who meets the academic and technical standards requisite to admission or participation in the recipient's education program or activity." 34 C.F.R. § 104.3(l)(3). An example of an "academic requirement" is a rule that students must maintain a 2.0 G.P.A. to remain enrolled at the institution. Examples of "technical standards" include rules that anyone in a firefighter training program must be able to lift 25 pounds, that students may not plagiarize or that students may not materially disrupt a class.

Individuals with disabilities are permitted to make use of necessary academic adjustment and auxiliary aids (i.e., reasonable accommodations) under Section 504 to meet these requirements as long as those adjustments neither represent a fundamental alteration in the nature of the academic program nor an undue burden. Similarly, ADA Titles II and III require that covered entities must provide students with disabilities with reasonable modifications.

This chapter will discuss (1) definition of qualified individual (2) admissions to postsecondary educational institutions, (3) documentation of disability, (4) reasonable modifications, (5) direct threat issues, and (6) the requirement that students participate in programs and activities in integrated settings.

B. QUALIFIED INDIVIDUAL WITH A DISABILITY

1. Generally

A postsecondary educational institution governed by Section 504 and ADA Titles II or III may not exclude an otherwise qualified student from any part of its programs or services, or otherwise discriminate against an applicant or student with a disability. The Section 504 regulations provide that "qualified handicapped persons may not, on the basis of handicap, be denied admission or be subjected to discrimination." 34 C.F.R. § 104.42(a). Similarly, the Section 504 regulations provide that a postsecondary educational institution "may not, on the basis of handicap, exclude any qualified handicapped student from any course, course of study, or other part of its education program or activity." 34 C.F.R. § 104.43(c). ADA Titles II and III are premised on similar principles.

ADA Title III provides that public accommodations, such as private colleges and universities, may not discriminate against an individual on the basis of disability with respect to the full enjoyment of its programs and services. 42 U.S.C. § 12182(a). The Department of Justice's (DOJ's) Title III regulations provide that a private entity may not impose eligibility requirements for admission that screen out or tend to screen out people with disabilities. 28 C.F.R. § 36.301(a). Under ADA Title II, a public postsecondary educational institution may not deny an equal opportunity to participate in its educational programs to a qualified individual with a disability, and may not impose or apply eligibility criteria for admission that screen out or tend to screen out qualified applicants with disabilities. *See* 28 C.F.R. § 35.130. These regulations are very similar to the principles applied in *Griggs v. Duke Power*, discussed in Chapter One.

Section 504 and the ADA require that *qualified* individuals with disabilities not be subjected to discrimination. To qualify for a postsecondary educational program or maintain good standing, an individual with a disability must be capable of fulfilling the essential requirements of the program, with or without the provision of reasonable accommodations. A disability does not entitle a student to waive an essential program requirement.

Although *Southeastern Community College v. Davis* was described in Chapter 1, the text of the decision is provided here, as it contains the principles applied by the Supreme Court to determine whether someone is a qualified individual with a disability.

SOUTHEASTERN COMMUNITY COLLEGE v. DAVIS
442 U.S. 397 (1979)

Mr. Justice Powell delivered the opinion of the Court.

This case presents a matter of first impression for this Court: Whether § 504 of the Rehabilitation Act of 1973, which prohibits discrimination against an "otherwise qualified handicapped individual" in federally funded programs solely by reason of his handicap, forbids professional schools from imposing physical qualifications for admission to their clinical training programs.

I

Respondent, who suffers from a serious hearing disability, seeks to be trained as a registered nurse. During the 1973–1974 academic year she was enrolled in the College Parallel program of Southeastern Community College, a state institution that receives federal funds. Respondent hoped to progress to Southeastern's Associate Degree Nursing program, completion of which would make her eligible for state certification as a registered nurse. In the course of her application to the nursing program, she was interviewed by a member of the nursing faculty. It became apparent that respondent had difficulty understanding questions asked, and on inquiry she acknowledged a history of hearing problems and dependence on a hearing aid. She was advised to consult an audiologist.

On the basis of an examination at Duke University Medical Center, respondent was diagnosed as having a "bilateral, sensory-neural hearing loss." A change in her hearing aid was recommended, as a result of which it was expected that she would be able to detect sounds "almost as well as a person would who has normal hearing." But this improvement would not mean that she could discriminate among sounds sufficiently to understand normal spoken speech. Her lipreading skills would remain necessary for effective communication: "While wearing the hearing aid, she is well aware of gross sounds occurring in the listening environment. However, she can only be responsible for speech spoken to her when the talker gets her attention and allows her to look directly at the talker."

Southeastern next consulted Mary McRee, Executive Director of the North Carolina Board of Nursing. On the basis of the audiologist's report, McRee recommended that respondent not be admitted to the nursing program. In McRee's view, respondent's hearing disability made it unsafe for her to practice as a nurse.[1] In addition, it would be impossible for respondent to participate safely in the normal clinical training program, and those modifications that would be necessary to enable safe participation would prevent her from realizing the benefits of the program: "To adjust patient learning experiences in keeping with [respondent's] hearing limitations could, in fact, be the same as denying her full learning to meet the objectives of your nursing programs."

After respondent was notified that she was not qualified for nursing study because of her hearing disability, she requested reconsideration of the decision. The entire nursing staff of Southeastern was assembled, and McRee again was consulted. McRee repeated her conclusion that on the basis of the available evidence, respondent "has hearing limitations which could interfere with her safely caring for patients." Upon further deliberation, the staff voted to deny respondent admission.

Respondent then filed suit in the United States District Court for the Eastern District of North Carolina, alleging both a violation of § 504 of the Rehabilitation Act of 1973, 87 Stat. 394, as amended, 29 U.S.C. § 794 (1976 ed., Supp. II), and a denial of equal protection and due process. After a bench trial, the District Court entered judgment in favor of Southeastern. 424 F. Supp. 1341 (1976). It confirmed the findings of the audiologist that even with a hearing aid respondent cannot understand speech directed to her except through lipreading, and further found:

> [I]n many situations such as an operation room intensive care unit, or post-natal care unit, all doctors and nurses wear surgical masks which would make lip reading impossible. Additionally, in many situations a Registered

---

[1] McRee also wrote that respondent's hearing disability could preclude her practicing safely in any setting allowed by a license as L[icensed] P[ractical] N[urse]. App. 132a. Respondent contends that inasmuch as she already was licensed as a practical nurse, McRee's opinion was inherently incredible. But the record indicates that respondent had not worked as a licensed practical nurse except to do a little bit of private duty, *id.* at 32a, and had not done that for several years before applying to Southeastern. Accordingly, it is at least possible to infer that respondent in fact could not work safely as a practical nurse in spite of her license to do so. In any event, we note the finding of the District Court that a Licensed Practical Nurse, unlike a Licensed Registered Nurse, operates under constant supervision and is not allowed to perform medical tasks which require a great degree of technical sophistication. 424 F. Supp. 1341, 1342–1343 (E.D.N.C. 1976).

> Nurse would be required to instantly follow the physician's instructions concerning procurement of various types of instruments and drugs where the physician would be unable to get the nurse's attention by other than vocal means.

Id., at 1343.

Accordingly, the court concluded:

> [Respondent's] handicap actually prevents her from safely performing in both her training program and her proposed profession. The trial testimony indicated numerous situations where [respondent's] particular disability would render her unable to function properly. Of particular concern to the court in this case is the potential of danger to future patients in such situations.

Id., at 1345.

Based on these findings, the District Court concluded that respondent was not an "otherwise qualified handicapped individual" protected against discrimination by § 504. In its view, "[o]therwise qualified, can only be read to mean otherwise able to function sufficiently in the position sought in spite of the handicap, if proper training and facilities are suitable and available." 424 F. Supp. at 1345. Because respondent's disability would prevent her from functioning "sufficiently" in Southeastern's nursing program, the court held that the decision to exclude her was not discriminatory within the meaning of § 504.

On appeal, the Court of Appeals for the Fourth Circuit reversed. 574 F.2d 1158 (1978). It did not dispute the District Court's findings of fact, but held that the court had misconstrued § 504. In light of administrative regulations that had been promulgated while the appeal was pending, *see* 42 Fed. Reg. 22676 (1977), the appellate court believed that § 504 required Southeastern to "reconsider plaintiff's application for admission to the nursing program without regard to her hearing ability." It concluded that the District Court had erred in taking respondent's handicap into account in determining whether she was "otherwise qualified" for the program, rather than confining its inquiry to her "academic and technical qualifications." The Court of Appeals also suggested that § 504 required "affirmative conduct" on the part of Southeastern to modify its program to accommodate the disabilities of applicants, "even when such modifications become expensive."

Because of the importance of this issue to the many institutions covered by § 504, we granted certiorari. We now reverse.

II

As previously noted, this is the first case in which this Court has been called upon to interpret § 504. It is elementary that "[t]he starting point in every case involving construction of a statute is the language itself." . . . Section 504 by its terms does not compel educational institutions to disregard the disabilities of handicapped individuals or to make substantial modifications in their programs to allow disabled persons to participate. Instead, it requires only that an "otherwise qualified handicapped individual" not be excluded from participation in a federally funded program "solely by reason of his handicap," indicating only that mere possession of a handicap is not a permissible ground for assuming an inability to function in a particular context.

The court below, however, believed that the "otherwise qualified" persons protected by § 504 include those who would be able to meet the requirements of a particular program in every respect except as to limitations imposed by their handicap. Taken literally, this holding would prevent an institution from taking into account any limitation resulting from the handicap, however disabling. It assumes, in effect, that a person need not meet legitimate physical requirements in order to be "otherwise qualified." We think the understanding of the District Court is closer to the plain meaning of the statutory language. An otherwise qualified person is one who is able to meet all of a program's requirements in spite of his handicap.

The regulations promulgated by the Department of HEW to interpret § 504 reinforce, rather than contradict, this conclusion. According to these regulations, a "[q]ualified handicapped person" is, "[w]ith respect to postsecondary and vocational education services, a handicapped person who meets the academic and technical standards requisite to admission or participation in the [school's] education program or activity. . . ." 45 CFR § 84.3(k)(3) (1978). An explanatory note states:

> The term "technical standards" refers to *all* nonacademic admissions criteria that are essential to participation in the program in question.

45 CFR pt. 84, App. A, p. 405 (1978) (emphasis supplied). A further note emphasizes that legitimate physical qualifications may be essential to participation in particular programs. We think it clear, therefore, that HEW interprets the "other" qualifications which a handicapped person may be required to meet as including necessary physical qualifications.

III

The remaining question is whether the physical qualifications Southeastern demanded of respondent might not be necessary for participation in its nursing program. It is not open to dispute that, as Southeastern's Associate Degree Nursing program currently is constituted, the ability to understand speech without reliance on lipreading is necessary for patient safety during the clinical phase of the program. As the District Court found, this ability also is indispensable for many of the functions that a registered nurse performs.

Respondent contends nevertheless that § 504, properly interpreted, compels Southeastern to undertake affirmative action that would dispense with the need for effective oral communication. First, it is suggested that respondent can be given individual supervision by faculty members whenever she attends patients directly. Moreover, certain required courses might be dispensed with altogether for respondent. It is not necessary, she argues, that Southeastern train her to undertake all the tasks a registered nurse is licensed to perform. Rather, it is sufficient to make § 504 applicable if respondent might be able to perform satisfactorily some of the duties of a registered nurse or to hold some of the positions available to a registered nurse.[8]

Respondent finds support for this argument in portions of the HEW regulations discussed above. In particular, a provision applicable to postsecondary educational programs requires covered institutions to make "modifications" in their programs to accommodate handicapped persons, and to provide "auxiliary" aids such as sign-language interpreters.[9] Respondent argues that this regulation imposes an obligation to ensure full participation in covered programs by handicapped individuals and, in particular, requires Southeastern to make the kind of adjustments that would be necessary to permit her safe participation in the nursing program.

We note first that on the present record it appears unlikely respondent could benefit from any affirmative action that the regulation reasonably could be interpreted as requiring. Section 84.44(d)(2), for example, explicitly excludes "devices or services of a personal nature" from the kinds of auxiliary aids a school must provide a handicapped individual. Yet the only evidence in the record indicates that nothing less than close, individual attention by a nursing instructor would be sufficient to ensure patient safety if respondent took part in the clinical phase of the nursing program. Furthermore, it also is reasonably clear that § 84.44(a) does not encompass the kind of curricular changes that would be necessary to accommodate respondent in the nursing program. In light of respondent's inability to function in clinical courses without close supervision, Southeastern, with prudence, could allow her to take only academic classes. Whatever benefits respondent might realize from such a course of study, she would not receive even a rough equivalent of the training a nursing program normally gives. Such a fundamental alteration in the nature of a program is far more than the "modification" the regulation requires.

Moreover, an interpretation of the regulations that required the extensive modifications necessary to include respondent in the nursing program would raise grave doubts about their validity. If these regulations were to require substantial adjust-

---

[8] The court below adopted a portion of this argument: [Respondent's] ability to read lips aids her in overcoming her hearing disability; however, it was argued that in certain situations such as in an operating room environment where surgical masks are used, this ability would be unavailing to her. Be that as it may, in the medical community, there does appear to be a number of settings in which the plaintiff could perform satisfactorily as an RN, such as in industry or perhaps a physician's office. Certainly [respondent] could be viewed as possessing extraordinary insight into the medical and emotional needs of those with hearing disabilities. If [respondent] meets all the other criteria for admission in the pursuit of her RN career, under the relevant North Carolina statutes, N.C. Gen. Stat. §§ 90-158, et seq., it should not be foreclosed to her simply because she may not be able to function effectively in all the roles which registered nurses may choose for their careers. 574 F.2d 1158, 1161 n.6 (1978).

[9] This regulation provides:

> (a) *Academic requirements.* A recipient [of federal funds] to which this subpart applies shall make such modifications to its academic requirements as are necessary to ensure that such requirements do not discriminate or have the effect of discriminating, on the basis of handicap, against a qualified handicapped applicant or student. Academic requirements that the recipient can demonstrate are essential to the program of instruction being pursued by such student or to any directly related licensing requirement will not be regarded as discriminatory within the meaning of this section. Modifications may include changes in the length of time permitted for the completion of degree requirements, substitution of specific courses required for the completion of degree requirements, and adaptation of the manner in which specific courses are conducted.

ments in existing programs beyond those necessary to eliminate discrimination against otherwise qualified individuals, they would do more than clarify the meaning of § 504. Instead, they would constitute an unauthorized extension of the obligations imposed by that statute.

The language and structure of the Rehabilitation Act of 1973 reflect a recognition by Congress of the distinction between the evenhanded treatment of qualified handicapped persons and affirmative efforts to overcome the disabilities caused by handicaps. Section 501(b), governing the employment of handicapped individuals by the Federal Government, requires each federal agency to submit "an affirmative action program plan for the hiring, placement, and advancement of handicapped individuals. . . ." These plans "shall include a description of the extent to which and methods whereby the special needs of handicapped employees are being met." Similarly, § 503(a), governing hiring by federal contractors, requires employers to "take affirmative action to employ and advance in employment qualified handicapped individuals. . . ." The President is required to promulgate regulations to enforce this section.

Under § 501(c) of the Act, by contrast, state agencies such as Southeastern are only "encourage[d] . . . to adopt and implement such policies and procedures." Section 504 does not refer at all to affirmative action, and except as it applies to federal employers it does not provide for implementation by administrative action. A comparison of these provisions demonstrates that Congress understood accommodation of the needs of handicapped individuals may require affirmative action and knew how to provide for it in those instances where it wished to do so.

Although an agency's interpretation of the statute under which it operates is entitled to some deference, "this deference is constrained by our obligation to honor the clear meaning of a statute, as revealed by its language, purpose, and history." . . . Here, neither the language, purpose, nor history of § 504 reveals an intent to impose an affirmative-action obligation on all recipients of federal funds. Accordingly, we hold that even if HEW has attempted to create such an obligation itself, it lacks the authority to do so.

IV

We do not suggest that the line between a lawful refusal to extend affirmative action and illegal discrimination against handicapped persons always will be clear. It is possible to envision situations where an insistence on continuing past requirements and practices might arbitrarily deprive genuinely qualified handicapped persons of the opportunity to participate in a covered program. Technological advances can be expected to enhance opportunities to rehabilitate the handicapped or otherwise to qualify them for some useful employment. Such advances also may enable attainment of these goals without imposing undue financial and administrative burdens upon a State. Thus, situations may arise where a refusal to modify an existing program might become unreasonable and discriminatory. Identification of those instances where a refusal to accommodate the needs of a disabled person amounts to discrimination against the handicapped continues to be an important responsibility of HEW.

In this case, however, it is clear that Southeastern's unwillingness to make major adjustments in its nursing program does not constitute such discrimination. The uncontroverted testimony of several members of Southeastern's staff and faculty established that the purpose of its program was to train persons who could serve the nursing profession in all customary ways. This type of purpose, far from reflecting any animus against handicapped individuals is shared by many if not most of the institutions that train persons to render professional service. It is undisputed that respondent could not participate in Southeastern's nursing program unless the standards were substantially lowered. Section 504 imposes no requirement upon an educational institution to lower or to effect substantial modifications of standards to accommodate a handicapped person.

One may admire respondent's desire and determination to overcome her handicap, and there well may be various other types of service for which she can qualify. In this case, however, we hold that there was no violation of § 504 when Southeastern concluded that respondent did not qualify for admission to its program. Nothing in the language or history of § 504 reflects an intention to limit the freedom of an educational institution to require reasonable physical qualifications for admission to a clinical training program. Nor has there been any showing in this case that any action short of a substantial change in Southeastern's program would render unreasonable the qualifications it imposed.

V

Accordingly, we reverse the judgment of the court below, and remand for proceedings consistent with this opinion.

NOTES AND PROBLEMS FOR DISCUSSION

1. The factual record in the *Davis* case was not very well developed by the plaintiff. The only evidence the plaintiff offered concerning her qualifications was that she was a licensed practical nurse, with a license in good standing. She offered no evidence concerning her qualifications at trial other than "an admission on cross examination that with special training and individual supervision she could perform adequately in some selected fields of nursing." 424 F. Supp. 1341, 1346 (E.D.N.C. 1976). The district court did not appear to give any weight to the stipulation that Davis had successfully worked as an LPN nor that "she is an excellent lip reader and . . . is skillful in communicating with other people if she wears her hearing aid and is allowed to see the talker and use her vision to aid her in interpreting the speech of others." *Id.* at 1343. Given this limited factual record, it is not surprising that the United States Supreme Court deferred to the judgment of the trial court concerning Davis' lack of qualifications.

An interesting question is whether the *Davis* case would have been resolved differently if the courts had been better educated about the qualifications of individuals like Ms. Davis who are hearing impaired yet can communicate very effectively through lip reading. In making that assessment, consider the following passage from the autobiography of a deaf respiratory therapist, Bonnie Poitras Tucker, who worked with people whose spinal cords were damaged at the C-2 level and were paralyzed from the neck down. Because the tracheostomy tubes those patients were required to utilize to allow them to breathe interfered with their vocal cords, the patients were unable to speak:

> So I walked up to one fellow, a big guy who looked like he might've been a football player, and asked him a question.
>
> . . . I checked his tracheostomy tube, part of the daily routine on this ward. "Are you comfortable?" It was a question we asked even though these patients were anything but comfortable. . . .
>
> The man smiled, then winked at me. "I can't feel a thing," he said. I laughed at his sense of humor, rare under the circumstances. But no sooner had I laughed than the man began to cry. "What is it?" I asked, immediately sorry. Perhaps he hadn't wanted me to find his joke funny.
>
> "Is this a dream?" he asked.
>
> "No," I said, "I'm afraid not."
>
> "I mean a good dream. Can you really understand me?"
>
> "Of course," I said. "Why shouldn't I?"
>
> "How? Do you read lips or something?"
>
> I nodded. And then it dawned on me. These patients couldn't talk. The tube interfered with the vocal cords. I was the only human being on the ward who had understood this man in all the days he'd been here.
>
> I wiped the tears from the side of his face.
>
> [The author then describes assisting another patient, "John," who ultimately lapsed into a coma and died. The author had decided to leave respiratory therapy to become a lawyer and had shared this news with John's widow Shirley. Shirley had accompanied the author on a cookout and hay ride with their children and various strangers.]
>
> In the midst of our ride home dusk fell, and as the sun went down I lost the conversation. As we pulled up to the front of the lodge and parked under the bright lights, I was shocked to see that everyone in the wagon was crying.
>
> "What happened?" I asked, frightened.
>
> Shirley, it seemed, had told our fellow guests that her husband had just died, and that I had been his "nurse." She had shared with those strangers her distress that I had chosen to leave the field of "nursing," because I was the only person at the hospital who could understand patients like John. At the end of her story there wasn't a dry eye in the wagon.

BONNIE POITRAS TUCKER, THE FEEL OF SILENCE 116–17 (1995).

Do you think that the court's characterization of Davis "suffering" from deafness is consistent with Bonnie Tucker's characterization of how her disability impacted her life?

2. With little experience in disability matters, the Supreme Court drew upon its race-based civil rights experience, mixing in the term "affirmative action" into its consideration of reasonable accommodations. In the context of race, "affirmative action" is subject to strict scrutiny, requiring a very high level of justification. Did the use of this term with regard to reasonable accommodation reflect a confusion in the Court's thinking and place Davis at a disadvantage?

3. Do you think it helpful or hurtful to the disability community if, once she had completed her education, the state of North Carolina had agreed to issue Davis a restricted or specialized RN license, one prohibiting her from some forms of traditional RN practice such as working in an operating room? On the one hand, Davis had unique insights and experiences that would benefit deaf persons who needed medical care. Imagine the value of a nurse who was fluent in American Sign Language (ASL) at a school for deaf children. On the other hand, Davis' degree or license would have been inferior to those issued to nondisabled persons; setting a precedent other individuals with disabilities may well not want to follow.

4. The Court unanimously decided *Davis*. The decision constituted a serious disappointment to disability rights advocates. However, a subsequent characterization by the Court helped to reframe it into a more balanced interpretation of the law. In *Alexander v. Choate*, 469 U.S. 287 (1985), the Supreme Court spoke again on the subject of Section 504. The Court distinguished "substantial" and "fundamental" changes (which it called affirmative action) from "changes that would be reasonable accommodations." *Id.* at 300 n.20. The Court stated:

> The balance struck in *Davis* requires that an otherwise qualified handicapped individual must be provided with meaningful access to the benefit that the grantee offers. The benefit, itself, of course, cannot be defined in a way that effectively denies otherwise qualified handicapped individuals the meaningful access to which they are entitled; to assure meaningful access, reasonable accommodations in the grantee's program or benefit may have to be made.

Id. at 301.

In accord with the Court's reasoning in *Alexander v. Choate*, should the nursing school have been required to engage in a more individualized inquiry about what accommodations might make it possible for her to complete the essential requirements of the nursing program? (They did meet with Davis, sent her to an audiologist and consulted with the state licensing agency. They also contacted other nursing schools to see if they had any experience educating deaf nursing students.)

5. The Court held in *Davis* that Section 504, and thus the ADA, do not require substantial modifications or fundamental alterations in the nature of a postsecondary education program. What constitutes such a "substantial modification" or "fundamental alteration"? *See PGA v. Martin*, 532 U.S. 661 (2001). Also consider this issue as you read the cases below.

6. The definitions section of the Section 504 regulations, 34 C.F.R. § 104.3, contains multiple definitions of a "qualified individual with a disability." For example the definition of a qualified employee and a qualified post-secondary student are quite different. What is the reason for these differences?

7. Consider the *Davis* case in light of the 2008 Amendments to the ADA. The term "auxiliary aids and services" is now defined to include "qualified interpreters or other effective methods of making aurally delivered materials available to individuals with hearing impairments." The Amendments also provide:

> Fundamental alteration.
>
> Nothing in this Act alters the provision of section 302(b)(2)(A)(ii) [42 USC § 12182(b)(2)(A)(ii)], specifying that reasonable modifications in policies, practices, or procedures shall be required, unless an entity can demonstrate that making such modifications in policies, practices, or procedures, including academic requirements in postsecondary education, would fundamentally alter the nature of the goods, services, facilities, privileges, advantages, or accommodations involved.

42 U.S.C. § 12201(f).

Is this allocation of the burden of proof consistent with *Southeastern Community College v. Davis?* Would Southeastern Community College still be able to argue that the requested accommodation was a "fundamental alteration" of their program or activity?

8. Twenty-seven years after the Court decided *Southeastern v. Davis*, Michael Argneyi entered Creighton University Medical School. After acceptance, he disclosed that he was deaf, had bilateral cochlear implants, and had relied upon cued speech interpreting and CART (computer assisted real time captioning) services to be successful as an undergraduate. Argenyi requested the same auxiliary aids to allow him to follow lectures and communicate with patients in clinical training. The School refused to provide Argenyi the aids he had requested. Instead, the School provided Argenyi with an FM microphone system that transmitted sound directly to his implants. Argenyi later testified that the system was inadequate, and one doctor stated that it actually reduced Argenyi's ability to understand his professors. Argenyi took out more than $100,000 in loans to pay for CART services, but concluded that he had to take a leave of absence in his third year when the university refused to allow him to have an interpreter to interact with clinical patients.

In 2009, Argenyi sued Creighton for its alleged failure to provide him with necessary auxiliary aids and modifications. Argenyi's claims were dismissed on a motion for summary judgment at the federal district court, but that decision was reversed by the Eighth Circuit. *Argenyi v. Creighton Univ.*, 703 F.3d 441 (8th Cir. 2013). Subsequently, a federal jury found that the School had discriminated against Argenyi, although it failed to find him a victim of intentional discrimination thereby denying him punitive damages. Although the School was ordered to commence the aids and modifications that Argenyi had requested and to pay his $500,000 in legal fees, it was not required to reimburse him for his CART expenses.

In July of 2014, Argenyi will return to Creighton to complete his medical education with the ordered aids and modifications. In the meantime however, the School has filed notice of an appeal, focusing on the issue of undue burden.

How does one square *Southeastern v. Davis* with *Argenyi v. Creighton*? In his opinion in *Davis*, Justice Powell states: "Technological advances can be expected to enhance opportunities to rehabilitate the handicapped or otherwise to qualify them for some useful employment." Since Davis applied to the nursing program, many technological changes have taken place, such as the development of visual stethoscopes. Does the basic logic of *Davis*, that a deaf medical service provider would represent a threat to patient safety, still make sense? Are there other differences? Has society's understanding of disability changed? Does it help that under Section 504 regulation, 34 C.F.R. § 104.42, Argenyi did not have to disclose his disability until he was admitted to Creighton? See Admissions discussion, Part C, below.

2. Essential Requirements

Although the question of what are essential qualifications comes up at the point of admission, it remains an important question throughout a course of study. It is particularly pertinent when an individual seeks a waiver and course substitution as an accommodation. See the discussion of this issue in the second presentation of *Guckenberger v. Boston University*, Part [E][1], discussed below.

When a college and a student assert differing perspectives on whether a student is otherwise qualified, a difference of opinion may arise as to what are the "essential eligibility requirements," ones that bear more than a marginal relationship to the tasks that an individual must be able to perform with or without reasonable accommodations. These questions can become particularly challenging when the requirement is not about substantive knowledge or the ability to demonstrate a particular skill, but rather matters of personality and character, requirements that are hard to measure and of contestable importance to the mastery of a profession. Consider the following case that deals with this issue.

HALPERN v. WAKE FOREST UNIVERSITY HEALTH SCIENCES
669 F.3d 454 (4th Cir. 2012)

FLOYD, Circuit Judge:

Appellant Ronen Halpern brought an action alleging that his dismissal from medical school for unprofessional behavior violated the Rehabilitation Act of 1973, 29 U.S.C. § 794, and the Americans with Disabilities Act (ADA), 42 U.S.C. § 12182. The district court granted summary judgment in favor of Appellee Wake Forest University Health Sciences (Wake Forest or the Medical School). Halpern filed this timely appeal. Because we agree with the district court that, with or without a reasonable accommodation, Halpern was not "otherwise qualified" to participate in the Medical School's program, we affirm.

I.

A.

Halpern was enrolled in Wake Forest's Doctor of Medicine program from July 2004 to March 2009. As at most medical schools, Wake Forest's curriculum is designed as a four-year program. During the first two years, students take classes to acquire knowledge in core areas, and for the last two years, students participate in rotations in different clinical environments. Prior to beginning these rotations, students must pass Step One of the United States Medical Licensure Examination (the Step One Exam).

The Medical School's Student Bulletin outlines the seven fundamental educational goals of its curriculum. One of these is that students establish "[p]rofessional [a]ttitudes and [b]ehavior." The Bulletin instructs that to satisfy this goal, students must demonstrate, prior to graduating, their respect for and ability to work with other health care professionals, adherence to the highest standards of integrity, ability to admit mistakes and lack of knowledge, and other identified aspects of professional behavior.

B.

Halpern has been diagnosed with Attention Deficit Hyperactivity Disorder (ADHD) and anxiety disorder — not otherwise specified, both of which he treats with prescription medications. He received his ADHD diagnosis while he was an undergraduate student at Emory University, and Emory provided accommodations for this disability. Upon matriculating at Wake Forest in July 2004, Halpern failed to disclose his ADHD diagnosis, and he did not request any disability-related accommodations.

Halpern's difficulties with professionalism began almost immediately after his arrival at the Medical School and continued throughout the first two years of his enrollment. In August 2004, Academic Computing staff reported that Halpern had acted in a "very abusive" manner that was "far and beyond worse" than anything they had experienced with other students. Dr. Joseph Ernest, then-Associate Dean of Student Services, met with Halpern and convinced him to apologize for his behavior so as to "set[] a more professional standard for his interactions" with Academic Computing.

During the fall of his second year of medical school, Halpern was absent from a small group session without notice. He falsely represented to faculty members inquiring into his absence that he had given advance notice to the group facilitators that he would not be present. When confronted, he retorted that he "got more out of" a different small group session that he had opted to attend without permission "than any . . . lecture, small group, or . . . class assignment to date." Subsequently, he was late to a lecture but signed the attendance sheet as though he had arrived on time. Faculty members contacted him regarding the discrepancy, and he replied that he was already "well aware of" the issues discussed. Halpern now attributes his conduct during this period to side effects of his ADHD medication.

Halpern experienced a severe reaction to this medication during the spring of his second year of school. He first informed the Medical School of a potential problem in March 2006, when he asked to postpone his Step One Exam. After Halpern presented a doctor's note explaining that he was suffering an adverse reaction to medication, the Medical School approved Halpern's request to delay the exam until May 2006. In May, Halpern asked to delay the exam further, initially because of car problems. After the school informed him that this was an insufficient reason and that the school was unable to provide him with an alternate vehicle as he had requested, he sought and received an additional medical postponement. He successfully took the Step One Exam in June 2006.

From June 2006 to August 2006, Halpern participated in an internal medicine clinical rotation. It is undisputed his performance in this rotation was deficient. His evaluation indicates he had numerous problems, including a below-average fund of medical knowledge and difficulty forming differential diagnoses. His "largest obstacle," however, "was his frequent lapses in professionalism": He was resistant to feedback, lacked interpersonal skills, and was absent without permission for more than one week. Additionally, Halpern failed to use an electronic log system, and he resisted efforts to help correct what he insisted was a technical problem, claiming that he had "more important things to do, like see patients." Academic Computing staff ultimately concluded that he was refusing to enter the necessary data, thereby preventing staff and faculty from recording feedback on his performance. After failing this rotation, Halpern met with Dr. Ernest and revealed that he had not slept in twelve days. Shortly thereafter, Halpern went on medical leave to address the severe side effects of his medications.

Halpern returned to the Medical School in February 2007. During conversations with Dr. Ernest discussing his return to rotations, Halpern indicated that he might seek accommodations for his medication-related insomnia, but he did not reveal his ADHD diagnosis. Dr. Ernest suggested that Halpern meet with each clerkship director prior to beginning a rotation to discuss their policy regarding absences, but he noted that some of the accommodations Halpern wanted — including the ability to call out of work without prior notice if he had been unable to sleep — likely would be infeasible. Dr. Ernest explained that, like practicing physicians, medical students were expected to provide advance notice of absences whenever possible and to coordinate coverage for patient care. Halpern reports that he felt discouraged from seeking an accommodation, and he failed to submit a formal request for any accommodation. In this meeting with Dr. Ernest, Halpern signed an acknowledgement that he was on "Academic or Professional Probation" as a result of failing a rotation.

Halpern resumed clinical rotations in April 2007. From April 2007 to October 2008, he successfully completed ten clinical rotations. The evaluations for these rotations show he received either passing or honors marks in the "Patient Rapport/ Professionalism" category, and many of the comments regarding his performance were positive. But, these records also reveal several incidents of unprofessional behavior in connection with his rotations. His neurology evaluation noted he missed a required lecture with the clerkship director. He also failed to appear for a family medicine examination in October 2007 and did not respond when paged. Although Dr. Ernest recommended that the family medicine faculty give him a failing grade for this exam, they permitted him to take it at a later date. The evaluation of his obstetrics/gynecology (OB/GYN) rotation was particularly critical. The evaluator reported Halpern had difficulty with constructive criticism and recommended that he "[b]e more humble," "accept feedback graciously," and "[r]ealize that rules apply to [him] as well as everyone else."

His interaction with staff members revealed more, and more acute, problems with professionalism. In April 2007, shortly after his return from medical leave, he paced back and forth in the financial aid office for forty-five minutes stating that someone should give him a scholarship to become a trauma surgeon. The financial aid director reported this bizarre behavior made her "very nervous."

In December 2007, Halpern requested, for the first time, an accommodation for his ADHD — specifically, testing accommodations for a surgery examination. He emailed this request to Dr. Ernest. Although Dr. Ernest informed him that the school required him to meet with a faculty member prior to receiving accommodations, he repeatedly sought to receive accommodations without first attending such a meeting. Halpern neglected to produce documentation of his disability until the day of the exam; nevertheless, the Medical School provided the requested accommodations.

Halpern failed to respond in October 2008 to repeated requests from student services staff that he review the "Dean's Letter" to be mailed out with his residency applications. Several hours after the deadline to respond had passed, he appeared at the student services office, "rude[ly]" insisting that the letter contained numerous errors and expressing disbelief that the staff member responsible for the letter was not there.

Finally, in November 2008, Halpern failed to send letters of appreciation to scholarship donors, despite numerous reminders. Although typically this would not have resulted in expulsion, because Halpern was on probation due to his failure of the internal medicine rotation, the Medical School referred his file to the Student Progress and Promotions Committee (SPPC), which makes disciplinary recommendations to the Medical School's dean. A student may appeal the SPPC's recommendation to the Academic Appeals Committee, but the dean of the Medical School makes the ultimate determination regarding discipline.

Halpern appeared before the SPPC in December 2008. During this appearance, he maintained that his medical condition did not affect his ability to "perform optimally in the medical curriculum." He further asserted his belief that the incidents of unprofessionalism "were isolated" and that he had "addressed them." After reviewing his records, the SPPC voted to recommend Halpern's dismissal based on a pattern of unprofessional behavior.

Halpern appealed to the Academic Appeals Committee through a letter to Associate Dean of Education, Dr. K. Patrick Ober. Halpern wrote that he was aware of his "behavioral tendencies" — including excessive defensiveness, intolerance of others, and rudeness — which he attributed both to his ADHD and to cultural differences between Israel, where he grew up, and the United States. Halpern suggested a "special remediation" plan including a comprehensive assessment by a treatment team, participation in a program for distressed physicians, continuing treatment by his psychiatrist, and "strict probation." He also submitted letters from his psychiatrist, Dr. Doreen Hughes, who ascribed his behavior to ADHD, an anxiety disorder, and childhood exposure to trauma, family modeling, and first-hand accounts of the Holocaust. After reviewing these materials and Halpern's record, the Academic Appeals Committee upheld the SPPC's recommendation.

Halpern then appealed to the Dean of the Medical School, Dr. William Applegate. Dr. Applegate considered and rejected alternatives to dismissal, including Halpern's suggested plan. Dr. Applegate explained that he believed, in light of the pattern of behavior Halpern engaged in both before and after his medical leave, Halpern inevitably would revert to unprofessional conduct. Particularly concerning was Halpern's treatment of staff members. While Halpern might be able to control his behavior towards other physicians, Dr. Applegate worried that the incidents with Medical School staff indicated he would treat nonphysician health care providers in a disrespectful and unprofessional manner. Such an attitude would undermine the team-centered approach to health care that Wake Forest sought to instill and would have a deleterious effect on patient care. Concluding that no accommodation could adequately alleviate these concerns, Dr. Applegate adopted the SPPC's recommendation of dismissal.

C.

Halpern brought suit in the Western District of North Carolina, alleging that his dismissal violated the Rehabilitation Act and ADA because the Medical School failed to make reasonable accommodations for his disability. The district court, adopting the magistrate judge's report and recommendation, granted summary judgment in favor of Wake Forest on the ground that Halpern was not "otherwise qualified" as a medical student because demonstrating professionalism was a fundamental aspect of the Medical School's program. The court further held that Halpern's proposed accommodation — obtaining therapeutic treatment, participating in a distressed physicians program, and continuing as a student on strict probation — was unreasonable "because of the uncertainty of the duration and the prospects for success of such behavior modification efforts."

II.

. . . .

In the context of a student excluded from an educational program, to prove a violation of either Act, the plaintiff must establish that (1) he has a disability, (2) he is otherwise qualified to participate in the defendant's program, and (3) he was excluded from the program on the basis of his disability . . . . Wake Forest concedes that Halpern has satisfied the first element. His ADHD and anxiety disorder constitute disabilities giving rise to protection under the Rehabilitation Act and ADA. Accordingly, we consider whether the district court erred in determining as a matter of law that Halpern was not "otherwise qualified" to participate in the Medical School's program.

B.

A "qualified" individual is one "who, with or without reasonable modifications to rules, policies, or practices,. . . meets the essential eligibility requirements" for participation in a program or activity . . . . To determine whether a plaintiff has satisfied this burden, a court must decide whether he has presented sufficient evidence to show (1) that he could satisfy the essential eligibility requirements of the program, i.e., those requirements " 'that bear more than a marginal relationship to the [program] at issue,' and (2) if not, whether 'any reasonable accommodation by the [defendant] would enable' " the plaintiff to meet these requirements. [*Tyndall v. Nat'l Educ. Ctrs., Inc.*, 31 F.3d 209, 213 (4th Cir. 1994)] (quoting *Chandler v. City of Dallas*, 2 F.3d 1385, 1393–94 (5th Cir. 1993)).

The parties dispute whether we should accord deference to the Medical School's professional judgment regarding Halpern's ability to satisfy the School's essential eligibility requirements. In the context of due-process challenges, the Supreme Court has held that a court should defer to a school's professional judgment regarding a student's academic or professional qualifications. *See Regents of the Univ. of Mich. v. Ewing*, 474 U.S. 214, 225, 106 S.Ct. 507, 88 L.Ed.2d 523 (1985) (stating that a court may not override a school's decision "unless it is such a substantial departure from accepted academic norms as to demonstrate that the person or committee responsible did not actually exercise professional judgment"); *Bd. of Curators of the Univ. of Mo. v. Horowitz*, 435 U.S. 78, 92, 98 S.Ct. 948, 55 L.Ed.2d 124 (1978) ("Courts are particularly ill-equipped to evaluate academic performance.").

Based on these cases, our sister circuits have overwhelmingly extended some level of deference to schools' professional judgments regarding students' qualifications when addressing disability discrimination claims . . . . And we have observed in dicta that, in general, "great deference to a school's determination of the qualifications of a hopeful student" is appropriate "because courts are particularly ill-equipped to evaluate academic performance." *Davis v. Univ. of N.C.*, 263 F.3d 95, 101–02 (4th Cir.2001) (dictum) (quoting *Horowitz*, 435 U.S. at 92, 98 S.Ct. 948) (internal quotation marks omitted).

Because we are likewise at a comparative disadvantage in determining whether Halpern is qualified to continue in the Doctor of Medicine program and whether his proposed accommodations would effect substantial modifications to the Medical School's program, we accord great respect to Wake Forest's professional judgments on these issues. But, in doing so, we must take care "not to allow academic decisions to disguise truly discriminatory requirements," *Zukle*, 166 F.3d at 1048, so we assiduously review the record to ensure that the educational institution has "conscientiously carried out [its] statutory obligation" to provide reasonable accommodations to persons with disabilities, *id.* (quoting *Wynne*, 932 F.2d at 25–26) (internal quotation marks omitted).

Adopting an appropriately deferential view, we find that professionalism was an essential requirement of the Medical School's program and that, without an accommodation, Halpern could not satisfy this requirement. Throughout the period of Halpern's enrollment at Wake Forest, the Medical School identified professionalism as a fundamental goal of its educational program, and it required that students demonstrate professional behavior and attitudes prior to graduating. The Student Bulletin explicated different aspects of professional behavior that the school sought to instill, such as the ability to collaborate with others and to admit mistakes gracefully. As Dr. Applegate explained in his affidavit, the Medical School emphasized professionalism based on evidence that inappropriate and disruptive behavior by physicians increases adverse patient outcomes.

Halpern does not dispute that the Medical School's professionalism requirement is essential. Instead, he maintains that because he received passing marks in professionalism in his clinical rotations after returning from medical leave, a question of fact exists as to whether he satisfied the requirement. This argument, however, fails to take into account Halpern's treatment of staff both before and after his medical leave. We accept Dr. Applegate's reasonable inference that Halpern's unprofessional treatment of staff, in contrast with his behavior towards faculty, suggests that he would interact poorly with health care providers who are not physicians, thereby undermining the team approach to health care. Halpern's contention also ignores the instances of unprofessional conduct reflected in his clinical evaluations, such as his resistance to constructive criticism during his OB/GYN rotation and failure to appear for a family medicine exam. Although, in isolation, these may not have warranted his evaluators giving him failing grades in professionalism, the school reasonably considered them as part of an ongoing pattern of unprofessional behavior.

Halpern's own admissions support the conclusion that without an accommodation he is unqualified to participate in the Doctor of Medicine program. In his letters appealing the SPPC's recommendation of dismissal, Halpern acknowledged his problematic behavioral tendencies. He did not argue that the professionalism requirement was nonessential or that he should be exempted. Instead, he requested the opportunity to undergo treatment and demonstrate he could satisfy the School's professionalism standards. Similarly, when deposed, he conceded that his past behavior had been perceived as rude, and he stated that the Medical School should not permit him to become a doctor if he was rude or hostile.

In light of the extensive evidence of Halpern's unprofessional behavior — both before and after his medical leave — and the potential for such behavior to undermine patient care, we have no difficulty concluding that, absent an accommodation, Halpern was not "otherwise qualified" for the Medical School's program. Therefore, we next consider whether there was a reasonable accommodation available by which Halpern would have become qualified.

C.

Federal law mandates that federal grantees and public accommodations make "reasonable," but not "substantial" or "fundamental," modifications to accommodate persons with disabilities. . . . As discussed above, we find that the requirement that students demonstrate professional behavior is an essential aspect of Wake Forest's Doctor of Medicine program. Accordingly, Halpern could not reasonably seek to avoid or lessen the professionalism requirement; rather, he must show that a reasonable accommodation would have permitted him to satisfy this criterion. He contends that his proposed special remediation plan, which included ongoing psychiatric treatment, participation in a program for distressed physicians, and continuing in the Medical School on strict probation, constituted a reasonable accommodation for his disability through which he could have met Wake Forest's standards for professionalism. We disagree. For the following reasons, we conclude that Halpern's proposed special remediation plan was unreasonable on its face and, as a result, that the district court properly granted summary judgment in favor of Wake Forest.

First, Halpern's request for an accommodation was untimely. The school was not obligated to accommodate Halpern's disability until he "provided a proper diagnosis . . . and requested specific accommodation." *Kaltenberger*, 162 F.3d at 437. Halpern failed to inform Wake Forest that he was disabled until December 2007, and when he did so, he requested only testing accommodations. Even when he appeared before the SPPC, he maintained that his medical conditions did not impact his ability to participate in the Medical School. He suggested, for the first time, that his behavioral problems were manifestations of a disability in his letter to Dr. Ober appealing the SPPC's recommendation of dismissal.

We have previously observed that "misconduct — even misconduct related to a disability — is not itself a disability" and may be a basis for dismissal. *Martinson v. Kinney Shoe Corp.*, 104 F.3d 683, 686 n. 3 (4th Cir.1997); *see also Tyndall*, 31 F.3d at 214–15 (finding the dismissal of an employee for attendance problems did not constitute discrimination, even if her disability caused her absences); *Little v. FBI*, 1 F.3d 255, 259 (4th Cir.1993) (holding that employee could be terminated for intoxication, although it was related to alcoholism, a disability). By the time Halpern requested that the Medical School implement his special remediation plan, he had already engaged in numerous unprofessional acts that warranted his dismissal, including acting abusively towards staff, multiple unexcused absences, repeated failure to meet deadlines, and tardiness. Thus, Halpern sought not a disability accommodation, but "a second chance to better control [his] treatable medical condition." *Hill v. Kan. City Area Transp. Auth.*, 181 F.3d 891, 894 (8th Cir.1999). This, however, "is not a cause of action under the ADA." *Id.* A school, if informed that a student has a disability with behavioral manifestations, may be obligated to make accommodations to help the student avoid engaging in misconduct. But, the law does not require the school to ignore misconduct that has occurred because the student subsequently asserts it was the result of a disability. Halpern's argument that he was owed an opportunity to continue at the Medical School and correct his misbehavior is, therefore, without merit.

Second, the indefinite duration and uncertain likelihood of success of Halpern's proposed accommodation renders it unreasonable. In *Myers v. Hose*, 50 F.3d 278 (4th Cir.1995), we held that the Rehabilitation Act and ADA do not require an employer to give a disabled employee "an indefinite period of time to correct [a] disabling condition" that renders him unqualified. *Id.* at 280. The plaintiff in *Myers* had worked as a bus driver until health problems prevented him from passing mandatory physical examinations. *See id.* at 280–81. After his forced retirement, he filed suit, arguing that federal disability laws compelled his employer to provide a grace period to treat his medical conditions. *Id.* at 282. We rejected this accommodation as unreasonable because it required the employer "to wait indefinitely" for an uncertain cure. *Id.* at 283.

A "reasonable accommodation," we declared, "is by its terms most logically construed as that which presently, or in the immediate future, enables the employee to perform the essential functions of the job in question." *Id.*

Likewise, the Rehabilitation Act and ADA do not obligate a school to permit a student to continue in an educational program with the hope that at some unknown time in the future he will be able to satisfy the program's essential requirements. At the time Halpern proposed the special remediation plan, he had already delayed his graduation by one year due to his medical leave, and he was seeking to further extend his medical education to have an opportunity to demonstrate his ability to behave professionally. Neither Halpern nor his expert could specify a time at which his treatment would be complete; indeed, they acknowledged there was no guarantee Halpern's treatment plan would be successful. Consequently, it was unreasonable to demand that Wake Forest wait to determine if and when the plan would enable Halpern to meet its professionalism standards.

Finally, we reject Halpern's argument that even if his proposed accommodation was unreasonable, Wake Forest violated the ADA by failing to engage in an "interactive process to identify a reasonable accommodation." *Haneke v. Mid-Atl. Capital Mgmt.*, 131 Fed.Appx. 399, 400 (4th Cir.2005) (per curiam). An interactive effort to identify an accommodation would not have corrected the untimeliness of Halpern's request or erased his record of prior misconduct. Dr. Applegate's affidavit indicates that he carefully considered alternatives to dismissal, but, because Halpern had consistently reverted to unprofessional conduct even after the Medical School's officials attempted to intervene, he was unable to identify any accommodation that could ensure Halpern would not engage in such behavior as a practicing physician. Thus, he concluded that all possible accommodations permitting Halpern to remain in the program would be unreasonable because they would allow Halpern to graduate with a medical degree.

We disagree with Halpern's contention that this conclusion reflects stereotypes that persons who experience depression or anxiety disorders are unable to change or modify their behavior. We believe, instead, that Dr. Applegate's decision was based on a careful consideration of Halpern's student record and, in particular, the fact that, despite numerous attempts by Medical School faculty to assist Halpern in rectifying his conduct, he continually lapsed into problematic practices. Although Halpern failed se his ADHD diagnosis until December 2007 and did not request accommodations for behavioral manifestations of his disability until after the SPPC recommended his dismissal, the Medical School made significant efforts throughout the period of Halpern's enrollment to help him satisfy its academic and professional standards. The record shows that Dr. Ernest, in his role as Associate Dean of Student Services, often interceded when Halpern had an altercation or incident with faculty or staff and attempted to counsel Halpern on appropriate behavior. In addition, the School granted Halpern the medical leave and testing accommodations that he requested. Despite these efforts, Halpern's lack of professionalism remained an issue. Where a professional school has reasonably determined based on an identifiable pattern of prior conduct that a student is unfit to join his chosen profession, federal law does not obligate the school to allow that student to remain in and graduate from its educational program. As the evidence in the record amply justifies Dr. Applegate's conclusion, we find that the Medical School did not violate the Rehabilitation Act or the ADA.

III.

Because, with or without reasonable accommodations, Halpern is unqualified for Wake Forest's Doctor of Medicine program, we affirm the district court's grant of summary judgment.

NOTES AND PROBLEMS FOR DISCUSSION

1. Do you agree with the court, that Halpern's proposed accommodations were inherently unreasonable and their prospective effect too speculative? What harms would have come from giving them a try?

2. Do you think Halpern might have defeated the motion for summary judgment if:

a. he had asked for an accommodation as soon as he learned that the medical school faculty found his conduct objectionable,

b. he had been studying to be a physical education teacher rather than a doctor, or

c. the defendant entity had been an employer rather than a college or university?

3. What do you think is the best way for courts to balance deference to academic decision-making and their duty to provide a meaningful forum for implementing anti-discrimination statutes? *See Wynne v. Tufts University School of Medicine*, 976 F.2d 791 (1st Cir. 1992), *cert. denied*, 507 U.S. 1030 (1993); *Guckenberger v. Boston University*, 974 F. Supp. 106 (D. Mass. 1997); *Zukle v. Regents of the University of California*, 166 F.3d 1041 (9th Cir. 1999); *Wong v. Regents of University of California*, 192 F.3d 807 (9th Cir. 1999); *Button v. Board of Regents of University and Community College System of Nevada*, 289 F.2d 964 (9th Cir. 2008).

4. Students and universities often disagree about whether a student is "qualified." Consider this fact pattern:

> Carrie Johnson is a student with dyslexia who was admitted into defendant's surgical technologist program. She requested various accommodations include extended time to take tests, a reader to use while taking tests, scanning of course materials into the reader, and a word bank to use on tests. The reader had various functional problems and lacked Internet access (which plaintiff needed to access all of its functionality). Although the defendant provided plaintiff with access to the scanner, it refused to provide the scanning service itself to plaintiff. Plaintiff was not provided with a word bank for her medical terminology class because her instructor thought such an accommodation was not fair to the other students in the class. Whereas the other students received the results of their tests and quizzes soon after they took tests, plaintiff did not receive her results until two weeks before the final exam, and after the in-class review session had ended. When she failed the final exam in her medical terminology class, she was allowed to retake the final but the "retest" was unlike the original test, requiring correct spelling throughout. When plaintiff

was not able to attain a passing 70% score in that course (to continue in the program), she brought suit arguing that she had not been provided reasonable accommodations and had been subject to disparate treatment. The defendant moved for summary judgment, arguing that she was not "qualified" for the program because of her inability to meet the neutral requirement of 70% proficiency. *See Johnson v. Washington County Career Center*, 2013 U.S. Dist. LEXIS 161138 (S.D. Ohio 2013).

C. ADMISSIONS

1. Pre-Admission Inquiries

(a) Generally

To assist in preventing discrimination against applicants with disabilities in the admissions process, the Section 504 regulations provide that a college or university may not make pre-admission inquiries as to whether an applicant for admission is disabled. Exceptions to this rule are made where "a recipient is taking remedial action to correct the effects of past discrimination," or where "a recipient is taking voluntary action to overcome the effects of conditions that resulted in limited participation in its federally assisted program or activity." 34 C.F.R. § 104.42(c). Even in the latter situations, however, the recipient must clearly state: (1) "that the information requested is intended for use solely in connection with its remedial action obligations or its voluntary action efforts"; and (2) "that the information is being requested on a voluntary basis, that it will be kept confidential, [and] that refusal to provide it will not subject the applicant to any adverse treatment." *Id.*

The Office for Civil Rights (OCR) at the United States Department of Education (E.D.) has frequently cited schools for making pre-admission inquiries where they were not doing so for one of the two allowed purposes. This is true even where the inquiry states that it is voluntary and has no effect on admission. For example, in *Glendale Community College (AZ)*, 5 Nat'l Disab. L. Rep. ¶ 36 (1993), the school's "Admission Form" asked if the applicant had "any disability or handicap" and provided a place to check "yes" or "no." A list of disabilities with code numbers was then listed and the applicant was requested to enter the appropriate code(s). The form stated that responses were voluntary, were used to comply with federal reporting, and had no effect on admission to the school. OCR concluded that these inquiries were in violation of the regulations.

Similarly, in a case involving Gwinnett College, the Department of Justice reached a settlement involving an admissions application to a medical assistant program that required disclosure of a student's HIV status. As part of the enrollment process, the applicant disclosed that she has HIV. She was admitted to the program. On the first day of class during the second quarter, the President of Gwinnett College informed her that she would have to switch to the Medical Office Administrator or Massage Therapy program, or leave Gwinnett College. The Department of Justice brought an action on her behalf, which resulted in a settlement. In addition to providing the complainant with damages for her harm and loss of tuition, Gwinnett agreed to stop asking: "Are you free of all blood-borne pathogens such as HIV/AIDS?" *See* Settlement Agreement Between The United States of America and Gwinnett College, available at http://www.ada.gov/gwinnett-col-sa.htm. *But see College of Charleston (SC)*, 17 Nat'l Disab. L. Rep. ¶ 164 (June 18, 1999) (OCR found no violation under Section 504 or Title II where college asked transfer students and students requesting readmission to "address any special circumstances or give information you would like us to know about you in considering your application;" the college indicated that it did not ask students to include a personal statement for the purpose of getting them to disclose information about a disability and did not consider disability related information in its admissions process).

The Section 504 regulations do not prohibit a student with a disability from discussing their disability in an admissions essay. But disclosure in an admission essay is not treated by OCR as notice to a college's disabled student services office that a student needs or wants academic adjustments or auxiliary aids. Unlike the requirements that apply to elementary and secondary students, post-secondary students must initiate any request for an accommodation.

After admission, a school may request documentation, on a confidential basis, when a student is requesting an accommodation. 34 C.F.R. § 104.42(b)(4). *See also Three Rivers Community College (MO)*, 19 Nat'l Disab. L. Rep. ¶ 60 (Nov. 23, 1999) (open enrollment college had form included in the acceptance package sent to students which contained a section for confidential emergency information regarding students' past or current illnesses or health problems for official use only; OCR found that this did not violate ADA Title II or Section 504).

Typically, courts are fairly deferential in reviewing decisions of admissions committees, but the Sixth Circuit recently reversed an award of summary judgment on that issue. The plaintiff was an applicant to a graduate program and she was denied admission after disclosing she had Crohn's disease at the interview. Applying a classic disparate treatment analysis, the Sixth Circuit reversed the grant of summary judgment in light of the fact that the applicant's disability was known by the admissions committee, she had strong paper qualifications in comparison to the other admitted applicants, and she was not given clear or consistent reasons for her rejection. In the face of strong qualifications, do colleges have a duty to clearly explain to a student why he or she was denied admission? *See Sjostrand v. Ohio State University*, 2014 U.S. App. LEXIS 7868 (6th Cir. 2014). Unless the case settles, there should be a trial on her allegations of discrimination.

(b) Programs for Students with Disabilities

The bar on pre-admission inquiries, however, does not apply where a college or university operates a program specifically for students with disabilities and admits students to that special program. For example, in *Halasz v. University of New England*, 816 F. Supp. 37 (D. Me. 1993), the court rejected a claim brought by a student with learning disabilities that the university had violated Section 504. The student, who had contacted the university about a special program for students with learning disabilities, claimed that questions on the school's application form regarding the special program violated the regulations. The court rejected this argument noting that the school's application form did not require an applicant to disclose his or her disability. Instead, if the applicant wished to be considered for the special program, which was only available to the students with learning disabilities, he or she could indicate that on the form. The court found that this pre-admission inquiry was not in violation of the regulations:

> When a university operates a program specifically for the handicapped, it clearly needs to know about an applicant's handicaps before it can make a decision about admission to the program, for the program may be appropriate for some handicapped individuals and not for others. Section 504 is designed in part to assure that handicapped applicants and students are not, because of their handicaps, denied the benefits of programs offered by federally subsidized universities to non-handicapped students. None of the purposes of the statute would be served by enforcing the inquiry prohibition when a university offers a program available only to handicapped students and a handicapped person seeks to participate in that program.

Id. at 46.

Accordingly, the court held that the university did not violate the regulations by requiring the student to provide information about his disability before being admitted to the special program.

(c) "Character" Questions

The prohibition on disability-related pre-admission inquiries also applies to questions concerning applicants' mental health and known behavioral problems. For example, in *Pennsylvania State Univ.*, 2 Nat'l Disab. L. Rep. ¶ 35 (May 3, 1991), an applicant identified himself to university personnel as having been diagnosed as a paranoid schizophrenic, and behaved in a disruptive manner during his contacts with them — at times using threatening and abusive language. The university sent the applicant a letter asking for, among other things, a release of information from psychiatrists and several letters of reference. This letter was sent in connection with the university's "Policy on Pre-Admission Review for Applicants With Known Behavioral Problems," which was designed to protect the members of the university community by limiting the risk of disruptive or harmful activities. The university implemented the policy where known or observed facts suggested an applicant's behavior could endanger the health, safety, or property of university community members, and adversely affect the university's educational mission.

The Office for Civil Rights found that the policy, as administered, violated Section 504 because the university did not distinguish between applicants with disabling health conditions which could pose a substantial risk of harm and those who merely had a history of certain handicapping conditions. According to OCR:

> [U]nder current practice the University has conducted pre-admission inquiries based solely upon undocumented indications of the existence of a condition, whether or not there is actual evidence that the individual has engaged in harmful or disruptive behavior. Therefore, OCR finds that the

University's implementation of its Policy violated the Section 504 regulation at 34 C.F.R. 104.42(a) and (b)(2) and (c)(4).

In *North Dakota State Univ.*, 2 Nat'l Disab. L. Rep. ¶ 174 (Sept. 6, 1991), however, OCR found that applicants to a counseling program could be asked about past mental health treatment. The counseling program's bulletin stated that as a part of the application process, it "reserve[d] the privilege of obtaining information about the student's professional competence from qualified professionals." During the course of an admissions interview, the school learned that an applicant had received substantial personal counseling, which included three psychiatrists, several counselors, and non-traditional therapies. The school requested that the applicant grant it access to her mental health professionals in order to determine whether she had adequately worked through her personal problems to the extent that she would be able to handle the emotional, personal, and psychological issues encompassed as part of the counseling program. The applicant refused, and the school stated that without this information it could not complete its processing of her application.

OCR found that this request did not violate the prohibition on pre-admission inquiries. While the admissions interview form for the counseling program included an inquiry as to the applicant's receipt of personal counseling, it made no direct inquiry regarding a "handicap." OCR found that "[t]he purpose of the inquiry in the admissions interview is to determine whether the applicant is an appropriate candidate for the program, has the motivation and emotional stability to be a human services worker, and has adequately resolved any personal/therapeutic issues before attempting to counsel others with similar issues." *See also Conception Seminary College (MO)*, 18 Nat'l Disab. L. Rep. ¶ 216 (Mar. 17, 2000) (students preparing for the priesthood were required to submit the results of psychological and physical examinations; college used the psychological and physical information to determine which applicants met the church's requirements for service as a member of the clergy; because the college used the information for this limited purpose, OCR concluded that it would not be appropriate to proceed with the complaint); *Arkansas Baptist College*, 19 Nat'l Disab. L. Rep. ¶ 61 (Oct. 26, 1999) (OCR concluded that there is no prohibition under the applicable regulations with respect to pre-admission inquiries regarding the use of illegal drugs or excessive alcoholic beverage use).

Broad questions about past mental health history are unlikely to be allowed outside a counseling or similar program, however. Both OCR and the courts have found mental health history questions on law school and bar applications violate Section 504 or the ADA. For example, in *Thomas M. Cooley Law School*, 2 Nat'l Disab. L. Rep. ¶ 130 (Aug. 9, 1991), OCR held that a school violated Section 504 when it included mental health questions in its application. For applicants who answered yes to these questions, the admissions director requested a note from the applicant's physician describing the diagnosis, treatment, and prognosis.

Several recent court decisions have similarly held that questions asking bar examination and medical board applicants whether they have been treated for any mental, emotional, or nervous disorders violate ADA. *See, e.g., Ellen S. v. Florida Board of Bar Examiners*, 859 F. Supp. 1489 (S.D. Fla. 1994); *Medical Society of New Jersey v. Jacobs*, 1993 U.S. Dist. LEXIS 14294, 4 Nat'l Disab. L. Rev. (LRP

Publications) ¶ 220 (D.N.J. Oct. 5, 1993); *Doe v. Judicial Nominating Comm'n for the Fifteenth Judicial Circuit of Florida*, 906 F. Supp. 1534 (S.D. Fla. 1995). For further discussion, see Jon Bauer, *The Character of the Questions and the Fitness of the Process: Mental Health, Bar Admissions and the Americans with Disabilities Act*, 49 UCLA L. Rev. 93 (2001).

NOTES AND PROBLEMS FOR DISCUSSION

1. Could a law school or medical school ask on its application form, "Have you been treated or hospitalized for a stress related mental illness within the past five years?"

2. Would it be different if the above application was for a bar exam or medical certification exam? Why or why not?

3. May a postsecondary educational institution ask applicants whether they have physical or mental impairments that might limit their ability to complete a course of study? If a school does ask such questions, can it require a response? Are there safeguards the school must provide?

4. May a postsecondary educational institution conduct preadmission interviews? Would an applicant who is blind have a good claim under Section 504 or the ADA if he or she was denied admission after such an interview? What if an applicant who is deaf applied to medical school, where preadmission interviews are common, and was thereafter rejected?

2. Admissions Tests

For private colleges and universities, the topic of testing is governed directly by ADA Title III § 12189. The regulation implementing this provision, 28 C.F.R. § 36.309(b), elaborated on the scope of this responsibility. The applicable Section 504 regulations provide that a college or university may "not make use of any test or criterion for admission that has a disproportionate, adverse effect" on applicants with disabilities unless the test or criterion has been validated as a predictor of success in the program and alternative tests or criteria that have a less disproportionate adverse effect are not available. 34 C.F.R. § 104.42(b). Admissions tests must be selected and administered so as to "best ensure" that when a test is administered to an applicant who has impaired sensory, manual, or speaking skills, the test does not reflect those impaired skills, but actually measures the applicant's aptitude or achievement level. *Id.* With regard to individuals with disabilities that impair sensory, manual, or speaking skills, very similar "best ensure" language is found in the Section 504 regulations: 34 C.F.R. § 104.42(b) (admissions examinations); 34 C.F.R. 104.44(c) (course examinations). This topic is discussed extensively below, at Part [E][5].

NOTES AND PROBLEMS FOR DISCUSSION

1. May a postsecondary educational institution receiving a flagged test ask an applicant why his or her test was taken under non-standard conditions or what accommodations were provided? May the educational institution ignore or devalue the

scores of applicants who took such tests under non-standard conditions (*i.e.*, with accommodations)? *Compare SUNY Health Science Center at Brooklyn College of Medicine*, 5 Nat'l Disab. L. Rep. (LRP Publications) ¶ 77 (1993) (OCR emphasized that schools may not give different weight to standardized tests given under non-standard conditions), *with Duke Univ*, 4 Nat'l Disab. L. Rep. (LRP Publications) ¶ 87 (1993) (OCR stated it would "not hold a postsecondary education institution in noncompliance for using test scores indicating that the test was taken under nonstandard conditions, so long as the test score is not the only criterion used for admission, and a person with a disability is not denied admission because the person with a disability took the test under nonstandard testing conditions"). For a discussion of the "stigma" of flagging, see Diana C. Pullin & Kevin J. Heaney, *The Use of "Flagged" Test Scores in College and University Admissions: Issues and Implications Under Section 504 of the Rehabilitation Act and the Americans with Disabilities Act*, 23 J.C. & U.L. 797 (1997).

2. In *Halasz v. University of New England*, 816 F. Supp. 37 (D. Me. 1993), the court rejected a challenge to the use of standardized tests in the admissions process. The applicant objected to a university's use of the SAT in evaluating his admission, pointing to a regulation prohibiting the use of any tests or criteria for admission which have a disproportionate, adverse effect on handicapped persons unless they have been validated as a predictor of success in the education program and alternate tests which have less disproportionate, adverse effects are shown not to be available. 34 C.F.R. § 104.42(b)(2). The court found no violation of this regulation because the SAT's availability in special formats for the disabled showed it did not have a disproportionate, adverse effect on persons with disabilities. 816 F. Supp. at 42 n.6. The LSAT survived a similar complaint. *See Mallett v. Marquette Univ*, 65 F.3d 170 (Table), 1995 U.S. App. LEXIS 24324, at *7–*8 (7th Cir. Aug. 24, 1995).

D. DOCUMENTATION OF DISABILITY

One problem faced by many individuals seeking accommodations on admissions exams or post-admissions accommodations has been the extensive documentation that the applicant finds unreasonable, especially if the individual was already assessed or evaluated and classified as disabled under the IDEA or Section 504 and educated under the terms of an IEP or 504 plan. This documentation issue is discussed in Chapter Two. In part, in response to years of standardized testing and entities nonetheless rejecting the adequacy of applicant documentation, DOJ has promulgated regulations under Title III to ease the burden on applicants. In its explanation of the new regulations, DOJ noted that the same requirements should also apply to testing provided under Title II. *See* Title III Regulation 2010 Guidance and Section-by-Section Analysis for Section 36.309.

DOJ added the following language to its Title III testing regulations:

> (1) Any private entity offering an examination covered by this section must assure that —
>
> . . .

(iv) Any request for documentation, if such documentation is required, is reasonable and limited to the need for the modification, accommodation, or auxiliary aid or service requested.

(v) When considering requests for modifications, accommodations, or auxiliary aids or services, the entity gives considerable weight to documentation of past modifications, accommodations, or auxiliary aids or services received in similar testing situations, as well as such modifications, accommodations, or related aids and services provided in response to an Individualized Education Program (IEP) provided under the Individuals with Disabilities Education Act or a plan describing services provided pursuant to section 504 of the Rehabilitation Act of 1973, as amended (often referred to as a Section 504 Plan).

28 C.F.R. § 36.309(b).

An applicant to a postsecondary educational institution may always voluntarily disclose a disability and ask that it be considered in the admissions determination. Further, once accepted, students who wish to receive accommodations or adjustments for their disabilities will have to identify the disability and the functional limitations associated with the disability. It is also preferable to list proposed accommodations and explain how they are related to the identified functional limitations. The educational institution may require documentation of the disability, as provided in section 36.309. Unlike students in the public elementary and secondary school setting, it is the responsibility of applicants to provide such documentation at their own expense.

OCR and the courts have been supportive of, or at least reluctant to second-guess, reasonable documentation requests of post-secondary institutions. Only time will tell whether the new Title III regulations and guidance which references Title II will lead to more activity by OCR, DOJ and others to challenge rigorous documentation requirements. Nonetheless, there have been a few instances where OCR and the courts have decided that unnecessarily burdensome requirements were being imposed as a pretext for discrimination. An important example is found in the case of *Guckenberger v. Boston University*, 974 F. Supp. 106 (D. Mass. 1997). *Guckenberger* was brought by Disability Rights Advocates on behalf of a number of students with learning disabilities who were attending Boston University (BU), when they found that its new President, Jon Wesling, an individual with a reputation for a hostility toward accommodating such students, suddenly imposed newer and stricter documentation requirements. The decision of the court in *Guckenburger* is particularly interesting because with regard to documentation requirements, it is very disposed to the students' claims. With regard to their claim that it is discriminatory to deny them certain course substitutions as an accommodation, a matter that more directly implicates questions of fundamental alteration and academic freedom, the court is disposed to the claims of the University. A portion of the court's decision pertaining to documentation is excerpted below.

GUCKENBERGER v. BOSTON UNIVERSITY
974 F. Supp. 106 (D. Mass. 1997)

Saris, District Judge.

. . . .

BU's eligibility requirements for receiving such accommodations are summarized as follows:

> (1) Learning-disabled students must be tested for a learning disorder by a physician, licensed clinical psychologist or a person with a doctorate degree in neuropsychology, educational or child psychology, or another appropriate specialty. The evaluator must have at least three year's experience in diagnosing learning disorders.
>
> (2) Documentation must be current, as it is recognized by BU for only three years after the date of the evaluation. A learning-disabled student whose documentation is too old at the time he matriculates, or whose documentation "expires" during his time at BU, must be reevaluated (including retesting). If retesting is deemed unnecessary by the student's evaluator, the evaluator is required to fill in a form explaining why it is not "medically necessary."

IX. *Learning Disorders, ADD, and ADHD — A Primer*

Seven expert witnesses testified at trial about the nature, diagnosis, and accommodation of the conditions known as learning disorders, ADD, and ADHD. . . .

A. *The Disabilities*

1. *Dyslexia*

Dyslexia has been traditionally defined as an "unexpected difficulty learning to read despite intelligence, motivation and education." . . .

. . . A dyslexic's ability to break down written words into their basic linguistic units is impaired. However, her higher-level cognitive comprehension abilities — vocabulary, reasoning, concept formation, and general intelligence — may remain intact despite the deficit in phonological processing. About 80 percent of people with learning disabilities have dyslexia. If an individual has a learning disability that makes phonological processing difficult, that individual will have a difficulty with any aspect of learning that involves language, including the acquisition of proficiency in a foreign language.

2. *Attention Deficit Disorder ("ADD")/Attention Deficit Hyperactivity Disorder ("ADHD")*

ADD and ADHD, as described in volume four of the *Diagnostical Statistical Manual* of the American Psychiatric Association ("DSM-IV"), have the following diagnostic feature: "a persistent pattern of inattention and/or hyperactivity-impulsivity that is more frequent and severe than is typically observed in individuals at a comparable level of development." . . . Although ADD and ADHD may interfere with a student's ability to perform effectively, they are not technically learning disabilities, in that the person's ability to acquire basic academic skills is not compromised.

. . . .

C. *Possibility for Change*

Once diagnosed, learning disorders and ADD/ADHD have significantly different possibilities of change or remission . . . . [S]pecific learning disorders do not disappear over time. . . .

. . . .

CONCLUSIONS OF LAW

I. *Discrimination Claims under the ADA and Section 504*

The plaintiff class claims that BU discriminates against students with learning disabilities in violation of the Americans with Disabilities Act ("ADA"), and the Rehabilitation Act of 1973 ("Section 504").

A. *The Laws*

The ADA and Section 504 specifically prohibit discrimination against the handicapped, not just based on invidious "affirmative animus," but also based on thoughtlessness, apathy and stereotypes about disabled persons. . . .

B. *Documentation Requirements*

Plaintiffs argue that BU's new accommodations policy makes it unnecessarily difficult for students to document their learning disabilities when requesting accommodation.[25]

. . . .

---

[25] Plaintiffs also contend that BU's documentation requirements are discriminatory to the extent that they apply to students with learning disabilities and not to students with physical or mental disabilities. Because it is fairly well established that "the ADA does not mandate equality between individuals with different disabilities," *Parker v. Metro. Ins. Co.*, 121 F.3d 1006 (6th Cir. 1997) (citing *Traynor v. Turnage*, 485 U.S. 535, 549 (1988)), this assertion fails.

1. *BU's Eligibility Criteria*

At present, students who seek reasonable accommodation from BU on the basis of a learning disability are required to document their disability by: a) being tested by a physician, or a licensed psychologist, or an evaluator who has a doctorate degree in neuropsychology, education, or another appropriate field; b) producing the results of testing conducted no more than three years prior to the accommodation request; and c) providing the results of I.Q. tests in addition to the results of the normal battery of tests designed to assess the nature and extent of a learning disability. These requirements are "eligibility criteria" within the meaning of the ADA and Section 504 because they are policies that allow the university to judge which students are eligible for the learning disability services and to tailor reasonable academic accommodations provided by BU. . . .

2. *Screen Out*

The ADA permits a university to require a student requesting a reasonable accommodation to provide current documentation from a qualified professional concerning his learning disability. . . .

Nevertheless, a university cannot impose upon such individuals documentation criteria that unnecessarily screen out or tend to screen out the truly disabled. 42 U.S.C. § 12182(b)(2)(i); *see also* 34 C.F.R. § 104.4(b)(4) (interpreting Section 504 so as to prohibit eligibility criteria that "have the purpose or effect of defeating or substantially impairing the accomplishment of the objectives of the recipient's program"). . . .

In determining whether BU's documentation requirements "screen out or tend to screen out" students with learning disabilities, the Court considers separately each of the contested eligibility criteria and takes into account the changes that BU has made to its policies in response to this litigation.

a. *Currency Requirement*

During the 1995–1996 school year, BU's policy required that a student seeking accommodations on the basis of a learning disability submit documentation that had been completed within three years of the request for accommodation. This meant that students essentially had to be retested every three years. Based on the evidence, I easily find that this initial "currency" requirement imposed significant additional burdens on disabled students. For example, Elizabeth Guckenberger testified that her retesting process took four days and cost $800.00. Jill Cutler's retesting took four hours and cost $650.00. Dean Robert Shaw testified that the evaluations could cost up to $1,000 and involve multiple visits. Cutler's tearful testimony was particularly compelling with respect to the emotional impact of the retesting because it was a poignant reminder that she was not "normal." BU's initial requirement mandating retesting for students with learning disabilities screened out or tended to screen out the learning disabled within the meaning of the federal law.

However, BU's retesting policy at present has been changed substantially to provide for a waiver of the reevaluation requirement. A recent statement of policy provides:

> Reevaluation is required to ensure that services and accommodations are matched to the student's changing needs. Comprehensive re-testing is not required. A student need only be re-tested for his previously diagnosed learning disability. The issue of what specific re-testing is required is, in the first instance, left to the discretion of the student's physician or licensed clinical psychologist. *If the student's physician or licensed psychologist believes that retesting is not necessary to reevaluate the student's learning disability, the physician or licensed clinical psychologist should write to DS to explain why. Re-testing that is not medically necessary will be waived.*

(Emphasis added). This waiver process was reconfirmed in the procedural pronouncements that BU distributed in March of 1997. Thus, it is clear that the retesting can now be obviated if a qualified professional deems it not medically necessary.

I am not persuaded that BU's current retesting policy tends to screen out disabled students. The university's new waiver position appears consistent with plaintiffs' position that the need for retesting should be examined on a student-by-student basis. This policy permits a qualified professional to evaluate the noncurrent testing data, examine issues of co-morbidity (whether other psychological or physical problems are contributing to the learning problem), and talk with the student to determine whether re-testing is desirable, thereby meeting BU's goals without placing an undue burden on the students. In any event, the waiver provision is so new this Court has an insufficient record for determining how this policy is being implemented, and whether it tends to screen out students.

b. *Credentials of Evaluators*

BU accepts evaluations and test results that document a learning disability only if the student's evaluator has certain qualifications. Plaintiffs appear to concede that a university can require credentialed evaluators; however, they argue that BU's policy of accepting only the evaluations of medical doctors, licensed clinical psychologists, and individuals with doctorate degrees is too restrictive. With respect to BU's narrow definition of the acceptable qualifications of the persons performing an evaluation, plaintiffs have proven that, both in its initial and current form, these eligibility criteria tend to screen out learning disabled students.

Many students . . . with long histories of learning disorders in elementary and high school were tested by trained, experienced professionals whose credentials do not match BU's criteria but were deemed acceptable by the student's secondary school, and are acceptable under the guidelines set forth by the Association for Higher Education and Disabilities ("AHEAD"). BU's policy raises a high hurdle because it seemingly requires students with current testing to be retested if the evaluation has not been performed by a person with credentials acceptable to BU. As initially drafted and implemented, the policy tends to screen out students because of the time, expense and anxiety of having to be completely retested, even if their documentation has been recently performed by an evaluator who specialized in learning disabilities and who had a masters degree in education or developmental psychology.

To complicate things further, BU's implementation of the credentials policy has been uneven. . . .

One caveat. With respect to BU students who have not been tested for a learning disability prior to matriculation at the university, there is no evidence that testing by evaluators with doctorate degrees is significantly more expensive or burdensome than testing by a person with a masters degree. Also, there is no evidence that it is more difficult to locate or to schedule an appointment with a person with credentials acceptable to BU, particularly in an academic mecca like Boston. This Court finds that BU's credentials requirement does not tend to screen out students who do not have to bear the burden of being *retested* in order to satisfy BU's qualifications mandate.

. . . .

d. *BU's Response*

BU argues that neither its initial or its current documentation criteria "screen out" the learning disabled within the meaning of federal law because there is no persuasive evidence that its requirements have had the effect of actually preventing students with learning disabilities from getting accommodations from the university. . . .

Contrary to BU's assertions, plaintiffs have demonstrated that BU's initial eligibility criteria actually screened out students. The number of enrolled students who self-identify as learning-disabled dropped 40 percent between the 1994–1995 academic year and the 1996–1997 academic year. Moreover, as considered in detail above, plaintiffs have established that as initially implemented, the currency and qualifications requirements were burdensome and, thus, they at least tended to screen out the disabled students. . . .

3. *Necessity*

Documentation requirements that screen out or tend to screen out disabled students — in this case, the qualification criteria and the currency requirement as it was initially imposed — still do not violate the ADA and Rehabilitation Act if BU can demonstrate that the requirement is a "necessary" part of the accommodations process. . . .

a. *Currency*

Because every expert who testified agreed that there is no demonstrable change in a specific learning disorder, such as dyslexia, after an individual reaches age 18, BU has failed to demonstrate that the three-year retesting requirement, as initially written, was necessary for students who had been diagnosed with specific learning disorders . . . .

b. *Qualifications Requirements*

BU argues that it is necessary to set a high standard for the qualifications of evaluators in order to prevent overdiagnoses for learning disabilities like dyslexia, and to ensure proper documentation of conditions such as ADD and ADHD. To support its assertion that a master's degree does not meet its quality litmus test, it argues in its legal briefs that "[a] doctorate degree is more likely to bring an evaluator into contact with new research and changes in the field. Evaluators with lower degrees tend not to have the sophistication necessary to properly evaluate people with attention deficit disorders and learning disabilities." . . . .

BU's burden is a heavy one because it must show that the more stringent eligibility criterion is "necessary" to achieve its goal of ensuring proper documentation. The record is sparse on the point. While concerns about improving the quality of documentation of learning disabilities are valid, there is no evidence that reports or testing by those evaluators with masters degrees are worse than those by Ph.D.'s, nor is there evidence that a Ph.D. gets better training than a person with a masters in the specific standardized testing that must be conducted to diagnose learning disabilities. . . .

The best argument advanced in support of a doctorate requirement is that an evaluator with a lesser level of education may be too focused on learning disabilities and have insufficient training to pick up other "co-morbid" causes for poor academic performance (like medical or psychological problems). However, this myopia concern could be alleviated with a waiver policy akin to the one followed for Nodelman which required an evaluator with a doctorate to evaluate the prior testing to determine its adequacy. In short, BU bears the burden of proving a complete re-evaluation by a person with doctorate degree or a licensed psychologist is "necessary" to accomplish its goal of improving the quality of evaluations. Because it has not met its burden, the Court concludes that the blanket policy requiring students to be retested if the prior evaluator has only a masters degree violates federal law.

On the other hand, BU has met its burden of proof with respect to the credentials necessary to evaluate ADD and ADHD. These conditions are primarily identified through clinical evaluations rather than through standardized testing, and a well-trained eye is essential for proper diagnosis. Defendants' expert Professor Klein testified credibly that an evaluator with a Ph.D. or an M.D. is more likely to distinguish between ADD/ADHD and medical or psychological conditions that present comparable symptoms. The Court is persuaded that, in regard to ADD/ADHD, a doctorate level of training is "necessary" within the meaning of the federal law.

C. *BU's Evaluation Procedure*

Plaintiffs contend that BU's process for evaluating accommodation requests is discriminatory because Westling and Klafter, who are actively participating in closed-door evaluations of student files, have no expertise in learning disabilities and are motivated by false stereotypes about learning disabled students. Moreover, the class contends that BU's evaluation process is insufficiently "interactive" and that students with learning disabilities have been denied the right to due process (as guaranteed by Section 504 regulations) because BU has failed to provide a neutral grievance procedure when a student's requests for accommodations has been denied.

1. *Process for Reviewing Accommodation Requests*

The ADA and Section 504 forbid both intentional discrimination against learning disabled students and "methods of administration" that "have the effect of discriminating on the basis of disability." *See* 42 U.S.C. § 12182(b)(1)(D); *see also* 34 C.F.R. § 104.4(b)(4). In considering these allegations, the Court distinguishes between the review process that existed during the 1995–1996 school year, when the policy was first implemented, and the procedure that exists at present.

The concerns about the nitty-gritty involvement of Westling and Klafter in the accommodations process during the 1995-1996 school year are well founded. There is no dispute that Westling and Klafter, who have no expertise in learning disabilities and no training in fashioning reasonable accommodations for the learning disabled, were actively involved in the process of approving accommodation requests at that time. Worse still, during that year, these administrators expressed certain biases about the learning disabilities movement and stereotypes about learning disabled students. Westling and Klafter indicated repeatedly that many students who sought accommodations on the basis of a learning disability were lazy or fakers (e.g., "Somnolent Samantha"), and Klafter labeled learning disabilities evaluators "snake oil salesmen." If not invidiousness, at the very least, these comments reflect misinformed stereotypes that, when coupled with Westling and Klafter's dominant role in the implementation of BU's accommodations policy during the 1995–1996 school year, conflicted with the university's obligation to provide a review process "based on actual risks and not on speculation, stereotypes, or generalizations about disabilities." . . .

BU's internally-contentious, multi-tiered evaluation process involving evaluators who were not only inexperienced but also biased caused the delay and denial of reasonable accommodations and much emotional distress for learning disabled students. The Court concludes that the implementation of BU's initial accommodations policy violated the ADA and Section 504 during the 1995–1996 academic year.

. . . .

NOTES AND PROBLEMS FOR DISCUSSION

1. Are more title II and III regulations needed to address the challenges to persons with learning disabilities or AD/HD? *See* Dept. of Justice, Amendment of Americans with Disabilities Act Title II and Title III Regulations to Implement ADA Amendments Act of 2008 (Jan. 22, 2014), available at http://www.ada.gov/ nprm_adaaa/ nprm_adaaa.htm.

2. What kinds of documentation requests are appropriate for institutions of higher education? *See* Supporting Accommodation Requests: Guidance on Documentation Practices — April 2012, available at https://www.ahead.org/ resources/ documentation-guidance.

E. REASONABLE MODIFICATIONS

1. Generally

Postsecondary educational institutions must make reasonable modifications or adjustments for qualified students with documented disabilities. However, a modification is not reasonable if it would constitute an undue burden or hardship to provide it, or if it would require a fundamental alteration of the program at issue. Although ADA Title I (employment) refers to "reasonable accommodations," ADA Title II and Title III refer to "reasonable modifications." *See, e.g.*, 42 U.S.C. § 12182(b)(2)(A)(ii) ("a failure to make reasonable modifications in policies, practices, or procedures"). Similarly, the Section 504 regulations refer to "modifications" to academic requirements. *See* 34 C.F.R. § 104.44(a). As we will see below, however, courts frequently use the phrase "reasonable accommodation."

The Section 504 regulations suggest three types of modifications that are available to a student with a disability in obtaining a postsecondary education: 1) "academic adjustments," 2) modification or alteration of course examinations, and 3) the provision of "auxiliary aids." 34 C.F.R. § 104.44. An example of an academic adjustment is a change in the length of time permitted for the completion of degree requirements. An example of a test modification is extra time to complete an examination or provision of the examination in a distraction free environment. Auxiliary aids include CART (computer-assisted, real-time captioning), sign-language interpreters, and alternate media such as a digitized book for an audio screen reader. The ADA Title II and Title III regulations provide generally that covered entities must provide auxiliary aids and services necessary to provide non-discriminatory treatment to persons with disabilities. The Section 504 regulations, because of their specific coverage of higher education, are often most useful for claims such as denial of an accommodation. However, for students with sensory impairments attending public institutions, the Title II regulations, at 28 C.F.R. § 35.160(a), which require "equal communication," may be more useful; particularly because 34 C.F.R. § 35.160 (b)(2) requires "primary consideration" of the auxiliary aid "requests" of the student. Given the very individualized nature of which type of auxiliary aid will work for a particular student with a sensory impairment, it is evident that this additional deference to the students' requests needs to be taken seriously.

Under 34 C.F.R. § 104.44(a), colleges and universities must make such modifications to its academic requirements as are necessary to ensure that such requirements do not discriminate or have the effect of discriminating, on the basis of disability, against a qualified applicant or student with a disability. Nonetheless, a college or university may deny a student's request for several reasons. First, an institution can decline requests that represent a fundamental alteration in the nature of an academic program, such as excusing a premed student from laboratory classes. Second, when providing modifications for students who do not have sensory impairments, a college may offer less costly but equally effective alternatives to the modifications proposed by students. Third, an institution need not incur an undue economic or administrative burden in providing modifications for students with disabilities. However, this defense is rarely effective, particularly for public institutions with large budgets. Fourth, colleges and universities need not bear the expense of "personal services," such as an aide or attendant. 34 C.F.R. § 104.44(d)(2). But, when needed, postsecondary schools must allow individuals, such as persons with mobility-impairments, to use their "personal attendants" for activities such as feeding, dressing, or bathing.

The courts and OCR accord colleges considerable deference in determining which modifications will or will not entail a fundamental alteration in the nature of a program. Several factors affect the degree of deference accorded a college in any given instance. Courts are unlikely to accord any deference to a college's decisions when there is simultaneous evidence of purposeful bias, when the denial is just a pretext for discrimination or retaliation. Similarly, little deference is accorded individuals in academia who reach conclusions they are not qualified to reach, such as a mathematics teacher deciding that an individual is not really disabled. Courts may also be reluctant to grant deference at an early stage in the litigation where the record is incomplete and the student has a plausible claim. On the other hand, considerable deference is accorded to institutions that promulgate well-developed procedures for considering and implementing requests for modifications. OCR encourages ongoing communication between students and colleges at every step of the modification process. Although no regulation pertaining to students requires an "interactive process," institutions that fail to engage in it are unlikely to prevail on a motion for summary judgment and may face burdens of proof they would not otherwise have to bear. This result is consistent with the duties the courts and the Equal Employment Opportunity Commission have widely required of employers.

Courts face a dilemma when a student proposes or requests a modification, the request is denied on the grounds that it would constitute a fundamental alteration, and the student alleges that the denial is a violation of Section 504 or the ADA. On the one hand, on First Amendment grounds and in recognition that courts should not make decisions on matters they are not qualified to decide, courts are reluctant to second-guess the decisions of academic institutions. *See Regents of the Univ. of Michigan v. Ewing*, 474 U.S. 214, 225 (1985). On the other hand, if courts simply defer to colleges and universities whenever they refuse to implement a modification request, Section 504 and the ADA effectively would be nullified. In a fairly consistent set of cases, the courts have concluded that colleges are entitled to deference to an academic decision to refuse to implement a modification, but only after they earn such deference. *See Wynne v. Tufts*, 976 F.2d 791 (1st Cir. 1992), *cert. denied*, 507 U.S. 1030 (1993); *Guckenberger v. Boston University*, 974 F. Supp. 106 (D. Mass. 1997); *Zukle v. Regents of the University of California*, 166 F.3d 1041 (9th Cir. 1999); *Wong v. Regents of University of California*, 192 F.3d 807 (9th Cir. 1999); *Button v. Board of Regents of University and Community College System of Nevada*, 289 F.2d 964 (9th Cir. 2008). Deference withheld: *Johnson v. Washington County Career Center*, 2013 U.S. Dist. LEXIS 161138 (S.D. Ohio Nov. 12, 2013); *Weiss v. Rutgers University*, 2014 U.S. Dist. LEXIS 80397 (D.N.J. June 10, 2014); *Palmer College of Chiropractic v. Davenport Civ. Rights Comm'n*, 2014 Iowa Sup. LEXIS 75 (Iowa Sup. Ct. June 27, 2014).

To earn this deference, courts have required that the "relevant officials" of the institution meet to "diligently" consider both the requested modification and alternatives to the requested modification, their feasibility, cost and effect on the academic program and come to a "rationally justifiable conclusion" that both the requested modification and available alternatives would result either in lowering academic standards or requiring substantial program alteration. *See* Paul D. Grossman, *Making Accommodations: The Legal World of Students with Disabilities*, 87 Academe: Bulletin of the American Association of University Professors, 41–46 (Nov.–Dec. 2001). The seminal case in this line of decisions is provided below.

WYNNE v. TUFTS UNIVERSITY SCHOOL OF MEDICINE
976 F.2d 791 (1st Cir. 1992)

Selya, Circuit Judge.

This appeal requires us to revisit a longstanding dispute between Tufts University School of Medicine and Steven Wynne, a former student. On a previous occasion, we vacated the district court's entry of summary judgment in Tufts' favor. *See Wynne v. Tufts Univ. School of Medicine*, 932 F.2d 19 (1st Cir. 1991) (en banc). After further proceedings, the district court again entered summary judgment for the defendant. This time around, on an augmented record, we affirm.

Prior Proceedings

In his court case, Wynne alleged that he was learning-disabled and that Tufts had discriminated against him on the basis of his handicap. In short order, Wynne refined his claim to allege that his disability placed him at an unfair disadvantage in taking written multiple-choice examinations and that Tufts, for no good reason, had stubbornly refused to test his proficiency in biochemistry by some other means. Eventually, the district court granted summary judgment in Tufts' favor on the ground that Wynne, because of his inability to pass biochemistry, was not an "otherwise qualified" handicapped person within the meaning of Section 504 of the Rehabilitation Act of 1973, 29 U.S.C. § 794 (1988), as explicated by the relevant caselaw.

On appeal, a panel of this court reversed. That opinion was withdrawn, however, and the full court reheard Wynne's appeal. We concluded that, in determining whether an aspiring medical student meets Section 504's "otherwise qualified" prong, it is necessary to take into account the extent to which reasonable accommodations that will satisfy the legitimate interests of both the school and the student are (or are not) available and, if such accommodations exist, the extent to which the institution explored those alternatives. . . . Recognizing the unique considerations that come into play when the parties to a Rehabilitation Act case are a student and an academic institution, particularly a medical school training apprentice physicians, we formulated a test for determining whether the academic institution adequately explored the availability of reasonable accommodations:

> If the institution submits undisputed facts demonstrating that the relevant officials within the institution considered alternative means, their feasibility, cost and effect on the academic program, and came to a rationally justifiable conclusion that the available alternatives would result either in lowering academic standards or requiring substantial program alteration, the court

> could rule as a matter of law that the institution had met its duty of seeking reasonable accommodation. In most cases, we believe that, as in the qualified immunity context, the issue of whether the facts alleged by a university support its claim that it has met its duty of reasonable accommodation will be a purely legal one. Only if essential facts were genuinely disputed or if there were significantly probative evidence of bad faith or pretext would further fact finding be necessary.

Id. at 26 (citation and internal quotation marks omitted).

Because the summary judgment record did not satisfactorily address this issue, we vacated the judgment and remanded for further proceedings, leaving the district court "free to consider other submissions [and] to enter summary judgment thereon if [an expanded record] meet[s] the standard we have set forth." *Id.* at 28.

Following remand, Tufts filed a renewed motion for summary judgment accompanied by six new affidavits. The plaintiff filed a comprehensive opposition supported, *inter alia*, by his own supplemental affidavit. The court below read the briefs, heard oral argument, reviewed the parties' updated submissions, and determined that Tufts had met its burden under *Wynne*. In the lower court's view, the expanded record clearly showed that Tufts had evaluated the available alternatives to its current testing format and had reasonably concluded that it was not practicable in this instance to depart from the standard multiple-choice format. Accordingly, the court again entered summary judgment in Tufts' favor. This appeal ensued.

Issues

The principal issue on appeal is whether, given those facts not genuinely in dispute, Tufts can be said, as a matter of law, either to have provided reasonable accommodations for plaintiff's handicapping condition[2] or to have demonstrated that it reached a rationally justifiable conclusion that accommodating plaintiff would lower academic standards or otherwise unduly affect its program. There is also a secondary issue: whether plaintiff has advanced significantly probative evidence sufficient to ground a finding that Tufts' reasons for not making further accommodations were pretextual or asserted in bad faith.

Discussion

We have carefully reviewed the amplitudinous record and are fully satisfied that the district court did not err in granting summary judgment. Fairly read, the record presents no genuine issue as to any material fact. Because this case has consumed so many hours of judicial time, we resist the temptation to wax longiloquent. Instead, we add only a few decurtate observations embellishing what the en banc court previously

[2] There is a lingering question as to whether Wynne's disability is such that he should be deemed "an individual with handicaps" within the purview of 29 U.S.C. § 794. Since the court below resolved the case against Wynne on summary judgment, we must take the facts and the reasonable inferences from them in the light most congenial to his cause. Thus, we assume, as the district court apparently assumed *sub silentio*, that Wynne suffers from a recognizable handicap.

wrote and remarking the significance of the new materials adduced below.

First: Following remand, Tufts satisfactorily filled the gaps that wrecked its initial effort at summary judgment. The expanded record contains undisputed facts demonstrating, in considerable detail, that Tufts' hierarchy "considered alternative means" and "came to a rationally justifiable conclusion" regarding the adverse effects of such putative accommodations. *Wynne*, 932 F.2d at 26. Tufts not only documented the importance of biochemistry in a medical school curriculum, but explained why, in the departmental chair's words, "the multiple choice format provides the fairest way to test the students' mastery of the subject matter of biochemistry." Tufts likewise explained what thought it had given to different methods of testing proficiency in biochemistry and why it eschewed alternatives to multiple-choice testing, particularly with respect to make-up examinations. In so doing, Tufts elaborated upon the unique qualities of multiple-choice examinations as they apply to biochemistry and offered an exposition of the historical record to show the background against which such tests were administered to Wynne. In short, Tufts demythologized the institutional thought processes leading to its determination that it could not deviate from its wonted format to accommodate Wynne's professed disability. It concluded that to do so would require substantial program alterations, result in lowering academic standards, and devalue Tufts' end product — highly trained physicians carrying the prized credential of a Tufts degree.

To be sure, Tufts' explanations, though plausible, are not necessarily ironclad. For instance, Wynne has offered evidence that at least one other medical school and a national testing service occasionally allow oral renderings of multiple-choice examinations in respect to dyslexic students. But, the point is not whether a medical school is "right" or "wrong" in making program-related decisions. Such absolutes rarely apply in the context of subjective decisionmaking, particularly in a scholastic setting. The point is that Tufts, after undertaking a diligent assessment of the available options, felt itself obliged to make "a professional, academic judgment that [a] reasonable accommodation [was] simply not available." *Wynne*, 932 F.2d at 27–28. Phrased another way, Tufts decided, rationally if not inevitably, that no further accommodation could be made without imposing an undue (and injurious) hardship on the academic program. With the diligence of its assessment and the justification for its judgment clearly shown in the augmented record, and with the fact of the judgment uncontroverted, the deficiency that spoiled Tufts' original effort at *brevis* disposition has been cured.

Second: The undisputed facts show that Tufts neither ignored Wynne nor turned a deaf ear to his plight. To the contrary, the defendant (a) warned Wynne in 1983 that he was failing biochemistry and suggested he defer his examination (a suggestion that Wynne scotched); (b) arranged for a complete battery of neuropsychological tests after Wynne failed eight courses in his freshman year; (c) waived the rules and permitted Wynne to repeat the first-year curriculum; (d) furnished Wynne access to tutoring, taped lectures, and the like; (e) allowed him to take untimed examinations; and (f) gave him make-up examinations in pharmacology and biochemistry after he again failed both courses. Given the other circumstances extant in this case, we do not think that a reasonable factfinder could conclude that Tufts, having volunteered such an array of remedial measures, was guilty of failing to make a reasonable accommodation merely because it did not *also* offer Wynne, unsolicited, an oral rendering of the biochemistry examination.

Third: Reasonableness is not a constant. To the contrary, what is reasonable in a particular situation may not be reasonable in a different situation — even if the situational differences are relatively slight. . . .

Ultimately, what is reasonable depends on a variable mix of factors.

In the Section 504 milieu, an academic institution can be expected to respond only to what it knows (or is chargeable with knowing). This means, as the Third Circuit has recently observed, that for a medical school "to be liable under the Rehabilitation Act, [it] must know or be reasonably expected to know of [a student's] handicap." *Nathanson v. Medical College of Pa.*, 926 F.2d 1368, 1381 (3d Cir. 1991). A relevant aspect of this inquiry is whether the student ever put the medical school on notice of his handicap by making "a sufficiently direct and specific request for special accommodations." *Id.* at 1386. Thus, we must view the reasonableness of Tufts' accommodations against the backdrop of what Tufts knew about Wynne's needs while he was enrolled there.

Several factors are entitled to weight in this equation, including the following: (a) Wynne was never diagnosed as dyslexic while enrolled at Tufts; (b) the school gave him a number of special dispensations and "second chances" — including virtually every accommodation that he seasonably suggested; (c) Wynne had taken, and passed, multiple-choice examinations in several courses; and (d) he never requested, at any time prior to taking and failing the third biochemistry exam, that an oral rendering be substituted for the standard version of the multiple-choice test. Under these circumstances, we do not believe a rational factfinder could conclude that Tufts' efforts at accommodation fell short of the reasonableness standard.

Fourth: Wynne's allegations of pretext do not raise prohibitory doubts about the reasonableness of Tufts' attempted accommodations or about the honesty of its assessment of alternatives to multiple-choice examinations vis-a-vis the school's educational plan. When pretext is at issue in a discrimination case, it is a plaintiff's duty to produce specific facts which, reasonably viewed, tend logically to undercut the defendant's position. . . . The plaintiff may neither "rest[ ] merely upon conclusory allegations, improbable inferences, and unsupported speculation," . . . nor measurably bolster his cause by hurling rancorous epithets and espousing tenuous insinuations. . . . Here, Wynne's charges comprise more cry than wool. They consist of unsubstantiated conclusions, backed only by a few uncoordinated evidentiary fragments. More is required to forestall summary judgment. . . .

Conclusion

We need go no further. In our earlier opinion, we recognized the existence of a statutory obligation on the part of an academic institution such as Tufts to consider available ways of accommodating a handicapped student and, when seeking summary judgment, to produce a factual record documenting its scrupulous attention to this obligation. *Id.* at 25–26. Of course, the effort requires more than lip service; it must be sincerely conceived and conscientiously implemented. We think that Tufts, the second time around, has cleared the hurdle that we envisioned: the undisputed facts contained in the expanded record, when considered in the deferential light that academic decisionmaking deserves, *id.* at 25, meet the required standard.

NOTES AND PROBLEMS FOR DISCUSSION

1. Do you agree with the First Circuit's reasoning with respect to the appropriate deference to be given decisions of academic personnel?

2. Does the affidavit submitted by Tufts on remand warrant a substantive finding different than the finding of the First Circuit in its original decision?

3. If *numerous* other medical schools permitted oral renderings of multiple choice examinations, would the First Circuit have reached a contrary result? *Should* it reach a contrary result if numerous other medical schools permit oral exams? *See Guckenberger v. Boston University*, 8 F. Supp. 2d 82, 89 (D. Mass. 1998).

4. Consider the following fact pattern:

> Robert Betts attended a state university medical school's post-baccalaureate program designed for economically disadvantaged and minority students. Students who successfully completed that program were automatically admitted into the university's medical school. To complete the program, a student was required to maintain a 2.75 grade point average. Betts received a 2.223 GPA for the fall term. He was then diagnosed as having a mild learning disability and allotted double time on his spring examinations. With the additional time, he obtained a 2.838 GPA but still had less than a 2.75 GPA for the year. (His GPA was 2.5313.) Betts, nonetheless, sought automatic admission into the medical school program, arguing that only his spring semester grades should be considered in determining whether he was qualified for admission. The university rejected that argument, and held that Betts was not qualified for admission.

How should a court resolve the issue of whether Betts is qualified for admission into medical school? Assuming that Betts is a person with a disability under the ADA, should a court second-guess the judgment of the educational institution? *See Betts v. Rector and Visitors of the Univ. of Virginia*, 967 F. Supp. 882 (W.D. Va. 1997), *aff'd in part, rev'd in part, remanded*, 1999 U.S. App. LEXIS 23105, 191 F.3d 447 (unpublished table decision) (4th Cir. Sept. 22, 1999).

5. A challenging issue that universities can face is whether they are entitled to apply their student code of conduct against a student with a disability who has purportedly violated their rules. Consider the following facts:

> Brett Rhodes was involved in a car accident that left him with substantial physical and mental disabilities. He enrolled at Southern Nazarene University, initially to pursue a degree in nursing. He documented his disabilities and made various requests for accommodations. The university agreed to his requests, and granted additional requests, upon additional documentation. Nonetheless, the University did not grant his request to receive syllabi,

assignments and his textbooks six weeks in advance of classes because professors did not always have material available that far in advance.

The biggest source of controversy arose over how much support he should receive from faculty. He believed his professors did not give him adequate support. Rhodes had many communications with one faculty member who felt threatened by some of his communications because they, for example, made reference to guns in his home. After this professor reported to university officials that she felt threatened, Rhodes "began sending [the university's disability officer] a flood of emails over the course of one day — most sent minutes from each other — containing lengthy, agitated, and threatening content."

A school judicial hearing was conducted and Rhodes was placed on disciplinary probation under which limitations were placed on his communications with staff but he was allowed to return to class immediately. Rhodes never returned to the university but filed a claim against them under Section 504 and ADA Title III.

Does Rhodes have a viable claim for failure to accommodate or for retaliation? The student, proceeding pro se, lost at both the trial court and court of appeals. *See Rhodes v. Southern Nazarene University*, 2014 U.S. App. LEXIS 1851 (10th Cir. 2014).

In Part D, above, excerpts were presented from a *Guckenberger* decision wherein the court clearly expressed its dissatisfaction with the unnecessarily burdensome documentation requirements of Boston University. Below, is the court's decision on a much more complex question, the autonomy of Boston University to cease granting accommodations in the form of course substitutions for math and foreign languages on the grounds that such substitutions would constitute a fundamental alteration in the academic program of Boston University. Ultimately, the analytical path the court followed was the one originally set out in *Wynne v. Tufts*.

GUCKENBERGER v. BOSTON UNIVERSITY

8 F. Supp. 2d 82 (D. Mass. 1998)

MEMORANDUM AND ORDER ON THE ISSUE OF COURSE SUBSTITUTIONS

SARIS, U.S.D.J.

INTRODUCTION

A class of students with learning disabilities brought this action against defendant Boston University ("BU") alleging that BU's policies toward them violated the Americans With Disabilities Act ("ADA"), 42 U.S.C. §§ 12101-12213, the Rehabilitation Act, 29 U.S.C. § 794, and state law. The Court issued its findings of fact, conclusions of law, and order of judgment on August 15, 1997, after a ten-day bench trial. *See Guckenberger v. Boston Univ.*, 974 F. Supp. 106 (D. Mass. 1997) ("*Guckenberger II*"). In paragraph two of its order, the Court required BU to propose and to implement a "deliberative procedure" for considering whether course substitutions for the foreign language requirement of BU's College of Arts and Sciences (the "College") would "fundamentally alter the nature" of BU's undergraduate liberal arts degree. *Id.* at 154-55. BU, using the College's existing Dean's Advisory Committee to consider the issue, decided that course substitutions would constitute such a fundamental alteration. Plaintiffs challenge that determination. After hearing, the Court holds that BU has complied with the order.

BACKGROUND

A. *Procedural History*

As part of a wholesale attack on BU's policies toward the learning disabled, plaintiffs alleged that BU's refusal to allow learning disabled students at the College to satisfy its foreign language requirement by completing selected non-language courses constituted a violation of federal and state discrimination law. Unlike some other portions of the case, the dispute over foreign language course substitutions involves *only* the College of Arts and Sciences and not other BU faculties. The Court rejected plaintiffs' sweeping argument that "any across-the-board policy precluding course substitutions" violates discrimination law. 974 F. Supp. at 149. Rather, the Court concluded that "neither the ADA nor the Rehabilitation Act requires a university to provide course substitutions that the university rationally concludes would alter an essential part of its academic program." *Id.* Plaintiffs did not appeal this or any other aspect of the Court's order of judgment.

Plaintiffs were successful, however, in pressing an inquiry into reasonable accommodation. Based on an administrative regulation that course substitutions "might" be a reasonable means of accommodating the disabled, 34 C.F.R. Pt. 104, App. A P31 (1997), and evidence introduced at trial, the Court held that plaintiffs had "demonstrated that requesting a course substitution in foreign language for students with demonstrated language disabilities is a reasonable modification." *Guckenberger II*, 974 F. Supp. at 147. Therefore, the burden of demonstrating "that the requested course substitution would fundamentally alter the nature of [BU's] liberal arts degree program" shifted to the University. *Id.*

The Court determined, for two reasons, that BU had failed to meet its burden at trial of demonstrating why it should not have to accommodate plaintiffs' request. First, BU's president, defendant Jon Westling, had been substantially motivated by uninformed stereotypes (as reflected in the "Somnolent Samantha" metaphor) when he made the decision to deny the request. Second, President Westling did not engage in any form of "reasoned deliberation as to whether modifications would change the essential academic standards of [the College's] liberal arts curriculum." *Guckenberger II*, 974 F. Supp. at 149. The Court's conclusion was directly guided by two opinions of the First Circuit in *Wynne v. Tufts University School of Medicine*, which concerned a request for reasonable accommodations by a learning disabled medical student with dyslexia who challenged the multiple choice format of medical school examinations. *See* 932 F.2d 19 (1st Cir. 1991) (en banc) ("*Wynne I*"); 976 F.2d 791 (1st Cir. 1992) ("*Wynne II*").

Because of BU's failure to "undertake a diligent assessment of the available options," *Guckenberger II*, 974 F. Supp. at 149 (quoting *Wynne II*, 976 F.2d at 795), the Court ordered BU:

> to propose, within 30 days of the receipt of this order, a deliberative procedure for considering whether modification of its degree requirement in foreign language would fundamentally alter the nature of its liberal arts program. Such a procedure shall include a faculty committee set up by the College of Arts and Sciences to examine its degree requirements and to determine whether a course substitution in foreign languages would fundamentally alter the nature of the liberal arts program. The faculty's determination will be subject to the approval of the president, as university by-laws provide. As provided in *Wynne*, BU shall report back to the Court by the end of the semester concerning its decision and the reasons.

974 F. Supp. at 154-55.

B. *BU's Deliberative Procedure*

The Court considers the following facts to be undisputed. *See Wynne I*, 932 F.2d at 26.

On October 6, 1997, the Court approved the use of the existing Dean's Advisory Committee (the "Committee") of the College as the mechanism for deliberating the issue of course substitutions for the foreign language requirement in accordance with the Court's order. In the course of normal business, the Committee "is charged by the by-laws of the College with advising the Dean on issues involving academic standards." (Berkey Dec. 8 Aff. P 4.) During the relevant time period, the Committee was composed of eleven faculty members of the College, including professors of mathematics, English, philosophy, natural sciences, engineering and foreign languages. [Footnote omitted.] The Committee is normally chaired by Dennis D. Berkey, who is the Dean of the College and the Provost of BU. However, Dean Berkey removed himself as chairman of proceedings relating to course substitutions because of his role in the "central administration" of BU. (*Id.* P 10.) In his place, Associate Professor of Mathematics Paul Blanchard assumed the role of Acting Chairman. (*Id.*)

The Committee convened to consider the issue of course substitutions on seven occasions. In keeping with its practice for general business, the Committee meetings were closed to interested parties and the public, with two exceptions. The first meeting on this issue was attended by Attorneys Lawrence Elswit and Erika Geetter, counsel for BU, who "set out the Committee's responsibilities as outlined in the Court's decision." (*Id.* P 10.) Also, several College students addressed the Committee at the November 14, 1997 meeting. Their involvement was directed by the Court at a October 6, 1997 hearing and was solicited through notice posted on an internet bulletin board and an advertisement published in BU's student newspaper, *The Daily Free Press*, on October 27, October 29 and November 3. (*Id.* P 7.) The opportunity for student input was also reported on the second page of a front-page story in the October 24 issue of *The Daily Free Press*. (*Id.* Ex.) Only current College students were permitted to address the Committee, and only five students did so. Among the students who spoke was Catherine Hays Miller, who had testified at trial. Neither President Westling nor his direct staff had any involvement with the Committee proceedings, and the Committee did not officially seek any other input from non-members.

The Committee kept minutes of four of its seven meetings. No minutes were recorded during the first two meetings, but, following the Court's order to do so at the October 6 hearing, minutes were kept for all but the last of the remaining meetings. The minutes are topical summaries of the discussions that took place at the covered meetings. They do not identify speakers. The Committee had never before kept minutes in the course of normal business.

On December 2, 1997, the Committee completed its eight-page report (plus attachments) and submitted it to President Westling in accordance with the BU by-laws. (Berkey Feb. 19 Aff. P 3 & Ex.) Its final recommendation was:

> After extensive review and deliberation, the [Committee's] professional and academic judgment is that the conjunction of the foregoing considerations (which we have merely summarized here) entails but one conclusion: the foreign language requirement is fundamental to the nature of the liberal arts degree at Boston University. The [Committee] therefore recommends against approving course substitutions for any student as an alternative to fulfilling the foreign language requirement.

(*Id.* Ex.)

Two days later, President Westling, in a letter to Dean Berkey, accepted the recommendation of the Committee. (*Id.* P 4 & Ex.) The completed report, along with minutes and attachments, was filed with the Court on December 5, 1997 and refiled as an attachment to an affidavit of Dean Berkey on February 19, 1998.

DISCUSSION

A. *The Test*

The First Circuit crafted the following test for evaluating the decision of an academic institution with respect to the availability of reasonable accommodations for the learning disabled:

> If the institution submits undisputed facts demonstrating that the relevant officials within the institution considered alternative means, their feasibility, cost and effect on the academic program, and came to a rationally justifiable conclusion that the available alternatives would result either in lowering academic standards or requiring substantial program alteration, the court could rule as a matter of law that the institution had met its duty of seeking reasonable accommodation.

Wynne I, 932 F.2d at 26, *quoted in Guckenberger II*, 974 F. Supp. at 148. "The point is not whether a [university] is 'right' or 'wrong' in making program-related decisions. Such absolutes rarely apply in the context of subjective decisionmaking, particularly in a scholastic setting." *Wynne II*, 976 F.2d at 795.

B. *Basic Facts Showing Reasoned Deliberation*

The Court's first task under this test is "to find the basic facts, giving due deference to the school. . . ." *Wynne I*, 932 F.2d at 27. Those "basic facts" must include showings of the following: (1) an "indication of who took part in the decision [and] when it was made"; (2) a "discussion of the unique qualities" of the foreign language requirement as it now stands; and (3) "a consideration of possible alternatives" to the requirement. *Id.* at 28. As these elements suggest, the required showing of undisputed facts refers to the "consideration" of the request by BU and not, as plaintiffs suggest, to a broad-ranging consensus of expert or university opinion on the value of foreign languages to a liberal arts curriculum.

The Court concludes that BU has presented sufficient undisputed essential facts, satisfying each of the three aspects of *Wynne*'s requirements. . . .

C. *Professional, Academic Judgment*

Having found undisputed facts of a reasoned deliberation, the Court must "evaluate whether those facts add up to a professional, academic judgment that reasonable accommodation is simply not available." *Wynne I*, 932 F.2d at 27-28. In the unique context of academic curricular decision-making, the courts may not override a faculty's professional judgment "unless it is such a substantial departure from accepted academic norms as to demonstrate that the person or committee responsible did not actually exercise professional judgment." *Id.* at 25 (quoting *Regents of Univ. of Mich. v. Ewing*, 474 U.S. 214, 225, 106 S. Ct. 507, 88 L. Ed. 2d 523 (1985)).

This standard is in keeping with the policy of judicial deference to academic decision making. The Court previously indicated that BU's decision would be given "great deference" so long as it occurred "after reasoned deliberations as to whether modifications would change the essential academic standards of its liberal arts curriculum." *Guckenberger II*, 974 F. Supp. at 149. Such deference is appropriate in this arena, because "when judges are asked to review the substance of a genuinely academic decision, . . . they should show great respect for the faculty's professional judgment." *Wynne I*, 932 F.2d at 25 (quoting *Ewing*, 474 U.S. at 225) (omission in original); *cf. Bercovitch v. Baldwin Sch., Inc.*, 133 F.3d 141, 153 (1st Cir. 1998). While, of course, "academic freedom does not embrace the freedom to discriminate," the First Circuit has observed that "we are a society that cherishes academic freedom and recognizes that universities deserve great leeway in their operations." *Cohen v. Brown Univ.*, 101 F.3d 155, 185 (1st Cir. 1996) (citations omitted), *cert. denied*, 520 U.S. 1186, 117 S. Ct. 1469, 137 L. Ed. 2d 682 (1997).

Plaintiffs attack the academic judgment of the Committee in three ways. First, they argue that BU's decision does mark "a substantial departure from accepted academic norms" because a majority of other colleges and universities — including Princeton, Harvard, Yale, Columbia, Dartmouth, Cornell and Brown — either do not have a general foreign language requirement or permit course substitutions for foreign languages. They also point out that the academic program would not be substantially affected because at BU only 15 students (out of 26,000) a semester would require such course modifications and suggest that similar low numbers of students requesting accommodations in other universities inform their willingness to allow substitutions. (*See* Shaw Decl. P 9). The evidence that BU is only among a handful of schools of higher education in its decision to deny course substitutions in language requirements is relevant to an evaluation of its decision to deny a reasonable accommodation. However, a court should not determine that an academic decision is a "substantial departure from accepted academic norms" simply by conducting a head-count of other universities. This approach is particularly inappropriate in the protean area of a liberal arts education. The liberal arts curriculum cannot be fit into a cookie cutter mold, unlike the medical school curriculum in *Wynne*, where no one disputed that mastery of biochemistry was necessary.

The *Wynne* decisions indicate that the appropriate question is whether BU's decision is "rationally justifiable" rather than the only possible conclusion it could have reached or other universities have reached. *See Wynne I*, 932 F.2d at 26. In *Wynne II*, the First Circuit endorsed the professional, academic judgment of Tufts Medical School officials, who had concluded after deliberation that allowing a requested accommodation "would require substantial program alterations, result in lowering academic standards, and devalue Tufts' end product. . . ." *Wynne II*, 976 F.2d at 795; *see also Bercovitch*, 133 F.3d at 154 ("The law does not require an academic program to compromise its integral criteria to accommodate a disabled individual."). The Court of Appeals there rejected a similar argument that at least one other medical school and a national testing service had permitted oral renderings of multiple-choice examinations. 976 F.2d at 795. Instead, because "Tufts decided, rationally if not inevitably, that no further accommodation could be made without imposing an undue (and injurious) hardship on the academic program," *Wynne II*, 976 F.2d at 795, the First Circuit ruled as a matter of law that the medical school had met its burden under the ADA.

This Court concludes that so long as an academic institution rationally, without pretext, exercises its deliberate professional judgment not to permit course substitutions for an academic requirement in a liberal arts curriculum, the ADA does not authorize the courts to intervene even if a majority of other comparable academic institutions disagree.

Second, plaintiffs challenge the substance of the Committee's conclusions and analysis. Specifically, they argue that there are sixteen "material facts" in dispute, such as the following: (1) the two year (four semester) foreign language requirement is not "sufficient to permit the vast majority of students to read major works of literature in a foreign language," thus debunking the *Madame Bovary* line of argument as involving an imperfect logic, not an imperfect tense; (2) a "foreign language requirement does not provide students with educational benefits regarding a foreign culture"; (3) there is "no particular thinking process involved in learning a foreign language that is distinct from any other type of learning"; and (4) BU's "foreign language requirement does not address ethnocentrism among students."

In particular, Naomi S. Baron, a chair of the Department of Language and Foreign Studies at American University, criticized the foreign language "mystique" on plaintiffs' behalf. Nevertheless, even Professor Baron acknowledges that many academic and governmental institutions in recent years have espoused foreign language requirements, indicating the existence of a genuine academic dispute on this issue. *See*

Naomi S. Baron, *Rationales and Rationalizations in Foreign Language Requirements*, Liberal Educ., Fall 1982, at 181. For example, she cites a study commissioned by then President Carter (*Strength through Wisdom*, 1979) which suggested that foreign language study was in the national interest. *Id.* at 184. Many colleges and universities (like Harvard and Haverford) have required proficiency in foreign languages based on the rationale that they deepen the students' appreciation of their own language, promote mental discipline, improve understanding between languages and thought, and make students less ethnocentric. *Id.* at 186-88. While plaintiffs have submitted affidavits of Professor Baron and other academics who strongly disagree with BU's conclusions and label them as "trite," "idealistic" or "cliches," these issues raise the kinds of academic decisions that universities — not courts — are entrusted with making.

Plaintiffs' final mode of attack is to argue that BU's report does not meet the minimum accepted standards of academic study and inquiry, especially in the Committee's not having referred to outside experts. Prior to the initiation of this litigation, President Westling did not substantially consult experts in learning disabilities or engage in any deliberative process in reaching his decision to preclude course substitutions. In *Guckenberger II*, I held that a decision involving reasonable accommodations must involve more than an *ipse dixit* or blind adherence to the status quo. *See* 974 F. Supp. at 149. However, the Committee's deliberative process occurred after a lengthy trial in which experts in the field of learning disabilities testified about the difficulty which students with learning disabilities experience in their efforts to gain proficiency in a foreign language. This testimony summarized in *Guckenberger II* was available to the members of the Committee. In light of the tight timetable which the litigation imposed on the Committee, and the expert evidence in prior proceedings, I am unpersuaded that further academic study (like a "longitudinal" study) would have refined or altered the decision-making process, which ultimately involved a qualitative evaluation: What is essential to a liberal arts education?

Plaintiffs' vigorous attacks on BU's submission generally overstate the Court's level of scrutiny at this stage of litigation. My opinion as to the value of foreign languages in a liberal arts curriculum is not material so long as the requirements of *Wynne* have been met. Despite plaintiffs' attempts to pull truly academic policy debates into the courtroom, the facts "essential" to this order are actually undisputed: BU implemented a deliberative procedure by which it considered in a timely manner both the importance of the foreign language requirement to this College and the feasibility of alternatives. Plaintiffs' argument that the procedure should have been more extensive and inclusive — effectively, more like a legal proceeding — does not have any support in the *Wynne* opinions.

BU's deliberations and conclusions pass muster under *Wynne*. The Court has no cause to doubt the academic qualifications and professionalism of the eleven members of the Committee. There is no evidence that the Committee's decision was mere lip service to the Court's order or was tainted by pretext, insincerity, or bad faith, beyond plaintiffs' unsubstantiated speculation that President Westling's bias infected the Committee. *See Wynne II*, 976 F.2d at 796 (placing burden on plaintiffs "to produce specific facts" of pretext). The Report is rationally premised on the Committee's conclusion that the liberal arts degree is "in no sense a technical or vocational degree" like other degrees and that, in its view, the foreign language requirement "has a primarily intellectual, non-utilitarian purpose." (Report at 5.) With the justifiable belief in mind that this decision could not be made empirically, the Committee concluded that "knowledge of a foreign language is one of the keys to opening the door to the classics and so to liberal learning. It is not the only key, but we do judge it as indispensable." (*Id.* at 7.)

The Court concludes that the Committee's judgment that "a person holding a liberal arts degree from Boston University ought to have some experience studying a foreign language," (*id.*), is "rationally justifiable" and represents a professional judgment with which the Court should not interfere. Therefore, the Court concludes as a matter of law that BU has not violated its duty to provide reasonable accommodations to learning disabled students under the ADA by refusing to provide course substitutions.

ORDER

Defendant Boston University has proven that it complied with paragraph two of the Court's order of August 15, 1997. *See Guckenberger v. Boston Univ.*, 974 F. Supp. 106, 154-55 (D. Mass. 1997).

NOTES AND PROBLEMS FOR DISCUSSION

1. In an earlier decision involving the *Guckenberger* case, *Guckenberger v. Boston Univ.*, 957 F. Supp. 306 (D. Mass. 1997), the plaintiffs alleged that two speeches by Boston University's president — in which the president referred to students with learning disabilities as " 'a plague,' and an indication of a 'silent genetic catastrophe' " — and the University's new accommodations policy created a hostile educational environment (or hostile learning environment) for students with learning disabilities in violation of the ADA and Section 504. 957 F. Supp. at 312. The court held that a valid claim for creation of a hostile learning environment can exist if a plaintiff can show that he or she was harassed on the basis of his or her disability and that the harassment was "sufficiently severe or pervasive that it alters the conditions of her education and creates an abusive educational environment." 957 F. Supp. at 314. The court found that the actions of Boston University and its president did not rise to that level. The court characterized the president's speeches as "critiques of the learning disabilities movement" as opposed to pervasively hostile expressions, and noted that the speeches occurred off-campus.

Under what circumstances do you think a plaintiff would prevail on an action for creation of a hostile learning environment in violation of the ADA and Section 504?

Why do you suppose that President Wesling was not a member of the fundamental alteration committee reviewed by the court? Why do you suppose that the committee included individuals who did not teach a foreign language?

Today, Boston University has an office to work with students with learning disabilities. *See* http://www.bu.edu/disability/services/lds.html. Why this apparent change in philosophy about such students?

2. Disputes frequently arise as to whether it would constitute a reasonable modification to waive or substitute certain course requirements for students with disabilities. Consider the following problems:

a. Would it constitute a reasonable modification of a medical school program to allow a student who is blind to substitute another course for a required radiology course?

b. Would it constitute a reasonable modification of a liberal arts degree program to eliminate a foreign language requirement for a student who is deaf? Would it make a difference if the student was majoring in physical education (to be a physical education teacher), or if the student was attending a program to be a member of the foreign service? *See Guckenberger v. Boston Univ.*, 8 F. Supp. 2d 82 (D. Mass. 1998); *Ouachita Baptist University*, 27 Nat. Disability L. Rep. ¶ 28 (2003); *Indiana University Northwest*, 3 Nat. Disab. L. Rep. ¶ 150 (1992).

c. Under what circumstances would it be reasonable for a college to eliminate or modify math requirements for students whose learning disabilities preclude them from performing complex math problems? *See OCR letter to Mt. San Antonio Community College*, OCR Complaint No. 09-96-2151 (San Francisco 1997). What if a student was majoring in political science? *See, e.g., Bennett College (NC)*, 7 Nat'l Disability L. Rep. (LRP Publications) ¶ 26, 1995 NDLR (LRP) LEXIS 1735 (OCR 1995). What if a student was majoring in journalism? *See, e.g., Northern Illinois Univ.*, 7 Nat'l Disability L. Rep. (LRP Publications) ¶ 393, 1995 NDLR (LRP) LEXIS 2018 (OCR 1995). What about a student enrolled in the university's teacher education program? *See University of Hawaii at Manoa*, 22 Nat. Disability L. Rep. ¶ 160 (2001).

Are there circumstances where academic deference should be withheld or accorded less weight?

1) Should deference be denied or deferred in early stages of proceedings before a complete record is developed? *See Weiss v. Rutgers University*, 2014 U.S. Dist. LEXIS 80397 (D.N.J. June 10, 2014). Plaintiff, an individual with a learning disability, sued Rutgers University under Section 504 of the Rehabilitation Act and Title II of the ADA following her dismissal from the Graduate School of Psychology. Early in the proceeding, calling for traditional academic deference, Rutgers moved for dismissal on the grounds that the Plaintiff was not academically qualified, as in the practicum setting, she asked inappropriate questions, required too much direction, and failed to meet deadlines. Ms. Weiss countered that she performed well academically in the classroom, had passed her comprehensive examinations, and met practicum expectations when she received positive feedback and one-on-one training. The court denied the motion to dismiss unwilling to let academic deference outweigh its responsibility to resolve all doubt in favor of the Plaintiff at this early stage in the proceeding; particularly as the Plaintiff had identified an "accommodation" with which she could "plausibly" be qualified: "hands on training." The court did not preclude the application of academic deference at

a later summary judgment stage when it expected to have a more complete record.

2) Should deference be denied when the court apprehends intentional discrimination or deliberate indifference on the part of the school? *See Johnson v. Washington County Career Center*, 2013 U.S. Dist. LEXIS 161138 (S.D. Ohio Nov. 12, 2013). Student with dyslexia was admitted into Defendant's surgical technologist program. She requested various accommodations including extended time to take tests, a reader to use while taking tests, scanning of course materials into a Kurzweil Reader, and a "word bank" to use on tests. The Reader had various operating problems and lacked Internet access (which Plaintiff needed to access all of its functionality). Although the Career Center provided Plaintiff with access to the scanner, it refused to provide the scanning service itself to Plaintiff. Plaintiff was not provided with a word bank for her medical terminology class, because her instructor thought such an accommodation was not fair to the other students in the class. Whereas the other students received the results of their tests and quizzes soon after they took tests, Plaintiff did not receive her results until two weeks before the final exam, and after the in-class review session had ended. When she failed the final exam in her medical terminology class, she was allowed to retake the final but the "retest" was unlike the original test, requiring correct spelling throughout. When Plaintiff was not able to attain a passing 70% score in that course (to continue in the program), she brought suit arguing that she had not been provided reasonable accommodations and had been subject to disparate treatment. The Defendant moved for summary judgment, arguing that she was not "qualified" for the program because of her inability to meet the neutral requirement of 70% proficiency.

The court concluded that the denial of accommodations was pertinent to determining whether the student was otherwise qualified to remain in the program and whether the student was subject to retaliation for having previously filed a disability discrimination suit against the Career Center:

> In light of the fact that several requested accommodations were denied without any stated reasons; that the word bank was denied despite the fact that it was permitted the prior year; that employees of Defendant interrupted and limited Plaintiff's ability to study and use the Reader; that the Reader itself could not properly read medical terminology, a fact of which Defendant was aware from the start of the 2009 Program; that Plaintiff's tests were graded differently and returned to her late; and that her final exam re-test was substantially changed to increase its difficulty for Plaintiff, a reasonable jury could find that Plaintiff would not have been dismissed "but for" her disability.

Id. at *29-30.

3. The National Collegiate Athletic Association (NCAA) established a "core course" requirement, pursuant to which students must take 13 core courses and earn a minimum GPA on a sliding scale between 2.0 and 2.5 (depending on standardized test scores) to be eligible to play college athletics. Students with learning disabilities (and

the DOJ) challenged this rule as violating the ADA, in that it unlawfully screened out students with learning disabilities from playing college sports. Must the NCAA modify its rules to accommodate students with learning disabilities? *Compare Ganden v. National Collegiate Athletic Ass'n*, 1996 U.S. Dist. LEXIS 17368, 9 Nat'l Disab. L. Rep. (LRP Publications) ¶ 33 (N.D. Ill. Nov. 19, 1996), *and Bowers v. National Collegiate Athletic Ass'n*, 974 F. Supp. 459 (D.N.J. 1997) (NCAA's requirement does not violate the ADA), *with Butler v. National Collegiate Athletic Ass'n*, 1996 WL 1058233 (W.D. Wash. 1996) (issuing a preliminary injunction prohibiting the NCAA from declaring plaintiff ineligible to participate in the University of Washington's football program or to receive the benefits of an athletic scholarship). Following these cases, the NCAA and the Department of Justice entered into a consent decree in which the NCAA agreed to, among other things, adopt a policy on waivers for students with learning disabilities that would be applied by a special committee consisting of individuals with expertise on learning disabilities. This committee would be required to look at the student's overall academic record and not place any "undue emphasis" on standardized test scores. United States Department of Justice, *Consent Decree*. http://www.usdoj.gov/crt/ada/ncaa.htm (last viewed on Apr. 25, 2013).

4. The extent to which postsecondary educational institutions should modify test taking requirements has also been a frequent subject of dispute under Section 504 and the ADA. In *McGregor v. Louisiana State Univ. Bd. of Supervisors*, 3 F.3d 850 (5th Cir. 1993), the court held that a law school need not allow a law student with learning disabilities to take exams at home. And in *Wynne v. Tufts Univ. Sch. of Med.*, discussed above, the court held that a medical school did not have to substitute oral or essay exams for multiple-choice exams to accommodate a student with learning disabilities. *See also Rawdin v. Am. Bd. of Pediatrics*, 985 F. Supp. 2d 636 (E.D. Pa. 2013), appeal pending (3rd Cir. 2014) (finding it would be a fundamental alteration of the test to allow the test-taker to use reference material and substitute an essay format for the multiple choice format).

What constitutes reasonable testing accommodations will vary from case to case. Consider the following problems:

a. May a college instructor deny the request of a student with a learning disability for extra time to take a chemistry exam on the ground that the instructor would have to provide all students with such additional time? *See, e.g., Big Bend Community College (WA)*, Complaint No. 10-90-2035 (OCR Region X, 1991).

b. May a college refuse to permit a reader for a student with a visual or learning impairment to edit the student's exam answers? *See, e.g., University of North Carolina at Chapel Hill*, Complaint No. 04-91-2144 (OCR Region IV, 1992).

c. May a college instructor refuse to modify the method of testing a student with visual dysfunctions in a manner that would not "involve filling in little circles"? *See, e.g., Eastern Iowa College District*, Complaint No. 07-90-2036 (OCR Region VII, 1991).

d. Does the duty to accommodate include providing a student more opportunities to pass a medical licensing examination than is generally granted to nondisabled students? Should there be any limit to the number of chances a student with a disability may receive to pass a certification or licensing exam? What ought to be the critieria for when an extra opportunity should be extended and when such student is being given too many chances? *See Doe v. Samuel Merritt College*, 2013 U.S. Dist. LEXIS 18252 (N.D. Cal. Feb. 8, 2013)

2. Burden and Order of Proof

The cases that follow concern students who have been dismissed on academic grounds. Student conduct is not a critical issue in these cases, a topic considered later in this chapter. In some cases, the courts conclude that the college or university met its responsibility to accommodate the student. In others, the courts are unsure. Consider whether this distinction affects the analysis of the courts. Consider also whether the duty to consider matters "diligently," as articulated in *Wynne v. Tufts*, discussed above, has been expanded to encompass more than just fundamental alteration questions.

ZUKLE v. REGENTS OF THE UNIVERSITY OF CALIFORNIA
166 F.3d 1041 (9th Cir. 1999)

O'Scannlain, Circuit Judge:

We must decide whether a medical school violated the Americans with Disabilities Act or the Rehabilitation Act when it dismissed a learning disabled student for failure to meet the school's academic standards.

I

Sherrie Lynn Zukle entered the University of California, Davis School of Medicine ("Medical School") in the fall of 1991 for a four year course of study. The first two years comprise the "basic science or "pre-clinical" curriculum, consisting of courses in the function, design and processes of the human body. The final two years comprise the "clinical curriculum." In the third year, students take six consecutive eight-week clinical clerkships. During the fourth year, students complete clerkships of varying lengths in more advanced areas. Most clerkships involve treating patients in hospitals or clinics, and oral and written exams.

From the beginning, Zukle experienced academic difficulty. During her first quarter, she received "Y" grades in Anatomy and Biochemistry.[1] Upon reexamination, her Biochemistry grade was converted to a "D." She did not convert her Anatomy

---

[1] The Medical School assigns letter grades of A, B, C, D, F, I and Y to measure academic performance. A "Y" grade in a pre-clinical course is provisional; it means that a student has earned a failing grade but will be or has been permitted to retake the exam. However, a "Y" grade in a clinical clerkship indicates unsatisfactory performance in a major portion of that clerkship and may not be converted until the student repeats that portion of the clerkship.

grade at that time. In her second quarter, she received a "Y" grade in Human Physiology, which she converted to a "D" upon reexamination.

In April 1992, the Medical School referred Zukle to the Student Evaluation Committee ("SEC"). Although subject to dismissal pursuant to the Medical School's bylaws, Zukle was allowed to remain in school. The SEC (1) placed Zukle on academic probation, (2) required her to retake Anatomy and Biochemistry, (3) required her to be tested for a learning disability, and (4) placed her on a "split curriculum," meaning that she was given three years to complete the pre-clinical program, instead of the usual two years. Zukle continued to experience academic difficulty. For the spring quarter of 1992 (while on academic probation) she received a "Y" grade in Neurobiology. In the fall, she received a "Y" grade in Medical Microbiology and in the winter she received a "Y" in Principles of Pharmacology. In total, Zukle received eight "Y" grades during the pre-clinical portion of her studies. Five were converted to "C" after reexamination, two to "D" and one to "F."

In November 1992, Zukle was tested for a learning disability. The results received in January 1993, revealed that Zukle suffered from a reading disability which "affects visual processing as it relates to reading comprehension and rate when under timed constraints." In short, it takes Zukle longer to read and to absorb information than the average person.[5] Zukle asked Christine O'Dell, Coordinator of the University's Learning Disability Resource Center, to inform the Medical School of her test results in mid-July 1993. O'Dell informed Gail Currie of the Office of Student Affairs in a letter dated July 21, 1993. O'Dell recommended that the Medical School make various accommodations for Zukle's disability and recommended various techniques for Zukle to try to increase her reading comprehension. The Medical School offered all of these accommodations to Zukle.

After completing the pre-clinical portion of Medical School, Zukle took the United States Medical Licensing Exam, Part I ("USMLE") in June 1994. Shortly thereafter, she began her first clinical clerkship, OB-GYN. During this clerkship, Zukle learned that she had failed the USLME. The Medical School allowed Zukle to interrupt her OB-GYN clerkship to take a six-week review course to prepare to retake the USMLE, for which the Medical School paid.

Before leaving school to take the USMLE review course offered in Southern California, Zukle asked Donal A. Walsh, the Associate Dean of Curricular Affairs, if she could rearrange her clerkship schedule. At this point, Zukle had completed the first half of her OB-GYN clerkship. She asked Dean Walsh if, instead of completing the second half on her OB-GYN clerkship upon return from retaking the USMLE, she could start the first half of a Family Practice Clerkship, and then repeat the OB-GYN clerkship in its entirety at a later date. Zukle testified that she made this request because she was concerned about how far behind she would be when she returned from the USMLE review course. She further asserted that she thought that if she started the Family Practice clerkship (which apparently requires less reading than the OB-GYN clerkship), she would be able to read for her upcoming Medicine clerkship at

[5] Under timed conditions, Zukle's reading comprehension is in the 2nd percentile, whereas when untimed her comprehension is in the 83rd percentile.

night. Zukle testified that Dean Walsh, and several other faculty members, including the Instructor of Record for Family Practice and the Instructor of Record for OB-GYN, initially approved her request. Later, however, Dean Walsh denied Zukle's request and informed her that she had to complete the OB-GYN clerkship before beginning another clerkship.

In September 1994, Zukle took and passed the USMLE on her second attempt. She returned to the Medical School and finished her OB-GYN clerkship. Without requesting any accommodations, she began her Medicine clerkship. During this clerkship, she learned that she had earned a "Y" grade in her OB-GYN clerkship. Because of this grade, Zukle was automatically placed back on academic probation.

Two weeks before the Medicine written exam, Zukle contacted her advisor, Dr. Joseph Silva, and expressed concern that she had not completed the required reading. Dr. Silva offered to speak with Dr. Ruth Lawrence, the Medicine Instructor of Record, on Zukle's behalf. According to Zukle, she then spoke with Dr. Lawrence in person and requested time off from the clerkship to prepare for the exam. Dr. Lawrence denied Zukle's request. Zukle passed the written exam, but failed the Medicine clerkship because of unsatisfactory clinical performance. On Zukle's grade sheet, Dr. Lawrence rated Zukle as unsatisfactory in clinical problem solving skills, data acquisition, organization and recording; and skill/ability at oral presentations. Dr. Lawrence also reported negative comments from the people who worked with Zukle during the clerkship. Because Zukle had earned a failing grade while on academic probation, she was again subject to dismissal pursuant to the Medical School's bylaws.

On January 13, 1995, Zukle appeared before the SEC. The SEC recommended that Zukle (1) drop her current clerkship, Pediatrics; (2) start reviewing for the OB-GYN exam, and retake it; (3) repeat the Medicine clerkship in its entirety; (4) obtain the approval of the SEC before enrolling in any more clerkships; and (5) remain on academic probation for the rest of her medical school career.

On January 17, 1995, the Promotions Board met to consider Zukle's case. The Promotions Board voted to dismiss Zukle from the Medical School for "failure to meet the academic standards of the School of Medicine." According to Dr. Lewis, who was a member of the Promotions Board and was present when it reached its decision, "the Promotions Board considered Plaintiff's academic performance throughout her tenure at the medical school and determined that it demonstrated an incapacity to develop or use the skills and knowledge required to competently practice medicine."

In June 1995, Zukle appealed her dismissal to an *ad hoc* Board on Student Dismissal composed of faculty and students ("the Board"). Zukle appeared before the Board on November 12, 1995, and requested that her dismissal be reconsidered and that she be given extra time to prepare prior to some of her clerkships to accommodate her disability. The Board also heard testimony from Dr. Silva, who spoke favorably on her behalf, Dr. Ernest Lewis, Associate Dean of Student Affairs and Dr. George Jordan, the Chair of the Promotions Board at the time of Zukle's dismissal. When asked about Zukle's request to remain in Medical School on a decelerated schedule, Dean Lewis testified:

> There is a certain point when everyone has to be able to respond in the same time frame. A physician does not have extra time when in the ER, for example. Speed of appropriate reaction to crisis is essential.

The Board on Student Dismissal voted unanimously to uphold the Promotions Board's decision of dismissal.

[Zukle filed suit in district court.] On Zukle's Americans with Disabilities Act ("ADA") and Rehabilitation Act claims, the district court found that "[b]ecause the evidence before the court shows that Zukle could not meet the minimum standards of the UCD School of Medicine with reasonable accommodation, she is not an otherwise qualified individual with a disability under the Rehabilitation Act of the ADA." [Zukle appealed.]

II

The Regents do not dispute that Zukle is disabled and that the Medical School receives federal financial assistance and is a public entity. The Regents argue, however, that Zukle was not "otherwise qualified" to remain at the Medical School. Zukle responds that she *was* "otherwise qualified" with the aid of reasonable accommodations and that the Medical School failed reasonably to accommodate her.[12]

C

Before turning to the merits of Zukle's claims, we must decide whether we should accord deference to academic decisions made by the school in the context of an ADA or Rehabilitation Act claim, an issue of first impression in this circuit.

In *Regents of the Univ. of Michigan v. Ewing*, the Supreme Court analyzed the issue of the deference a court should extend to an educational institution's decision in the due process context. *See* 474 U.S. 214 (1985). In *Ewing*, the plaintiff-medical student challenged his dismissal from medical school as arbitrary and capricious in violation of his substantive due process rights. *See id.* at 217. The Court held that:

> When judges are asked to review the substance of a genuinely academic decision, such as this one, they should show great respect for the faculty's professional judgment. Plainly, they may not override it unless it is such a substantial departure from accepted academic norms as to demonstrate that the person or committee responsible did not actually exercise professional judgment.

Id. at 225 (footnote omitted).

---

[12] Zukle does not argue that she could meet the Medical School's essential eligibility requirements *without* the aid of reasonable accommodations. Indeed, Zukle could not make this argument. As discussed below, Zukle had failed to meet the Medical School's essential eligibility requirements at the time she was dismissed. Because she had received a failing grade while on academic probation, she was subject to dismissal pursuant to the Medical School's bylaws. Accordingly, Zukle must show that she can meet the academic standards of the Medical School *with* the aid of reasonable accommodations. *See Barnett v. U.S. Air, Inc.*, 157 F.3d 744, 748 n.2 (9th Cir. 1998).

While the Court made this statement in the context of a due process violation claim, a majority of circuits have extended judicial deference to an educational institution's academic decisions in ADA and Rehabilitation Act cases. *See Doe v. New York Univ.*, 666 F.2d 761 (2d Cir. 1981); *McGregor v. Louisiana State Univ. Bd. Of Supervisors*, 3 F.3d 850 (5th Cir. 1993); *Wynne v. Tufts Univ. Sch. of Med. ("Wynne I")*, 932 F.2d 19 (1st Cir. 1991). *But see Pushkin v. Regents of the Univ. of Colorado*, 658 F.2d 1372 (10th Cir. 1981) (refusing to adopt deferential, rational basis test in evaluating educational institution's decisions in Rehabilitation Act case). These courts noted the limited ability of courts, "as contrasted to that of experienced educational administrators and professionals," to determine whether a student "would meet reasonable standards for academic and professional achievement established by a university," and have concluded that " '[c]ourts are particularly ill-equipped to evaluate academic performance.' " *Doe*, 666 F.2d at 775–76 [citation omitted].

We agree with the First, Second and Fifth circuits that an educational institution's academic decisions are entitled to deference. . . .

We recognize that extending deference to educational institutions must not impede our obligation to enforce the ADA and the Rehabilitation Act. Thus, we must be careful not to allow academic decisions to disguise truly discriminatory requirements. The educational institution has a "real obligation . . . to seek suitable means of reasonably accommodating a handicapped person and to submit a factual record indicating that it conscientiously carried out this statutory obligation." *Wynne I*, 932 F.2d at 25–26. Once the educational institution has fulfilled this obligation, however, we will defer to its academic decisions.

III

Having answered several preliminary questions, we now turn to the ultimate question — did Zukle establish a prima facie case of discrimination under the ADA or the Rehabilitation Act? As noted before, only the "otherwise qualified" prong of the prima facie case requirements is disputed by the parties. Zukle argues that she was otherwise qualified to remain at the Medical School, with the aid of the three accommodations she requested. The Medical School argues that Zukle's requested accommodations were not reasonable because they would have required a fundamental or substantial modification of its program. . . .

Zukle bears the burden of pointing to the existence of a reasonable accommodation that would enable her to meet the Medical School's essential eligibility requirements. Once she meets this burden, the Medical School must show that Zukle's requested accommodation would fundamentally alter the nature of the school's program. We must determine, viewing the evidence in the light most favorable to Zukle, if there are any genuine issues of material fact with regard to the reasonableness of Zukle's requested accommodations. . . .

We note at this stage that "[r]easonableness is not a constant. To the contrary, what is reasonable in a particular situation may not be reasonable in a different situation — even if the situational differences are relatively slight." *Wynne v. Tufts Univ. Sch. of Med. ("Wynne II")*, 976 F.2d 791, 795 (1st Cir. 1992). Thus, we must evaluate Zukle's requests in light of the totality of her circumstances. . . .

The evidence is undisputed that the Medical School offered Zukle all of the accommodations that it normally offers learning disabled students. When the Medical School first learned of Zukle's disability she was offered double time on exams, notetaking services and textbooks on audio cassettes. Further, Zukle was allowed to retake courses, proceed on a decelerated schedule and remain at the Medical School despite being subject to dismissal under the Medical School's bylaws.

Even with these accommodations, Zukle consistently failed to achieve passing grades in her courses. Though Zukle was on a decelerated schedule, she continued to receive "Y" grades in her pre-clinical years and failed the USMLE on her first attempt. Further, although she was unable to remedy some of her failing grades in her pre-clinical years, she was only able to do so by retaking exams. Moreover, she received a "Y" grade in her first clinical clerkship, automatically placing her on academic probation, and an "F" in her second. Because Zukle received a failing grade while on academic probation, she was subject to dismissal pursuant to the Medical School's bylaws. Clearly, Zukle could not meet the Medical School's essential eligibility requirements without the additional accommodations she requested.

The issue, then, is whether the ADA and Rehabilitation Act required the Medical School to provide Zukle with those additional accommodations. As noted above, the Medical School was only required to provide Zukle with *reasonable* accommodations. Accordingly, we examine the reasonableness of Zukle's requested accommodations.

A

Zukle claims that the Medical School should have granted her request to modify her schedule by beginning the first half of the Family Practice Clerkship instead of finishing the second half of her OB-GYN clerkship when she returned from retaking the USMLE. She proposed that she would then begin the Medicine clerkship, and finish Family Practice and OB-GYN at a later time.

The Regents presented evidence that granting this request would require a substantial modification of its curriculum. While the Medical School has granted some students reading time prior to the commencement of a clerkship, Dean Walsh testified that once a clerkship begins "all students are expected to complete the reading and other requirements of the clerkship, including night call and ward care, and to prepare themselves for the written exam which is given only at the end of the 8-week clerkship." Zukle's request would have entailed interrupting her OB-GYN clerkship, and starting the Medicine clerkship before finishing the Family Practice clerkship. Thus, by the time Zukle began the Medicine clerkship she would have had two uncompleted clerkships.

Dean Walsh testified that the only time the Medical School allows a student to begin a clerkship, interrupt it, and return to that clerkship at a later point is when a student has failed the USMLE and needs time off to study. However, the student is still required to return to the same clerkship. Given that no student had been allowed to rearrange her clerkships, in the manner Zukle requested and that Zukle's request would entail Zukle interrupting two courses to complete them at some later date, we have little difficulty concluding that this would be a substantial alteration of the Medical School's curriculum. . . .

Zukle argues that the Medical School allowed numerous students to rearrange their clerkship schedules, and thus there is a material issue of fact as to whether her request was reasonable. However, while the students that Zukle mentions were allowed to remedy failing grades by retaking clerkships or exams, *none* was allowed to begin a clerkship, interrupt it, begin another clerkship, and retake the second half of the first clerkship at a later point. The facts are undisputed that no student had been allowed to rearrange their clerkship schedule as Zukle requested. Indeed, Zukle admitted in the district court that "no student has been permitted to finish an interrupted course in the fashion [she] requested because it would require substantial curricular alteration." We defer to the Medical School's academic decision to require students to complete courses once they are begun and conclude, therefore, that this requested accommodation was not reasonable.

B

Two weeks before the scheduled written exam in her Medicine clerkship, Zukle asked Dr. Silva, her advisor, if she could have more time to prepare for the exam because she was behind in the readings. Zukle testified that she specifically requested to leave the hospital early every day so that she could spend more time preparing for the written exam in Medicine. Dr. Silva and Zukle spoke with the Instructor of Record in Zukle's Medicine clerkship, Dr. Lawrence. Dr. Lawrence told Zukle that she could not excuse her from the in-hospital part of the clerkship. Dr. Lawrence testified that she denied this request because she thought that it would be unfair to the other students.

The Medical School presented uncontradicted evidence that giving Zukle reduced clinical time would have fundamentally altered the nature of the Medical School curriculum. The Medical School presented the affidavit of Dean Lewis in which he explained the significance of the clinical portion of the Medical School curriculum:

> The third-year clinical clerkships are designed to simulate the practice of medicine. . . . Depending on the specialty and the setting, students are generally required to be "on call" at the hospital through an evening and night one or more times each week. Other than these call nights, students remain at the hospital or clinic during day time hours on a schedule similar to that expected of clinicians. . . . Releasing a student from a significant number of scheduled hours during the course of a rotation would compromise the clerkship's curricular purpose, i.e. the simulation of medical practice.

We defer to the Medical School's academic decision that the in-hospital portion of a clerkship is a vital part of medical education and that allowing a student to be excused from this requirement would sacrifice the integrity of its program. Thus, we conclude that neither the ADA nor the Rehabilitation Act require the Medical School to make this accommodation.

WONG v. THE REGENTS OF THE UNIVERSITY OF CALIFORNIA
192 F.3d 807 (9th Cir. 1999)

KRAVITCH, Circuit Judge:

Plaintiff-appellant Andrew H.K. Wong appeals the district court's order granting summary judgment in favor of defendant-appellee Regents of the University of California ("the University") on Wong's claim that the University discriminated against him in violation of Title II of the Americans with Disabilities Act, 42 U.S.C. § 12132 ("the ADA") and section 504 of the Rehabilitation Act, 29 U.S.C. § 794. Wong alleges that the University violated the Acts when, after refusing to grant his request for accommodation of his learning disability, it dismissed him for failing to meet its academic requirements. The district court ruled that summary judgment was appropriate on two grounds: (1) the accommodation Wong requested was not reasonable, and (2) Wong was not qualified to continue his course of study in the School of Medicine because with or without accommodation, he could not perform the tasks required of an effective medical doctor. We conclude, however, that Wong created a question of fact with respect to both of these issues and that the district court therefore erred in granting the University's motion.

I. FACTS

After excelling in his undergraduate and master's degree programs, Wong entered the School of Medicine at the University of California at Davis in the fall of 1989. The School of Medicine consists of a four-year curriculum: typically, in the first two years, students take academic courses in basic sciences; in the third year, they complete six consecutive clinical "clerkships" in core areas of medical practice; and in the fourth year, they take a series of more specialized clerkships. The clinical clerkships teach the students to integrate their academic knowledge with the skills necessary to practice medicine and test them on their progress in developing these skills.

Wong completed the first two years of medical school on a normal schedule and with a grade point average slightly above a "B"; he also passed the required national board examination immediately following the second year. He began his third year on schedule, enrolling in the Surgery clerkship in the summer of 1991 and, upon its conclusion, in the Medicine clerkship. When he was approximately four weeks into the Medicine clerkship, Wong learned that he had failed Surgery. In accordance with school policy, Wong appeared before the Student Evaluation Committee ("SEC"), a body that meets with students having academic problems and makes recommendations to another group, the Promotions Board, which ultimately decides what action, if any, the school should take with respect to that student. The Promotions Board placed Wong on academic probation, decided that he should repeat the Surgery clerkship, and recommended that he continue in the Medicine clerkship at least until the midterm evaluation. Wong withdrew from the Medicine clerkship in November 1991 when his midterm evaluation showed significant problems with his performance to that point. Wong's instructor of record then assigned a senior resident to work with Wong one-on-one, focusing upon taking patient histories and making oral presentations. These sessions continued through the winter of 1992.

In March 1992, Dr. Ernest Lewis, associate dean of student affairs, granted Wong's request to take time off from school to be with his father, who had just been diagnosed with lung cancer. Wong spent at least some of this time doing extra reading in preparation for his upcoming clerkships, Psychiatry and Pediatrics. He returned to school in July 1992 and between July and December passed clerkships in Psychiatry (with a "B"), Pediatrics ("C+"), and Obstetrics/Gynecology ("C"). Wong generally received positive comments on his final evaluation forms for these courses. Instructors noted that he was "competent," "prompt," "enthusiastic," "a very hard worker," and "an extremely pleasant student who related exceptionally well with the staff"; they also stated that he had "a good fund of knowledge," "contributed meaningfully to the discussions at hand," "made astute observations of patients," and "did a good job of presenting on [gynecology] rounds." Evaluators also observed, however, that Wong "seem[ed] to have difficulty putting things together" and "limited abilities to effectively communicate his thoughts," and they recommended that he work on "organizational skills" and "setting priorities."

Wong re-enrolled in the Medicine clerkship in January 1993. Three weeks later, his father died, an event that by all accounts had a devastating impact on Wong. He continued in the Medicine clerkship for a brief period of time, but after his midterm evaluation showed a borderline performance in the first half of the clerkship, Wong, with Dean Lewis's approval, withdrew from the course and left the Davis campus to be closer to his family, who lived in the San Francisco area. In order to prevent Wong from falling further behind, Dean Lewis permitted him to take several fourth-year level clerkships at hospitals in the San Francisco area. He earned A's and B's in these courses, with positive comments. Two evaluators thought that Wong needed to improve his fund of knowledge, but both attributed the deficiency to the fact that he was taking classes in the fourth-year curriculum without having completed his third year "core" clerkships. When Wong returned to the School of Medicine at Davis in the summer of 1993, he again enrolled in Medicine. He asserts that although he did not feel prepared for this course and attempted to drop it, Dean Lewis did not permit the withdrawal, and he ultimately failed the class, triggering another appearance before the SEC and Promotions Board.

The Promotions Board adopted strict conditions for Wong to remain a student in the School of Medicine: it required him to take only reading electives for the next three quarters; to meet again with the SEC and Dean Lewis following that period to assess his progress; and, assuming he received approval to reenter the clerkship program, to repeat the entire third year, including the courses he already had passed. During the meeting with the Promotions Board, Wong stated that he thought he might have a learning disability and learned from members of the Promotions Board about the University's Disability Resource Center ("DRC"). DRC staff members and doctors to whom they referred Wong administered a battery of tests and concluded that Wong has a disability that affects the way he processes verbal information and expresses himself verbally.

When Dean Lewis learned the results of the tests, he referred Wong to Dr. Margaret Steward, a psychologist and School of Medicine faculty member, so that she could counsel him regarding coping skills and help him determine what accommodations would allow him to complete his courses successfully. Dr. Steward suggested several strategies for Wong to employ, including telling people that he has a "hearing problem" and may need them to slow down or repeat messages; using a tape recorder; and double-checking his understanding of information he has received verbally. Dr. Steward reported to Dean Lewis in a memorandum that "[t]here is no doubt that [Wong] will need extra time to complete the clerkship years." In the same memorandum, she also specifically recommended giving Wong extra time to read before his next two clerkships, Medicine and Surgery; in a later memorandum, she informed Dean Lewis that she had discussed with Wong that he needed to pass the Medicine clerkship to provide "empirical support" for extra reading time before his next clerkship and that "if he passes Medicine that he needs to anticipate extra time in order to complete the clerkship years." Finally, Dr. Steward recommended that Dean Lewis assign Wong an "SLD [Student Learning Disability] advisor" with whom he could meet to review strategies for coping with his disability. Dean Lewis never appointed this advisor. Wong also contends (and the University does not dispute) that Dr. Steward told him that the School of Medicine "would set up a learning disability resource team to ensure that Wong received adequate accommodations," but the school never did so.

After completing the requisite three quarters of elective reading under the supervision of a faculty member, Wong planned to retake the Medicine clerkship in July 1994. After attending orientation, however, he felt unprepared for the course and asked for another eight weeks off for additional reading. Dean Lewis granted this request, although he noted that he did not know how the extra time would help Wong. In September 1994, Wong took and passed Medicine, earning a "B" and receiving overwhelmingly positive comments on his grade report, including observations of his "excellent fund of knowledge," "excellent retention of new material," and compassionate manner with patients as he performed effective physical exams and formulated diagnoses. The instructor noted some difficulty in making verbal presentations, including uncertainty and taking extra time to answer, but concluded that Wong was a "solid third year medical student" who performed satisfactorily "in all areas of the clerkship." Wong then received eight weeks off to read in preparation for his Surgery clerkship, which commenced in January 1995 and in which he earned a "B." The comments on his grade report were similar to those for the preceding clerkship: generally positive remarks mitigated by reference to his need for time and a calm setting to make good oral presentations. The instructor of record concluded:

> [T]he department was very pleased with [Wong]'s performance on the clerkship. We thought that he had turned in a solid performance and that he had improved markedly over the past year. We think that he has everything it takes to become a safe and effective physician.

Before completing the Surgery clerkship, Wong contacted Dean Lewis's office and requested eight weeks off to read for his next clerkship, Pediatrics. Dean Lewis denied this request through the registrar; he has offered several different reasons for this decision, giving rise to an issue of fact on this point. In an October 1997 deposition, Dean Lewis stated that he received Wong's request through the registrar, who told him that Wong wanted time off for reading but also asked to intersperse fourth year electives with his remaining third year clerkships because he wanted to graduate on time without having to take the core clerkships in straight succession. According to Dean Lewis's testimony, he did not grant Wong's request because Wong needed to finish his third year before proceeding to fourth year courses and because giving Wong time off to read would keep him from graduating the following year. Wong denies that he pressed for permission to take fourth year courses in order to keep from delaying his graduation date; he contends that he only mentioned this alternative after Dean Lewis denied his request for eight weeks off to read for Pediatrics and told Wong that he must take courses in succession for the remainder of the year.

In the same deposition, Dean Lewis also explained his denial of Wong's request for reading time as follows: Wong already had received time off before the previous two clerkships and had passed the Pediatrics clerkship three years earlier. For these reasons, Dean Lewis opined that Wong did not need the extra time for this Pediatrics clerkship. In the course of this explanation, however, Dean Lewis again mentioned his belief that Wong wanted to graduate on time; furthermore, Dean Lewis acknowledged that Pediatrics, as well as Obstetrics/Gynecology and Psychiatry, which he expected Wong to take in succession following Pediatrics, had become much more rigorous and demanding over the past few years. Wong concurred in Dean Lewis's evaluation of the relative difficulty of the 1995 Pediatrics course as compared to the 1992 Pediatrics course.

Finally, in his December 1997 declaration, Dean Lewis repeated as reasons for denying Wong's requested accommodation that he already had granted Wong a significant amount of time off for additional reading and directed studies and that Wong previously had passed Pediatrics (and the next scheduled clerkship, Obstetrics/Gynecology) with no accommodation. Lewis also advanced a third set of explanations: "In that he was presumed to have previously read the material for those courses, I decided that allowing additional time off to read before repeating those clerkships would have been unreasonable, unfair to other students and contrary to the purposes of the curriculum."

Wong received a "Y" grade in the Pediatrics clerkship. A "Y" signifies work of failing quality in one area of a clerkship; Wong's evaluations showed that he passed the written and oral examinations but that his ward performance was unsatisfactory. His final grade sheet reported that his "clinical judgment was poor" and that his evaluators "had concerns with his ability to synthesize information." The grade sheet also noted reporting inaccuracies that in at least one instance "would have resulted in inappropriate dosages," although Wong contends that his supervisor was responsible for this particular error. Some evaluators wondered whether Wong "could safely practice clinical medicine." At the time Wong learned of his unsatisfactory performance in Pediatrics, he already had begun his Obstetrics/Gynecology clerkship. A preliminary report from his instructor in that course stated that for the first two weeks, Wong's performance had been "borderline" and "lower than expected." This evaluation particularly noted that Wong did not communicate effectively and seemed unsure of himself when examining patients, causing them to react with anger or anxiety.

Wong's "Y" grade in Pediatrics triggered another appearance before the SEC and Promotions Board. In a letter to the Promotions Board, Wong attributed his poor performance in the pediatric ward to a flu-like virus that affected him during the first two weeks of the clerkship. He stated that during this time, he was extremely ill, once requiring IV fluids, and that he fell behind in his reading which affected his performance in the wards. Wong also mentioned being preoccupied with his mother's health; she recently had been diagnosed with cancer. Wong contends that Dean Lewis's refusal to grant him an eight-week reading period prior to this clerkship also contributed to his failing grade; he did not tell the Promotions Board about the refused accommodation because, according to Wong, Dean Lewis ordered him not to mention that issue, an allegation that the University has not disputed.

The SEC recommended dismissal from the School of Medicine, and the Promotions Board concurred. Although the Promotions Board does not keep records of its proceedings, Wong was present during some of the Board's debate and contends that Dean Lewis (a member of both the SEC and Promotions Board) dominated the discussion. The written recommendation of the Promotions Board stated that it had "considered at length the academic record of Mr. Wong, [including] his current academic deficiency, a 'Y' grade in [the] Pediatrics Clerkship. . . . After a discussion, it was . . . approved to recommend Mr. Wong['s dismissal] for failure to meet the academic standards of the School of Medicine." The Dean of the School of Medicine accepted this recommendation and dismissed Wong on May 17, 1995. Wong did not appeal his dismissal through the procedure for appeal outlined in the School of Medicine Bylaws and Regulations.

II. DISCUSSION

To establish a prima facie case of discrimination based upon his disability in violation of the Acts, Wong must produce evidence that: (1) he is "disabled" as the Acts define that term; (2) he is qualified to remain a student at the School of Medicine, meaning that he can meet the essential eligibility requirements of the school with or without reasonable accommodation; (3) he "was dismissed solely because of [his] disability;" and (4) the school "receives federal financial assistance (for the Rehabilitation Act claim) or is a public entity (for the ADA claim)." *Zukle v. Regents of the Univ. of California*, 166 F.3d 1041, 1045 (9th Cir. 1999). For summary judgment purposes, the University concedes that Wong has met the first and last elements of this test. The dispute focuses upon the second element: the University argues that Wong was not qualified because he could not satisfy the academic standards of the School of Medicine, even with reasonable accommodation.

Wong bears the "initial burden of producing evidence" both that a reasonable accommodation exists and that this accommodation "would enable [him] to meet the educational institution's essential eligibility requirements." *Zukle*, 166 F.3d at 1047. Production of such evidence shifts the burden to the University to produce rebuttal evidence that either (1) the suggested accommodation is not reasonable (because it would substantially alter the academic program), or (2) that the student is not qualified (because even with the accommodation, the student could not meet the institution's academic standards). *See id.* Wong argues that, viewing the evidence in his favor, he has created an issue of fact as to whether allowing him eight weeks of additional reading time between the Surgery and Pediatrics clerkships was a reasonable modification of the School of Medicine's academic program. If extra reading time was reasonable, Wong contends, the evidence shows that he was qualified to continue in the School of Medicine because when granted that accommodation, he met the school's standards, performing satisfactorily in both the academic and interactive portions of his courses. According to the University, however, it is entitled to summary judgment because it has rebutted Wong's evidence on both of these points as a matter of law.

A. *Standards of Review*

In this case, we must consider another standard of review as well: the degree of deference (if any) with which we should treat an educational institution's decisions involving its academic standards and curriculum. We recently observed that the Supreme Court, in the context of examining whether a university violated a student's constitutional rights to due process when it dismissed him, has held that judges "should show great respect for [a] faculty's professional judgment" when reviewing "the substance of a genuinely academic decision." *Regents of the Univ. of Michigan v. Ewing*, 474 U.S. 214, 225 (1985), *quoted in Zukle*, 166 F.3d at 1047. Extending this reasoning to the realm of the ADA and Rehabilitation Act, we concluded, as most other circuits have, "that an educational institution's academic decisions are entitled to deference." *Zukle*, 166 F.3d at 1047 (citing with approval cases from the First, Second, and Fifth Circuits). We typically defer to the judgment of academics because courts generally are "ill-equipped," as compared with experienced educators, to determine whether a student meets a university's "reasonable standards for academic and professional achievement." *Id.* (internal quotations omitted).

This deference is not absolute, however: courts still hold the final responsibility for enforcing the Acts, including determining whether an individual is qualified, with or without accommodation, for the program in question. We must ensure that educational institutions are not "disguis[ing] truly discriminatory requirements" as academic decisions; to this end, "[t]he educational institution has a 'real obligation . . . to seek suitable means of reasonably accommodating a handicapped person *and to submit a factual record indicating that it conscientiously carried out this statutory obligation.*' " *Zukle*, 166 F.3d at 1048 (quoting *Wynne v. Tufts Univ. Sch. of Med.*, 932 F.2d 19, 25–26 (1st Cir. 1991) (en banc) (*Wynne I*)) (emphasis added). Subsumed within this standard is the institution's duty to make itself aware of the nature of the student's disability; to explore alternatives for accommodating the student; and to exercise professional judgment in deciding whether the modifications under consideration would give the student the opportunity to complete the program without fundamentally or substantially modifying the school's standards. *See Wynne I*, 932 F.2d at 26 (explaining that institution needs to submit "*undisputed facts*" showing that "relevant officials" "considered alternative means, their feasibility, [and] cost and effect on the academic program") (emphasis added); *id.* at 28 (refusing to defer when institution presented no evidence regarding "who took part in the decision" and finding "simple conclusory averment" of head of institution insufficient to support deferential standard of review). We defer to the institution's academic decisions only after we determine that the school "has fulfilled this obligation." *Zukle*, 166 F.3d at 1048. Keeping these standards in mind, we examine the two issues in contention: whether the accommodation Wong requested was reasonable and whether, with accommodation, he was "qualified" to continue his studies at the School of Medicine.

B. *Reasonable Accommodation*

A public entity must "make reasonable modifications in policies, practices, or procedures when the modifications are necessary to avoid discrimination on the basis of disability." *Zukle*, 166 F.3d at 1046 (quoting 28 C.F.R. § 35.130(b)(7)). The Acts do not require an academic institution "to make fundamental or substantial modifications to its programs or standards," however. *Id*. . . .

In the typical disability discrimination case in which a plaintiff appeals a district court's entry of summary judgment in favor of the defendant, we undertake this reasonable accommodation analysis ourselves as a matter of course, examining the record and deciding whether the record reveals questions of fact as to whether the requested modification substantially alters the performance standards at issue or whether the accommodation would allow the individual to meet those requirements. In a case involving assessment of the standards of an academic institution, however, we abstain from an in-depth, *de novo* analysis of suggested accommodations that the school rejected if the institution demonstrates that it conducted such an inquiry itself and concluded that the accommodations were not feasible or would not be effective. *See supra* Part II.A. We do not defer to the academic institution's decision in the present case because the record that the University presented falls short of this requirement.

Dean Lewis's denial of Wong's requested accommodation is not entitled to deference because the University failed to present us with a record undisputedly showing that Dean Lewis investigated the proposed accommodation to determine whether the School of Medicine feasibly could implement it (or some alternative modification) without substantially altering the school's standards. First, Dean Lewis rejected Wong's request for an eight-week reading period before the Pediatrics clerkship without informing himself of Wong's need for accommodation of his learning disability. Despite Dr. Steward's earlier statement to Dean Lewis to the effect that Wong was certain to need additional time to finish the third-year clerkships, Dean Lewis failed to discuss Wong's proposal with any of the professionals who had worked with Wong to pinpoint his disability and help him develop skills to cope with it. This omission is particularly noteworthy when considered in light of the following testimony that Dean Lewis gave at his deposition:

Q: Am I correct, Dr. Lewis, that you are the person within the School of Medicine who has the ultimate authority to determine what accommodations should be made available to students with disabilities?

A: I'm not responsible for determining which accommodations will be offered to students[;] my office is responsible for seeing that the suggested accommodations are provided to the students, but we don't make the decisions as to what the accommodations are.

Q: Who does?

A: The Disability Resources Center.

Given Dean Lewis's own description of the limitations upon his responsibility in assessing appropriate accommodations, the fact that he simply passed messages to Wong through the registrar stating his decision to deny Wong's request — without consulting Wong or any person at the University whose job it was to formulate appropriate accommodations — strikes us as a conspicuous failure to carry out the obligation "conscientiously" to explore possible accommodations.

Second, the evidence creates real doubts that Dean Lewis gave any consideration to the effect the proposed accommodation might have upon the School of Medicine's program requirements or academic standards at the time he denied Wong's request. In his October 1997 deposition, Dean Lewis stated that he denied Wong's requested accommodation because (1) Wong wanted to graduate on time, and (2) Wong already had taken Pediatrics and had received a significant amount of time off for reading, and Dean Lewis therefore did not believe Wong needed additional time off. Neither of these reasons is relevant to the School of Medicine's or standards. Only in a declaration dated two months after this deposition did Dean Lewis assert that he denied the requested accommodation because it was "contrary to the purposes of the curriculum." A jury reasonably could find that Dean Lewis did not formulate this final rationale for denying the accommodation until long after Wong's dismissal from the School of Medicine. Such after-the-fact justification obviously does not satisfy the University's obligation to present "undisputed facts" showing that it conscientiously considered whether possible modification would fundamentally or substantially alter the school's standards when it decided that it could not reasonably accommodate the disabled student. *See Wynne I*, 932 F.2d at 26. We therefore do not defer to the institution's decision; we examine the rejection of Wong's request for an eight-week reading period *de novo*.

We briefly note that both parties have met their burdens of production as to whether the accommodation was reasonable. Among other things, Wong has shown that the University granted this accommodation in the past. The University, on the other hand, has produced the testimony of Dean Lewis that the eight-week break Wong requested was unreasonable because it required the School of Medicine to alter its curriculum. It contends that the schedule was designed for students to complete consecutively to allow them to practice skills consistently and frequently and to allow the faculty to evaluate the steady development of those skills. Allowing extra time for reading before every clerkship does not comport with this goal, the University argues. Our analysis focuses upon whether this evidence shows as a matter of law that the proposed accommodation is unreasonable; we conclude for the reasons discussed below that the evidence creates an issue of fact as to the reasonableness of granting Wong an eight-week reading period prior to his Pediatrics clerkship.

First, Dr. Steward, the Coordinator of the Student Learning Disability Resource Teams and a member of the medical school faculty, informed Dean Lewis soon after Wong's diagnosis that Wong certainly would need additional time to complete the clerkship portion of the curriculum. Dr. Steward also stated that if Wong passed the Medicine clerkship after receiving additional reading time, that success would provide empirical support for Wong to receive the same accommodation for his next clerkship. A jury could have found Dr. Steward a persuasive authority on the issue whether the decelerated schedule fundamentally altered the curriculum. *See also* 34 C.F.R. § 104.44(a) (regulation interpreting Rehabilitation Act as it applies to postsecondary education stating that "[m]odifications may include changes in the length of time permitted for the completion of degree requirements" (emphasis added)).

Second, the School of Medicine had granted Wong this same accommodation for his two previous clerkships. An institution's past decision to make a concession to a disabled individual does not obligate it to continue to grant that accommodation in the future, nor does it render the accommodation reasonable as a matter of law. *See, e.g.*, *Myers v. Hose*, 50 F.3d 278, 284 (4th Cir. 1995) (holding that fact that employer had offered accommodation to employees in the past did not require employer to grant same accommodation to plaintiff as a matter of federal law). The fact that the school previously made the exact modification for the Surgery and Medicine clerkships that Wong requested for the Pediatrics clerkship, however, is certainly persuasive evidence from which a jury could conclude that the accommodation was reasonable. *Cf. Hunt-Golliday v. Metropolitan Water Reclamation Dist.*, 104 F.3d 1004, 1013 (7th Cir. 1997) (observing fact that employer previously had restricted employee's lifting requirements to 50 pounds in response to back injury indicated that this accommodation was reasonable). The School of Medicine also deviated from the consecutive clerkship standard when it allowed Wong to take a leave of absence during the third year to spend time with his ailing father. Both of these occurrences imply that consecutive completion of the third-year clerkships was not an essential element of the curriculum.

Third, that Wong had earned "B's" and received generally positive comments in the Medicine and Surgery clerkships for which Dean Lewis granted him eight weeks of reading time indicates that it may have been reasonable for Wong to continue receiving this same accommodation. *Cf. Roberts v. Progressive Indep., Inc.*, 183 F.3d 1215, 1220 (10th Cir. 1999) (in the employment context, holding that "[r]easonable accommodation[s are] those accommodations which presently, or in the near future, enable the employee to perform the essential functions of his job") (internal quotations and citations omitted). From this evidence, a jury could conclude that the decelerated schedule allowed Wong to meet the substantive academic standards of the two clerkships for which he received the eight-week reading period. Allowing disabled individuals to fulfill the "essential eligibility requirements for . . . participation in programs" is, after all, the principle behind the statutory mandate that public entities provide disabled individuals with reasonable accommodations. 42 U.S.C. § 12131(2).

Our holding that Wong has created an issue of fact as to the reasonableness of an eight-week reading period between clerkships does not conflict with our opinion in *Zukle*, in which we decided that the plaintiff did not create an issue of fact as to the reasonableness of the same accommodation that Wong requested. *See* 166 F.3d at 1050–51. In *Zukle*, we reached the conclusion that a disabled medical student's requested decelerated schedule for clerkships was not a reasonable accommodation only after determining that a deferential standard of review was appropriate. We noted that the Promotions Board had considered the plaintiff's previous failure to perform adequately even when granted a decelerated schedule. *See id.* at 1050–51. Given that plaintiff's inability to perform even *with* accommodation, we concluded that the school made a rationally considered decision that allowing her to remain in the program would negatively impact the school's academic standards. Here, however, Wong has presented evidence that when granted the decelerated schedule, his performance drastically improved, and that the University failed to consider fully the effect of this modification on its program and on his abilities. *See id.* at 1048 ("[R]easonableness is not a constant. To the contrary, what is reasonable in a particular situation may not be reasonable in a different situation-even if the situational differences are relatively slight.") (internal punctuation and citation omitted).

We re-emphasize that at this stage of the litigation, we examine all of the record evidence in the light most favorable to Wong. We do not hold that allowing Wong to take eight weeks off between each of the third-year clerkships would have been a reasonable accommodation; in fact, we recognize that a jury may well find that, despite the evidence we have just discussed, this modification to the school's curriculum was not reasonable. Under the summary judgment standard, however, we do not consider whether a jury could find in favor of the defendant: we affirm the entry of summary judgment only if a jury could not find for the plaintiff. Here, a jury could decide that the modification he requested in the School of Medicine's program was reasonable. The district court erred in concluding otherwise.[33]

C. *Qualified Individual*

The ADA provides that "no qualified individual with a disability shall, by reason of such disability, be excluded from participation in or be denied the benefits of the services, programs, or activities of a public entity. . . ." 42 U.S.C. § 12132. The statute defines a "qualified individual with a disability" as "an individual with a disability who, with or without reasonable modifications to rules, policies, or practices . . . meets the essential eligibility requirements for the . . . participation in programs or activities provides by a public entity." *Id.* § 12131(2). The Rehabilitation Act creates similar rights and duties. In the context of postsecondary education, administrative regulations define "qualified" as "meet[ing] the academic and technical standards requisite to . . . participation in the . . . education program or activity." 34 C.F.R. § 104.3(k)(3). For purposes of resolving the summary judgment issue, Wong concedes that he is not qualified to continue in the School of Medicine without reasonable accommodation; the issue we must consider, therefore, is whether, with the accommodation of time off between clerkships for additional reading, Wong has created an issue of fact that he could satisfy the school's academic standards.

---

[33] In its order granting the University's motion for summary judgment, the district court stated that it would disregard the parties' discussion of "time off" as an "accommodation," essentially concluding as a matter of law that additional time "dilute[d] appropriate academic standards" and thus fell outside of the Acts' requirements. District Ct. Order, R37 at 12 n.5; *see also id.* at 13 & n.6 (accepting as a matter of law the University's argument that granting additional time between clerkships for reading fundamentally altered the academic program and *sua sponte* applying this reasoning to the reading periods the school granted Wong for the Surgery and Medicine clerkships, stating: "Why this was considered an appropriate accommodation by the university, even at the outset, is puzzling to this court."). The district court misguidedly incorporated into its decision its own perception that the time Wong requested (and the University originally granted) significantly modified the curriculum.

> We have determined in this case that we could not treat the University's denial of the requested accommodation with deference because it did not demonstrate that it conscientiously exercised professional judgment in considering the feasibility of the modification in making that decision. Even so, where record evidence indicates that an institution determined that certain modifications to its program were acceptable, courts may not as a matter of law disregard that evidence in favor of their own ideas about what constitutes "appropriate academic standards."

Again, our analysis begins with a determination of whether we defer to the University's decision to dismiss Wong for "failure to meet the academic standards of the School of Medicine." We will not defer to a school's decision if the ostensibly professional, academic judgment "disguise[s] truly discriminatory requirements." *Zukle*, 166 F.3d at 1048. Moreover, the academic institution bears the burden of presenting us with a factual record that shows it conscientiously considered all pertinent and appropriate information in making its decision. Far from demonstrating a conscientious effort to consider all relevant factors in deciding that Wong could not meet the school's academic requirements even with reasonable accommodation, the record contains evidence that the University eschewed its obligation to consider possible modifications it could make (or could have made) in the program to accommodate Wong and the past and potential effects of such accommodations (and lack thereof) on Wong's performance.

The University has not disputed Wong's assertion that Dean Lewis instructed him not to mention the requested accommodation — or Dean Lewis's denial of it — to the Promotions Board. In fact, the record contains evidence that at least two Promotions Board members believed that Dean Lewis *had* given Wong accommodations and erroneously believed that Wong had been unable to perform adequately even with those modifications. These same two individuals also identified Wong's failure of the Pediatrics clerkship as the determining factor in their decision to dismiss him. Finally, Dean Lazarus, who issued the letter formally dismissing Wong, testified that Dean Lewis told him that Wong had been accommodated and that based upon this representation and the Promotions Board's recommendation for dismissal, he issued the school's decision without considering the matter independently. The University has presented no evidence that the Promotions Board considered the fact that in his previous two clerkships, Wong had performed well after receiving an eight-week reading period as an accommodation but that in the Pediatrics clerkship, Wong performed poorly after failing to receive the same accommodation. *Cf. Zukle*, 166 F.3d at 1050–51 (in deferring to University's decision not to grant accommodation to that plaintiff, noting that Promotions Board had considered fact that the student previously had "experienced severe academic difficulties" "even on a decelerated schedule").

This failure to take Wong's disability and need for accommodation into account shows that the school's system for evaluating a learning disabled student's abilities and its own duty to make its program accessible to such individuals fell short of the standards we require to grant deference to an academic institution's decision-making process. We therefore analyze whether Wong has created an issue of fact with respect to his qualifications *de novo*.

Wong has produced enough evidence that he could meet the University's eligibility requirements to shift the burden of production to the University: his final grade sheets from the Medicine and Surgery clerkships for which he received the accommodation show that he received satisfactory grades and generally positive comments from his evaluators. The University argues, however, that an examination of Wong's entire academic record demonstrates that he did not have the capacity to become an effective physician. Evaluators from multiple courses reported flaws in his performance — such as Wong's inability to comprehend verbal information, accurately respond to questions posed to him on the wards, think on his feet, and relate to patients and staff — that the University argues could not be corrected simply by allowing Wong additional time to read before each clerkship. Thus, the University contends, Wong was not qualified because even with the accommodation he requested, he could not satisfy the School of Medicine's standards. We acknowledge that Wong's performance in some areas of the clerkship program were less than ideal, and a jury may eventually determine that Wong simply does not have and cannot acquire — even with reasonable modifications to the program — skills that are indispensable for the receipt of a license to practice medicine. For the reasons discussed below, however, we cannot say as a matter of law that he was unqualified to continue participating in the medical program.

Most importantly, a comparison of Wong's final grade sheets from his 1991 Surgery and 1993 Medicine clerkships (which he failed and for which he received no accommodation) and his 1994 Medicine and 1995 Surgery clerkships (which he passed with grades of "B" and for which he received eight weeks of reading time prior to starting) show a marked improvement, not only in Wong's performance on written and oral examinations, *but also in his performance in the clinical setting.* For example, the final grade sheet for the 1993 Medicine clerkship reported that Wong's clinical performance was "below that expected" because, for example, he could not collect data from patients and use it to formulate a diagnosis; his oral presentations were problematic; and he had difficulty with interpersonal interactions. In contrast, his 1994 Medicine clerkship evaluation stated that his clinical performance was "satisfactory in all areas." It noted some difficulty with verbal presentations, including taking a little extra time or repeating a question, but stated that he nonetheless answered questions satisfactorily. Significantly, this grade sheet reported excellent performance in two areas with which Wong earlier had struggled: interpersonal relationships (both with patients and with other professionals) and synthesizing a diagnosis while taking a patient's history.

Wong's poor performance in the 1995 Pediatrics clerkship for which he did not receive the accommodation he requested mimicked his earlier failures. The comments he received regarding his clinical performance were similar to the assessments of his work in the 1993 Medicine and 1991 Surgery clerkships: he could not synthesize information; his oral presentation skills were poor; and he lacked confidence. From all of this evidence, a reasonable jury could discern a pattern: Wong failed when he did not have extra time to prepare before a clerkship, but with the modified schedule, he succeeded in all areas of the clerkship.

The University points out that Wong's scores on the written and oral examinations in the 1995 Pediatrics clerkship were good; only his clinical and ward performance was less than satisfactory. Based upon these facts, the University contends that Wong still was not qualified because the accommodation he requested, additional reading time, would not have improved the "hands-on" skills with which he had so much difficulty. In addition to Wong's performance in the 1994 Medicine and 1995 Surgery clerkships, which tend to disprove the University's assertion, evidence from one of the School of Medicine's own faculty members discounts this argument. In a memorandum to Dean Lewis written soon after Wong received his learning disability diagnosis, Dr. Steward reported that two of the professionals who helped diagnose Wong concurred in Wong's own perception that his problems with processing verbal information increased "when he is anxious, worried, and/or nervous, and *when the vocabulary includes new, technical information.*" Similarly, "negative and anxious emotions can interrupt or exacerbate [Wong's difficulty expressing himself verbally], and new or not-quite-mastered terms and concepts are more likely to be difficult to retrieve than older material." From this analysis of Wong's disability, a reasonable jury could conclude that having reading time between clerkships allowed him to perform satisfactorily by (1) enabling him to familiarize himself with new, technical information so that he could communicate more easily on these topics and (2) easing his anxiety about the new information, thus making him more comfortable in the clinical setting.

The University emphasizes that Wong passed the Pediatrics clerkship the first time he took it, in 1992, without any accommodation. Although this fact does bolster the school's argument that the lack of extra reading time should not have affected Wong's performance in Pediatrics in 1995, the fact that Pediatrics had become "a lot more rigorous in the last five [or] six years" mitigates the support this evidence lends to the University's position. Finally, we give little credence to the University's argument that the total amount of time Wong already had spent in the third year of medical school — nearing four years at the time of his dismissal — indicates that he simply could not master the skills that the school's curriculum demanded. The majority of this time was attributable to the death of Wong's father; courses Wong failed prior to his diagnosis; and courses that Wong had passed but that the school required him to retake. If a jury were to find that the schedule modification Wong requested was reasonable, we could attribute at the most one year of additional time in the third year curriculum to the accommodation of his disability. Neither the University's argument regarding Wong's prior passing grade in Pediatrics nor the emphasis it places upon the amount of time he had spent in the third year is sufficient to overcome, as a matter of law, the evidence Wong presented that when given extra time to read between clerkships, he could meet the academic standards of the School of Medicine.

III. CONCLUSION

Faculty members and administrators of a professional school are unquestionably in the best position to set standards for the institution and to establish curricular requirements that fulfill the school's purpose of training students for the work that lies ahead of them. However, "extending deference to educational institutions must not impede our obligation to enforce the ADA and the Rehabilitation Act. . . . The educational institution has a 'real obligation . . . to seek suitable means of reasonably accommodating a handicapped person and to submit a factual record indicating that it conscientiously carried out this statutory obligation.' " *Zukle*, 166 F.3d at 1048 (quoting *Wynne I*, 932 F.2d at 25–26). Here, school administrators accepted the recommendation of a faculty member (and learning disability services coordinator) to grant Wong the schedule modification he requested for two courses, and Wong performed well with this accommodation. The School of Medicine did not present any evidence that during this time period, it believed that Wong's decelerated schedule impeded his attainment of the goals of the program or lowered the school's academic standards. Then, however, for reasons about which there is a dispute of fact, the school refused to continue granting Wong the accommodation and dismissed him when he could not perform satisfactorily without it.

The deference to which academic institutions are entitled when it comes to the ADA is a double-edged sword. It allows them a significant amount of leeway in making decisions about their curricular requirements and their ability to structure their programs to accommodate disabled students. On the other hand, it places on an institution the weighty responsibility of carefully considering each disabled student's particular limitations and analyzing whether and how it might accommodate that student in a way that would allow the student to complete the school's program without lowering academic standards or otherwise unduly burdening the institution. Here, although the record shows that the University failed to undertake this task properly, the University still asks that we hold as a matter of law and at a very early stage of this litigation that it has satisfied its legal obligations under the ADA. Under the circumstances, we cannot grant this request. We will not sanction an academic institution's decision to refuse to accommodate a disabled student and subsequent dismissal of that student when the record contains facts from which a reasonable jury could conclude that the school made those decisions for arbitrary reasons unrelated to its academic standards.

Because genuine issues of fact remain as to both the reasonableness of the accommodation in question and Wong's qualifications, summary judgment was inappropriate. Resolving these factual disputes is the province of a jury. We REVERSE the order of the district court and REMAND this case for further proceedings consistent with this opinion.

CHRISTOPHER L. FALCONE v. UNIVERSITY OF MINNESOTA

388 F.3d 656 (8th Cir. 2004)

OPINION

Loken, Chief Judge.

When Christopher Falcone was admitted to the University of Minnesota Medical School, he advised the University's Disability Services Office that he suffers from learning disabilities. Falcone received accommodations but was dismissed from the medical school after failing three clinical courses. He then commenced this action, claiming the dismissal violated Section 504 of the Rehabilitation Act of 1973, 29 U.S.C. § 794(a). The district court granted summary judgment in favor of the University, and Falcone appeals. Reviewing the grant of summary judgment de novo, and viewing the facts in the light most favorable to Falcone, we affirm. See *Amir v. St. Louis Univ.*, 184 F.3d 1017, 1024 (8th Cir. 1999) (standard of review).

. . . .

II. Discussion.

Section 504 provides, "No otherwise qualified individual with a disability . . . shall, solely by reason of her or his disability . . . be denied the benefits of . . . any program or activity receiving Federal financial assistance. . . ." Section 504 applies to postgraduate education programs that receive or benefit from Federal financial assistance. See 45 C.F.R. § 84.41. However, the statute does not require an educational institution to lower its standards for a professional degree, for example, by eliminating or substantially modifying its clinical training requirements. "An otherwise qualified person is one who is able to meet all of a program's requirements in spite of his handicap." *Southeastern Cmty. Coll. v. Davis*, 442 U.S. 397, 406, 99 S. Ct. 2361, 60 L. Ed. 2d 980 (1979); see 45 C.F.R. § 84.44(a) & App. A P 31.

To avoid summary judgment on his wrongful dismissal claim, Falcone must present sufficient evidence that he was disabled, otherwise qualified, and dismissed solely because of his disability. See *Jeseritz v. Potter*, 282 F.3d 542, 546 (8th Cir. 2002); *Amir*, 184 F.3d at 1029 n.5. The University concedes for purposes of summary judgment that Falcone is disabled. The issues, then, are whether Falcone presented sufficient evidence that he was "otherwise qualified" to remain in medical school but was nonetheless dismissed solely because of his disability.

A.

Taking up the easier issue first, we agree with the district court that no rational factfinder could conclude that Falcone was dismissed *solely* because of his learning disabilities. The University explained that Falcone was dismissed because "you have been unable to demonstrate, with or without accommodations, that you can synthesize data obtained in a clinical setting to perform clinical reasoning, which is an essential element of functioning as a medical student and ultimately as a physician." Falcone presented no evidence that this explanation was pretextual, or that the University's decision was a bad faith exercise of its virtually unrestricted discretion to evaluate academic performance. See *Bd. of Curators of the Univ. of Mo. v. Horowitz*, 435 U.S. 78, 95, 98 S. Ct. 948, 55 L. Ed. 2d 124 (1978) (Powell, J., concurring) (evaluating performance in clinical courses "is no less an 'academic' judgment . . . than assigning a grade to . . . written answers on an essay question"). "We will not invade a university's province concerning academic matters in the absence of compelling evidence that the academic policy is a pretext for [disability] discrimination." *Amir*, 184 F.3d at 1029.

Falcone argues that he presented sufficient evidence of bad faith because he was not provided all the accommodations listed in the Disability Specialist's letter in every clinical rotation. However, it is uncontroverted that the University made numerous accommodations throughout Falcone's medical school career, bending its policies and giving him additional chances when his performances raised serious concern about his ability to function as a physician. Despite these accommodations, Falcone failed three clinical courses, after he failed numerous classroom courses before finally completing that part of the curriculum. "Nothing in the record suggests that the University's decision was based on stereotypes about [Falcone's disability] as opposed to honest judgments about how [he] had performed in fact and could be expected to perform." *Anderson v. Univ. of Wis.*, 841 F.2d 737, 741 (7th Cir. 1988); see *Hines v. Rinker*, 667 F.2d 699, 703 (8th Cir. 1981) ("no genuine issue of material fact is presented . . . where the record provides ample evidence of the dismissed student's scholastic ineptitude") (quotation omitted).

The University was not required to tailor a program in which Falcone could graduate with a medical degree without establishing the ability to care for patients. Based on the uncontroverted evidence of Falcone's academic deficiencies, the only reasonable inference from this record is that he was dismissed because of the University's genuine concern about his inability to synthesize clinical data.

B.

In addition, we agree with the district court's alternative ground, that Falcone failed to present sufficient evidence that he was otherwise qualified to remain in the University's medical school program. It is undisputed that Falcone was not qualified to remain in medical school without accommodations. He then bears the burden "to establish that reasonable accommodations for his disability would render him qualified for the medical school program." *Stern v. Univ. of Osteopathic Med. & Health Scis.*, 220 F.3d 906, 909 (8th Cir. 2000).

Falcone argues that genuine issues of material fact preclude summary judgment on this issue because he did not receive one of the agreed accommodations in all his clinical courses — access to at least weekly, regularly scheduled feedback meetings with each instructor — and because his performance improved in clinical rotations when he received that level of feedback. In prior medical school cases, the issue has been whether the students requested reasonable accommodations that the universities refused to provide. See *Stern, 220 F.3d at 908-09*; *Zukle v. Regents of the Univ. of Cal.*, 166 F.3d 1041, 1048-51 (9th Cir. 1999). Here, on the other hand, the parties agreed on the accommodations to be provided, but Falcone argues they were imperfectly delivered. The University's COSSS disagreed and also concluded that he was, in any event, academically unfit. The latter point is critical — even if there is a genuine fact dispute over whether the feedback accommodation was perfectly implemented, Falcone must still show that, if it had been perfectly implemented, he would have passed the clinical courses that he failed. We agree with the district court that Falcone did not meet this burden.

The University presented abundant evidence supporting its conclusion that no amount of additional feedback would have made Falcone "otherwise qualified" to remain in school and receive a medical degree. In Emergency Medicine, Falcone acknowledged that he received feedback at the end of each shift from the residents with whom he worked and never approached the course instructors for additional feedback, yet he failed that course, his third failure in a clinical rotation. In Renal Medicine, a clinical course in which Falcone praised the level of feedback provided, the instructor did not issue a grade because Falcone's "fundamental abilities for clinical medicine were not sufficient," and he was "not able to handle the load and working pace of an intern in an internal medicine program." In addition, Falcone's Pediatric Neurology instructor had "great reservations about [his] ability to practice medicine." His Otolaryngology instructor noted his inability "to synthesize the information at hand into a practical, workable plan." And his Surgery instructor noted that all faculty and residents who worked with Falcone "expressed concern with his ineptitude to relate with patients."

Falcone did not controvert this evidence, nor did he present evidence other than his own opinion that he would have become "otherwise qualified" had he been provided more or better instructor feedback. Falcone failed an unacceptable number of clinical courses because he could not "synthesize data obtained in a clinical setting to perform clinical reasoning." He failed to present evidence showing that more feedback or better delivery of any other agreed accommodation would have cured this deficiency. Accordingly, the grant of summary judgment on this issue was proper.

The judgment of the district court is affirmed.

NOTES AND PROBLEMS FOR DISCUSSION

1. Does the Ninth Circuit's discussion of academic deference in *Zukle* give full recognition to all aspects of the problem? Why did the Ninth Circuit hold that the school in *Zukle* had met its burden of production, but the school in *Wong* did not? For a case that is quite critical of the *Zukle* analysis, see *Singh v. George Washington University School of Medicine and Health Sciences*, 508 F.3d 1097 (2007).

2. In *Pushkin v. Regents of the Univ. of Colorado*, 658 F.2d 1372 (10th Cir. 1981), the court rejected the rule of deference to academic decisions as inconsistent with the plain language of Section 504 forbidding discrimination against otherwise qualified individuals with disabilities. The school administrators in *Pushkin* argued that their decision not to admit Pushkin to a medical residency program should be reviewed under equal protection standards using the rational basis test. More specifically, they argued that "judicial deference to [an] administrative decision, *especially academic decisions relating to admissions criteria*, must be followed whenever the decision of the public body is rationally related to legitimate governmental needs. In other words they say that the rational basis test of equal protection must be applied when considering § 504." *Id.* at 1383 (emphasis added). The court disagreed, stating that the statute:

> provides that a recipient of federal financial assistance may not discriminate on the basis of handicap, regardless of whether there is a rational basis for so discriminating. The inquiry has to be on whether the University has, in fact, discriminated on the basis of handicap. The mere fact that the University acted in a rational manner is no defense to an act of discrimination. Thus, while application of the rational basis test may be used to lend credence to the proposition that no discriminatory action has been taken, a finding of rational behavior on the part of the University is only the start of our search to determine whether the mandate of § 504 has been followed.

Id. See also Lane v. Pena, 867 F. Supp. 1050, 1053 (D.D.C. 1994), *aff'd*, 1995 U.S. App. LEXIS 20039 (D.C. Cir. June 5, 1995), *aff'd*, 518 U.S. 187 (1996) (holding that the Merchant Marine Academy's requirement that cadets be able to be accepted for a naval reserve commission after graduation was not essential to its purpose; thus the Academy violated Section 504 when it expelled a student who could not fulfill the reserve requirement because of insulin dependent diabetes). Although *Pushkin* was decided in 1981, the issue of how much deference courts should give to the judgments of academic institutions is still a lively issue today.

3. On remand, the University no longer conceded that Wong was an individual with a disability. Instead, it sought summary judgment on that issue. The court granted the motion for summary judgment. "Given his previous academic success the issue translates to whether he can demonstrate that most people, or the average person, would not have difficulty with the third and fourth years of medical school." *Wong v. Regents of the Univ. of California*, 410 F.3d 1052, 1065–66 (9th Cir. 2005). Framing the issue in that way, the court concluded that Wong was not disabled in learning or reading. The court also concluded that Wong was not precluded, by virtue of his disability, from engaging in a broad range of jobs. Thus, he was not substantially limited in the major life activity of working. The Ninth Circuit affirmed that holding. "The level of academic success Wong achieved during the first two years of medical school, without any special accommodation provided to him by the school, made that proposition [that his impairment substantially limited his ability to learn as a whole] implausible. His record was to the contrary." *Id.* How would that issue be resolved under the 2008 Amendments to the ADA? Would he be considered disabled?

4. A postsecondary educational institution may not condition the provision of academic adjustments and auxiliary aids on a student's ability to pay for such accommodations, nor may the institution require the student to attempt to obtain accommodations from other sources. *See, e.g., United States v. Board of Trustees for Univ. of Alabama*, 908 F.2d 740 (11th Cir. 1990) (holding that requiring students with hearing impairments to show that they lacked the financial means to pay for their own interpreters or other auxiliary aids violated Section 504); *State University of New York*, Complaint No. 02-92-2106 (OCR Region II, 1993) (university violated Section 504 by requiring a student with learning disabilities to request books on tape from service organizations whose names the university provided to the student). It is the responsibility of the postsecondary educational institution to ensure that necessary aids and accommodations are provided. *See Notre Dame Technical Assistance letter*, March 16, 2012 (OCR Cleveland) (regarding charging for services allegedly not required by Section 504 and the ADA).

5. Should the burden and order of proof vary with whether the student has received all the accommodations he or she requests (or the court finds necessary) as compared to situations where the student has received only some promised accommodations or the accommodations have been poorly implemented? *Compare Chen v. Univ. of Washington*, 2008 U.S. Dist. LEXIS 16902 (W.D. Wash. 2008) (accommodations provided), *and Falcone v. Univ. of Minnesota*, 388 F.3d 656 (8th Cir. 2004) (en banc) (above); *with Johnson v. Washington County Career Center*, 2013 U.S. Dist. LEXIS 161138 (S.D. Ohio Nov. 12, 2013) (some accommodations poorly implemented and others denied without sound justification).

3. Students with Sensory Impairments

Students, visiting parents, other program participants such as individuals who enroll in on-line classes with "sensory impairments," individuals who are blind or have low vision or are deaf or are hard-of-hearing, can face considerable challenges in accessing the information available to other students in academic and other school-sponsored activities. *See Thomas M. Cooley Law School*, OCR Complaint No.

15082067 (Seattle 2011) (law school responsible for insuring that CART services were provided to deaf students attending law student association open tutoring sessions).

Among the difficulties faced by students with sensory impairments is a reluctance by some colleges and universities to spend the considerable amount of money that may be entailed in hiring sign-language interpreters, real-time captionists, or alternate-media production specialists. Moreover, in some geographic areas, there may be a serious shortage of these specially-trained individuals, though technology, such as remote video-captioning, may both reduce the shortage problems and modestly reduce costs.

The Department of Justice recently published technical assistance on effective communication. *See* U.S. Dept. of Justice, Technical Assistance: ADA Requirements — Effective Communication (January 2014), available at http://www.ada.gov/ effective-comm.htm (Titles II and III guidance for individuals with "communications disabilities"). This publication is reprinted below:

Overview

People who have vision, hearing, or speech disabilities ("communication disabilities") use different ways to communicate. For example, people who are blind may give and receive information audibly rather than in writing and people who are deaf may give and receive information through writing or sign language rather than through speech.

The ADA requires that title II entities (State and local governments) and title III entities (businesses and nonprofit organizations that serve the public) communicate effectively with people who have communication disabilities. The goal is to ensure that communication with people with these disabilities is equally effective as communication with people without disabilities.

This publication is designed to help title II and title III entities ("covered entities") understand how the rules for effective communication, including rules that went into effect on March 15, 2011, apply to them.

- The purpose of the effective communication rules is to ensure that the person with a vision, hearing, or speech disability can communicate with, receive information from, and convey information to, the covered entity
- Covered entities must provide auxiliary aids and services when needed to communicate effectively with people who have communication disabilities.
- The key to communicating effectively is to consider the nature, length, complexity, and context of the communication and the person's normal method(s) of communication.
- The rules apply to communicating with the person who is receiving the covered entity's goods or services as well as with that person's parent, spouse, or companion in appropriate circumstances.

Auxiliary Aids and Services

The ADA uses the term "auxiliary aids and services" ("aids and services") to refer to the ways to communicate with people who have communication disabilities.

- For people who are blind, have vision loss, or are deaf-blind, this includes providing a qualified reader; information in large print, Braille, or electronically for use with a computer screen-reading program; or an audio recording of printed information. A "qualified" reader means someone who is able to read effectively, accurately, and impartially, using any necessary specialized vocabulary.
- For people who are deaf, have hearing loss, or are deaf-blind, this includes providing a qualified notetaker; a qualified sign language interpreter, oral interpreter, cued-speech interpreter, or tactile interpreter; real-time captioning; written materials; or a printed script of a stock speech (such as given on a museum or historic house tour). A "qualified" interpreter means someone who is able to interpret effectively, accurately, and impartially, both receptively (i.e., understanding what the person with the disability is saying) and expressively (i.e., having the skill needed to convey information back to that person) using any necessary specialized vocabulary.
- For people who have speech disabilities, this may include providing a qualified speech-to-speech transliterator (a person trained to recognize unclear speech and repeat it clearly), especially if the person will be speaking at length, such as giving testimony in court, or just taking more time to communicate with someone who uses a communication board. In some situations, keeping paper and pencil on hand so the person can write out words that staff cannot understand or simply allowing more time to communicate with someone who uses a communication board or device may provide effective communication. Staff should always listen attentively and not be afraid or embarrassed to ask the person to repeat a word or phrase they do not understand.

In addition, aids and services include a wide variety of technologies including 1) assistive listening systems and devices; 2) open captioning, closed captioning, real-time captioning, and closed caption decoders and devices; 3) telephone handset amplifiers, hearing-aid compatible telephones, text telephones (TTYs), videophones, captioned telephones, and other voice, text, and video-based telecommunications products; 4) videotext displays; 5) screen reader software, magnification software, and optical readers; 6) video description and secondary auditory programming (SAP) devices that pick up video-described audio feeds for television programs; 7) accessibility features in electronic documents and other electronic and information technology that is accessible (either independently or through assistive technology such as screen readers).

Real-time captioning (also known as computer-assisted real-time transcription, or CART) is a service similar to court reporting in which a transcriber types what is being said at a meeting or event into a computer that projects the words onto a screen. This service, which can be provided on-site or remotely, is particularly useful for people who are deaf or have hearing loss but do not use sign language.

The free nationwide **telecommunications relay service** (TRS), reached by calling 7-1-1, uses communications assistants (also called CAs or relay operators) who serve as intermediaries between people who have hearing or speech disabilities who use a text telephone (TTY) or text messaging and people who use standard voice telephones. The communications assistant tells the telephone user what the other party is typing and types to tell the other party what the telephone user is saying. TRS also provides speech-to-speech transliteration for callers who have speech disabilities.

Video relay service (VRS) is a free, subscriber-based service for people who use sign language and have videophones, smart phones, or computers with video communication capabilities. For outgoing calls, the subscriber contacts the VRS interpreter, who places the call and serves as an intermediary between the subscriber and a person who uses a standard voice telephone. The interpreter tells the telephone user what the subscriber is signing and signs to the subscriber what the telephone user is saying.

Video remote interpreting (VRI) is a fee-based service that uses video conferencing technology to access an off-site interpreter to provide real-time sign language or oral interpreting services for conversations between hearing people and people who are deaf or have hearing loss. The new regulations give covered entities the choice of using VRI or on-site interpreters in situations where either would be effective. VRI can be especially useful in rural areas where on-site interpreters may be difficult to obtain. Additionally, there may be some cost advantages in using VRI in certain circumstances. However, VRI will not be effective in all circumstances. For example, it will not be effective if the person who needs the interpreter has difficulty seeing the screen (either because of vision loss or because he or she cannot be properly positioned to see the screen, because of an injury or other condition). In these circumstances, an on-site interpreter may be required.

If VRI is chosen, *all* of the following specific performance standards must be met:

- real-time, full-motion video and audio over a dedicated high-speed, wide-bandwidth video connection or wireless connection that delivers high-quality video images that do not produce lags, choppy, blurry, or grainy images, or irregular pauses in communication;
- a sharply delineated image that is large enough to display the interpreter's face, arms, hands, and fingers, and the face, arms, hands, and fingers of the person using sign language, regardless of his or her body position;

- a clear, audible transmission of voices; and
- adequate staff training to ensure quick set-up and proper operation.

Many deaf-blind individuals use support service providers (SSPs) to assist them in accessing the world around them. SSPs are not "aids and services" under the ADA. However, they provide mobility, orientation, and informal communication services for deaf-blind individuals and are a critically important link enabling them to independently access the community at large.

Effective Communication Provisions

Covered entities must provide aids and services when needed to communicate effectively with people who have communication disabilities.

The key to deciding what aid or service is needed to communicate effectively is to consider the nature, length, complexity, and context of the communication as well as the person's normal method(s) of communication.

Some easy solutions work in relatively simple and straightforward situations. For example:

- In a lunchroom or restaurant, reading the menu to a person who is blind allows that person to decide what dish to order.
- In a retail setting, pointing to product information or writing notes back and forth to answer simple questions about a product may allow a person who is deaf to decide whether to purchase the product.

Other solutions may be needed where the information being communicated is more extensive or complex. For example:

- In a law firm, providing an accessible electronic copy of a legal document that is being drafted for a client who is blind allows the client to read the draft at home using a computer screen-reading program.
- In a doctor's office, an interpreter generally will be needed for taking the medical history of a patient who uses sign language or for discussing a serious diagnosis and its treatment options.

A person's method(s) of communication are also key. For example, sign language interpreters are effective only for people who use sign language. Other methods of communication, such as those described above, are needed for people who may have lost their hearing later in life and do not use sign language. Similarly, Braille is effective only for people who read Braille. Other methods are needed for people with vision disabilities who do not read Braille, such as providing accessible electronic text documents, forms, etc., that can be accessed by the person's screen reader program.

Covered entities are also required to accept telephone calls placed through TRS and VRS, and staff who answer the telephone must treat relay calls just like other calls. The communications assistant will explain how the system works if necessary.

Remember, the purpose of the effective communication rules is to ensure that the person with a communication disability can receive information from, and convey information to, the covered entity.

Companions

In many situations, covered entities communicate with someone other than the person who is receiving their goods or services. For example, school staff usually talk to a parent about a child's progress; hospital staff often talk to a patient's spouse, other relative, or friend about the patient's condition or prognosis. The rules refer to such people as "companions" and require covered entities to provide effective communication for companions who have communication disabilities.

The term "companion" includes any family member, friend, or associate of a person seeking or receiving an entity's goods or services who is an appropriate person with whom the entity should communicate.

Use of Accompanying Adults or Children as Interpreters

Historically, many covered entities have expected a person who uses sign language to bring a family member or friend to interpret for him or her. These people often lacked the impartiality and specialized vocabulary needed to interpret effectively and accurately. It was particularly problematic to use people's children as interpreters.

The ADA places responsibility for providing effective communication, including the use of interpreters, directly on covered entities. They cannot require a person to bring someone to interpret for him or her. A covered entity can rely on a companion to interpret in only two situations.

(1) In an emergency involving an imminent threat to the safety or welfare of an individual or the public, an adult or minor child accompanying a person who uses sign language may be relied upon to interpret or facilitate communication only when a qualified interpreter is not available.

(2) In situations *not* involving an imminent threat, an adult accompanying someone who uses sign language may be relied upon to interpret or facilitate communication when a) the individual requests this, b) the accompanying adult agrees, and c) reliance on the accompanying adult is appropriate under the circumstances. This exception does not apply to minor children.

Even under exception (2) , covered entities may not rely on an accompanying adult to interpret when there is reason to doubt the person's impartiality or effectiveness. For example:

- It would be inappropriate to rely on a companion to interpret who feels conflicted about communicating bad news to the person or has a personal stake in the outcome of a situation.
- When responding to a call alleging spousal abuse, police should never rely on one spouse to interpret for the other spouse.

Who Decides Which Aid or Service Is Needed?

When choosing an aid or service, title II entities are required to give primary consideration to the choice of aid or service requested by the person who has a communication disability. The state or local government must honor the person's choice, unless it can demonstrate that another equally effective means of communication is available, or that the use of the means chosen would result in a fundamental alteration or in an undue burden (see limitations below). If the choice expressed by the person with a disability would result in an undue burden or a fundamental alteration, the public entity still has an obligation to provide an alternative aid or service that provides effective communication if one is available.

Title III entities are *encouraged* to consult with the person with a disability to discuss what aid or service is appropriate. The goal is to provide an aid or service that will be effective, given the nature of what is being communicated and the person's method of communicating.

Covered entities may require reasonable advance notice from people requesting aids or services, based on the length of time needed to acquire the aid or service, but may not impose excessive advance notice requirements. "Walk-in" requests for aids and services must also be honored to the extent possible.

Limitations

Covered entities are required to provide aids and services unless doing so would result in an "undue burden," which is defined as significant difficulty or expense. If a particular aid or service would result in an undue burden, the entity must provide another effective aid or service, if possible, that would not result in an undue burden. Determining what constitutes an undue burden will vary from entity to entity and sometimes from one year to the next. The impact of changing economic conditions on the resources available to an entity may also be taken into consideration in making this determination.

State and local governments: in determining whether a particular aid or service would result in undue financial and administrative burdens, a title II entity should take into consideration the cost of the particular aid or service in light of all resources available to fund the program, service, or activity and the effect on other expenses or operations. The decision that a particular aid or service would result in an undue burden must be made by a high level official, no lower than a Department head, and must include a written statement of the reasons for reaching that conclusion.

Businesses and nonprofits: in determining whether a particular aid or service would result in an undue burden, a title III entity should take into consideration the nature and cost of the aid or service relative to their size, overall financial resources, and overall expenses. In general, a business or nonprofit with greater resources is expected to do more to ensure effective communication than one with fewer resources. If the entity has a parent company, the administrative and financial relationship, as well as the size, resources, and expenses of the parent company, would also be considered.

In addition, covered entities are not required to provide any particular aid or service in those rare circumstances where it would fundamentally alter the nature of the goods or services they provide to the public. In the performing arts, for example, slowing down the action on stage in order to describe the action for patrons who are blind or have vision loss may fundamentally alter the nature of a play or dance performance.

Staff Training

A critical and often overlooked component of ensuring success is comprehensive and ongoing staff training. Covered entities may have established good policies, but if front line staff are not aware of them or do not know how to implement them, problems can arise. Covered entities should teach staff about the ADA's requirements for communicating effectively with people who have communication disabilities. Many local disability organizations, including Centers for Independent Living, conduct ADA trainings in their communities. The Department's ADA Information Line can provide local contact information for these organizations.

NOTES AND PROBLEMS FOR DISCUSSION

1. How does a college effectively ascertain the auxiliary aid choices of individuals with disabilities? Does it make sense that a private institution subject to Title III has a lesser duty to address the preferences of individuals with sensory impairments than does a public institution? Because all private colleges and universities are likely to be subject to Section 504, is the duty actually the same irrespective of whether they are covered by Title II or Title III?

2. The above guidance from DOJ delves into the issue of undue burden. Is it suggesting that for a large institution there is virtually no limit as to how much must be spent to provide auxiliary aids for persons with sensory impairments? Can a college require students who need similar aids for the same course to register for the same course section so as to control costs?

3. The above guidance may be very helpful, but how does a disability compliance officer ensure that all faculty are aware of its requirements?

(a) Students Who Are Blind or Have Low Vision

The preparation of alternate media for students who are blind, have low vision or a reading disability, such as dyslexia, requires cooperation and coordination between faculty, the disabled student services office, and "alternate media specialists," the persons who acquire or produce the alternate media. Most commonly, these persons must convert traditional text books to digital media that can be used on computers with adaptive technology programs such as Kurzweil, Jaws, Dragon Dictate, Naturally

Speaking and Zoom Text. *See Authors Guild, Inc. v. Hathitrust*, 902 F. Supp. 2d 445 (S.D.N.Y. 2012), *aff'd*, ___ F.3d ___, 2014 U.S. App. LEXIS 10803 (2d Cir. June 10, 2014). These screen-reading programs can produce text to speech, speech to text, refreshable braille and enlarged text. While the conversion of a basic piece of English literature may be fairly straightforward with the right equipment, the conversion of scientific, mathematical, graphical, and second language materials can be quite challenging. For more information about adaptive technology for students with disabilities in higher education, *see* https://www.washington.edu/doit/; www.htctu.net/ (last viewed on Apr. 26, 2013). As a result of the decision in *Hathitrust*, millions of books are available as digital books for purposes of text search and accessibility for readers who are visually impaired within the limits of fair use under the copyright laws.

CALIFORNIA STATE UNIVERSITY FULLERTON

OCR Docket Number 09-03-2166
http://www.galvin-group.com/media/48594/CA_OCR_CSU_Fullerton%5B1%5D.pdf
(last viewed on August 26, 2013)

The U.S. Department of Education (Department), Office for Civil Rights (OCR), has completed its investigation of the above referenced complaint against the California State University, Fullerton. The complainant alleged that the University discriminated against her based on her disability, visual impairment/legally blind. The issues OCR investigated were whether the complainant's documented and authorized academic adjustments were implemented in a timely manner and whether the method of administration utilized to produce electronic text materials (alternative print format) created barriers to the complainant's ability to participate in the educational program.

This letter is to inform you that OCR has completed its investigation of these allegations. OCR enforces Section 504 of the Rehabilitation Act of 1973 and its implementing regulation. Section 504 prohibits discrimination on the basis of disability in programs and activities operated by recipients of Federal financial assistance. OCR also has jurisdiction as a designated agency under Title II of the Americans with Disabilities Act of 1990 and its implementing regulation over complaints alleging discrimination on the basis of disability that are filed against certain public entities. The University receives Department funds, is a public entity, and is subject to the requirements of Section 504 and Title II.

OCR initiated its resolution process by requesting and reviewing information from the complainant and the University, and by conducting telephone conferences with relevant University staff. OCR concluded that the evidence established that the University did not provide the Student academic material in an appropriate, accessible alternative format and in a timely manner for classes that she registered for in spring 2003, summer 2003, or and fall 2003.

After discussions with OCR, the University agreed, without admitting to any violation of law, to take actions to resolve the issues raised by this complaint. The facts gathered during the investigation, the applicable legal standards, and the reasons for our determination are summarized below.

Legal Standard

The Regulation implementing Section 504 at 34 C.F.R. § 104.44 (d) provides in pertinent part:

> (d) Auxiliary Aids.
>
> (1) A recipient to which this subpart applies shall take such steps as are necessary to ensure that no individual with a disability is denied the benefits of . . . an educational program because of the absence of educational auxiliary aids for students with impaired sensory, manual, or speaking skills.
>
> (2) Auxiliary aids may include taped texts, interpreters or other effective methods of making orally delivered materials available to students with hearing- impairments, readers in libraries for students with visual impairments, classroom equipment adapted for use by students with manual impairments, and other similar services and actions . . .

Further, at § 104.4(4):

> Discriminatory actions prohibited.
>
> (1) A recipient, in providing any aid, benefit, or service, may not . . . on the basis of disability:
>
> (4) . . . [U]tilize criteria or methods of administration [that] (i) that have the effect of subjecting qualified individuals with disabilities to discrimination on the basis of disability, [or] (ii) that have the purpose or effect of defeating or substantially impairing accomplishment of the objectives of the recipient's program or activity with respect to individuals with disabilities. . . .

The regulation implementing Title II of the Americans with Disabilities Act found at 28 C.F.R. Part 35 provides in pertinent part:

> § 35.130 General prohibitions against discrimination.
>
> (b)(1) A public entity, in providing any aid, benefit, or service, may not . . . on the basis of disability-
>
> (iii) Provide a qualified individual with a disability with an aid, benefit, or service that is not as effective in affording equal opportunity to obtain the same result, to gain the same benefit, or to reach the same level of achievement as that provided to others.
>
> § 35.160 General Communications
>
> (a) A public entity shall take appropriate steps to ensure that communications with applicants, participants, and members of the public with disabilities are as effective as communications with others.

> (b)(1) A public entity shall furnish appropriate auxiliary aids and services where necessary to afford an individual with a disability an equal opportunity to participate in, and enjoy the benefits of, a service, program, or activity conducted by a public entity.
>
> (2) In determining what type of auxiliary aid and service is necessary, a public entity shall give primary consideration to the requests of the individual with disabilities.

OCR has interpreted the term "communication" in this context to mean the transfer of information, including (but not limited to) the verbal presentation of a lecturer, the printed text of a book, and the resources of the Internet. In construing the conditions under which communication is "as effective as" that provided to non-disabled persons, on several occasions OCR has regarded the three basic components of effectiveness as timeliness of delivery, accuracy of the translation, and provision in a manner and medium appropriate to the significance of the message and the abilities of the individual with the disability.

Our investigation found the following:

- The complainant has substantially impaired vision, and ordinarily does not use printed text as a means obtaining information.
- The complainant prefers to use "JAWS", a computer program that converts electronic text (e-text) files to auditory language, to review educational materials assigned by her instructors.
- The complainant is registered with Disabled Student Services (DSS), and has substantially followed DSS procedures for requesting coursework, mainly textbooks, in alternative format, i.e. e-text, since fall of 2000.
- The DSS of California State University, Fullerton has established for itself standards for providing educational materials in an alternative accessible format: timely delivery, equal in quality to the materials utilized by non-disabled students, and produced in a manner and medium appropriate to the abilities of the individual with the disability.
- The complainant requested e-text on December 19, 2004 for spring 2003, i.e. Sociology 301-Social Theories, Sociology 302-Research Methods, and Spanish310-Spanish in the Business World. The due date she requested was mid-January 2003.
- The DSS notified the complainant that the McTavish textbook for Soc 301 was scanned January 17, 2003, and the audiocassette was mailed January 21, 2003. This was a delay of approximately a week.
- The DSS notified the complainant by an e-mail on January 27, 2003 that the Farganis textbook for Sociology 301 was completed and ready for pick up. This was a delay of approximately two weeks.
- The DSS notified the complainant by an e-mail on January 29, 2003, the book for Spanish 310 came in and DSS would be working on that. This was a delay of approximately two weeks.

- The DSS notified the complainant by an e-mail dated February 27, 2003, the Cuzzort book for Sociology 301 ready for pick-up. This was delay of approximately six weeks.
- Because the books for Sociology 301, Sociology 302, and Spanish 310 were untimely produced, the complainant was behind in class work, homework, group work and preparing for exams. The complainant reported to OCR that the untimely receipt of alternative format materials caused her to become anxious and stressed. She stated that, by April 2003, she felt compelled to drop all her classes.
- The complainant later took these classes again, but had incurred additional expenses for textbooks that were not covered by state rehabilitation funds.
- The complainant requested e-text for summer 2003 for English 301; Advanced College Writing on May 12th — which were due on June 2, 2003. She made a request for another English text on June 3, 2003 which complainant needed on June 4, 2003.
- The complainant requested e-text for "To Kill a Mockingbird" on May 12, 2003 and she needed the required reading by June 2, 2003. The DSS notified the complainant that, "To Kill a Mockingbird" was ready for pick up June 13, 2003. This was a delay of approximately ten days. Further, the complainant had difficulties with chapters one through five, which were not readable by her computer e-text recognition program. She eventually had to drop the English 301 class.
- The complainant requested e-text for fall 2003 in early September, i.e. Sociology 301 Social Theories, Sociology 302 -Research Methods, and Spanish 315 -Spanish Culture.

  OCR found evidence that the complainant timely requested a Spanish dictionary be scanned for fall 2003.
- The DSS scanned the dictionary in three parts: On September 30, 2003, letters A-E were ready; on October 20, 2003, sections F, G, H were ready; and October 30, 2003, sections N, 0, V, W, X, Y, Z were ready for pick-up. The piecemeal production of this resource meant that it was not practically usable until mid-term.
- In interviews with OCR, DSS staff, who were quite knowledgeable and insightful about e-text preparation, identified these recurring obstacles to producing the e- text in a timely manner:
  1) Inability/unwillingness of professors to provide the bookstore with a class syllabus in advance of registration;
  2) Insufficient number of editors, especially for specialty texts;
  3) A lack of coordination of work on e-text requests when the job function is split between two or three people;
  4) There is no back up if the sole e-text conversion coordinator is absent due to illness, family emergency, etc.;
  5) Use of an outdated scanner;

6) Conflicting use of the scanner by students and by editors;
7) The existing on-line request system can be difficult for some students since there is no immediate confirmation that their request was received;
8) Inability of the current alternative text conversion system to track the progress of pending e-text jobs; and
9) The request process is not sufficiently interactive.

Conclusion

Based on the facts gathered during the investigation, OCR concluded that the University's "method of administration" for receiving requests, processing, and producing alternative format requests, established legally appropriate standards, but did not provide the complainant access to alternative media educational materials in the same time frame as educational materials are made available to non-disabled students. The delays in receiving alternative media materials had a negative effect on complainant's opportunities to achieve the same educational opportunity, and "effective communication" as that afforded to non-disabled students.

On April 29, 2004, the University provided OCR with a Resolution Agreement to develop a plan that will commit sufficient trained and qualified personnel resources to ensure that students who require text and other written materials to be converted to an alternative format will receive those alternative media materials that are equal in quality and received at the same time as educational materials provided to non-disabled students, in accordance with Section 504. This plan reflects the considerable expertise that currently exists at the University with regard to the production of alternative media.

The University also undertook to improve the on-line request process by making a range of options available for requesting alternative media, making staff available to assist the complainant and other visually impaired students to make requests online, track progress toward completion of conversion of text, and provide students with progress reports.

The University has also agreed to reimburse the complainant for out-of-pocket expenses related to the courses she re-took because the alternate format text materials were not provided to her in a timely manner. The University undertook to establish dates for faculty to provide departments with a list of reading material for courses and communicate these dates to all faculty so as to allow more time to produce alternative media materials.

OCR concludes that the Resolution Agreement, when fully implemented, will resolve this complaint under appropriate legal standards. Therefore, we are closing the investigative phase of this complaint as of the date of this letter. The complainant is being notified concurrently. OCR will monitor implementation of the agreement through reports from the University.

OCR wishes to thank the University for its cooperation and resolution of this complaint.

NOTES AND PROBLEMS FOR DISCUSSION

1. One of the most common problems in the production of timely alternate media is that students may give little or no advance notice to the disabled student services program or alternate media production center of which courses they intend to take or the books required for their chosen courses. Shouldn't some level of cooperation be expected from students with disabilities who want accommodations that require advanced planning, arrangements, or production? Do you think colleges should be excused from providing timely alternate media when students are uncooperative in meeting reasonable deadlines?

2. A second common problem is that teachers provide their syllabi at the last minute, and may modify them over the course of the semester. Generally, disabled student service providers have little leverage over faculty. Should a college or university be able to require faculty to provide their syllabi well before the semester starts in order to provide equal access to information for students with sensory and print impairments? What if a faculty member refuses to cooperate on the grounds that such a requirement violates the principle of academic freedom as well as constitutes an undue burden and a fundamental alteration. *See* Settlement between the University of California, Disability Rights Advocates, and Several Named Students (May 2013). http://dralegal.org/sites/dralegal.org/files/casefiles/settlement-ucb.pdf (last viewed on August 26, 2013) (faculty required to provide syllabi on a timely basis to enable the production of alternate media); *Rhodes v. Southern Nazarene University*, 554 Fed. Appx. 685 (10th Cir. 2014) (receiving syllabi six weeks in advance when courses are presented in five week blocks is not a required accommodation).

3. A recently filed case involving a student who is blind may offer further guidance on a university's obligations to a student who is blind. Aleeha is an undergraduate student at Miami University in Ohio. She enrolled at Miami University in the fall of 2011 to pursue a bachelor's degree in zoology so that she might secure admission to veterinary school. According to her complaint, the university sent a letter to her instructors suggesting only two modifications: offering all classroom material in Rich Text Format and allowing double-time for exams and quizzes. The letter made no mention of Braille textbooks, tactile graphics, human assistants, timely course materials or accessible learning management software. Her lecture instructors used LearnSmart to manage homework assignments, which was not accessible to her. She was not permitted to participate fully in lab activities. In the complaint, she alleged that Miami University made technology procurement decisions with indifference to the accessibility of the technology in question, even though accessible technology existed and was being used at other universities. *See Aleeha Dudley v. Miami University*, No. 1:14-cv-38 (filed January 10, 2014). *See* https://nfb.org/images/nfb/documents/pdf/miami%20teach.pdf (last viewed on May 22, 2014).

(b) Students Who Are Deaf or Hard-of-Hearing

i. Systemic practices

The degree of coordination and advanced planning necessary to provide equal communication for deaf students may even be greater than that necessary to provide timely alternate media. The form of accommodation that works for one student who is deaf, such as American Sign Language (ASL) or cued speech, may not be appropriate for another student who is deaf, such as a veteran who has only recently become deaf. The veteran, instead, is likely to need CART services. Colleges may find that there are simply not enough interpreters to go around. One college may be competing with another or even a local school district for interpreting services. Those interpreters with whom a college contracts may be qualified to interpret for some individuals in some courses, but not for other individuals or in other, more advanced courses. To meet their responsibilities to deaf or hard-of-hearing students, colleges must plan ahead and carefully organize and schedule their resources.

HAYDEN v. REDWOODS COMMUNITY COLLEGE DISTRICT

2007 U.S. Dist. LEXIS 835, 33 NDLRP 250 (N.D. Cal. Jan. 8, 2007)

NANDOR J. VADAS, United States Magistrate Judge.

AMENDED ORDER DENYING THE PARTIES' MOTIONS FOR SUMMARY JUDGMENT AND FOR INJUNCTIVE RELIEF

In this action for discrimination by denying meaningful access to a public accommodation in violation of Title II of the Americans with Disabilities Act of 1990 (ADA), section 504 of the Rehabilitation Act, and the Unruth Civil Rights Act [citations omitted], brought by Plaintiff Mandi Hayden against Defendants Redwoods Community College District et al., both parties have filed motions for summary judgment in whole, or in the alternative, in part. For the reasons set forth below, the parties' motions are denied.

I. BACKGROUND

Plaintiff Mandi Hayden attended the College of the Redwoods ("the College") between Spring of 2003 and Fall of 2005. (Joint Statement of Stipulated Facts in Support for Mot. for Summ. J. #5.) The College is part of the Redwoods Community College District, which is part of the California Community College system, and is a state agency subject to Title II of the ADA. [All stipulation citations hereinafter omitted.] A violation of the ADA is, per se, a violation of the Unruth Act. (*Lentini v. Cal. Center for the Arts*, 370 F.3d 837, 847 (9th Cir. 2004).) The Redwoods Community College District is also a recipient of federal funds and is therefore subject to section 504 of the Rehabilitation Act.

Plaintiff was born with the inability to hear and is completely deaf. Plaintiff attended a deaf program from preschool through grade 6 at Magnalia Elementary

School in Carlsbad, California from teachers who signed, and then grades 7 through 12 at the School for the Deaf in Riverside, California, also taught by teachers who signed. Thus, Plaintiff received her early education in American Sign Language (ASL), which is also her first language. ASL is not a visual representation of English or any other spoken language, but an entirely distinct visual language.

In the Spring of 2003, Plaintiff enrolled at College of the Redwoods. At the College, the Disabled Student Programs and Services (DSPS) is responsible for the provision of auxiliary aids. While Plaintiff was enrolled at the College, Tracey Thomas was the Director of DSPS. The State Chancellor's Office oversees the College and has issued guidelines that 5% of the College budget must be kept in reserve, leaving 95% to be allocated. The annual budget of the College, from which DSPS's budget comes, is based on the number of students enrolled.

The annual budget of DSPS is determined by a set formula based on the number of students who receive disabled student services from the College. The annual budget of DSPS in 2000-2001 was $1,213,662.57, $1,361,630.20 in 2001-2002, $1,288,247.45 in 2002-2003, $1,314,464.45 in 2003-2004, and $1,367,093.95 in 2004-2005. DSPS served 1,316 students in 2000-2001, 1,227 in 2001-2002, 1,401 in 2002-2003, 1,247 in 2003-2004, and 1,199 in 2004-2005. In terms of students receiving interpreter services from DSPS, 3 students in 2001-2002, 4 in 2002-2003, 6 in 2003-2004, 8 in 2004-2005, and 8 in 2005-2006.

On November 2, 2002, Plaintiff applied for DSPS services. In order to receive services, students must agree to abide by policies and procedures designed to "maximize administrative efficiency when providing DSPS services." On November 6, 2002, Plaintiff applied specifically for Interpreter Services. That application process included signing a document entitled "DSPS Guidelines for Interpreter Services" that outlined the College's policies for interpreter requests, absences, and the appeals process for grievances. Plaintiff signed this document. Plaintiff never told anyone at DSPS if she understood the document. Nor does it appear if anyone from the College asked her if she understood it.

Among the provisions of the Interpreter Guidelines were those regarding absences. In relevant part the guidelines stated that "if you plan to miss one or more classes, please notify DSPS at least 24 hours before the missed class(es). If the office is closed, please leave a message. This will allow DSPS to promptly inform your interpreter and make any needed changes to the interpreting schedule. If you are ill or if an emergency situations arises please contact DSPS within 24 hours. [sic] If you do not show up for a class and DSPS has not been notified, the absence will be considered unexcused. If there are three or more unexcused absences, or other such situations occur that are perceived by DSPS as abusing the interpreting services, DSPS will suspend your interpreting services. In order to clear an unexcused absence, please bring a doctor's note, etc., to the DSPS office. If you would like your services reinstated, you will need to make an appointment with DSPS."

Also included in the guidelines is a section named "Appeals Process." In that section, the policy states that "if you have a concern about academic programs or college services, and feel you have been denied services or access to a program, we encourage you to meet with the appropriate program or department manager. If you cannot resolve the issue, please contact the Vice President of Student Services."

On November 15, 2002, Plaintiff submitted medical documentation that she is a deaf individual with "severe-to-profound sensorineural hearing loss bilaterally" with "limited hearing even using hearing aids" and lip reading skills that allow for "50% understanding." The form indicated a "possible benefit from interpreter (sign language) and notetaker." Plaintiff received a copy of the DSPS Student Resource Guide, which outlined the services available to disabled students, the procedure to obtain such services, and the procedure for grievances. All of the text in the Guide consists of a bold topic heading, followed by single-spaced paragraphs of a few sentences each. None of the text in the Guide is in fine print.

The Student Resource Guide contains several sections relevant to the motions at hand. Under "Sign Language Interpreters," the Guide notes, *"An Interpreter will be provided through the DSPS office for students who are deaf or hard of hearing and who wish to use sign language as their primary and preferred mode of communication." When a student completes an application for such services, "DSPS will then recruit qualified Interpreters for the classes the student will be attending."* [emphasis added].

A later section of the Guide notes the "Grievance Process." There, the Guide states that "Every effort will be made to resolve the matter through the informal process. This may include a meeting with the Coordinator at DSPS, the faculty member and the student to determine a reasonable accommodation or service for the student. In situations when an agreement can not be reached informally, the Academic Accommodations panel will review the grievance. . . . The student still has the right of external appeal to the Office of Civil Rights under Section 504 of the Rehabilitation Act of 1973." This final sentence regarding the Rehabilitation Act of 1973 is its own paragraph.

Over the course of the next seven semesters, Plaintiff received Interpreter Services from DSPS from seven different interpreters. Prior to the start of each semester, DSPS would send Plaintiff a letter with the Interpreter assignments, and attach a copy of the Guidelines for Interpreter Services that Plaintiff signed on November 6, 2002. Plaintiff consistently refused real-time captioning and transcription services, though DSPS offered them to her several times. Instead, Plaintiff exclusively preferred Interpreters as her auxiliary aids. Most classes only require a single Interpreter. For particularly long classes, teams of two may be assigned so that one person is not signing for several hours, which can become painful for the Interpreter's hands. Instead, the Interpreters alternate, giving the other a chance to rest.

. . . .

Plaintiff received Interpreting services for 91.5% of her classes (580/637) from. Spring 2003 through Spring 2005, which does not include class meetings after Plaintiff dropped her classes in Fall 2004 and Spring 2005. (Stipulated Facts # 77.) Between Spring 2003 and Summer 2004, Plaintiff received an interpreter for 96.5% of her classes (491/509). (Stipulated Facts # 76.) A full-time permanent sign language interpreter is estimated to cost $85,244.01, with a base yearly salary of $60,008.00 and benefits totaling $25,236.01.

II. DISCUSSION

. . . .

B. Plaintiff's Motion

I. Plaintiff claims Defendant has discriminated by requiring Plaintiff to sign away her "rights" in order to receive services

II. Plaintiff claims Defendant is attempting to screen Plaintiff from services by use of its DSPS agreement and its policy and procedures in violation of 28 C.F.R. § 35.130(b)-(f)

III. Plaintiff claims Defendant has failed to meet its burden regarding fundamental alteration or undue financial or administrative burden

IV. Plaintiff claims Defendant should be prohibited from continuing its discriminatory behavior

. . . .

C. Defendant's Motion

I. Defendant claims no duty to provide a sign language interpreter

II. Defendant claims Plaintiff cannot show that the accommodations offered by the College were unreasonable

III. Defendant claims Plaintiff cannot establish a *prima facie* case for an ADA violation

IV. Defendant claims Plaintiff should be estopped from asserting an ADA violation for the Spring 2005 semester

V. Defendant claims compensatory damages are not available because the College did not act with deliberate indifference to Plaintiff's requests

VI. Defendant claims Plaintiff's, request for injunctive relief are moot and should be dismissed

D. Analysis

. . . .

In this case Defendant must provide Plaintiff with "meaningful access" to its programs. *Hunsaker v. Contra Costa County*, 149 F.3d 1041, 1043 (9th Cir. 1998). To that end, it may be required to make reasonable, but not fundamental or substantial, modifications to its programs See *Alexander v. Choate*, 469 U.S. 287, 300, 105 S. Ct. 712, 83 L. Ed 2d 661 (1985). Reasonableness requires a "fact-specific, individualized analysis of the disabled individual's circumstances and the accommodations that might allow him to meet the program's standards." *Vinson v. Thomas*, 288 F.3d 1145, 1154 (9th Cir. 2002).

28 CFR § 35.160 requires public entities to "take appropriate steps to ensure that communications with applicants, participants, and members of the public with disabilities are as effective as communications with others." 28 CFR § 35.160(a). These appropriate steps include furnishing "appropriate auxiliary aids and services where necessary to afford an individual with a disability an equal opportunity to participate in, and enjoy the benefits of, a service, program, or activity conducted by a public entity. In determining what type of auxiliary aid and service is necessary, a public entity shall give primary consideration to the requests of the individual with disabilities." 28 CFR § 35.160(b)(1)-(2).

In relevant part, the Appendix to Title II of the ADA provides: "the public entity must provide an opportunity for individuals with disabilities to request the auxiliary aids and services of their choice. This expressed choice shall be given primary consideration by the public entity (§ 35.160(b)(2)). The public entity shall honor the choice unless it can demonstrate that another effective means of communication exists or that use of the means chosen would not be required under § 35.164 [the affirmative defenses]. Deference to the request of the individual with a disability is desirable because of the range of disabilities, the variety of auxiliary aids and services, and different circumstances requiring effective communication." 28 C.F.R. Pt. 35, App. A

Among the auxiliary aids listed by the statute for individuals with hearing disabilities are "qualified interpreters, notetakers, transcription services, written materials, telephone handset amplifiers, assistive listening devices, assistive listening systems, telephones compatible with hearing aids, closed caption decoders, open and closed captioning, telecommunications devices for deaf persons (TDD's), videotext displays, or other effective methods of making aurally delivered materials available to individuals with hearing impairments." 28 C.F.R. § 35.104(1).

Defendant correctly acknowledges its duty under the ADA to make reasonable modifications to accommodate disabled individuals. However, Defendant argues that interpreter services, Plaintiff's preferred auxiliary aid, are not the only effective auxiliary aid, and that Defendant has the discretion to offer other aids. It is true that Defendant is not necessarily required to provide Plaintiff with her preferred auxiliary aid, but in giving her request primary consideration, Defendant may refuse her request only in limited circumstances, i.e. if there are other equally effective means of communication, or Defendant has an affirmative defense.

Defendant does not dispute it is a public entity subject to the ADA, and that it must "furnish appropriate auxiliary aids" where necessary to afford Plaintiff an equal opportunity to participate in the College. (Joint Stipulated Facts 1.) Nor does Defendant dispute that it must give "primary consideration" to Plaintiff's requested auxiliary aid, which Defendant acknowledges to be a ASL interpreter.

Where the parties differ is whether "another equally effective means of communication exists" as a form of auxiliary aid that affords Plaintiff an equal opportunity to participate in the College's programs besides an SLI. Defendant offered other auxiliary aids including transcription, real-time captioning, and audiotaping services to Plaintiff, all of which are listed by the statute as auxiliary aids for individuals with hearing disabilities. While it is true that Plaintiff rejected these options without trying them, it is Defendant's burden under the statute to demonstrate the proffered aid's effectiveness.

Though Plaintiff's application indicated her to have "50% lip reading ability" and possibly benefit from notetakers as well as SLIs, that does not necessarily mean that auxiliary aids that complement these abilities are sufficient to satisfy the ADA's "equally effective communication" standard. It is not clear from the record sufficient to satisfy the summary judgment standard whether the auxiliary aids offered by Defendant in alternative to an SLI are sufficiently "equally effective" to satisfy the ADA. Not only does the efficacy of an auxiliary aid vary with the hearing abilities of each individual, but an auxiliary aid that provides Plaintiff with an equal opportunity to participate in one particular class may not be sufficient in another class. Such findings cannot be made here.

It is for the trier of fact to determine whether the auxiliary aids offered by Defendant to Plaintiff meet the standards created in the ADA.

The Supreme Court has noted that "the "undue hardship" inquiry requires not simply an assessment of the cost of the accommodation in relation to the recipient's overall budget, but a "case-by-case analysis weighing factors that include: (1) the overall size of the recipient's program with respect to number of employees, number and type of facilities, and size of budget; (2) the type of the recipient's operation, including the composition and structure of the recipient's workforce; and (3) the nature and cost of the accommodation needed." " (*Olmstead v. L. C. by Zimring*, 527 U.S. 581, 606, 119 S. Ct. 2176, 144 L. Ed. 2d 540 (1999) citing 28 CFR § 42.511(c) (1998).) Further, "if applicable, the overall financial resources of the parent corporation and the number of facilities; and if applicable, the type of operation of the parent corporation" are to be considered. 28 C.F.R § 36.104.

DSPS has 36 staff who served 1,199 students. across 3 campuses in the 2004-2005 school year with a budget of $1,233,172. (#55, 19:9; Joint Stipulated Facts #3, 71, 72.) The staff include not only employees who assist hearing impaired students, but those who assist students with mobility disabilities, learning disabilities, and other challenges, as well as administrative staff. (#55, 19:10.) The budget comes from the California legislature and is dependent upon the number of disabled students enrolled at the College, as well as the type(s) of disability (or disabilities) they have. (#55, 19:18-19.)

Defendant cites *Roberts v. KinderCare Learning Ctrs., Inc.*, 86 F.3d 844 (8th Cir. 1996) an 8th Circuit decision, to support its contention that the budget of the College should not be taken into account, since financial operation of DSPS is separate. In *KinderCare*, the particular center was responsible for being independently profitable and could not rely on the parent corporation's resources. Here, however, DSPS is not intended to be a profitable operation, though it is responsible for managing its budget.

Defendant has provided the Court with financial information indicating that Plaintiff's demand for a personal interpreter would constitute nearly 7% of the DSPS annual budget. Personal interpreters for each of the 8 deaf students would constitute nearly 50% of the DSPS annual budget. With these figures, Defendant claims an undue financial hardship to accommodate Plaintiff's demand of a personal interpreter.

Again, it is for the trier of fact to determine whether or not this constitutes an "undue hardship" on the Defendant.

Regarding the remaining issues that the parties raise in their respective motions for summary judgment, the court comes to a similar conclusion. That is without "weighing the evidence" there remain genuine issues of material fact that must be decided by a jury. The core issue in this litigation appears to the court to be whether the College complied with its obligations under the ADA to provide adequate interpretation services to a hearing-impaired student that has been characterized by the Defendant as difficult and demanding. Plaintiff submits a very different picture of what took place over several semesters at the College. Plaintiff's version of events paints a picture of bureaucratic incompetence on the part of the Disabled Student Programs and Services Department of the College of the Redwoods and an attempt on their part to supply her with substandard assistance for her hearing disability. This analysis is by its nature fact driven.

. . . .

IV. DEFENDANT'S CLAIM OF UNDUE ADMINISTRATIVE BURDEN

Defendant asserts an undue administrative burden in allowing Plaintiff to choose her own interpreter. Defendant states that Plaintiff cannot claim an ADA violation "by simply asserting that the full-time interpreter could not communicate effectively for her." If she could, Defendant argues, the College would have to include Plaintiff in the interviewing process, as the College would have to for all disabled students receiving interpreter services. Plaintiff demands a certified full-time interpreter, but "certification is not required in order for an interpreter to be considered to have the skills necessary to facilitate communication." Indeed, the ADA requires only a "qualified interpreter" as an auxiliary aid for effective communication. Defendant claims that "qualified" does not necessarily demand that the student like the interpreter, only that the interpreter communicate "effectively, accurately, and impartially." To require the College to include Plaintiff in assigning interpreters, claims Defendant, would be an undue administrative burden.

As for Spring 2005, Defendant argues that it was unable to assign a new interpreter to Plaintiff's two uncovered classes, and to require it to do so would also be an undue administrative burden. Defendant claims that despite the efforts of DSPS Director Tracey Thomas, who contacted multiple schools and agencies, no interpreters were available. Plaintiff declined alternate auxiliary aids such as transcription and captioning because she claimed they could not provide the necessary level of communication skills required. Thomas also looked at VRI [Video Remote Interpreting], which turned out to require significant equipment installations and upgrades and was not feasible as a solution for Spring 2005. Thus, the only way to assign an interpreter for Plaintiff would be to reassign an interpreter from another student's class to Plaintiff's. Such a reassignment, Defendant states, is also an undue administrative burden.

Defendant argues that Plaintiff's request to choose her own interpreter and include Plaintiff in the process of assigning her an interpreter would constitute an undue administrative burden. Defendant cites two Ninth Circuit cases to support this contention, *Zukle v. Regents of the Univ. of Cal.*, 166 F.3d 1041 (9th Cir. 1999) and *Memmer v. Marin County Courts*, 169 F.3d 630 (9th Cir. 1999) In *Zukle* the Court held that:

> Deference is also appropriately accorded an educational institution's determination that a reasonable accommodation is not available. Therefore, we agree with the First Circuit that "a court's duty is to first find the basic facts, giving due deference to the school, and then to evaluate whether those facts add up to a professional, academic judgment that reasonable accommodation is not available." *Wynne II*, 932 F.2d at 27-28; *see also McGregor*, 3 F.3d at 859 (the court must "accord deference to [the school's] decisions not to modify its programs [when] the proposed modifications entail academic decisions").
>
> We recognize that extending deference to education institutions must not impede our obligation to enforce the ADA and the Rehabilitation Act. Thus, we must be careful not to allow academic decisions to disguise truly discriminatory requirements. The educational institution has a "real obligation . . . to seek suitable means of reasonably accommodating a handicapped person and to submit a factual record indicating that it conscientiously carried out this statutory obligation. *Wynne I*, 932 F.2d at 25-26. Once the educational institution has fulfilled this obligation, however, we will defer to its academic decisions.

Zukle at 1046.

In *Memmer* the Court noted that being deaf is required a very special skill:

> Memmer's disability, however, differs from Duffy's in a crucial respect. Duffy was deaf; Memmer is visually impaired. Accommodating a deaf person requires a special skill, the ability to converse in sign language not possessed by the ordinary person. Memmer's evidence did not show that accommodating her required more than a helper with the ability to observe, to read, and to communicate verbally with her. These skills are possessed by the average person, and more importantly, were possessed by Calderon, the Spanish-language interpreter offered by MCC.

Memmer at 634.

Given the totality of the circumstances, the facts in this case and viewing the evidence in the light most favorable to Plaintiff. It cannot be held that as a matter of law Plaintiff's requests constitute an undue administrative burden on Defendant. In fact, as to one of those issues, the College allowed Plaintiff to use Christopher Gardner, a person she found, as an interpreter when it suited the College's needs. Unlike other disabilities, interpreting for a deaf student requires not only special skills but the ability to effectively communicate through ASL. This almost by definition requires the input and, at times, the inclusion of the Plaintiff in the process of assigning a qualified interpreter to assist her.

V. CONCLUSION

For the reasons set forth above, and based on the entire record herein, the parties' cross-motions for summary judgment are DENIED.

NOTES AND PROBLEMS FOR DISCUSSION

1. In 2012, a complaint was filed with the Office for Civil Rights against the College of Redwoods in which the complainants argued that the College was not providing sufficient services for students who are deaf and attending remote campuses. College of Redwoods agreed to take further steps to provide auxiliary aids to students who are deaf and attending remote campuses. College agreed that Video Remote Captioning and sign language interpreter are not always equally effective services and that student-by-student, class-by-class, determinations will be necessary. Where effective services cannot be provided, the student will be permitted to withdraw from the class without penalty or cost. *See* OCR Case No. 09-12-2164 (San Francisco 2012).

2. Given the expense entailed in providing sign-language interpreters, colleges and universities have tried various approaches to using interpreters efficiently, including refusing to provide interpreting services to students who are repeatedly late for class, making use of technology such as cell phone and pagers to resolve last minute scheduling problems and fining students who repeatedly fail to show up for classes to which interpreters have been assigned. *Compare* the approved class action settlement in *Siddiqi v. Regents of California*, No. C 94-0790 SI, 2000 U.S. Dist. LEXIS 19930 (N.D. Cal. Sept. 6, 2000), *with Utah Valley College*, OCR Complaint No. 08102026 (Denver 2011). In the *Utah Valley* matter, OCR found no violation of Section 504 or Title II on the basis of a College policy that, with notice, an emergency exception, a right to appeal and provision for fine mitigation, provided that the College may impose a modest fine on deaf students who habitually fail to show up for class without giving advance notice of their absences.

By contrast, the court-approved *Siddiqi* settlement provides in pertinent parts:

> (1) . . . [T]hat the University of California at Berkeley and the University of California at Davis will no longer terminate the communication services of students who are deaf or hard of hearing. The prior statements of policy in this regard [will be] withdrawn,
>
> (2) . . . [T]hat communication service providers will remain on- site at the event or class for which they will provide services if they receive any notice that a deaf or hard of hearing student will be late for whatever reason. The settlement also provides that text pagers and other communication access features will be provided on the campuses so that it will be feasible for deaf and hard of hearing students to provide such notice. Further, the settlement provides that communication service providers will remain on-site for a somewhat longer period even if a deaf or a hard of hearing student does not provide advance notice of lateness.

(3) . . . [D]eaf and hard of hearing students can obtain communication services for extracurricular events directly through the disabled students programs at the two campuses.

(4) . . . [D]eaf and hard of hearing students are requested, but not required, to give three days advance notice of requests for services, and the policies provide that the Universities will continue making efforts to provide services up through the time that the event takes place. In addition, the new policies provide that additional efforts will be made to ensure that services are provided at scheduled events if a service-provider is unavailable at the last moment, and back-up services are necessary.

(5) . . . [T]he University of California at Davis and the University of California at Berkeley will provide auxiliary aids and services at university expense for those deaf and hard of hearing students who choose to participate in the Education Abroad Program.

(6) With respect to communications access, . . . the Universities will install a number of additional TDD's and assistive listening systems on the two campuses by no later than June 30, 2003. In addition, . . . a jointly selected panel of access experts . . . will review communications access and emergency evacuation procedures at the two campuses, and will make recommendations regarding what steps should be taken to improve the two campuses in these areas. . . .

(7) . . . [T]he disabled students programs give primary consideration to the type of communication service requested by deaf and hard of hearing students, rather than substituting their own judgment as to what communication service is effective for these university students.

(8) . . . [N]otetakers will receive training in how to take effective and complete notes for class members who utilize this service. Notetaker quality will be monitored on, a continuing basis by the Universities' disabled students programs, and remedial measures will be taken if a student complains of incomplete and ineffective notes.

(9) . . . [T]he Universities will ensure that deaf and hard of hearing students are provided with effective communication services with respect to video presentations that are shown in class. Such video presentations will be screened with captions with very few exceptions.

3. In *Bakersfield College*, OCR Complaint No. 09102048 (San Francisco 2012), OCR learned that due to a shortage of sign language interpreters, the College was videotaping class sessions and requiring hearing impaired students to set up a separate appointment, at a later time, to view the videotape with an interpreter. These students alleged that this practice prevented them from participating in classroom lectures and lessons and that this practice was burdensome because the College still required these students to go to the regular classroom session. In effect, they had to sit through each class twice. OCR's investigation revealed that a number of classes were not even videotaped, and that many of the videos were not captioned (even though the accommodation plans for some students called for it). When several of the

students complained, the Deaf Services Coordinator gave them a handout saying that they could talk to Disability Services, Student Affairs, or file a complaint with OCR — ultimately they chose OCR. What can a College do when there simply are not enough interpreters to meet the needs of all the students?

4. To what extent are colleges and universities responsible to provide auxiliary aids to students in practicum programs, such as student teaching and nursing internships? In *Central Michigan University*, OCR Complaint No. 15122009 (Cleveland 2012), a teaching student who was hard-of-hearing was required to sign a form stating that, although a candidate has the right to request an interpreter for all of her student teaching, the presence of an interpreter does not indicate the ability to independently demonstrate the necessary technical standards of independent teaching and good classroom management. In other words, if a student uses a sign language interpreter, she may not meet the technical standards for getting a teaching certificate. Further, even though the form starts by stating that a candidate has the right to request an interpreter for all of her student teaching, it goes on to state that the university would only provide an interpreter for the first few weeks of the student teaching (except for large group presentations outside the classroom, assemblies, and professional development).

The no-fault resolution agreement required the university to provide students with accommodations, and provide individual relief to the student who filed the complaint — an assurance that the use of an interpreter would not be factored into the evaluation of her student teaching performance and would not exclude her from being eligible for a provisional teaching license, a consistent team of qualified interpreters, and no gaps in interpreter coverage for all of her student teaching.

ii. Individual cases

In *Southeastern Community College v. Davis*, Justice Powell stated that, "technological advances can be expected to enhance opportunities to rehabilitate the handicapped or otherwise to qualify them for some useful employment." 442 U.S. at 412. In *Argenyi v. Creighton University*, 703 F.3d 441 (8th Cir. 2013), the Eighth Circuit again was confronted with the case of a medical student who was hard-of-hearing. Thirty-four years after *Southeastern*, the technology is quite different. The medical student, Argenyi, had a cochlear implant and the accommodation he sought was computer assisted real time captioning (CART). This time, the issue for the court was whether the auxiliary aid (accommodation) Argenyi claimed was necessary for him to be an otherwise qualified individual, CART, was actually "necessary" and whether it was the responsibility of Creighton University, a private entity, to provide CART in order to comply with Section 504 and Title III of the ADA.

ARGENYI v. CREIGHTON UNIVERSITY

703 F.3d 441 (8th Cir. 2013).

Murphy Circuit Judge.

Michael Argenyi, a young man with a serious hearing impairment, moved from Seattle to Omaha, Nebraska to attend medical school at Creighton University. Before enrolling Argenyi requested specific accommodations from Creighton for his hearing impairment. They were denied, but Argenyi repeatedly renewed them during his first two years at Creighton Medical School. He explained that without these accommodations he was unable to follow lectures, participate in labs, or communicate with patients.

Because Creighton failed to provide what he considered necessary and reasonable accommodations, Argenyi brought this action under Title III of the Americans with Disabilities Act (ADA), 42 U.S.C. § 12182, and § 504 of the Rehabilitation Act, 29 U.S.C. § 794. The district court decided that Argenyi had not shown his requested accommodations were necessary and granted summary judgment to Creighton while denying its motion for costs. Argenyi and Creighton both appeal. We reverse and remand.

I.

Argenyi began using hearing aids before he was one year old, but his parents primarily communicated with him through spoken language. To distinguish between sounds that appear the same on a speaker's lips Argenyi relied on "cued speech," which uses hand signals to represent sounds. He does not know sign language. In eighth grade Argenyi began using Communication Access Real-time Transcription (CART), a system which transcribes spoken words into text on a computer screen. Argenyi received a cochlear implant in his right ear in September 2004 before he began undergraduate studies at Seattle University. That university provided CART for Argenyi's lectures and a cued speech interpreter for his lab courses, and Argenyi graduated from Seattle in 2008 with a 3.87 grade point average.

Argenyi stated in his application to Creighton University Medical School in 2009 that he was "hearing-impaired." Upon his admission Argenyi explained to Michael Kavan, Creighton's associate dean for student affairs, that he would require accommodation "similar to what [he] had used in the past . . . primarily interpretation or captioning services during lectures teaching sessions." Dean Kavan asked for more information about the nature of his hearing disability and a more specific request for the type of accommodation he needed.

Argenyi's otolaryngologist, Dr. Douglas Backous, responded that Argenyi "would benefit from closed captioning" and an FM system which transmits sound directly into cochlear implants. Argenyi also renewed his requests that Creighton supply CART for his lectures, a cued speech interpreter for labs, and an FM system for small learning groups of eight students or fewer. Kavan replied that the written requests submitted by Dr. Backous and Argenyi were inadequate because they differed and the doctor had not made a "direct request."

Before starting medical school Argenyi received a bilateral cochlear implant, and his implant audiologist and Dr. Backous both recommended that to succeed in his studies he would also need CART, a cued speech interpreter, and the FM system. Dr. Backous wrote to Creighton that Argenyi "remains . . . deaf regardless of if he is or is not using his cochlear implants. . . . [He] has a bilateral profound sensorineural hearing loss." Before Argenyi's enrollment, Creighton's medical education management team met to review his requests for accommodation. Dean Kavan then informed Argenyi that Creighton would provide him with an FM system for lectures, small groups, and labs. Argenyi agreed to give the FM system "a wholehearted try."

Shortly before classes began on August 16, 2009, Argenyi renewed his original requests for accommodations. Creighton denied them. After trying the FM system for two weeks, Argenyi informed Dean Kavan that he needed to obtain CART for himself. He wrote the dean that "[t]he [university's] accommodations are inadequate as evidenced by the level of stress and fatigue I am experiencing, as well as the amount of information I am missing. . . . [They] do not provide for meaningful participation nor independence as a student, and also put me at a significant disadvantage academically." Dr. Backous wrote to Creighton in support of Argenyi's needs, urging that

> It is imperative that [Argenyi] have access to visual cues for everyday communication and education. Visual cues include, but are not limited to captioning on videos and films, real time captioning for lectures and discussions, and speech reading cues for one-on-one interactions.

The dean responded by offering Argenyi only enhanced note taking services. In late September 2009 Argenyi brought this action against Creighton, alleging violations of Title III of the ADA and § 504 of the Rehabilitation Act by the university's failure to provide "auxiliary aids and services to ensure effective communication and an equal opportunity to participate in and benefit from the School of Medicine." Argenyi sought a declaratory judgment compelling Creighton to provide him with "auxiliary aids and services to ensure effective communication," as well as compensatory damages and attorney fees.

Argenyi continued to attend class and pursue his medical education. In February 2010 he consulted ear specialist Dr. Britt Thedinger as an expert witness. Dr. Thedinger tested the Creighton FM system and found that with the background noise that Argenyi had only 38 percent speech perception. Dr. Thedinger determined that "the FM system does not provide any significant benefit and . . . actually reduces [Argenyi's] discrimination ability."

Creighton provided no further auxiliary support or services during Argenyi's first year of medical school, and Argenyi borrowed approximately $53,000 to pay for CART and interpreters himself. In a document publicly available on its website, Creighton estimates that the first year of its medical school costs approximately $71,000 for an average student before financial aid. After paying for his accommodations, the effective cost to Argenyi for his first year of medical school was therefore more than $120,000.

Argenyi renewed his request for accommodation before his second year of medical school. In response Creighton offered to provide an interpreter for lectures and a seat next to the instructor for small group discussions. Argenyi found the interpreter not sufficient to convey complex new vocabulary and again took out approximately $61,000 in loans to pay for CART.

The second year curriculum included clinical courses in which students interviewed and cared for patients. For those courses Creighton refused to allow Argenyi to use an interpreter even if he paid for one himself. Argenyi tried the clinical courses without an interpreter for approximately two weeks and then renewed his request for one. As he explained on September 21, 2010,

> I met with patients . . . and found that I could not understand all of what patients and others at the clinic said. With some patients I understood very little. . . . I know you said I only have to show up to pass, but I want to learn how to be a doctor and I think it is important to understand what the patients are saying to me.

Argenyi and Creighton entered into settlement negotiations in January 2011, and the university temporarily provided him with an interpreter in his clinical courses. Settlement talks ended the following month, however, and Argenyi was again prohibited from using an interpreter. Argenyi nevertheless succeeded in passing his clinical and other courses, but after his second year he took a leave of absence pending the resolution of his claims under the ADA and the Rehabilitation Act.

In July 2011 Argenyi and Creighton both moved for summary judgment. The district court granted summary judgment to Creighton after it concluded that (1) Argenyi had not shown the accommodations he requested were "necessary" within the meaning of the statutes and (2) that Creighton had provided "effective communication" as required by both laws. The court also rejected Argenyi's affidavit as "unsupported self-serving allegations," denied him relief, and ordered each party to pay its own costs.

Argenyi appeals the district court's grant of summary judgment to Creighton. Creighton cross appeals the denial of costs, asserting that the district court erred by failing to provide a supporting rationale.

II.

This court reviews a district court's grant of summary judgment de novo. *Minnesota ex rel. N. Pac. Ctr., Inc. v. BNSF R.R. Co.*, 686 F.3d 567, 571 (8th Cir. 2012). Facts must be construed favorably to the losing party, and Argenyi is to be given the benefit of all reasonable inferences in the record. *Id.* Summary judgment is appropriate only if no genuine dispute exists "as to any material fact and the movant is entitled to judgment as a matter of law." *Id.* (citation omitted). To establish a genuine issue of material fact, Argenyi may not "merely point to self-serving allegations, but must substantiate allegations with sufficient probative evidence that would permit a finding in [his] favor." *Davidson & Assocs. v. Jung*, 422 F.3d 630, 638 (8th Cir. 2005) (citation omitted). A "party's own testimony is often self-serving," but the mere fact that Argenyi's factual testimony is favorable to his legal claim does not render it incompetent. *C.R. Pittman Const. Co., Inc. v. Nat'l Fire Ins. Co. of Hartford*, 453 F. App'x 439, 443 (5th Cir. 2011).

A.

In granting summary judgment to Creighton the district court disregarded Argenyi's affidavit, termed it "self-serving," and concluded that "there [was] an absence of evidence to support [his] claim." There was, however, a variety of supporting evidence in the record. Argenyi's affidavit must be considered, and its particular factual allegations scrutinized for "independent documentary evidence" to support them. *O'Bryan v. KTIV Television*, 64 F.3d 1188, 1191 (8th Cir. 1995). In a case such as this it is especially important to consider the complainant's testimony carefully because "the individual with a disability is most familiar with his or her disability and is in the best position to determine what type of aid or service will be effective." U.S. Dep't of Justice, The Americans with Disabilities Act Title II Technical Assistance Manual, at II-7.1100 (1993).

Argenyi testified in his affidavit that without CART and interpreters he was "unable to follow class lectures and classroom dialogue" or "the rapid pace of dialogue in the clinical setting." He stated that he "began experiencing debilitating headaches and extreme fatigue" from his "fruitless attempts" to follow lectures, even though he had "utilized all of [his] time outside of the classroom trying to obtain the information the other students obtained in the classroom."

In clinical courses Argenyi and his patients frequently failed to communicate effectively. He described in his affidavit a "consult with the parents of a two month old, with communication limited such that [he] did not know . . . why the infant was hospitalized," as well as his struggle to communicate with "emotional family members, patients with accents, and . . . a patient with a history of a broken jaw." Argenyi stated that Creighton had done "nothing to remedy [his] inability to understand what was happening in the clinic" and eventually advised him to "refrain from making requests for additional auxiliary aids and services."

After a careful review of the record, we cannot agree with the district court's conclusion that Argenyi's allegations were "unsupported." The record contains five letters from Argenyi's doctors to Creighton confirming his need for additional auxiliary aids and services. Dr. Backous wrote to Creighton during Argenyi's first month of medical school that "[i]t is imperative that [Argenyi] have access to visual cues for everyday communication and education," including "but . . . not limited to" closed captioning, CART, and a cued speech interpreter. He urged Creighton to consider Argenyi's specific requests, explaining that Argenyi "is the best person to judge what [assistance may be necessary] since no one else can really understand what he is hearing through his cochlear implant systems."

Creighton also received a report from Dr. Thedinger prior to Argenyi's second year, stating that the FM system actually worsened Argenyi's speech discrimination ability to 38 percent comprehension. In addition the record contains correspondence between Argenyi and Creighton in which he repeated requests for an interpreter in clinical courses, which were all denied. During his first two years of medical school, Argenyi borrowed more than $100,000 to pay for the auxiliary aids and services he needed to obtain the medical education he sought, and which Creighton declined to provide.

Argenyi's affidavit, corroborated by evidence from Dr. Backous and Dr. Thedinger and his own need to obtain private loans for CART and interpreters, provides strong evidence that Creighton's accommodations were inadequate and that the university was not entitled to summary judgment. We conclude that the district court erred by disregarding Argenyi's affidavit, the "independent documentary evidence" offered in its support, and all aspects of the record before it. *O'Bryan*, 64 F.3d at 1191.

B.

The evidence presented by Argenyi must be viewed under the legal standard for ADA and Rehabilitation Act claims. To assert his discrimination claim under either statute, Argenyi must show that (1) he is disabled and academically qualified to attend Creighton, (2) Creighton is a "place of public accommodation (for ADA purposes) and receives federal funding (for Rehabilitation Act purposes)," and (3) Creighton discriminated against him based on his disability. *Mershon v. St. Louis Univ.*, 442 F.3d 1069, 1076-77 (8th Cir. 2006). There is no dispute here as to the first two elements. The key question is whether Creighton discriminated against Argenyi by failing to provide necessary auxiliary aids and services during his first year of medical school and by refusing to permit Argenyi to use an interpreter during his second year clinic.

1.

Congress recognized in enacting the ADA that "individuals with disabilities continually encounter various forms of discrimination, including . . . communication barriers." 42 U.S.C. § 12101(a)(5). The purpose of the ADA was to "provide clear, strong, consistent, enforceable standards" to remedy discrimination in employment (Title I), in the services of public entities (Title II), and in places of public accommodation (Title III). *Id.* § 12101(b)(2). Under Title III of the ADA, places of public accommodation include "undergraduate[] or postgraduate private schools" like Creighton. 28 C.F.R. § 36.104.

Discrimination is defined by the ADA as a failure to "make reasonable modifications in policies, practices, or procedures" that are "necessary to afford . . . privileges, advantages, or accommodations to individuals with disabilities" or a failure to "take such steps as may be necessary to ensure that no individual with a disability is . . . treated differently than other individuals because of the absence of auxiliary aids and services." *Id.* § 12182(b)(2)(A)(ii), (iii). In furtherance of the congressional purpose, Title III of the ADA prohibits places of public accommodation such as Creighton from discriminating against individuals with disabilities "in the full and equal enjoyment" of the "privileges, advantages, or accommodations" they offer. 42 U.S.C. § 12182(a).

Congress specifically intended the ADA to remedy "the discriminatory effects of . . . communication barriers" for individuals with hearing disabilities. 42 U.S.C. § 12101(a)(5). Regulations promulgated under Title III of the ADA require the provision of "appropriate auxiliary aids and services where necessary to ensure effective communication with individuals with disabilities," 28 C.F.R. § 36.303(c)(1), and instruct places of public accommodation to "consult with individuals with disabilities whenever possible to determine what type of auxiliary aid is needed to ensure effective communication," *id.* § 36.303(c)(1)(ii). The regulations specifically provide that appropriate aids and services for deaf individuals include interpreters and CART. *Id.* § 36.303(b)(1).

The Rehabilitation Act is similar to the ADA. Congress enacted the Rehabilitation Act as a "comprehensive federal program," *Consol. Rail Corp. v. Darrone*, 465 U.S. 624, 626 (1984), to ensure that individuals with disabilities would not "be denied the benefits of /or be subjected to discrimination under any program or activity" receiving federal funding, 29 U.S.C. § 794(a). To achieve that purpose the Rehabilitation Act requires entities receiving federal funding to furnish auxiliary aids which "afford handicapped persons equal opportunity to obtain the same result, to gain the same benefit, or to reach the same level of achievement" as others. 45 C.F.R. § 84.4(b)(2). Creighton receives financial assistance from federal agencies including the Department of Education, so it must comply with § 504 of the Rehabilitation Act.

Both the ADA and the Rehabilitation Act are intentionally broad in scope, but they do not require institutions to provide all requested auxiliary aids and services. Instead, each statute requires the responsible parties to provide "necessary" auxiliary aids and services to individuals with disabilities. 42 U.S.C. § 12182(b)(2)(A)(ii) (ADA); 34 C.F.R. § 104.44(d)(1) (Rehabilitation Act). Since the ADA and the Rehabilitation Act are "similar in substance," we treat the case law interpreting them as "interchangeable." *Gorman v. Bartch*, 152 F.3d 907, 912 (8th Cir. 1998). Our court has never determined the definition of "necessary" under Title III of the ADA so we must consult the Rehabilitation Act standards as we consider Argenyi's under that statute and under Title III of the ADA.

2.

The Supreme Court has held that § 504 of the Rehabilitation Act requires that "an otherwise qualified handicapped individual must be provided with meaningful access to the benefit that the grantee offers." *Alexander v. Choate*, 469 U.S. 287, 301 (1985). In applying *Alexander*, our court has concluded that the Rehabilitation Act requires a private medical school to provide "reasonable accommodations . . . when a disabled student would otherwise be denied meaningful access to a university." *Stern v. Univ. of Osteopathic Med. & Health Sciences*, 220 F.3d 906, 908 (8th Cir. 2000) (citing *Alexander*, 469 U.S. at 301). In that case, a dyslexic student at a private medical university sued the university under § 504 of the Rehabilitation Act for failing to provide reasonable accommodations in testing. *Id.* at 907. We affirmed the district court's grant of summary judgment to the university after concluding that the student had "failed to establish a nexus between his requested testing scheme and his dyslexia." *Id.* at 909.

We also applied a "meaningful access" standard to a Rehabilitation Act claim brought by a hearing impaired prisoner against the Missouri Department of Corrections for having denied him an interpreter during internal disciplinary proceedings. *Randolph v. Rodgers*, 170 F.3d 850, 858 (8th Cir. 1999). The district court in that case had granted the prisoner summary judgment after determining that "[t]he undisputed evidence . . . show[ed] that although he ha[d] been provided with some . . . benefits, he ha[d] not received the full benefits solely because of his disability." *Id.* We affirmed on appeal, concluding that the record did not "contain credible evidence to support a finding that [the prisoner] enjoyed meaningful access to the prison's internal disciplinary process." *Id.*

Under a "meaningful access" standard, we have decided that aids and services "are not required to produce the identical result or level of achievement for handicapped and nonhandicapped persons," but they nevertheless "must afford handicapped persons equal opportunity to . . . gain the same benefit." *Loye v. Cnty. of Dakota*, 625

F.3d 494, 499 (8th Cir. 2010) (citing *Alexander*, 469 U.S. at 305). The Eleventh Circuit has similarly concluded that the "proper inquiry" under the Rehabilitation Act to determine if a hospital had provided "necessary" auxiliary aids to a hearing impaired patient was whether the proffered aids "gave that patient an equal opportunity to benefit from the hospital's treatment." *Liese v. Indian River Cnty. Hosp. Dist.*, 701 F.3d 334, 343 (11th Cir. 2012). As the court observed in *Liese*, that inquiry "is inherently fact-intensive" and "largely depends on context." *Id.* at 342-43.

The meaningful access standard to ensure an equal opportunity is consistent with the purpose of Title III of the ADA, which is to ensure that all people have "full and equal enjoyment" of public accommodations regardless of disability. 42 U.S.C. § 12182(a). We conclude that § 504 of the Rehabilitation Act and Title III of the ADA each require Creighton to provide reasonable auxiliary aids and services to afford Argenyi "meaningful access" or an equal opportunity to gain the same benefit as his nondisabled peers.

The Ninth Circuit applied a similar standard to a claim arising under Title III of the ADA. *See Baughman v. Walt Disney World Co.*, 685 F.3d 1131, 1135 (9th Cir. 2012). There, the district court had granted summary judgment to the defendant after concluding that Baughman had failed to show that it was "necessary" for her to use a Segway to visit Disneyland because she would not have been "effectively excluded" without it. 691 F. Supp. 2d 1092, 1095 (C.D. Cal. 2010). The Ninth Circuit reversed, reasoning that the ADA "guarantees the disabled more than mere access to public facilities; it guarantees them 'full and equal enjoyment.' " 685 F.3d at 1135 (quoting 42 U.S.C. § 12182(a)). The appellate court instructed the Disney company to "start by considering how their facilities are used by non-disabled guests and then take reasonable steps to provide disabled guests with a like experience." *Id.*

Considering Argenyi's Rehabilitation Act and ADA claims together, the district court granted summary judgment to Creighton after concluding that Argenyi had failed to show that his requested accommodations were necessary as required under the ADA. The district court looked to guidance from the Supreme Court's decision in *PGA Tour, Inc. v. Martin*, 532 U.S. 661 (2001), a quite different case from the one brought by Argenyi. In *Martin*, a professional golfer with a degenerative circulatory disorder sought to travel in a golf cart between the eighteen holes at tournaments. The Court distinguished that golfer from "players with less serious afflictions that make walking the course uncomfortable or difficult, but not beyond their capacity. *In such cases, an accommodation might be reasonable but not necessary.*" *Id.* at 682 (emphasis added).

Here, the district court compared Argenyi's situation not with the golfer with the degenerative disorder who obtained relief in Martin but with those "players with less serious afflictions" for whom walking the course was "not beyond their capacity." With this faulty analogy the court reasoned that by use of the auxiliary aids and services Creighton did supply, Argenyi's medical school experience, although "uncomfortable or difficult," was not "beyond [his] capacity." Since Argenyi had not been "effectively excluded" from Creighton, his requested additional aids and services were not "necessary" under the ADA. Overlooking Argenyi's evidence which showed that aspects of his medical education at Creighton were beyond his capacity without the accommodations he requested, the court failed to make the appropriate comparison with the golfer with the degenerative disorder in *Martin.*

The *Martin* Court indicated that its ruling was narrow and most significantly, it stated that was not deciding the definition of "necessary" in the context of the ADA, since the PGA Tour had conceded that Martin's requested modification was both "reasonable" and "necessary." 532 U.S. at 683 n.38. The "narrow dispute" before the Court was "whether allowing Martin to use a golf cart, despite the walking requirement that applies to the PGA Tour . . . is a modification that would 'fundamentally alter the nature'" of the golf tournament. *Id.* at 682. That argument had been undermined by the district court's finding that "the fatigue [for other golfers] from walking during one of [its] tournaments cannot be deemed significant." *Id.* at 687. Here, there is no allegation that Argenyi is seeking any "competitive advantage" over other medical students. *See id.* at 670-71.

To the extent that the district court interpreted *Martin* to mean that the word "necessary" in the ADA requires a showing that the claimant has been effectively excluded from a place of public accommodation, it would be inconsistent with the congressional purpose of the ADA and the Rehabilitation Act. In Title III of the ADA and § 504 of the Rehabilitation Act, Congress required public accommodations and entities which receive public funding to furnish reasonable auxiliary aids and services so that all individuals have an equal opportunity to gain "a like" or "equal" benefit. *Baughman,* 685 F.3d at 1135; *Liese,* 701 F.3d at 343. Rather than merely ensure that Argenyi is not "effectively excluded" from its medical school, the ADA and the Rehabilitation Act require Creighton to "start by considering how [its educational programs] are used by non-disabled [medical school students] and then take reasonable steps to provide [Argenyi] with a like experience." *Baughman,* 685 F.3d at 1135.

We conclude that the evidence produced in this case created a genuine issue of material fact as to whether Creighton denied Argenyi an equal opportunity to gain the same benefit from medical school as his nondisabled peers by refusing to provide his requested accommodations. At this stage the record supports Argenyi's claim that he was unable to follow lectures and classroom dialogue or successfully communicate with clinical patients. From such evidence a reasonable factfinder could determine that Argenyi was denied an opportunity to benefit from medical school equal to that of his nondisabled classmates. The district court's grant of summary judgment to Creighton should therefore be reversed and the case remanded.

III.

Creighton has cross appealed, contending that the district court erred by denying its request for costs without providing a rationale for doing so. See Fed. R. Civ. P. 54(d)(1). We need not consider that argument because at this stage Creighton has not qualified as a prevailing party and therefore is not to cost recovery. See *Pottgen v. Mo. State High Sch. Activities Ass'n,* 103 F.3d 720, 723-24 (8th Cir. 1997).

IV.

Accordingly, we reverse the summary judgment granted to Creighton and remand for further proceedings consistent with this opinion.

NOTES AND PROBLEMS FOR DISCUSSION

1. On remand, before a jury, Argenyi prevailed on many but not all issues. Though Creighton University was found guilty of disability discrimination and ordered to provide CART in didactic settings and sign-supported oral interpreters in small-group and clinical settings, the jury declined to find that the University had discriminated against Argenyi with "deliberate indifference." Consequently, although Argenyi was the "prevailing party" and awarded $487,000 in attorney fees, expert fees, and costs, he did not qualify for punitive damages and did not obtain reimbursement for his $100,000 in prior CART expenses. Further, because Argenyi had not asked in advance for the court to authorize interpreter expenses for meetings with his attorney, the court declined to award attorney/client interpreting costs to Argenyi but suggested his attorney should bear the cost under Title III of the ADA. Argenyi, after taking a leave of absence, returns to Creighton this July to begin his last two years of medical school. In the meantime, Creighton University has filed a notice of appeal in the Eighth Circuit, focusing on the question of undue burden. Available at http://www.sfgate.com/news/article/Creighton-appeals-order-favoring-deaf-student-5536365.php.

2. How would you expect the Eighth Circuit to resolve the undue burden argument on appeal?

BUTTON v. BOARD OF REGENTS OF UNIVERSITY
289 F.2d 964 (9th Cir. 2008)

JUDGES: Before: Hawkins, Thomas, and Clifton, Circuit Judges. Clifton, Circuit Judge, dissenting.

OPINION

Plaintiff-Appellant Lezlie Button ("Button") appeals the adverse summary judgment grant on her Americans with Disabilities Act ("ADA") and Rehabilitation Act claims, arguing genuine issues of material fact exist about whether the Community College of Southern Nevada ("CCSN") and the University of Nevada, Las Vegas ("UNLV") (collectively "The Board") provided reasonable accommodations to ensure equal access in the classroom or acted with deliberate indifference.

Whether reasonable accommodations have been provided is ordinarily a question of fact. *Fuller v. Frank*, 916 F.2d 558, 562 n.6 (9th Cir. 1990). Whether a particular accommodation is reasonable depends on the individual circumstances of each case and requires a fact-specific, individualized analysis of the disabled individual's circumstances and the accommodations necessary to meet the program's standards. *Vinson v. Thomas*, 288 F.3d 1145, 1154 (9th Cir. 2002).

Reasonable Accommodation

1. Spelling 095

A triable issue of fact exists with respect to whether the institution provided Button with a "qualified interpreter" for this class. Button complained about the quality of interpreters on a number of occasions. Although the institution agreed to use Debra Scott's interpreting services for some classes as Button requested, the record reflects that Button complained about the quality of interpreters and the spotty attendance of interpreters on several occasions. In one e-mail, Button notes, "I already gave FIVE months for you to arrange to search [for] an interpreter. . . ." Button's expert testified that "the institutions in this case did not respond in a timely enough manner." The e-mail exchange, in combination with the expert testimony, points to a triable issue of fact as to whether the accommodations offered in response to Button's requests were reasonable.

2. Environmental Science

College officials acknowledged some insufficiency in note taking; at one point the administration sent an e-mail explaining that they had been looking for a "legitimate" note taker and finally found one. This indicates that there was a substantial period of time during which a "legitimate" note taker was not provided.

Button's e-mails confirm that she raised concerns about the delay in finding an adequate note taker. Button's expert also concluded that the institution's response was not adequate, stating that, while a single missed note taker might be understandable, it is not excusable "[w]hen you have a whole series of courses where note takers [and] notes were never provided, there is a problem, and it's a systemic problem. . . ." This indicates that there is a triable issue of fact regarding whether the Board's actions constituted "reasonable accommodations" of Button's requests.

3. Global Economics

With respect to Global Economics, the district court concluded that there was no evidence that Button complained about Dr. Robinson's speaking speed after the institution sent him a letter asking him to slow down. However, the evidence is undisputed that Button requested Real Time Captioning ("RTC") instead of an interpreter for this class, which was not provided. It appears the district court addressed only the initial RTC request and not the one made in the Global Economics class. The court justified the denial of the UNLV RTC request by stating that RTC in addition to an interpreter would be duplicative. However, in the e-mails pertaining to her Global Economics class, Button specifically requested RTC instead of an interpreter for this class. The institution apparently looked into the possibility of RTC but found it was not available. The stated lack of availability is odd in light of CCSN's utilization of RTC for her spelling class when an interpreter was unavailable. Button's expert also stated that when the quality of interpreters and note takers is spotty the school "does have the responsibility to have some kind of back-up plan." Given Button's continual e-mail complaints that she was unable to keep up with the class, in conjunction with the expert testimony, there is a genuine issue of material fact as to whether the university's response constituted a reasonable accommodation.

4. UNLV RTC Request

Button's expert stated that the institution's summary denial of the RTC in conjunction with note taking and interpreters was inappropriate because administrators did not try to determine why Button believed all three services were necessary. The Board's expert, on the other hand, opined that "it is totally inappropriate to have both [interpreters and RTC] at the same time." A conflict in expert testimony is a quintessential dispute of material fact. See e.g., *Schroeder v. Owens-Corning Fiberglas Corp.*, 514 F.2d 901, 903-904 (9th Cir. 1975). The Board does not argue that Button's expert was unqualified. Rather, it argues that her testimony is not supported by sufficient record evidence. However, different inferences could be drawn from the record evidence. See *Linn Gear Co. v. N.L.R.B.*, 608 F.2d 791, 796 (9th Cir. 1979).

The institution's denial and the reasons for the denial are undisputed, but there is no legal or factual barrier preventing a jury from reasonably concluding that the university's response constituted a denial of a reasonable accommodation. "[M]ere speculation that a suggested accommodation is not feasible falls short of the reasonable accommodation requirement; [both the ADA and the Rehabilitation Act] create a duty to gather sufficient information from the disabled individual and qualified experts as needed to determine what accommodations are necessary. . . ." *Duvall v. County of Kitsap*, 260 F.3d 1124, 1136 (9th Cir. 2001) (quoting *Wong v. Regents of the University of California*, 192 F.3d 807, 818 (9th Cir. 1999) (omission in original)). The denial of a request for accommodation "without consulting [plaintiff] or any person at the University whose job it was to formulate appropriate accommodations" has been found "a conspicuous failure to carry out the obligation 'conscientiously' to explore possible accommodations." *Wong*, 192 F.3d at 819.

Deliberate Indifference

To recover money damages, Button must show that the institution acted with "deliberate indifference," which requires both "knowledge that a harm to a federally protected right is substantially likely, and a failure to act upon that likelihood." *Duvall*, 260 F.3d at 1139. A denial of a request without investigation is sufficient to survive summary judgment on the question of deliberate indifference. See *id.* at 1139-41. In *Duvall*, the court stated, "if [plaintiff's] account of the timing and content of his requests for accommodation and defendants' reactions thereto are accurate, a trier of fact could conclude that defendants' decisions not to accommodate him were considered and deliberate." *Id.* at 1141. There, the plaintiff contacted the ADA coordinator of the court to request RTC; the coordinator responded that the courtroom would be equipped for the hearing impaired but that the plaintiff would have to file a motion for further accommodation; plaintiff made such a motion, and the judge denied it because they did not have the technology, and instead allowed the plaintiff to move about the courtroom freely wherever he could best hear the proceedings. *Id.* at 1131.

We cannot say that, if the jury concludes that the Board's accommodations were not reasonable, the jury could not also conclude that the Board's failure to provide greater accommodations was not "deliberate and considered," particularly in light of the Board's summary denial of Button's RTC request. It is not enough that the Board took some action — in *Duvall* the court made some effort to accommodate, but we held that a jury could find this effort both insufficient and deliberate. See *id.* This inquiry is nuanced and fact-intensive — precisely the province of the jury.

Disputed issues of material fact preclude summary judgment.

REVERSED and REMANDED.

Clifton, Circuit Judge, dissenting:

I respectfully dissent. Plaintiff Lezlie Button seeks only an award of damages, not injunctive relief. To recover money damages she must show that the Board acted with "deliberate indifference." *Duvall v. County of Kitsap*, 260 F.3d 1124, 1139 (9th Cir. 2001). Even viewing the evidence in the light most favorable to her, she has not identified sufficient evidence to support such a finding. Indeed, her brief does not even argue that she has.

The Board responded repeatedly to try to satisfy Button's concerns. The majority cites *Duvall* in support of the proposition that the denial of a request without investigation is sufficient to survive summary judgment on the question of deliberate indifference, but there is no evidence that the Board ever denied any of Button's requests without investigation. I infer from the majority's discussion that the denial allegedly without investigation was the Board's so-called summary denial of Button's request that she be provided at the same time with multiple accommodations: Real Time Captioning (RTC), note-taking, and an interpreter. But it did not require a special investigation for university administrators to know that it was not customary for a disabled student to require or to receive all three forms of assistance at the same time. Moreover, the record shows that university administrators did in fact consult other providers of deaf services about the feasibility of RTC as a form of note taking before denying that request. The denial was not without investigation and it did not demonstrate indifference.

The Board's responses might not have been effective or sufficient to solve the problems — and may not have satisfied the legal obligation to make reasonable accommodations — but there is no evidence of indifference, let alone the "deliberate indifference" needed to support a claim for money damages. I would affirm the judgment of the district court.

NOTES AND PROBLEMS FOR DISCUSSION

1. Consider the following problems:

a. Joan is an undergraduate student at Utopia State College, majoring in liberal arts. Joan is deaf, and communicates via oral speech and lipreading (she does not use sign language). Joan wants the college to provide her with computer assisted transcription (CART) services for all of her classes.

The college refuses to provide the CART services, saying they are too expensive. The college offers to provide sign language interpreters and/or notetakers. Who should prevail? What are the college's obligations under Section 504 and the ADA? Can a compromise resolution be worked out?

b. Suppose that Joan communicates via sign language rather than orally. Joan wants the college to provide her with two sign language interpreters during classes (so they may switch off every 20 minutes) *and* notetakers. The college says it will provide either the interpreters or the notetakers. Who should prevail?

c. Joan is a first year law student at Utopia State Law School. The law school provides Joan with interpreters and notetakers for all classes. Joan wants to participate in a study group with eight other first year students. The law school encourages first-year students to form such study groups, but does not sponsor or organize the groups. Must the law school provide Joan with interpreters for study group sessions? *See* OCR letter to Thomas M. Cooley Law School, OCR Complaint No. 15-08-2067 (Chicago 2011). If Joan requests a full-time interpreter during the school day so she may communicate with the other students during the day and discuss matters relating to law school classes and other events must the school provide such an interpreter? What if Joan requests an interpreter for school functions, such as a debate or play?

d. Jack, who is blind, is also a first year law student at Utopia State Law School. Jack wants the law school to provide him with an assistant/reader 20 hours a week while he does research at the library to complete his requirements for his legal research and writing class. Must the law school provide the assistant? What if Jack wants to read something tangentially related to law school, such as *The Death of Common Sense* by Phillip K. Howard?

2. Title II issues involving effective communication can also be raised with respect to K-12 students. The Ninth Circuit recently decided two cases brought under Title II against California school districts that refused to provide Communication Access Realtime Translation ("CART") to students. The plaintiffs conceded the school districts had complied with their IDEA obligations but argued they should still be able to argue a lack of compliance with their Title II obligation. The Ninth Circuit reversed the grant of summary judgment by the district courts, and held that the plaintiffs could go forward with their Title II claims because of three significant differences between IDEA and Title II: (1) the ADA regulations require the public entity to "give primary consideration to the requests of the individuals with disabilities," (2) the ADA has a fundamental alteration and undue burden defense, and (3) the Title II effective communication regulation requires schools to communicate "as effective[ly]" with disabled students as with other students, and to provide disabled students the "auxiliary aids . . . necessary to afford . . . an equal opportunity to participate in, and enjoy the benefits of," the school program. *K.M. v. Tustin Unified School District*, 725 F.3d 1088, 1100-1101 (9th Cir. 2013).

(c) Impact of Emerging Technology on Students with Sensory Impairments.

Recently, DOJ, OCR and advocacy organizations like the National Federation of the Blind (NFB) have been directing complaints and investigatory resources to the accessibility of digital information resources. Under scrutiny are websites, course management tools, library catalogues, on-line courses, and ticketing and registration systems. At the same time, colleges and universities face unsettled questions at the edges of technology. For example, what must be done to make a MOOC accessible or must recordings of classes posted on YouTube for use without charge, registration, or evaluation be captioned? Post-secondary institutions will need more DOJ and judicial guidance to answer these questions. Moreover, they will need to develop, share and scale both up and down models for achieving compliance. How does a large university ensure that the thousands of websites maintained by its faculty are accessible? What can a small college with no information officer do to accomplish this goal? Without the requisite expertise, how can a college ensure that it does not purchase technology, such as course management tools, that are inaccessible or not easily amenable to known "fixes."

Heretofore, courts have struggled with how to apply brick and mortar precedents and concepts of equality to the virtual world. Is the opposite about to happen? Are decisions and settlements that pertain to the virtual world going to expand how we measure equality for individuals with disabilities in all settings? Recent settlements, in particular, reflect consideration of the degree to which the digital information is readily amenable to adaptive technology such as screen readers; the ease of use of a new technology; how independently the information provided by the technology may be accessed, without reliance, for example, on a reader; the integration of the user into the information stream that is available to nondisabled individuals; the timeliness of delivery of displayed information or the provision of the provided information in an alternate format; and the completeness of the information that is made accessible to the user with a disability.

In 2009, the National Federation of the Blind (NFB) and the American Council of the Blind (ACB) filed suit against Arizona State University (ASU) to prevent the University from deploying Amazon's Kindle DX electronic reading device as a means of distributing electronic textbooks to its students on the grounds that the device could not be used by students with visual disabilities. According to the complaint, the Kindle DX featured text-to-speech technology that could read textbooks to such students. However, the pull-down menus of the device were allegedly not accessible to blind individuals. In addition to ASU, five other institutions of higher education were deploying the Kindle DX as part of a "pilot project" to assess the role of electronic textbooks and reading devices in the classroom. The NFB and ACB also filed complaints with the Office for Civil Rights of the U.S. Department of Education and the Civil Rights Division of the U.S. Department of Justice, asking for investigations of the five institutions. https://nfb.org/node/1129.

In June of 2010, in response to these complaints and subsequent investigations, OCR and DOJ issued joint guidance requiring that schools, colleges and universities not adopt emerging technology, if such technology is inaccessible to students with disabilities. In May of 2011, OCR issued a further clarification of this document in the form of questions and answers. The FAQs explain that the same principles apply to students with print disabilities, such as students with a learning disabilities who would otherwise get books on tape as an accommodation. If a college is providing electronic book readers to the rest of the students, it can no longer provide books on tape to this type of student. It would be required to provide an accessible electronic book reader because the book reader provides greater functionality than audio books. *See* http://aim.cast.org/learn/policy/federal/ocr (last viewed on Apr. 26, 2013).

June 29, 2010

Dear College or University President:

We write to express concern on the part of the Department of Justice and the Department of Education that colleges and universities are using electronic book readers that are not accessible to students who are blind or have low vision and to seek your help in ensuring that this emerging technology is used in classroom settings in a manner that is permissible under federal law. A serious problem with some of these devices is that they lack an accessible text-to-speech function. Requiring use of an emerging technology in a classroom environment when the technology is inaccessible to an entire population of individuals with disabilities — individuals with visual disabilities — is discrimination prohibited by the Americans with Disabilities Act of 1990 (ADA) and Section 504 of the Rehabilitation Act of 1973 (Section 504) unless those individuals are provided accommodations or modifications that permit them to receive all the educational benefits provided by the technology in an equally effective and equally integrated manner.

The Departments of Justice and Education share responsibility for protecting the rights of college and university students with disabilities. The Department of Justice is responsible for enforcement and implementation of title III of the ADA, which covers private colleges and universities, and the Departments of Justice and Education both have enforcement authority under title II of the ADA, which covers public universities. In addition, the Department of Education enforces Section 504 with respect to public and private colleges and universities that receive federal financial assistance from the Department of Education. As discussed below, the general requirements of Section 504 and the ADA reach equipment and technological devices when they are used by public entities or places of public accommodation as part of their programs, services, activities, goods, advantages, privileges, or accommodations.

Under title III, individuals with disabilities, including students with visual impairments, may not be discriminated against in the full and equal enjoyment of all of the goods and services of private colleges and universities; they must receive an equal opportunity to participate in and benefit from these goods and services; and, they must not be provided different or separate goods or services unless doing so is necessary to ensure that access to the goods and services is equally as effective as that provided to others.[1] Under title II, qualified individuals with disabilities may not be excluded from participation in or denied the benefits of the services, programs, or activities of, nor subjected to discrimination by, public universities and colleges.[2] Both title II and Section 504 prohibit colleges and universities from affording individuals with disabilities with an opportunity to participate in or benefit from college and university aids, benefits, and services that is unequal to the opportunity afforded others.[3] Similarly, individuals with disabilities must be provided with aids, benefits, or services that provide an equal opportunity to achieve the same result or the same level of achievement as others.[4] A college or university may provide an individual with a disability, or a class of individuals with disabilities, with a different or separate aid, benefit, or service only if doing so is necessary to ensure that the aid, benefit, or service is as effective as that provided to others.[5]

The Department of Justice recently entered into settlement agreements with colleges and universities that used the Kindle DX, an inaccessible, electronic book reader, in the classroom as part of a pilot study with Amazon.com, Inc. In summary, the universities agreed not to purchase, require, or recommend use of the Kindle DX, or any other dedicated electronic book reader, unless or until the device is fully accessible to individuals who are blind or have low vision, or the universities provide reasonable accommodation or modification so that a student can acquire the same information, engage in the same interactions, and enjoy the same services as sighted students with substantially equivalent ease of use. The texts of these agreements may be viewed on the Department of Justice's ADA Web site, www.ada.gov. (To find these settlements on www.ada.gov, search for "Kindle.") Consistent with the relief obtained by the Department of Justice in those matters, the Department of Education has also resolved similar complaints against colleges and universities.

As officials of the agencies charged with enforcement and interpretation of the ADA and Section 504, we ask that you take steps to ensure that your college or university refrains from requiring the use of any electronic book reader, or other similar technology, in a teaching or classroom environment as long as the device remains inaccessible to individuals who are blind or have low vision. It is unacceptable for universities to use emerging technology without insisting that this technology be accessible to all students.

Congress found when enacting the ADA that individuals with disabilities were uniquely disadvantaged in American society in critical areas such as education.[6] Providing individuals with disabilities full and equal access to educational opportunities is as essential today as it was when the ADA was passed. In a Proclamation for National Disability Employment Awareness Month, President Obama underscored the need to "*strengthen and expand* the educational opportunities for individuals with

---

[1] 28 C.F.R. § 36.201(a); 28 C.F.R. 36.202(a); and 28 § C.F.R. 36.202(c) (2009).

[2] 28 C.F.R. § 35.130(a) (2009).

[3] 28 C.F.R. § 35.130(b)(1)(ii) and 34 C.F.R. § 104.4(b)(1)(ii) (2009).

[4] *Cf.* 28 C.F.R. § 35.130(b)(1)(iii) and 34 C.F.R. § 104.4(b)(1)(iii) (2009).

[5] 28 C.F.R. § 35.130(b)(1)(iv) and 34 C.F.R. § 104.4(b)(1)(iv) (2009).

[6] 42 U.S.C. § 12101(a) (1990).

disabilities," noting that, "[i]f we are to build a world free from unnecessary barriers . . . we must ensure that every American receives an education that prepares him or her for future success." http://www.whitehouse.gov/the-press-office/presidential-proclamation-national-disability-employment-awareness-month (September 30, 2009) (emphasis added).

Technology is the hallmark of the future, and technological competency is essential to preparing all students for future success. Emerging technologies are an educational resource that enhances the experience for everyone, and perhaps especially for students with disabilities. Technological innovations have opened a virtual world of commerce, information, and education to many individuals with disabilities for whom access to the physical world remains challenging. Ensuring equal access to emerging technology in university and college classrooms is a means to the goal of full integration and equal educational opportunity for this nation's students with disabilities. With technological advances, procuring electronic book readers that are accessible should be neither costly nor difficult.

We would like to work with you to ensure that America's technological advances are used for the benefit of all students. The Department of Justice operates a toll-free, technical assistance line to answer questions with regard to the requirements of federal laws protecting the rights of individuals with disabilities. For technical assistance, please call (800) 514-0301 (voice) or (800) 514-0383 (TTY). Specialists are available Monday through Friday from 9:30 AM until 5:30 PM (ET) except for Thursday, when the hours are 12:30 PM until 5:30 PM. These specialists have been trained specifically to address questions regarding accessible electronic book readers. Colleges, universities, and other stakeholders can also contact the Department of Education's Office for Civil Rights for technical assistance by going to OCR's Web site at http://wdcrobcolp01.ed.gov/CFAPPS/OCR/contactus.cfm.

We appreciate your consideration of this essential educational issue and look forward to working with you to ensure that our nation's colleges and universities are fully accessible to individuals with disabilities.

Sincerely,

Thomas E. Perez
Assistant Attorney General Civil Rights Division U.S. Department of Justice

Russlynn Ali
Assistant Secretary for Civil Rights U.S. Department of Education

---

http://www2.ed.gov/about/offices/list/ocr/letters/colleague-20100629.html.

For a criticism of the Kindle Letter, see http://www.digitalsociety.org/2010/08/disabilities-civil-rights-the-kindle-letter (last viewed on Apr. 26, 2013). For an additional discussion of this issue, see Daniel Goldstein & Gregory Care, *Disability Rights and Access to the Digital World: An Advocates Analysis of an Emerging Field*, The Federal Lawyer (Dec. 2012). http://www.browngold.com/wbcntntprd1/wp-content/uploads/Disability-Rights-and-Access-to-the-Digital-World.pdf (last viewed on Apr. 26, 2013). *See also* Constance S. Hawke & Anne L. Jannarone, *Emerging Issues of Web Accessibility: Implications for Higher Education*, 160 Educ. L. Rep. 715 (2002).

NOTES AND PROBLEMS FOR DISCUSSION

1. How does a small college without the requisite expertise ensure that it does not purchase technology that is inaccessible or not easily amenable to known "fixes"?

2. Scrutiny of DOJ/OCR complaint and compliance reviews reveal a number of common deficiencies including missing tags for PDF files, graphics, identification of column headers, specified reading order, critical heading and watermarks; videos missing labels, keyboard controls, or captioning; missing labels for screen readers for fields that require filling in; tables missing headings; areas where keyboard-only users could not access information or use drop-down menus; content of course management tools missing captions and alt. text; and course management tools that are not fully accessible to screen readers. They also exemplify emerging solutions including requiring that information is posted only in formats that are compatible with common adaptive technology; making adaptive technology widely available around campus; adopting, dispersing, and monitoring digital information policies and practices that will make information readily available to all students as well as training faculty and staff on these policies; wisely prioritizing which barriers to accessing information will be removed first; implementing effective alternatives to address delays; placing compliance responsibility on specific individuals and giving them the authority to implement the necessary changes, and purchasing only technology, such as course management tools, that are accessible or at least easily amenable to known "fixes." *See* OCR Letter to South Carolina Technical College System, OCR Compliance Review No. 11-11-6002 (Metro 2013); http://www2.ed.gov/about/ offices /list/ocr/docs/investigations/11116002-a.doc (last viewed on August 25, 2013); Settlement Agreement Between the United States Department of Justice and Louisiana Technical College

(2013), http://www.ada.gov/louisiana-tech.htm (last viewed on August 25, 2013); Resolution Agreement, Among the University of Montana — the US Department of Education, Office for Civil Rights, DOJ DJ Number 169-44-9, OCR Case No. 10126001 (March 2014). Available at https://nfb.org/images/nfb/documents/pdf/agreement_university_of_montana_march_10_2014.pdf

4. Service Animals

The modifications in the regulations regarding the use of service animals was probably the most extensive, and the most subject to notice and comment, when the ADA regulations were revised in 2010. Because the same rules govern service animals under Titles II and III, this section will discuss issues and cases that involve both Title II and III entities. *See also* 34 C.F.R. § 104.44(b) "*Other rules*. A recipient to which this subpart applies may not impose upon . . . students [with disabilities] other rules, such as the prohibition of . . . dog guides in campus buildings, that have the effect of limiting the participation of [such] students in the recipient's education program or activity."

One issue that arises frequently is what kind of proof an entity can require before allowing an individual to bring a service animal into its facility. The regulations specify that an entity can make two inquiries to determine whether an animal qualifies as a service animal. It may ask (1) if the animal is required because of a disability and (2) what work or task the animal has been trained to perform. 28 C.F.R. § 36.302(c)(6). But a "public accommodation shall not require documentation, such as proof that the animal has been certified, trained, or licensed as a service animal." *Id.* OCR applies similar rules when universities seek what it considers overly extensive documentation from a student who seeks to use a service animal. *See* Complaint No. 01-12-2008 (Community College of Vermont) (Apr. 6, 2012), available at http://www.galvin-group.com/media/171481/ocr_letter_01_12_2008_service_animals.pdf (last viewed on Apr. 29, 2013).

The definition of a "service animal" was changed by the 2010 ADA regulations and is therefore very important to understand. For the purposes of Title II and III of the ADA, DOJ has promulgated regulations stating that a service animal is a *dog* "that is individually trained to do work or perform tasks for the benefit of an individual with a disability, including a physical, sensory, psychiatric, intellectual, or other mental disability. . . . The work or tasks performed by a service animal must be directly related to the individual's disability. . . . The crime deterrent effects of an animal's presence and the provision of emotional support, well-being, comfort, or companionships do not constitute work or tasks for the purposes of this definition." 28 C.F.R. § 36.104. The regulations also provide that public accommodations must allow for the use of a "miniature horse" so long as the facility can accommodate the type, size, and weight. 28 C.F.R. § 36.302(c)(9). In contrast to service animals (dogs), admission of a miniature horse is determined on a case by case basis. Neither species need be admitted if not house broken.

The DOJ regulations under ADA Titles II and III are different than those of the Department of Housing and Urban Development (HUD) under the FHA and the Department of Transportation (DOT) under ADA Title II. The FHA and DOT regulations permit the use of emotional support or comfort animals in covered entities; the DOJ regulations do not. This is how the DOJ explains these differences:

> The Department's position is based on the fact that the title II and title III regulations govern a wider range of public settings than the housing and transportation settings for which the Department of Housing and Urban Development (HUD) and the DOT regulations allow emotional support animals or comfort animals. The Department recognizes that there are situations not governed by the title II and title III regulations, particularly in the context of residential settings and transportation, where there may be a legal obligation to permit the use of animals that do not qualify as service animals under the ADA, but whose presence nonetheless provides necessary emotional support to persons with disabilities. Accordingly, other Federal agency regulations, case law, and possibly State or local laws governing those situations may provide appropriately for increased access for animals other than service animals as defined under the ADA. Public officials, housing providers, and others who make decisions relating to animals in residential and transportation settings should consult the Federal, State, and local laws that apply in those areas (e.g., the FHAct regulations of HUD and the ACAA) and not rely on the ADA as a basis for reducing those obligations.

28 C.F.R. § 36.302 app.

HUD has also explained its position in contrast to that of DOJ in the following memo (with the footnotes deleted).

> February 17, 2011
>
> TO: FHEO Region Directors
>
> FROM: Sara K. Pratt, Deputy Assistant Secretary for Enforcement and Programs
>
> SUBJECT: New ADA Regulations and Assistance Animals as Reasonable Accommodations under the Fair Housing Act and Section 504 of the Rehabilitation Act of 1973
>
> **I. Purpose**
>
> This memo explains that the Department of Justice's (DOJ) recent amendments to its Americans with Disabilities Act (ADA) regulations do not affect reasonable accommodation requests under the Fair Housing Act (FHAct) and Section 504 of the Rehabilitation Act of 1973 (Section 504). The DOJ's new rules limit the definition of "service animal" in the ADA to include only dogs. The new rules also define "service animal" to exclude emotional support animals. This definition, however, does not apply to the FHAct or Section 504. Disabled individuals may request a reasonable accommodation for assistance animals in addition to dogs, including emotional support animals, under the FHAct or Section 504. In situations where both laws apply, housing providers must meet the broader FHAct/Section 504 standard in deciding whether to grant reasonable accommodation requests.

II. Definitions of Service Animal

The DOJ's new ADA rules define "service animal" as any dog that is individually trained to do work or perform tasks for the benefit of an individual with a disability, including a physical, sensory, psychiatric, intellectual, or other mental disability. The new rules specify that "the provision of emotional support, well-being, comfort, or companionship do not constitute work or tasks for the purposes of this definition." Thus, trained dogs are the only species of animals that may qualify as service animals under the ADA (there is a separate provision regarding miniature horses) and emotional support animals are expressly precluded from qualifying as service animals.

Neither the FHAct, Section 504, nor HUD's implementing regulations contain a specific definition of the term "service animal." However, species other than dogs, with or without training, and animals that provide emotional support have been recognized as necessary assistance animals under the reasonable accommodation provisions of the FHAct and Section 504. The new ADA regulation does not change this FHAct/Section 504 analysis, and specifically notes, "[u]nder the FHAct, an individual with a disability may have the right to have an animal other than a dog in his or her home if the animal qualifies as a 'reasonable accommodation' that is necessary to afford the individual equal opportunity to use and enjoy a dwelling, assuming that the animal does not pose a direct threat." In addition, the preambles to the new rules state that emotional support animals do not qualify as service animals under the ADA but may "nevertheless qualify as permitted reasonable accommodations for persons with disabilities under the FHAct."

A distinguishing characteristic between service animals and companion animals is that a service animal must both respond to a stimulus or circumstance, such as a child with autism beginning to run off a school campus ("bolt") and respond to the stimulus or circumstance with as specific action, such as restraining the child. By contrast, a companion or assistance animal may meet its responsibilities passively, comforting an individual with a psychological disability merely by its presence. Such an animal is still more than just a pet. Not that the companion animal is an accommodation in the classic sense of the term, permitting the entity to require reasonable pertinent documentation and making a case-by-case determination. The inquiry into a service animal is fairly more limited and once the inquiry is satisfied, with rare exception, the animal must be admitted.

III. Applying the Law

Under the FHAct and Section 504, individuals with a disability may be entitled to keep an assistance animal as a reasonable accommodation in housing facilities that otherwise impose restrictions or prohibitions on animals. In order to qualify for such an accommodation, the assistance animal must be necessary to afford the individual an equal opportunity to use and enjoy a dwelling or to participate in the housing service or program. Further, there must be a relationship, or nexus, between the individual's disability and the assistance the animal provides If these requirements are met, a housing facility, program or service must permit the assistance animal as an accommodation, unless it can demonstrate that allowing the assistance animal would impose an undue financial or administrative burden or would fundamentally alter the nature of the housing program or services.

Under the ADA, the animal need only meet the definition of "service animal" to be covered by the law. No further test or reasonable accommodation analysis should be applied. An individual's use of a service animal in an ADA-covered facility should not be handled as a request for reasonable accommodation. If an animal qualifies as a "service animal," ADA-covered entities may not restrict access to a person with a disability on the basis of his or her use of that service animal unless the animal is out of control and its handler does not take effective action to control it or if the animal is not housebroken. The service animal must be permitted to accompany the individual with a disability to all areas of the facility where customers are normally allowed to go.

The new ADA definition of "service animal" applies to state and local government services, public accommodations, and commercial facilities; the FHAct covers housing services and facilities; and HUD's Section 504 regulations apply to all recipients of HUD-funds. Some types of entities, such as rental offices and housing authorities, are subject to both the service animal requirements of the ADA and the reasonable accommodation provisions of the FHAct or Section 504. Entities must ensure compliance under all relevant civil rights laws. Compliance with the ADA's regulations does not ensure compliance with the FHAct or Section 504. An entity that is subject to both the ADA and the FHAct or Section 504 must permit access to ADA covered "service animals" and, additionally, apply the more expansive assistance animal standard when considering reasonable accommodations for persons with disabilities who need assistance animals that fall outside the ADA's "service animal" definition.

IV. Conclusion

The ADA regulations' revised definition of "service animal" does not apply to reasonable accommodation requests for assistance animals in housing under either the FHAct or Section 504. Rules, policies, or practices must be modified to permit the use of an assistance animal as a reasonable accommodation in housing when its use may be necessary to afford a person with disabilities an equal opportunity to use an d enjoy a dwelling, common areas of a dwelling, or participate in, or benefit from, any housing program receiving Federal financial assistance from HUD, unless an exception applies.

NOTES AND PROBLEMS FOR DISCUSSION

1. Why do ADA and FHA have such different definitions and rules for service animals? The FHA often applies to common areas that are part of housing facilities. However, it does not apply to classroom structures. Should the Department of Education OCR extend the logic of the FHA, allowing for companion animals as a reasonable modification, to the classroom setting? What inferences may be drawn from the silence of DOJ on this topic other than its support for the guidance of HUD? As yet, OCR has not issued written guidance on this question. If you were in-house counsel training the security guards on your campus, what would you tell them do?

2. Because of the different rules between FHA and the ADA, whether housing is covered by the FHA rather than the ADA can impact the ability of an individual to live with a comfort animal. Should university housing be covered by the ADA or the FHA? *See United States v. University of Nebraska*, No. 4:11-CV-3209, 2013 U.S. Dist. LEXIS 56009 (D. Neb. Apr. 19, 2013).

3. Consider the following fact pattern:

> Kathleen Lentini is an individual with quadraplegia who uses a service animal, Jazz, who provides minimal protection and retrieves small dropped items. Lentini repeatedly attended concerts with Jazz at an arts center. On two occasions, Jazz barked during intermission but stopped barking as soon as Lentini said "okay." When Lentini sought to return to the arts center, she was told that she could not bring Jazz because he created a disturbance. Lentini brought suit under ADA Title III. The district court ordered the arts center to modify its policies to give persons with disabilities the "broadest feasible access" under the following rule:
>
>> The Center's policies, practices and procedures may not exclude a service animal who has made a noise on a previous occasion, even if such behavior is disruptive, if the noise was made and intended to serve as means of communication for the benefit of the disabled owner or if the behavior would otherwise be acceptable to the Center if engaged by humans.
>
> On appeal, the arts center argued that the rule requiring them to modify their policies were unnecessary and unreasonable and would fundamentally alter the services and facilities provided by the arts center.

How do you think the court of appeals should rule? *See Lentini v. California Center for the Arts*, 370 F.3d 837 (9th Cir. 2004).

4. The 1991 title III regulation, 28 C.F.R. § 36.104, defined a "service animal" as "any guide dog, signal dog, or other animal individually trained to do work or perform tasks for the benefit of an individual with a disability, including, but not limited to, guiding individuals with impaired vision, alerting individuals with impaired hearing to intruders or sounds, providing minimal protection or rescue work, pulling a wheelchair, or fetching dropped items." The revised Title III (and Title II) regulations, as discussed above, limit service animals to "dogs" except for the reference to "miniature horses" (which are not service animals but can be permitted on a case by case basis).

Read the comments criticizing this change. Do you think DOJ had ample reason to make this modification? The revised regulations also do not allow animals to qualify as "service" animals solely on the basis that they are providing "minimal protection" as provided in the 1991 Regulations. DOJ eliminated the "minimal protection" language because it thought that language generated confusion. In its opinion, aggression-trained animals are not appropriate service animals. *See* 28 C.F.R. § 36.104 app. However, it does recognize providing "non-violent protection or rescue work" as appropriate service activity. *See* 28 C.F.R. § 36.104.

5. One problem that individuals often face who use a service dog is that they are confronted with requests to document their need for the dog. The following language from a recent court case, *O'Connor v. Scottsdale Healthcare Corp.*, 871 F. Supp. 2d 900 (D. Ariz. 2012), reflects how this kind of interaction can occur:

> Plaintiff Kimberly O'Connor went to Scottsdale Healthcare Shea Medical Center on November 18, 2009 to visit her mother, who had been admitted to the hospital for atrial fibrillation. Plaintiff brought her service dog, Peaches, with her. Peaches was on a leash and wearing a collar and a blue cape with two patches reading "Service Dog."
>
> Plaintiff and Peaches entered the hospital from a side entrance, south of the emergency entrance. As they were walking in the corridor toward the north elevator, they passed a security guard. When Plaintiff had gotten about ten feet beyond the security guard, he stopped her.
>
> The security guard asked Plaintiff if she had registered her dog. Plaintiff politely informed the security guard that she had not and would not register Peaches because it was not necessary for her to do so. The security guard reasserted that Plaintiff needed to register Peaches and asked Plaintiff when Peaches was last groomed and vaccinated. Plaintiff told the security guard that her dog's vaccinations were current.
>
> The security guard continued to insist that Plaintiff register her dog. Plaintiff told the guard that his demands were improper and illegal. The guard told her that he was doing nothing illegal and that the registration of dogs was the policy of the Scottsdale Healthcare legal department. Plaintiff asked to speak with a member of the legal department, but no member was present at the Shea campus.
>
> Plaintiff then withdrew a publication distributed by the Disability Rights Task Force of the U.S. Department of Justice and the National Association of Attorneys General from the pocket of the dog's cape. The publication set forth the most commonly asked questions regarding service dogs' access to public accommodations. Plaintiff read to the guard a section from the publication discussing a disabled person's right to bring his or her service animal with him to public accommodations.
>
> The security guard nonetheless continued to ask Plaintiff to register her dog. He became increasingly irritated with Plaintiff's refusal to comply with his orders and told Plaintiff that he could call the police and have her arrested for trespassing if she did not leave. Plaintiff told the guard that she knew the

hospital policy was wrong because she was an attorney and had read the applicable disability laws.

When Plaintiff continued to stand her ground, the security guard asked her to leave by the door through which she had entered and to wait outside while he got his supervisor. The guard then escorted Plaintiff out of the hospital. The guard asked her to wait outside the hospital security office while he spoke with his supervisor.

The original security guard re-joined Plaintiff with two more security guards and a man who identified himself as the head of security for Scottsdale Healthcare. The head of security asked Plaintiff if she was disabled and if her dog was a service dog. When she answered yes to both questions, the head of security immediately allowed Plaintiff to enter the hospital with Peaches and without registering the dog.

Notice in this example that the plaintiff was a lawyer who was aware of her legal rights. Look at the regulations about inquiries regarding service animals. How did the security guard violate this regulation? What should he have asked? What kind of relief might be sought in such a situation? Is the injury too minor to necessitate relief, especially if the plaintiff has no trouble entering the facility in the future? *See also Hurley v. Loma Linda Univ. Med. Ctr.*, 2014 U.S. Dist. LEXIS 18018 (C.D. Calif. Feb. 12, 2014) (improper questioning whether dog was a service animal).

6. What if someone has a "dog in training" to be a service dog? Should the dog be allowed to enter facilities that ordinarily do not allow animals? *See Davis v. Ma*, 848 F. Supp. 2d 1105 (C.D. Cal. 2012) (no). *But see* 21 N.Y.C.R.R. § 1050.9(h)(1) (creating exception for "service animals or to animals which are being trained as service animals and are accompanying persons who disabilities, or to animals which are being trained as service animals by a professional trainer"). Is the breadth of that exception legally required under ADA?

7. It is a common fact pattern that security guards, even at court houses, are not trained on the proper protocol for allowing service animals to enter. *See Sears v. Bradley County Government*, 821 F. Supp. 2d 987 (E.D. Tenn. 2011) (security guard not allowing individual to enter court house with service animal for about two hours until the documentation she possessed was examined by a judge). Similarly, a lawsuit was brought against the New York City Transit Authority in which an individual who used a service dog demonstrated that workers were repeatedly hostile to her bringing a service dog with her on the public transportation system. *See Stamm v. New York City Transit Authority*, No. 04-CV-2163, 2013 U.S. Dist. LEXIS 8534 (E.D.N.Y. Jan. 18, 2013). In both *Sears* and *Stamm*, the plaintiffs had difficulty obtaining damages because the entity's official policy (which was not known or followed by the security personnel) was legally correct.

In *Stamm*, the plaintiff went to enormous lengths to demonstrate that the Transit Authority was not properly training its workers. She had numerous recorded conversations between bus operators and their supervisors in which even the supervisors often demonstrated ignorance of the Transit Authority's own rules regarding service animals. Further, she produced deposition testimony from the

Transit Authority's ADA officer in which he acknowledged that many of the employees did not understand their policies regarding service animals. With this mountain of evidence, the district court found that the plaintiff could survive the defendant's motion for summary judgment. *Id.* at *29.

It's one thing for the house counsel of a large institution to know the content of the law, for example, with regard to service animals. It's another, to protect your client from liability arising from a lack of familiarity with the law by lay-persons, temporary employees, trainees, etc. If you were the house counsel or ADA officer of a large institution, how would you ensure that every relevant employee and authorized volunteer (security guards, volunteer ushers, maintenance staff, etc.) knows what to say when someone claims that the animal at his or her side is a service animal? Is it unrealistic and unfair to hold such large institutions responsible for "perfect compliance" with such a "technical" provision of the law?

8. Another problem that continues to emerge is whether a city ordinance that prohibits pit bulls violates the ADA when the bit bull is a service animal. Consider the following facts:

> James Sak is a retired police officer who suffered a stroke which left him permanently disabled, with no control over the right side of his body, and the need to use a wheelchair. He has had a dog named Snickers, who is believed to be a pit bull mix, since the dog was ten weeks old. Although Snickers was originally a family pet, after Sak's stroke, Snicker was trained and certified as a service animal. He has been certified with the "National Service Animal Registry." His certification states that he is a "working animal" rather than a "pet." Snickers has been trained to assist Sak with tasks which mitigate his disability, including walking, balance and retrieving items around the house.
>
> The town in which Sak resides has an ordinance prohibiting anyone to have a pit bull dog. Thirty-six residents of Sak's community presented a petition to City Council, requesting it to enforce the pit bull ordinance. The City Council held a hearing and required that Sak kennel his dog outside the city. Sak complied with that ruling and had repeated falling accidents at his home because he could not get assistance from Snickers. He brought suit against the city arguing that it was violating ADA Title II by refusing to accommodate his service animal request.

Locate the language in the Interpretive Guidance where DOJ prohibits breed limitations as a result of city ordinances. Should a state or municipal court defer to DOJ Guidance just because it was issued by a Federal agency or should such courts make a case-by-case determination about the dangerousness of an animal rather than use breed as a proxy for dangerousness?

In *Sak v. City of Aurelia*, 832 F. Supp. 2d 1026 (N.D. Iowa 2011), Judge George Wittgraf entered a preliminary injunction on behalf of Sak with the following evocative language:

> Thus, I find that, whatever the legal bark of the City's Ordinance prohibiting pit bull dogs as a general matter of public health and safety, it is sufficiently likely that enforcement of that Ordinance against Snickers would take such an

> impermissible bite out of Title II of the ADA and the regulations and guidance promulgated to implement it that a preliminary injunction is warranted. There is also sufficient showing that enforcement of the Ordinance against Snickers is causing and will cause irreparable harm to Sak. Granting the injunction is not counterbalanced by any harm to the City. Finally, in my view, the public interest in allowing Sak to keep and use his certified and registered service dog, Snickers, substantially outweighs the City's interest in banning Snickers. This is one small, but vital step for Sak, one giant leap for pit bull service dogs.

If you were clerking for Judge Wittgraf, might you suggest he change some of this language? *See also Grider v. City and County of Denver*, Civil Action No. 10-cv-00722-MSK-MJW, 2012 U.S. Dist. LEXIS 44463 (D. Colo. Mar. 30, 2012) (pit bull ordinance).

9. One of the biggest areas of contention involves the exclusion of animals that are providing "emotional support" but not engaging in discrete tasks that could be considered "work." For example, Kyra Alejandro, a student at Palm Beach State College, has been diagnosed with post-traumatic stress disorder, major depressive disorder, attention deficit hyperactivity disorder and a learning disorder. After receiving her diagnosis, she began training her dog "to establish eye contact, nip her fingers, or snort when he perceives imminent panic attack." She provided the college with evidence of her diagnosis and a description of how the dog signals her when a panic attack is imminent. Is the college required to allow her to bring the dog on campus as an accommodation? Can it require more documentation? *See Alejandro v. Palm Beach State College*, 843 F. Supp. 2d 1263 (S.D. Fla. 2011) (granting temporary injunction to student).

Do you agree with the DOJ policy distinguishing between "emotional support" and "work" animals?

10. Given that service and emotional support animals on college campuses are present for extended periods of time (and that not all students may be mature enough to care for their animals), should colleges and universities be viewed more like municipalities with the authority to set reasonable health and safety regulations that apply to all animals on campus, such as rules requiring registration, proof of vaccinations, and setting health care standards (flea and tick prevention)?

11. One of the most complex and unsettled issues pertaining to service animals is how the ADA service animal regulations and guidance should be applied in public elementary and secondary schools. This question arises because elementary and secondary students with disabilities are protected under multiple legal authorities and standards including Section 504 of the Rehabilitation Act, Title II of the ADA, and the IDEA. This conundrum is particular likely to arise for students who want to bring to school dogs specifically trained to work with autistic children. Among other functions, these dogs are trained to prevent such children from "bolting" off of campus and as a way to attract the interest of other students in communicating with a classmate with autism, consequently helping to develop the child's impaired social communication skills. Some districts have welcomed autism dogs, others have not, fearing the child will be unable to independently control the dog, placing an additional burden on a teacher or aide or simply that the dog will be a disruptive attraction for the other students. When parents challenge a school district's refusal to admit such a dog, some

courts have analyzed this as a FAPE question, meaning that the decision to admit the dog is a placement matter to be resolved by an IEP team. *See Cave v. East Meadow Union Free School District*, 480 F. Supp. 2d 610 (E.D.N.Y. 2007), *rev'd on other grounds*, 514 F.3d 240 (2d Cir. 2008). This process generally leads to a denial of use of the dog on the grounds that teachers and classroom aides can do everything the dog can do for the student or better. Other courts have seen this as a preemptive reasonable modification question with all the protections found in the DOJ guidance ensuring the admittance of service animals to public entities. Generally, these courts require admission of the dog. *See Sullivan v. Vallejo City Unified School District*, 731 F. Supp. 947 (E.D. Cal. 1990); *CC by Ciriaks v. Cypress School District*, Case No. CV11-00352 AG, 2011 U.S. Dist. LEXIS 88287 (C.D. Cal. June 13, 2011). *See also* Statement of Interest of the United States in *CC by Ciriaks* (filed June 13, 2011), available at http://www.ada.gov/briefs/cc_interest.pdf.

If a dog is individually trained to do work or perform discrete tasks for the benefit of a child with autism, but it is the dog that controls the child, not the child who controls the dog, is the dog still a service animal? Should the rules for a child with a service animal be applied more flexibly while the child is learning to work with the service animal over a sustained period of time?

12. Assume that a university has a rule stating that a student who uses a service dog may only live in a limited portion of university housing that has no carpets and must place a sign at the entrance indicating she has a dog. Does this policy violate the ADA or Section 504? What if the sign leads to harassment of the student? *See* OCR Reference No. 10112060 (Portland State University) (Sept. 8, 2011), available at www.galvin-group.com/media/171636/ocr_letter_portland_state_university_1_.pdf (last viewed on Apr. 29, 2013). Following a settlement with OCR concerning these restrictions on students with service animals in residence halls, an original OCR complainant alleged in federal district court that she was not permitted to bring her service animal anywhere into a science building on the grounds that it contained toxic fumes, another student allegedly was taken to a disciplinary hearing for keeping a companion animal in her dorm room, and a Fair Housing Council tester alleged that Portland State was not complying with the terms of a settlement with OCR. Portland State alleged that it was not subject to the Fair Housing Act. Following complaint, Portland State settled for $160,000, policy changes, and training. Settlement Agreement between Leland and *Fair Housing Council of Oregon v. Portland State University*, 3:12-cv-00911-SI (D.C. Or. Feb. 13, 2014).

May a university prohibit service animals from entering its health service or food preparation facilities? Relying on DOJ and Center for Disease Control guidance, a federal district court concluded that, in only very few settings, may a hospital maintain a blanket policy against the use of service animals. "[L]imited-access areas that employ infection control measures" could qualify for an exception. A psychiatric ward does not qualify for an exception, as the presence of a service animal is not likely to require a fundamental alteration or present a direct threat that cannot be mitigated. Direct threat arguments concerning service animals in specialized treatment areas may exist, but they cannot be based on generalizations and speculation, as occurred in this case. *Tamara v. El Camino Hospital*, 964 F. Supp. 2d 1077 (N.D. Cal. 2013).

5. Examinations and Courses

a. Statutory and Regulatory Provisions

42 U.S.C. § 12189 provides:

> Any person that offers examinations or courses related to applications, licensing, certification, or credentialing for secondary or post-secondary education, professional, or trade purposes shall offer such examinations or courses in a place and manner accessible to persons with disabilities or offer alternative accessible arrangements for such individuals.

The regulations require that any private entity offering an examination covered by the statute must assure that it "is selected and administered so to as best ensure that examination results accurately reflect the aptitude or achievement level of individuals with disabilities rather than reflecting the individuals' impaired sensory, manual, or speaking skills." 28 C.F.R. § 36.309(b)(i). An appendix to the regulations notes that "[e]xaminations covered by the section would include a bar exam or the Scholastic Aptitude Test prepared by the Educational Testing Service." 28 C.F.R. pt. 36, app. B.

The "any person" referred to in this section is *not* limited to public accommodations. The DOJ has stated that Section 12189 was intended to fill in "the gap . . . created when licensing, certification, and other testing authorities are not covered by Section 504 of the Rehabilitation Act or Title II of the ADA." 56 Fed. Reg. 35,572 (1991). Although this section also applies to public accommodations already covered by Title III, those entities would arguably already be under such obligations even without the existence of Section 12189. *See, e.g.*, 42 U.S.C. § 12182(b)(2)(A)(ii) (requiring entities to make reasonable modifications in policies, practices, or procedures unless such alterations would result in a fundamental alteration of the good or service). The cases involving Section 12189 have therefore primarily arisen in the context of entities that are not clearly covered by the public accommodation section of the statute, such as medical and legal examiners.

In recent years, the most important legal development in the interpretation of section 12189 is the interpretation of the language "so as to best ensure that examination reflects accurately the aptitude or achievement level of individuals with disabilities." 28 C.F.R. § 36.309(b)(i). Consider the following case interpreting that rule.

ENYART v. NATIONAL CONFERENCE OF BAR EXAMINERS, INC.

630 F.3d 1153 (9th Cir. 2011)

Before: Robert E. Cowen, A. Wallace Tashima, and Barry G. Silverman, Circuit Judges.

Silverman, Circuit Judge:

Stephanie Enyart, a legally blind law school graduate, sought to take the Multistate Professional Responsibility Exam and the Multistate Bar Exam using a computer equipped with assistive technology software known as JAWS and ZoomText. The State Bar of California had no problem with Enyart's request but the National Conference of Bar Examiners refused to grant this particular accommodation. Enyart sued NCBE under the Americans with Disabilities Act seeking injunctive relief. The district court issued preliminary injunctions requiring NCBE to allow Enyart to take the exams using the assistive software, and NCBE appealed. We hold that in granting the injunctions, the district court did not abuse its discretion. We affirm.

I. Background

Enyart suffers from Stargardt's Disease, a form of juvenile macular degeneration that causes her to experience a large blind spot in the center of her visual field and extreme sensitivity to light. Her disease has progressively worsened since she became legally blind at age fifteen. Enyart relies on assistive technology to read.

Enyart graduated from UCLA School of Law in 2009. Before she could be admitted to practice law in California, Enyart needed to pass two exams: the Multistate Professional Responsibility Exam, a 60–question, multiple-choice exam testing applicants' knowledge of the standards governing lawyers' professional conduct; and the California Bar Exam. The Bar Exam spans three days, on one of which the Multistate Bar Exam is administered. The MBE is a six-hour, 200–question, multiple-choice exam that tests applicants' knowledge of the law in a number of subject areas. NCBE develops both the MPRE and the MBE. NCBE contracts with another testing company, ACT, to administer the MPRE and licenses the MBE to the California Committee of Bar Examiners for use in the Bar Exam.

Enyart registered to take the March 2009 administration of the MPRE and wrote to ACT requesting a number of accommodations for her disability: extra time, a private room, hourly breaks, permission to bring and use her own lamp, digital clock, sunglasses, yoga mat, and migraine medication during the exam, and permission to take the exam on a laptop equipped with JAWS and ZoomText software. JAWS is an assistive screen-reader program that reads aloud text on a computer screen. ZoomText is a screen-magnification program that allows the user to adjust the font, size, and color of text and to control a high-visibility cursor.

ACT granted all of Enyart's requests with the exception of the computer equipped with JAWS and ZoomText. ACT explained that it was unable to offer this accommodation because NCBE would not make the MPRE available in electronic format. In lieu of Enyart's requested accommodation, ACT offered her a choice between a live reader or an audio CD of the exam, along with use of closed-circuit television for text magnification. Enyart sought reconsideration of ACT's denial of her request to use JAWS and ZoomText, asserting that the options offered would be ineffective because they would not allow her to synchronize the auditory and visual inputs. After ACT denied Enyart's request for reconsideration, Enyart cancelled her registration for the March 2009 MPRE.

In April 2009, Enyart applied to take the July 2009 California Bar Exam, requesting the same accommodations she asked for on the MPRE. The California Committee of Bar Examiners granted all of Enyart's requested accommodations with the exception of her request to take the MBE portion of the test using a computer equipped with ZoomText and JAWS. The Committee denied this request because NCBE would not provide the MBE in electronic format. Because of this denial, Enyart cancelled her registration for the July 2009 Bar Exam.

Enyart registered for the November 2009 MPRE and requested the same accommodations she previously sought for the March 2009 administration. NCBE again declined to allow Enyart to take the MPRE using a computer equipped with ZoomText and JAWS. Instead, they offered to provide a human reader, an audio CD of the test questions, a braille version of the test, and/or a CCTV with a hard-copy version in large font with white letters printed on a black background. Because of NCBE's denial of her request to use a computer with ZoomText and JAWS, Enyart cancelled her registration for the November 2009 MPRE.

After these repeated denials of her requests to take the MPRE and MBE using assistive technology software, Enyart filed this action against NCBE, ACT, and the State Bar of California, alleging violations of the ADA and the Uhruh Act, California's civil rights law. Enyart sought declaratory and injunctive relief.

Enyart moved for a preliminary injunction, asking the district court to order NCBE to allow Enyart to use a computer equipped with ZoomText and JAWS on the February 2010 MBE and the March 2010 MPRE. After hearing oral argument, the court granted Enyart's motion, addressing the factors for deciding whether to issue a preliminary injunction in a well-reasoned order:

> Because the accommodations provided by NCBE will not permit Enyart to take the exam without severe discomfort and disadvantage, she has demonstrated the test is not "accessible" to her, and that the accommodations [offered by NCBE] therefore are not "reasonable." Therefore, this Court concludes, based on the current record and moving papers, that it is more likely than not that Enyart will succeed on the merits at trial. . . .
>
> NCBE spends a good portion of its brief disputing Enyart's factual claims that the accommodations offered by NCBE will not permit her to comfortably complete the exam. NCBE points out that in the past Enyart has "successfully utilized a number of different accommodations." Opp. at 2. She used readers and audiotapes during her undergraduate years at Stanford, and used CCTV while working as an administrative assistant before law school. *Id.* Further,

NCBE points out that Enyart used a reader to help her complete her LSAT prep program, and used audiotapes and the services of a human reader on her examinations. *Id.*

These factual claims, however, are somewhat beside the point. First, Enyart avers that hers is a progressive condition, so there is no reason to believe an accommodation that may or may not have been sufficient during Enyart's undergraduate coursework would be sufficient. Second, none of those examinations compare to the bar exam, which is a multi-day, eight hour per day examination. Hence, an accommodation that might be sufficient for a law school examination is not necessarily sufficient for the bar exam. Third, the relevant question is not whether Enyart would be able, despite extreme discomfort and disability-related disadvantage, to pass the relevant exams. NCBE points to no authority to support the position that an accommodation which results in "eye fatigue, disorientation and nausea within five minutes, which become fully developed several minutes after that" is "reasonable."

. . . .

The facts as outlined in the attachments to Plaintiff's motion therefore strongly suggest that the accommodations offered by NCBE would either result in extreme discomfort and nausea, or would not permit Enyart to sufficiently comprehend and retain the language used on the test. This would result in Enyart's disability severely limiting her performance on the exam, which is clearly forbidden both by the statute [42 U.S.C. § 12189] and the corresponding regulation [28 C.F.R. § 36.309].

NCBE's citation to other regulations and cases does not overcome this factual presentation. . . . [T]he examples [of auxiliary aids] offered in the regulation and the statute cannot be read as exclusive, nor do those examples support the conclusion that such accommodations are reasonable even where they do not permit effective communication. On the contrary, the statute and relevant regulations all emphasize access and effective communication. The statute itself illustrates that the central question is whether the disabled individual is able to employ an "effective method[ ] of making visually delivered materials available." The evidence submitted by Plaintiff strongly suggests that the only auxiliary aid that meets this criteria is a computer with JAWS and ZoomText. While NCBE may be successful at trial in establishing that this is not the case, the record presently before this Court more strongly supports the conclusion that only ZoomText and JAWS make the test "accessible" to Enyart. See 42 U.S.C. § 12189.

Order Granting Prelim. Inj. 5–9, Feb. 4, 2010 (footnotes omitted). The district court required Enyart to post a $5,000 injunction bond. NCBE immediately appealed the preliminary injunction.

Meanwhile, while NCBE's appeal of the preliminary injunction was pending, Enyart learned that her score on the March 2010 MPRE was not high enough to allow her to qualify for admission to the California Bar. She moved for a second preliminary injunction, asking the court to order NCBE to provide her requested accommodations on the August 2010 MPRE and "any other administration to Ms. Enyart of the California Bar Exam, the Multistate Bar Exam ('MBE') and/or the MPRE." After filing her motion, Enyart learned that she did not pass the July 2009 Bar Exam. The district court granted a second preliminary injunction ordering NCBE to allow Enyart to take the July 2010 MBE and the August 2010 MPRE on a computer equipped with ZoomText and JAWS, stating:

> The relevant question here is whether the auxiliary aids offered by NCBE make the test's "visually delivered materials available" to Enyart. As this Court has previously concluded, they do not. . . . NCBE continues to argue that Enyart is not entitled to her preferred accommodations, and in so doing continues to miss the point. She does not argue that she simply "prefers" to use JAWS and ZoomText. On the contrary, she has presented evidence that the accommodations offered by NCBE do not permit her to fully understand the test material, and that some of the offered accommodations result in serious physical discomfort. CCTV makes her nauseous and results in eye strain, and the use of human readers is not suited to the kind of test where one must re-read both questions and answers, and continually shift back and forth between different passages of text. . . . Such accommodations do not make the test accessible to Enyart, and so do not satisfy the standard under the ADA.

Order Granting Prelim. Inj. 5–6, June 22, 2010. The court required Enyart to post an additional $5,000 injunction bond. NCBE immediately appealed, and the appeal was consolidated with NCBE's appeal of the first preliminary injunction.

Enyart has since learned that she received a high enough score on the August 2010 MPRE to qualify for admission to the California Bar but that she did not pass the July 2010 California Bar Exam.

II. Discussion

A. Jurisdiction and Standard of Review

We have jurisdiction to review the district court's orders granting these preliminary injunctions pursuant to 28 U.S.C. § 1292(a)(1). Our review is for an abuse of discretion. *Does 1–5 v. Chandler*, 83 F.3d 1150, 1152 (9th Cir.1996). . . .

B. Mootness

As an initial matter, we hold that even though the injunctions only related to the March and August 2010 MPRE exams and the February and July 2010 California Bar Exams, which have since come and gone, NCBE's appeals are not moot because the situation is capable of repetition, yet evading review. . . .

C. Preliminary Injunctions

A plaintiff seeking a preliminary injunction must show that: (1) she is likely to succeed on the merits, (2) she is likely to suffer irreparable harm in the absence of preliminary relief, (3) the balance of equities tips in her favor, and (4) an injunction is in the public interest. *Winter v. Natural Res. Def. Council*, 555 U.S. 7, 129 S.Ct. 365, 374, 172 L.Ed.2d 249 (2008) (citations omitted). The district court correctly identified the Winter standard as controlling in this case.

1. Likelihood of Success on the Merits

Congress enacted the ADA in order to eliminate discrimination against individuals with disabilities. See 42 U.S.C. § 12101(b). The ADA furthers Congress's goal regarding individuals with disabilities: "to assure equality of opportunity, full participation, independent living, and economic self-sufficiency for such individuals[.]" 42 U.S.C. § 12101(a)(8). The ADA contains four substantive titles: Title I relates to employment; Title II relates to state and local governments; Title III relates to public accommodations and services operated by private entities; and Title IV relates to telecommunications and common carriers. See generally Americans with Disabilities Act of 1990, 42 U.S.C. §§ 12101–12213 and 47 U.S.C. §§ 225, 611.

42 U.S.C. § 12189, which falls within Title III of the ADA, governs professional licensing examinations. This section requires entities that offer examinations "related to applications, licensing, certification, or credentialing for . . . professional, or trade purposes" to "offer such examinations . . . in a place and manner *accessible* to persons with disabilities or offer alternative accessible arrangements for such individuals." 42 U.S.C. § 12189 (emphasis added). The purpose of this section is "to assure that persons with disabilities are not foreclosed from educational, professional, or trade opportunities because an examination or course is conducted in an inaccessible site or without an accommodation." H.R.Rep. No. 101–485(III), at 68–69 (1990), reprinted in 1990 U.S.C.C.A.N. 445, 491–92.

The Attorney General is charged with carrying out many of the provisions of the ADA and issuing such regulations as he deems necessary. Relevant here, the Attorney General is responsible for issuing regulations carrying out all non-transportation provisions of Title III, including issuing accessibility standards. 42 U.S.C. § 12186(b).

Pursuant to its authority to issue regulations carrying out the provisions of Title III, the Department of Justice has adopted a regulation interpreting § 12189. This regulation defines the obligations of testing entities:

> Any private entity offering an examination covered by this section must assure that . . . [t]he examination is selected and administered so as to *best ensure* that, when the examination is administered to an individual with a disability that impairs sensory, manual, or speaking skills, the examination results accurately reflect the individual's aptitude or achievement level or whatever other factor the examination purports to measure, rather than reflecting the individual's impaired sensory, manual, or speaking skills . . .[.]

28 C.F.R. § 36.309(b)(1)(i) (emphasis added). The regulation continues:

> A private entity offering an examination covered by this section shall provide appropriate auxiliary aids for persons with impaired sensory, manual, or speaking skills, unless that entity can demonstrate that offering a particular auxiliary aid would fundamentally alter the measurement of the skills or knowledge the examination is intended to test or would result in an undue burden.

Id. § 36.309(b)(3).

Enyart argues that DOJ's regulation requires NCBE to administer the MBE and MPRE "so as to best ensure" that her results on the tests accurately reflect her aptitude, rather than her disability. NCBE argues that the regulation is invalid and asks this court to apply a reasonableness standard in lieu of the regulation's "best ensure" standard. The district court declined to rule on the validity of 28 C.F.R. § 36.309, and instead held that "even assuming NCBE's more defendant-friendly standard applies," Enyart had demonstrated a likelihood of success on the merits.

We defer to an agency's interpretation of a statute it is charged with administering if the statute "is silent or ambiguous with respect to the specific issue" and the agency's interpretation is "based upon a permissible construction of the statute." *Contract Mgmt., Inc. v. Rumsfeld*, 434 F.3d 1145, 1146–47 (9th Cir.2006) (quoting *Chevron U.S.A. Inc. v. Natural Res. Def. Council, Inc.*, 467 U.S. 837, 842–43 (1984)). We hold that 28 C.F.R. § 36.309 is entitled to *Chevron* deference.

Section 12189 requires entities like NCBE to offer licensing exams in a manner "accessible" to disabled people or to offer "alternative accessible arrangements." 42 U.S.C. § 12189. Congress's use of the phrases "accessible" and "alternative accessible arrangements" is ambiguous in the context of licensing exams. Nowhere in § 12189, in Title III more broadly, or in the entire ADA did Congress define these terms. The phrase "readily accessible" appears in Titles II and III, but only with respect to physical spaces, i.e., facilities, vehicles, and rail cars. See 42 U.S.C. §§ 12142–12148, 12162–12165, 12182–12184. The phrase is not defined; instead, the Act directs the Secretary of Transportation to issue regulations establishing accessibility standards for public transportation facilities, vehicles, and rail cars, 42 U.S.C. §§ 12149, 12163–12164, and 12186(a), and directs the Attorney General to issue regulations establishing accessibility standards for new construction and alterations in public accommodations and commercial facilities, 42 U.S.C. § 12186(b). The text of these other ADA provisions does not resolve the ambiguity in § 12189's use of term "accessible" because an examination is not equivalent to a physical space.

Because § 12189 is ambiguous with respect to its requirement that entities administer licensing exams in a manner "accessible" to individuals with disabilities, we defer to DOJ's interpretation of the statute so long as that interpretation is based upon a permissible construction of the statute. *See Contract Mgmt., Inc.*, 434 F.3d at 1146–47. NCBE seeks to invalidate 28 C.F.R. § 36.309, arguing that the regulation imposes an obligation beyond the statutory mandate. Instead of the regulation's requirement that entities administer licensing exams in a manner "so as to best ensure" that the results reflect whatever skill or aptitude the exam purports to measure, NCBE argues that the ADA only requires such entities to provide "reasonable accommodations."

The "reasonable accommodation" standard advocated by NCBE originated in the Department of Health and Human Services' regulations implementing the Rehabilitation Act of 1973. See 45 C.F.R. 84.12(a) (requiring employers to make "reasonable accommodation to the known physical or mental limitations of an otherwise qualified handicapped applicant or employee unless the [employer] can demonstrate that the accommodation would impose an undue hardship on the operation of its program or activity."). When Congress enacted the ADA, it incorporated 45 C.F.R. 84.12's "reasonable accommodation" standard into Title I, which applies in the employment context. See H.R.Rep. No. 101–485(II), at 2 (1990), reprinted in 1990 U.S.C.C.A.N. 303, 304 ("Title I of the ADA . . . incorporates many of the standards of discrimination set out in regulations implementing section 504 of the Rehabilitation Act of 1973, including the obligation to provide reasonable accommodations unless it would result in an undue hardship on the operation of the business.").

Notably, Congress did not incorporate 45 C.F.R. 84.12's "reasonable accommodation" standard into § 12189. Instead, § 12189 states that entities offering licensing exams "shall offer such examinations . . . in a place and manner accessible to persons with disabilities or offer alternative arrangements for such individuals." 42 U.S.C. § 12189. One reasonable reading of § 12189's requirement that entities make licensing exams "accessible" is that such entities must provide disabled people with an equal opportunity to demonstrate their knowledge or abilities to the same degree as nondisabled people taking the exam — in other words, the entities must administer the exam "so as to best ensure" that exam results accurately reflect aptitude rather than disabilities. DOJ's regulation is not based upon an impermissible construction of § 12189, so this court affords *Chevron* deference to 28 C.F.R. § 36.309 and applies the regulation's "best ensure" standard.

Applying 28 C.F.R. § 36.309's "best ensure" standard, we conclude that the district court did not abuse its discretion by holding that Enyart demonstrated a likelihood of success on the merits. The district court found that the accommodations offered by NCBE did not make the MBE and MPRE accessible to Enyart. This finding is supported by evidence that Enyart would suffer eye fatigue, disorientation, and nausea if she used a CCTV, so CCTV does not best ensure that the exams are accessible to her; that auditory input alone is insufficient to allow Enyart to effectively comprehend and retain the language used on the exam; and that, according to Enyart's ophthalmologist, the combination of ZoomText and JAWS is the only way she can fully comprehend the material she reads.

NCBE argues that because Enyart has taken other standardized tests using accommodations comparable to those offered by NCBE, the district court erred in finding that those accommodations did not make the MPRE and MBE accessible to her. In support of this argument, NCBE points out that Enyart took the SAT college admissions test using large-print exam booklets; that she used CCTV for her Advanced Placement tests; and that she relied on a human reader and scribe during the LSAT. Although Enyart's prior experiences with the accommodations offered by NCBE may be relevant to establishing whether those accommodations make the MPRE and MBE accessible, they are not conclusive, especially as to whether those accommodations best ensure that the exams are accessible. Enyart graduated from college more than a decade ago, and took the LSAT six years ago. Enyart's disability is a progressive one, and as the district court noted, an accommodation that may or may not have been sufficient years ago is not necessarily sufficient today. Moreover, assistive technology is not frozen in time: as technology advances, testing accommodations should advance as well.

NCBE also argues that because it offered to provide auxiliary aids expressly identified in the ADA, the regulations, a DOJ settlement agreement, and a Resolution of the National Federation of the Blind, courts should not require it do more. We do not find this argument persuasive. The issue in this case is not what might or might not accommodate other people with vision impairments, but what is necessary to make the MPRE and MBE accessible to Enyart given her specific impairment and the specific nature of these exams.

As NCBE concedes, the lists of auxiliary aids contained at 42 U.S.C. § 12103 and at 28 C.F.R. § 36.309 are not exhaustive. See 42 U.S.C. § 12103(1) ("the term 'auxiliary aids and services' includes (A) qualified interpreters *or other effective methods* of making aurally delivered materials available to individuals with hearing impairments; (B) qualified readers, taped texts, *or other effective methods* of making visually delivered materials available to individuals with visual impairments; . . . and (D) *other similar services and actions*.") (emphases added); 28 C.F.R. § 36.309(c)(3) ("Auxiliary aids and services required by this section may include taped texts, interpreters or other effective methods of making orally delivered materials available to individuals with hearing impairments, Brailled or large print texts or qualified readers for individuals with visual impairments . . . and other similar services and actions.") (emphases added). To hold that, as a matter of law, an entity fulfills its obligation to administer an exam in an accessible manner so long as it offers some or all of the auxiliary aids enumerated in the statute or regulation would be inconsistent with Congressional intent:

> The Committee wishes to make it clear that technological advances can be expected to further enhance options for making meaningful and effective opportunities available to individuals with disabilities. Such advances may require public accommodations to provide auxiliary aids and services in the future which today they would not be required because they would be held to impose undue burdens on such entities.
>
> Indeed, the Committee intends that the types of accommodations and services provided to individuals with disabilities, under all of the titles of this bill, should keep pace with the rapidly changing technology of the times.

H.R. Rep. 101–485(II), at 108 (1990), reprinted in 1990 U.S.C.C.A.N. 303, 391.

NCBE points next to a July 2000 settlement between DOJ and the American Association of State Social Work Boards in which the AASSWB agreed to adopt a policy allowing vision-impaired candidates to choose among a list of available accommodations for the social work licensing exam. The list included an audiotaped version of the exam, a large print test book, a Braille version of the exam, extra time, a private room, a qualified reader, and a flexible start time. NCBE argues that because it offered Enyart the accommodations listed in the AASSWB settlement, the court should conclude that the accommodations offered satisfied NCBE's obligations under § 12189 as a matter of law. We find this argument unpersuasive. There is no reason that this decade-old settlement agreement should define the maximum NCBE can be required to do in order to meet its obligation to make the MBE and MPRE accessible to Enyart.

Finally, NCBE makes much of a Resolution of the National Federation of the Blind from 2000 that called upon the American Council on Education to ensure that it administered the GED exam in "the four standard media routinely used by blind persons to access standardized tests: large print, Braille, tape, and live reader." This NFB Resolution appears to have been written to address a specific problem identified in the administration of the GED exam, namely the prohibition on the use of live readers. Moreover, the NFB has no power to define testing entities' obligations under the ADA. The fact that the NFB ten years ago urged the American Council on Education to allow test-takers to choose among large print, Braille, tape, and live reader accommodations does not lead to the conclusion that, as a matter of law, the accommodations offered by NCBE made the MBE and MPRE accessible to Enyart.

The sources described above — the lists of auxiliary aids contained in the statute and regulation, the AASSWB settlement agreement, and the NFB's Resolution — possibly support a conclusion that the accommodations offered by NCBE are sufficient to meet their obligations with respect to many blind people in many situations. As we have tried to make clear already, accommodations that make an exam accessible to many blind people may not make the exam accessible to Enyart, and our analysis depends on the individual circumstances of each case, requiring a "fact-specific, individualized analysis of the disabled individual's circumstances." *Wong v. Regents of Univ. of Cal.*, 192 F.3d 807, 818 (9th Cir.1999).

Enyart provided the district court with evidence that the accommodations offered by NCBE will put her at a disadvantage by making her nauseated or by preventing her from comprehending the test material. Enyart presented evidence that she used JAWS and ZoomText for all but one of her law school examinations; that a combination of JAWS and ZoomText is the only way she can effectively access the exam; and that use of a CCTV causes her to suffer nausea and eye fatigue. In a sworn statement, Enyart's ophthalmologist stated that the only way Enyart can fully comprehend the material she reads is if she is able to simultaneously listen to and see magnified test material, as JAWS and ZoomText allow.

The district court reviewed the evidence of Enyart's disability and her history of using auxiliary aids including JAWS and ZoomText, and concluded that "the accommodations offered by NCBE would either result in extreme discomfort and nausea, or would not permit Enyart to sufficiently comprehend and retain the language used on the text. This would result in Enyart's disability severely limiting her performance on the exam, which is clearly forbidden both by the statute and the corresponding regulation." The court compared Enyart's evidence to that offered by NCBE, and found that the balance "more strongly supports the conclusion that only ZoomText and JAWS make the text 'accessible' to Enyart." This is a logical conclusion, supported by the evidence, and therefore we conclude that the district court did not abuse its discretion in holding that Enyart demonstrated a likelihood of success on the merits.

2. Irreparable Harm

A plaintiff seeking a preliminary injunction must demonstrate that irreparable injury is likely in the absence of preliminary relief. *Winter*, 129 S.Ct. at 375. Mere possibility of harm is not enough. *Id.* The district court correctly identified this legal rule and concluded that Enyart had established a likelihood of irreparable harm. Because the court "got the law right," this court should not reverse unless the district court clearly erred in its factual determinations. *Earth Island Institute v. Carlton*, 626 F.3d 462, 468–69 (9th Cir.2010).

The district court found that, in the absence of preliminary relief, Enyart would likely suffer irreparable harm in the form of (1) the loss of the chance to engage in normal life activity, i.e., pursuing her chosen profession, and (2) professional stigma. Enyart additionally argues that, as a matter of law, she faced irreparable injury from the fact of NCBE's violation of the ADA. We need not decide whether discrimination in violation of the ADA constitutes irreparable harm per se, or whether irreparable harm can be presumed based on such a statutory violation, because we agree with the district court's conclusion that Enyart demonstrated irreparable harm in the form of the loss of opportunity to pursue her chosen profession.

In her declaration in support of her first preliminary injunction motion, Enyart stated that she would not be able to complete a lengthy exam using NCBE's proposed accommodations, even with extended time. The district court was entitled to give credence to that declaration. If Enyart cannot complete the MPRE or the MBE using NCBE's proposed accommodations — and the evidence suggests that she can only use CCTV for about five minutes before becoming nauseated and disoriented, and that without simultaneous visual and auditory input, she cannot comprehend lengthy written material — then those proposed accommodations do not comply with the ADA, when other technology is readily available that will make the exam accessible.

The district court further inferred that, as a result of her likely failure, Enyart would probably suffer professional stigma and the loss of the opportunity to pursue her chosen profession. NCBE is correct that no evidence in the record supports a finding that, in the absence of preliminary relief, Enyart would likely suffer professional stigma. But the district court did not err in concluding that Enyart would likely lose the chance to pursue her chosen profession. If she fails the Bar Exam or scores too low on the MPRE to qualify for admission, Enyart cannot be licensed to practice law in California. This conclusion is not speculative, but rather is prescribed by California law. See State Bar Act, Cal. Bus. & Prof.Code § 6060(f) and (g) (requiring passage of general bar exam and professional responsibility exam to qualify for admission and licence to practice law).

NCBE argues that Enyart can pursue her chosen profession without admission to the bar, because California Rule of Court 9.42 allows Enyart to represent clients before passing the bar exam so long as she is supervised by a licensed attorney. Even if Enyart is eligible to represent clients under Rule 9.42, the rule only allows her to undertake limited activities under the supervision of an attorney. She is not allowed to hold herself out as an attorney or appear on behalf of a client in court without having a supervisor physically present, and she must obtain a signed consent from all clients acknowledging her status as a "certified law student." Cal. R. Court 9.42(d); see also Ninth Cir. R. 46–4 (permitting law students to participate in appeals under similar circumstances). Assisting clients as a certified law student is simply not the same as practicing law as an attorney. Enyart claims she is unable to take advantage of the opportunity afforded by her two-year, public-interest fellowship as a result of her inability to practice law. Because the fellowship is of limited duration, "[a] delay, even if only a few months, pending trial represents precious, productive time irretrievably lost" to Enyart. See *Chalk v. U.S. Dist. Ct.*, 840 F.2d 701 (9th Cir.1988) (holding that teacher suffered irreparable harm when he was transferred from classroom position to administrative role because of AIDS diagnosis). Because the district court's finding of irreparable harm in the form of Enyart's likely loss of the ability to pursue her chosen profession is supported by facts in the record, it does not constitute an abuse of discretion. See *Hinkson*, 585 F.3d at 1261.

3. Balance of Equities

The district court compared the harm Enyart would suffer in the absence of preliminary relief to the harm an injunction would cause NCBE, and concluded that the equities weighed in Enyart's favor. The district court rejected NCBE's argument that the injunction would cause NCBE harm that cannot be undone. NCBE argues that providing Enyart's requested accommodations is expensive and poses a security concern; however, as the district court noted, Enyart posted two $5,000 injunction bonds that will cover NCBE's costs in the event it prevails on the merits at trial, and the injunction minimized security risks by requiring Enyart to use NCBE's laptop rather than her own. Compared to the likelihood that Enyart would suffer irreparable harm by losing the chance to pursue her chosen profession in the absence of an injunction, the potential harm to NCBE resulting from injunctive relief was minimal. The district court did not abuse its discretion in holding that the balance of equities favored Enyart.

4. Public Interest

The district court held that "the public clearly has an interest in the enforcement of its statutes," and concluded that the public interest weighed in favor of granting the injunctions. NCBE argues that the public's interest in having statutes enforced is not sufficient to support a grant of a preliminary injunction.

In enacting the ADA, Congress demonstrated its view that the public has an interest in ensuring the eradication of discrimination on the basis of disabilities. 42 U.S.C. § 12101(a)(9) (finding that "the continuing existence of unfair and unnecessary discrimination and prejudice . . . costs the United States billions of dollars in unnecessary expenses resulting from dependency and nonproductivity"). This public interest is served by requiring entities to take steps to "assure equality of opportunity" for people with disabilities. See id. § 12101(a)(8). Although it is true that the public also has an interest in ensuring the integrity of licensing exams, NCBE never argued that allowing Enyart to take the MPRE and MBE using a computer equipped with JAWS and ZoomText would result in unreliable or unfair exam results. The district court did not abuse its discretion in concluding that the issuance of these preliminary injunctions served the public's interest in enforcement of the ADA and in elimination of discrimination on the basis of disability.

III. Conclusion

For the foregoing reasons, we affirm the district court's February 4, 2010 and June 22, 2010 orders issuing preliminary injunctions requiring NCBE to permit Enyart to take the MBE and MPRE using a laptop equipped with JAWS and ZoomText.

AFFIRMED.

NOTES AND PROBLEMS FOR DISCUSSION

1. Following the decision in *Enyart*, the Northern District of California, the District of Vermont and the D.C. District Court granted preliminary injunctions that required the National Conference of Bar Examiners to allow test-takers with visual disabilities to use their preferred technology in the form of special screen-access software to take the Multistate Professional Responsibility Exam or the Multistate Bar Exam. *See Elder v. NCBE*, No. C 11-00199 SI, 2011 U.S. Dist. LEXIS 15787 (N.D. Cal. Feb. 16, 2011); *Jones v. NCBE*, 801 F. Supp. 2d 270 (D. Vt. 2011); *Bonnette v. District of Columbia Court of Appeals*, 796 F. Supp. 2d 164 (D.D.C. 2011). In the Vermont case, the district court judge noted that the NCBE had "not even evaluated its own proposed accommodations for their reasonableness or efficacy in Plaintiff's case. In such circumstances, a court should give considerable weight to the opinions of Plaintiff's treating professionals who opine that the accommodation Plaintiff seeks are the only ones that will allow her to fully access the MPRE." 801 F. Supp. 2d at 288.

2. Before 2001, entities providing accommodations on tests such as the SAT, GRE, LSAT, and MCAT, frequently "flagged" scores on tests taken with accommodations as being taken under non-standard conditions. This "flag" indicates that the test, taken under non-standard conditions, has — in theory — not been validated as a predictor of success in the program at issue. When the test is flagged, the school receiving the test results becomes aware of the likelihood that the applicant has a disability.

In February 2001, the Educational Testing Service agreed to stop the practice of "flagging" scores on several tests, including the GRE, the Graduate Management Admission Test (GMAT), the Test of English as a Foreign Language (TOEFL), and Praxis by October 1, 2001. The settlement also required that an expert panel study whether to continue flagging SAT results. On July 15, 2002, the College Board announced that it would stop flagging SAT test scores effective September 2003. Immediately following the settlement, ACT officials, who flagged tests by marking them "special," said they were re-examining their own policies. Then, 11 days later, they decided to follow the SAT's lead and stop flagging scores. The groups that give the law school and medical school admissions tests, however, still flag the scores of students who receive accommodations.

The *New York Times* story about the SAT discontinuing its practice of flagging scores was headlined *Abuse Is Feared as SAT Test Changes Disability Policy*, http://www.nytimes.com/2002/07/15/national/15SAT.html. It quoted a high school counselor:

> In a perfect world, if students really need extended time to do as well as they can on a test, they should not have it flagged. But it's that flag, that asterisk, that helps cut down on abuse. This will open the floodgates to families that think they can beat the system by buying a diagnosis, and getting their kid extra time.

A college admission official expressed similar concerns:

> I think it's going to run amok and the kids who are going to get most hurt are the kids who do have real disabilities. It's very clear who's been getting extended-time: the highest-income communities have the highest rates of accommodations. I think what's going to have to happen now is that everyone will, in effect, get more time.

For a more scholarly critique expressing similar concerns, see Craig S. Lerner, *"Accommodations" for the Learning Disabled: A Level Playing Field or Affirmative Action for Elites?*, 57 Vand. L. Rev. 1043 (2004).

A member of the panel which recommended that the SAT stop flagging scores, University of Massachusetts Professor Stephen G. Sireci, acknowledged that there was a legitimate concern that affluent students without disabilities would find ways to take the SAT with extended time to increase their scores. He noted, however, that there are strong policies in place regarding who is eligible to take the exam with extended time that require medical documentation and an established history of testing accommodations in school. In addition, he said the new version of the SAT will likely have more generous time limits for all students, which would make extended time for non-disabled students irrelevant. "Therefore, I think the likelihood that this decision will inflate SAT scores for non-disabled students is very low." http://www.umass.edu/newsoffice/archive/2002/071702sat.htm. Do you agree with Prof. Sireci's assessment? What can the College Board do to alleviate the concerns about affluent families "buying" diagnoses of learning disabilities so students have more time to take standardized tests?

Until recently, the entities that administer the MCAT and LSAT still flagged test scores. For a defense of this practice, see Michael E. Slipsky, *Flagging Accommodated Testing on the LSAT and MCAT: Necessary Protections of the Academic Standards of the Legal and Medical Communities*, 82 N.C. L. Rev. 811 (2004). However, with regard to the LSAT, the matter was recently in litigation. *See California Department of Fair Employment and Housing v. Law School Admissions Counsel*, cv-01830-EMC, 2013 U.S. Dist. LEXIS 84205 (N.D. Cal. June 14, 2013). *See* University of Michigan, Civil Rights Litigation Clearinghouse. http://www.clearinghouse.net/detail.php?id=12446 (last viewed on Apr. 25, 2013).

The Law School Admission Council recently entered into an agreement with the United States Department of Justice regarding its testing practices. Under the consent decree, LSAC will pay $7.74 million in penalties and damages to compensate over 6,000 individuals nationwide who applied for testing accommodations on the LSAT over the past five years. LSAC will also end its practice of "flagging" or annotating, LSAT score reports for test takers with disabilities who have received extended time as an accommodation. *See* http://www.justice.gov/opa/pr/2014/May/14-crt-536.html (last viewed on May 22, 2014). *See also* http://www.ada.gov/defh_v_lsac/lsac_consentdecree.htm (last viewed on May 22, 2014) (consent decree). The consent decree also seeks to ensure that LSAC's documentation requests are reasonable and limited to the need for the testing accommodation requested.

3. *Enyart* involved the language in the regulation requiring the examination to be selected and administered so "as to best ensure that . . . the examination results accurately reflect the individual's aptitude or achievement level . . . rather than reflecting the individual's impaired sensory, manual, or speaking skills (except where those skills are the factors that the examination purports to measure.)" 28 C.F.R. § 36.309(b)(1)(i). In some cases, the defendant will argue that the parenthetical clause applies — that the accommodation sought by the test taker will preclude the testing entity from measuring the skills it seeks to measure. The next case involves that issue. Note that "best ensure" language is not just limited to licensing and certification examinations. Best ensure language is also found in the Section 504 regulations pertaining to post-secondary admissions examinations. *See*, 34 C.F.R. § 104.42(b)(3)(i). Does the "best ensure" standard extend to all post-secondary examinations or merely to all high stakes or gatekeeper examinations? *See* 34 C.F.R. § 104.44(a) and (c). Should it cover routine class examinations or semester final examinations? Should it be limited to individuals with vision or hearing impairments? Should it be extended to persons with learning disabilities?

FALCHENBERG v. NEW YORK STATE DEPARTMENT OF EDUCATION

2009 U.S. App. LEXIS 12213 (2d Cir. June 8, 2009), *cert. denied*, 558 U.S. 1136 (2010)

JUDGES: Present: Hon. John M. Walker, Jr., Hon. Richard C. Wesley, Hon. J. Clifford Wallace,* Circuit Judges.

OPINION

SUMMARY ORDER

UPON DUE CONSIDERATION, IT IS HEREBY ORDERED, ADJUDGED, AND DECREED that the judgment and orders of the United States District Court for the Southern District of New York be AFFIRMED.

Plaintiff-appellant Marsha Falchenberg appeals from various discovery orders and the amended opinion filed on July 10, 2008, 642 F. Supp. 2d 156, in the United States District Court for the Southern District of New York (Sweet, J.), (1) granting the

* The Honorable J. Clifford Wallace, United States Court of Appeals for the Ninth Circuit, sitting by designation.

motion of the State of New York, the New York State Education Department ("SED"), and National Evaluation Systems, Inc. ("NES") for summary judgment and denying plaintiff's cross-motion for summary judgment; (2) denying plaintiff's motion to preclude the defendants from introducing evidence; and (3) denying plaintiff discovery on the defenses raised by the defendants in their motion for summary judgment. We assume the parties' familiarity as to the facts, the procedural context, and the specification of appellate issues.

First, Falchenberg argues that the district court erred in holding that NES provided her with reasonable accommodations to take the Liberal Arts and Sciences Test ("LAST") and, thus, did not discriminate against her on the basis of her disability in violation of Titles II and III of the Americans with Disabilities Act ("ADA"), 42 U.S.C. § 12111 et seq., the Rehabilitation Act, 29 U.S.C. § 794a, the New York State Human Rights Law ("NYSHRL"), or the New York City Human Rights Law ("NYCHRL"). Disabled individuals are entitled to receive "reasonable accommodations" that permit them to have access to and take a meaningful part in public services and public accommodations. *Powell v. Nat'l Bd. of Med. Exam'rs*, 364 F.3d 79, 85 (2d Cir. 2004). However, "a defendant need not make an accommodation at all if the requested accommodation would fundamentally alter the nature of the service, program, or activity." *Id.* at 88 (internal quotation marks omitted); *see also* 42 U.S.C. § 12182(b)(2)(A)(ii); 28 C.F.R. § 35.130(b)(7). To be in compliance with the ADA, examinations like the LAST must be selected and administered so as to ensure that, when administered to an individual with a disability, the examination results do not reflect the individual's impaired ability or skill, "except where those skills are the factors that the examination purports to measure." 28 C.F.R. § 36.309(b)(1)(i); *see also* 28 C.F.R. § 36.309(b)(3) (requests for accommodation on examination need not be granted if they would "fundamentally alter the measurement of the skills or knowledge the examination is intended to test."). Thus, where a test applicant seeks an accommodation that would prevent her scores from accurately evaluating the skills intended to be measured by the test, the denial of the requested accommodation is not unlawful. *Powell*, 364 F.3d at 89.

Here, Falchenberg's request for an "oral" examination that does not require her to indicate spelling, punctuation, capitalization and paragraphing would effectuate precisely the type of fundamental alteration that need not be made as a matter of law. It is undisputed that spelling, punctuation, capitalization and paragraphing are among the skills tested on the LAST. Falchenberg's competency at these skills — competencies that all other examinees are required to demonstrate — cannot be tested without requiring her to actually spell, punctuate, capitalize and paragraph. NES granted Falchenberg every accommodation she requested that did not interfere with the measurement of skills actually tested on the LAST, including an offer to provide her with a reader to read each test question to her, a transcriber to write down her dictated written assignment for her, extra time to take the test, and a separate testing room to avoid distractions from other test takers. However, NES was not legally obligated to grant her additional accommodations fundamentally altering the LAST. Thus, the district court was correct to enter summary judgment in the Defendants' favor on Falchenberg's disability discrimination claim.

. . . .

Accordingly, for the reasons set forth above, the judgment and orders of the district court are AFFIRMED.

NOTES AND PROBLEMS FOR DISCUSSION

1. Falchenberg did not have the opportunity, on appeal, to argue that spelling and punctuation were not essential job functions for an elementary and secondary school teacher. Had she been given the opportunity to argue this point, do you think she would have been successful? Do all elementary and secondary school teachers make use of the common conventions of English grammar in their practice?

2. Deanna Jones is a 44-year-old student in her third year of a four year law program at Vermont Law School. She seeks to take the Multistate Professional Responsibility Exam under appropriate conditions of accommodation. Jones has been legally blind since age five. Her overall vision has progressively worsened during her lifetime. After struggling in college, she learned that she also has a reading disability due to deficits in phonological memory and phonological awareness. When she uses ZoomText, a computerized magnification program, and Kurzweil 1000, a text-to-speech software program, she has found that she has an ability to access written text in a manner that had previously eluded her. The National Conference of Bar Examiners denied her request and offered to let her use other accommodations such as Braille text and a CCTV. Jones, however, is not proficient in Braille. And she finds the use of CCTV unsatisfactory because it can display only a small section of text at a time and gives her significant eye fatigue. She was also offered a human reader but rejected that accommodation because of the difficult of going back and forth to figure out what she will need to do when the question is finished. Similarly, she has found digital audio to be time-consuming and confusing. The NCBE could load the required software on a laptop in a few hours at a cost at about $5000 (by their own estimates). Should the fact that other test takers and the DOJ in the past have found the NCBE's offer of accommodations to be reasonable have any impact on the decision in Jones' case? *See Jones v. NCBE*, 801 F. Supp. 2d 270 (D. Vt. 2011) (granting preliminary injunction).

3. Particularly effective use of the *Enyart* standard was demonstrated in *Bonnette v. District of Columbia Court of Appeals*, 796 F. Supp. 2d 164 (D.D.C. 2011), where the Plaintiff introduced expert witnesses, using concepts like "memory decay" and "regression," to specifically explain why the NCBE's proposed accommodations of a reader or examination questions on an audio CD were less significantly effective than those accommodations preferred by Bonnette, a legally blind individual. Similarly relying on an expert in electronic voting fraud, Bonnette presented a strong rebuttal to the assertions of the NCBE that putting its exams on computers might lead to cheating and other security risks. The court in Bonnette directly addressed the argument also asserted in Jones, that the accommodation requested would be so costly to implement that it would be unduly burdensome, noting that the DC Appellate court with a budget of $180 million had offered to pay for the costs associated with the accommodation.

4. On September 26, 2012, the state of California passed legislation making it illegal for LSAC to flag test scores of applicants to California schools who took the

exam under conditions of accommodation. *See* http://leginfo.legislature.ca.gov/faces/billTextClient.xhtml;jsessionid=2786d7a9a799535f9927d4efdd6e?bill_id=201120120AB2122 (Assembly Bill No. 2122) (last viewed on Apr. 30, 2013). The Law School Admission Council sued the state of California over this practice, arguing that it is unconstitutional because it violates its freedom of speech and does not apply to other testing entities. *See* http://www.law.com/jsp/nlj/PubArticleNLJ.jsp?id=1202583770614&California_law_school_test_council_spar_over_accommodations_for_disabled&slreturn=20130330181653 (last viewed on Apr. 30, 2013). Superior Court Judge Raymond Cadei issued a preliminary injunction on February 1, 2013, finding that it was problematic that the legislation singled out one entity for different treatment. (The Medical College Admission Test continues to flag scores and is not covered by California law.) *See* http://www.law.com/jsp/nlj/PubArticleNLJ.jsp?id=1202586925213&Ruling_allows_council_to_flag_disabled_Law_School_Admission_Test_takers (last viewed on Apr. 30, 2013).

F. SAFETY/DIRECT THREAT DEFENSE

The safety/direct threat defense first arose under Section 504 in *School Board of Nassau County v. Arline*, 480 U.S. 273 (1987), a case in which a school teacher was fired from her job because of her alleged susceptibility to tuberculosis. The trial court had ruled that individuals with contagious diseases are not covered by Section 504 and, even assuming coverage, that the school district could fire Arline because she was not qualified to teach elementary school due to her history of tuberculosis. *Id.* at 277. The Court of Appeals reversed on both issues, and the Supreme Court affirmed the Court of Appeals. The Supreme Court remanded the case to the district court to "conduct an individualized inquiry." It emphasized that an individualized inquiry was necessary if "Section 504 is to achieve its goal of protecting handicapped individuals from deprivations based on prejudice, stereotypes, or unfounded fear, while giving appropriate weight to such legitimate concerns of grantees as avoiding exposing others to significant health and safety risks." *Id.* at 287–88. The Court agreed with the American Medical Association that this inquiry should include

> [findings of] facts, based on reasonable medical judgments given the state of medical knowledge, about (a) the nature of the risk (how the disease is transmitted), (b) the duration of the risk (how long is the carrier infectious), (c) the severity of the risk (what is the potential harm to third parties) and (d) the probabilities the disease will be transmitted and will cause varying degrees of harm.

480 U.S. at 288.

Although this four-part test was developed in the context of contagious diseases, courts have applied it to consider the significance of other kinds of public safety risks as well. DOJ has codified the *Arline* test in both its Title II and Title III regulations. *See* 28 C.F.R. § 35.139 (Title II); 28 C.F.R. § 36.308 (Title III). As in *Arline*, both regulations consider only the risk that an individual might pose to *others*. Congress also codified the direct threat defense in ADA Title I. *See* 42 U.S.C. § 12113(b) ("The term 'qualification standards' may include a requirement that an individual shall not pose a direct threat to the health or safety of other individuals in the workplace.").

Unlike the ADA Title II and III regulations, the EEOC regulation interpreting the direct threat defense for purposes of ADA Title I defines a direct threat as "a significant risk of substantial harm to the health or safety *of the individual or others* that cannot be eliminated or reduced by reasonable accommodation," and states that "[a]n employer may require, as a qualification standard, that an individual not pose a direct threat to the health or safety of *himself/herself or others.*" 29 C.F.R. § 1630.2(r) (emphasis added). In *Chevron U.S.A. Inc. v. Echazabal*, 536 U.S. 73 (2002), discussed in Chapter 3, the Court held that the EEOC regulation authorizing refusal to hire an individual because his performance on the job would endanger his own health due to a disability did not exceed the scope of permissible rulemaking under the ADA. The Title II and III regulations, however, do not include the language about threat to *self*, and OCR is grappling with the issue of whether threat to self is a proper consideration in a nonemployment case under Titles II and III.

Before the ADA became law, safety issues arose frequently in higher education cases under Section 504. In *Southeastern Community College v. Davis*, 442 U.S. 397 (1979) and in *Doe v. Washington Univ.*, 780 F. Supp. 628 (E.D. Mo. 1991), plaintiffs were not allowed to graduate from university health-care programs containing clinical components due to their disabilities. Davis had a hearing impairment and was denied admission to a nursing program. Doe was disenrolled from a dentistry program after he tested positively for HIV. In both cases, the plaintiffs lost because the courts held that they were not "otherwise qualified" for their educational program due to their alleged inability to practice their professional safely.

Similarly, in *Pushkin v. Regents of the Univ. of Colorado*, 658 F.2d 1372 (10th Cir. 1981), the university denied a physician admittance to its psychiatric residency program because he suffered from multiple sclerosis. This denial was based on assumptions made by the admissions committee that the plaintiff was angry and so emotionally upset due to his disability that he would be unable to do an effective job as a psychiatrist and that his disability and use of steroids had led to difficulties with mentation, delirium and disturbed sensorium. The district court held, and the court of appeals affirmed, that the denial was based on incorrect assumptions or inadequate factual grounds.

Direct threat issues also arose in the readmission context under Section 504. For example, in *Doe v. New York University*, 666 F.2d 761 (2d Cir. 1981), *superseded on other grounds, Zervos v. Verizon New York, Inc.*, 252 F.3d 163 (2d Cir. 2001), the court denied the university's request for summary judgment, holding there was a fact issue regarding a medical school's denial of readmission to a medical student with a personality disorder which involved self-destructive and antisocial behavior. It stated, however, that, if there was significant risk of recurrence of her mental disturbances, the school was not required to give preference to her over other qualified applicants who did not pose any such appreciable risk at all.

Despite the language of the Title II and III regulations, some courts have considered the issue of whether an individual would arguably pose a risk to himself under the ADA. For example, in *Breece v. Alliance Tractor-Trailer Training II, Inc.*, 824 F. Supp. 576 (E.D. Va. 1993), the district court found that a tractor trailer training school did not violate the ADA by rejecting an applicant with severe hearing impairment who would be unable to communicate with his instructor in the cab. The court found that the applicant could not possibly keep his eyes on the road, gauges, and mirrors and simultaneously watch a sign-language interpreter translating his teacher's instructions. It also found that the severity of Breece's hearing impairment would make voice amplification devices useless in a noisy truck cab. The court found that the school could deny Breece admission because his presence on the road would pose a direct threat to the safety of himself, his instructor, and the public at large on the public highway system.

OCR has recently grappled with the issue of whether threat to self is a sufficient basis to deny admission or readmissions. In *Spring Arbor*, OCR Complaint No. 15102098 (Metro 2011), OCR found that a school may not set conditions for readmission upon a student who engages in a voluntary withdrawal while in good academic standing, even though the student had a serious record of self-destructive behavior. According to OCR (and DOJ), a threat to self, only, without more, is not a sufficient independent basis for adverse treatment, sanctions, or coercive terms of readmission.

A similar issue recently arose in a complaint against Princeton University. After a student took an overdose of medication, and checked himself into the university health center, the university tried to force him to withdraw from school. After securing legal counsel, he reached a settlement that allowed him to re-enroll at the university. *See* http://www.newsweek.com/2014/02/14/how-colleges-flunk-mental-health-245492.html (good discussion of mental health issues on college campuses). A redacted copy of the complaint is available for review at this address: http://www.bazelon.org/LinkClick.aspx?fileticket=KgxSxhU1XQM%3d&tabid=313. Is it unlawful for a university to impose different conditions on a student who is hospitalized because he broke his leg as compared to a student who is hospitalized due to a prescription drug overdose? In an interview about this matter, the student said that the university's treatment of him should forewarn other students to avoid a university medical center if he or she has suicidal ideations. What policy would you recommend a university maintain if it wants to encourage students to seek medical treatment without concern about adverse actions?

OCR has also grappled with the issue of what medical information a university can request before readmitting a student, applying the individualized requirement under *Arline*. In *Fordham University*, OCR Complaint No. 02102013 (New York 2012), a student requested a medical withdrawal for several psychological conditions. University policy provides that students who withdraw must apply for readmission. They approved the withdrawal but warned that when he applied for readmission, he would have to provide unspecified "medical documentation."

At the point of readmission, he completed all the requirements, but believing these terms to be discriminatory, also filed a complaint with OCR. OCR found the readmission practices of Fordham to be discriminatory because the University required all students with actual or perceived mental health conditions, regardless of the nature or severity of their conditions, to provide detailed information about their treatment, diagnosis, and mental state from both a psychiatrist and psychologist; be evaluated by a University clinician; sign a Statement of Expectations; and give permission for the University to review their medical records. There was no individualized evaluation to determine if all of these requirements are necessary, unlike for physical conditions or injuries, as to which the University determined on a case-by-case basis what documentation would be required.

The University signed a resolution agreement in which it committed to establishing a written procedure for reviewing students' requests for readmission following a medical withdrawal, which would ensure an individualized determination as to what documentation would be required. The procedure would apply to all medical withdrawals, including for physical and psychological reasons. *See also Georgetown University*, OCR Complaint No. 11112044 (Metro 2012).

In response to recent violent events on university campuses, some schools have tightened their policies to dismiss students who they perceive to be a direct threat to others. The following case reflects that fact pattern. Does the case involve a proper consideration of the *Arline* four-part test?

STEBBINS v. UNIVERSITY OF ARKANSAS

Civil No. 10-5125, 2012 U.S. Dist. LEXIS 182620 (W.D. Ark. Dec. 28, 2012)

JUDGES: Jimm Larry Hendren, United States District Judge.

MEMORANDUM OPINION

On December 3-4, 2012, the captioned matter came on for trial to the Court. Plaintiff appeared and represented himself. Defendants appeared by their representative Dr. Monica Holland and were represented by counsel. The Court received documentary evidence and heard testimony and the arguments of counsel, and now makes the following findings of fact and conclusions of law.

PROCEDURAL HISTORY

1. Plaintiff David Stebbins contends that the University of Arkansas ("UA") discriminated against him, in violation of Section 504 of the Rehabilitation Act of 1973, 29 U.S.C. § 794(a), by failing in 2010 to allow him to re-enroll as a student after he was banned from campus in 2007. Stebbins contends that he has a disability — Asperger's Syndrome — and that UA made no attempt to accommodate this disability. He seeks money damages and injunctive relief.

2. Stebbins also asserted claims that his First Amendment rights were violated by UA Chancellor David Gearhart, and that he was subjected to employment discrimination by UA. These claims were dismissed before trial, as lacking merit, and will not be addressed in this opinion.

. . . .

CONCLUSIONS OF LAW

34. UA contends that Stebbins' case should be dismissed because he failed to exhaust administrative remedies when he did not appeal the decision of the AUJ. The Court finds this contention without merit. UA did not plead failure to exhaust as an affirmative defense in its Answer. Generally speaking, "'failure to plead an affirmative defense results in a waiver of that defense'." *Sherman v. Winco Fireworks, Inc.*, 532 F.3d 709, 715 (8th Cir. 2008). While the Eighth Circuit has recognized that a trial court may exercise discretion to allow the defense to be untimely pled if it does not result in unfair surprise, UA never sought to amend its Answer, nor was the matter brought to the Court's attention until shortly before trial. Under these circumstances, the Court finds that UA has waived this defense.

35. To make out a prima facie case on his Rehabilitation Act claim, Stebbins must show the following:

(a) that he is a person with a disability, as defined by statute;

(b) that he is otherwise qualified for the benefit in question, enrollment at UA;

(c) that he was excluded from the benefit due to discrimination based on his disability; and

(d) that the program or activity from which he was excluded receives federal financial assistance.

Randolph v. Rodgers, 170 F.3d 850, 858 (8th Cir. 1999).

36. "Disability," for purposes of the Rehabilitation Act, has the meaning given in 42 U.S.C. § 12102. 29 U.S.C. § 705. It includes a person with a physical or mental impairment that substantially limits one or more major life activities, a person with a record of such impairment, and a person regarded as having such an impairment. Major life activities include learning, thinking, communicating, and working. Defendant admitted, in Responses to Requests for Admission, that Stebbins was eligible for accommodations based on the disability of Asperger's Syndrome. Thus, element (a) is not in dispute.

37. Stebbins presented a webshot of a UA description of available financial aid including statements relating to application for Federal Student Aid, and this was admitted without objection. It appears, therefore, that element (d) is also undisputed.

38. A person is "otherwise qualified" under the Rehabilitation Act if, with reasonable accommodations, he "can perform the essential functions of the position in question without endangering the health and safety of the individual or others." *Wood v. Omaha School District*, 25 F.3d 667, 669 (8th Cir. 1994). Failing to make reasonable accommodations is a form of disability discrimination. *Peebles v. Potter*, 354 F.3d 761, 765-67 (8th Cir. 2004).

39. Stebbins has the initial burden of proving that he requested reasonable accommodations from UA, and that those accommodations would render him "otherwise qualified." *Mershon v. St. Louis University*, 442 F.3d 1069, 1077 (8th Cir. 2006). He need not have used any particular words to request accommodations, but must have said enough to invoke the "interactive process" whereby he and UA would have

worked out what accommodations were appropriate for what disability. *Ballard v. Rubin*, 284 F.3d 957, 960 (8th Cir. 2002).

40. Stebbins failed to establish that he requested reasonable accommodations applicable to the reason for his suspension. The evidence shows that when he registered with the CEA [the disabled student services center] as having Asperger's Syndrome, the only accommodation he mentioned was "help negotiating my tactlessness w/my professors." His statements that if he did not get his medications refilled there could be another "Virginia Tech incident" are on a different order of magnitude than mere tactlessness. They could reasonably be interpreted as threats to the safety of the entire UA community, and in fact were so perceived.

Moreover, Stebbins failed to show that the accommodations he requested after having made the "Virginia Tech incident" comments — patience and understanding, giving him the benefit of the doubt, not taking his words as threatening unless he really meant them that way, giving him a second chance — were reasonable.

Jannarone [the CEA Director] testified that it would be unreasonable to accommodate behavior that rises to the level of a violation of the Code of Student Life, such as threats and profanity. The legal touchstone for reasonable accommodations supports this position. An accommodation is not reasonable if it imposes undue financial and administrative burdens on an institution. *Kohl by Kohl v. Woodhaven Learning Center*, 865 F.2d 930, 936 (8th Cir. 1989). For UA officials to have adopted a "wait and see" attitude in the face of Stebbins' "Virginia Tech incident" comments would have burdened UA with the risk of all the financial, administrative, and human toll that another Virginia Tech incident would have carried with it had they made the wrong decision. It cannot be seriously argued that such would be reasonable.

41. Stebbins also failed to establish that he was excluded from the benefit of UA enrollment due to discrimination based on his disability. The evidence shows that accommodations appropriate to Asperger's Syndrome were afforded Stebbins, and that he was not suspended for "tactlessness" or the social awkwardness and challenges with social interaction that characterize Asperger's Syndrome. He was suspended for making threats, which is not a characteristic of Asperger's Syndrome.

42. Not only did Stebbins fail to establish a prima facie case of discrimination, UA succeeded in establishing its affirmative defense that Stebbins constituted a direct threat to the UA community, as to which it had the burden of proof. *EEOC v. Wal-Mart Stores, Inc.*, 477 F.3d 561, 571 (8th Cir. 2007). The criteria to be used in assessing whether a student presents a direct threat are drawn from *School Board of Nassau County, Fla. v. Arline*, 480 U.S. 273, 287 (1987), wherein the Court said that the Rehabilitation Act has goals of protecting handicapped individuals from discrimination "while giving appropriate weight to such legitimate concerns of grantees as avoiding exposing others to significant health and safety risks."

Factors to consider in the evaluation of risk under *Arline* include:

(a) the nature of the risk;

(b) the duration of the risk;

(c) the severity of the risk; and

(d) the probability of the risk.

43. When the Arline factors are applied to the facts of this case, they lead ineluctably to the conclusion that UA officials properly evaluated Stebbins as a direct threat to UA on December 5, 2007, when he made repeated statements that if he did not get his medications refilled there could be another "Virginia Tech incident."

(a) The nature of the risk:

Stebbins' statements about a "Virginia Tech incident" went far beyond the tactlessness and "smarting off" he noted when registering with the CEA. Only a few months before, a student had shot and killed a large number of people on the campus of Virginia Tech, a highly publicized event that shocked the nation, and especially those on college campuses. UA was not required to prove that a threat was actually made and intended by Stebbins, but rather that those who heard his statements reasonably believed that a threat was made. *Mershon, supra*, 442 F.3d at 1075. Based on Stebbins' history at UA, Dr. Holland and the AJU could reasonably have believed that Stebbins might do the same thing.

(b) The duration of the risk:

By December 5, 2007, Stebbins had been a student at UA for about four months. In that short period of time, he had had significant difficulties in his interactions with dorm staff and Treasurer's Office staff. Dr. Holland, who made the decision to suspend Stebbins, knew about these difficulties, and it was reasonable for her to believe that the December 5, 2007, incident was not an isolated one, but rather a pattern that had existed from Stebbins' enrollment and was not likely to improve without significant intervention. Thus, the duration of the risk was indefinite.

(c) The severity of the risk:

The risk in this case was severe. Stebbins' statements implicated the safety — indeed, the lives — of students, faculty, and staff at UA. No reasonable administrator could afford to overlook them.

(d) The probability of the risk:

Given Stebbins' history since matriculation — reflecting a pattern of repeatedly becoming enraged over what others would perceive merely as minor annoyances — it was reasonable for Dr. Holland, and later the AUJ, to believe that there was a significant probability that Stebbins would carry out his threats of another "Virginia Tech incident."

44. Finally, the Court is not persuaded that there was any violation of law when UA decided not to allow Stebbins to re-enroll following his profanity-filled e-mail to Chancellor Gearhart. In addition to the fact that Stebbins still had not satisfied the conditions of re-enrollment established by the AUJ, there was the threatening tone of the e-mail itself.

While Stebbins argued at trial that the only threat to be found in the e-mail was a threat to sue Chancellor Gearhart, the Court does not agree.

* The e-mail is extremely profane, and Stebbins admitted at the AUJ hearing — long before he sent the e-mail — that he knew profanity could be perceived as threatening.
* The tone of the e-mail is intensely malicious.
* The e-mail is couched in terms of demands that must be met within hours.
* The threat to sue is obviously coercive in nature.

When viewed in light of Stebbins' past history at UA, and his mental health treatment records, the e-mail was clearly threatening, and the Court finds that it was reasonable for UA to conclude that Stebbins should not be allowed back in school, or even on campus.

45. Having concluded that Dr. Holland's interim suspension was reasonable; that the interim suspension of the AUJ was reasonable; and that the criminal trespass warning in 2010 was reasonable, it follows that Stebbins' claim that UA violated the Rehabilitation Act is without merit. There is, therefore, no need to address the issues of damages or injunctive relief. His claims will be denied and dismissed with prejudice, and a separate judgment to this effect will be entered contemporaneously herewith.

NOTES AND PROBLEMS FOR DISCUSSION

1. When Stebbins threatened individuals with lawsuits under Section 504 and the ADA, was he engaging in a protected activity? Was it retaliation to sanction him for engaging in these kinds of activities?

2. If Stebbins "turned his life around," engaged in long term therapy, adhered to a treatment and medication plan, would he be entitled to readmission, or could the University argue that he was entitled to "no more bites at the apple"?

3. Universities have often tightened their rules regarding students who they perceive to be a danger to others in response to recent, well-publicized instances of violence on college campuses. Yet, studies suggest that college campuses are a relatively safe environment for 18-to-24-year-olds. "When compared to the mortality of 18-to-24-year-olds in the general population, college student death rates are significantly lower for such causes as suicide, alcohol-related deaths and homicide." Further, the workplace for college professors ranks among the safest occupations studied, with the rate of workplace violence for college teachers being 1.9 per 1,000 employed person as compared, for example, to 10.1 per 1,000 for physicians. *See* Gary Pavela, THE PAVELA REPORT: LAW AND POLICY IN HIGHER EDUCATION (Apr. 6, 2012) (last viewed on Apr. 28, 2013), at: .

https://docs.google.com/document/d/
1UMXdMVlitBII8BjkxTBCk3heUaopniJSJscFk1cLWbE/edit

4. Consider the following fact pattern:

An investigator for the Office for Civil Rights, U.S. Department of Education, reported to a federal law enforcement officer that Craig Mershon had twice stated during her interview with him about his complaint of disability-related discrimination that "My professor makes me so mad that I want to put a bullet in his head." University officials were contacted; they decided to prohibit Mershon from entering the campus because he had made threats against a professor in violation of university policy. Mershon filed suit against the university claiming that he was expelled from campus in retaliation for complaining about his treatment at the university. The district court held that the university was entitled to summary judgment even if Mershon disputed that he made the threatening statement and even if the university would not have known of the threatening statement absent OCR's investigation of Mershon's discrimination complaint. Mershon appealed.

What should be the result? *See* ***Mershon v. St. Louis University***, 442 F.3d 1069 (8th Cir. 2006).

5. In *Davis* and *Does v. Washington*, had the plaintiffs been allowed to continue with their course of study, they probably would have been able to pass the requisite certifying exam. Should the latter fact be relevant to the resolution of these cases? Could a nursing program, for example, exclude an individual with diabetes from the program because it might be more difficult for that individual to do shift work (usually required of nurses) due to a lack of stamina?

6. The interplay between safety and athletics is often an issue of dispute in the context of both secondary and postsecondary educational programs. Under Section 504 and the ADA, an educational institution must allow qualified students with disabilities an equal opportunity to participate in intercollegiate, club, or intramural athletics. The question sometimes arises as to whether an individual with a disability is qualified to play a certain sport, or whether the educational institution can claim a safety defense within the meaning of the law. Consider the following problems:

a. A university refuses to allow a student who is blind in one eye to play intercollegiate football, due to fear that the student will injure his other eye and thus become blind. Has the university violated Section 504 and the ADA? Should it matter whether experts testify that playing football does or does not pose a serious risk of eye injury? *See, e.g.*, ***Wright v. Columbia Univ.***, 520 F. Supp. 789 (E.D. Pa. 1981).

b. Should it make a difference if the student was a high school freshman, and the student was prohibited from participating in all contact sports? *See, e.g.*, *Kampmeier v. Nyquist*, 553 F.2d 296 (2d Cir. 1977). Should a high school be permitted to prohibit a student with only one kidney from participating on the wrestling team due to fear that the student would injure his remaining kidney?

c. Joe is a freshman at Utopia State College, admitted on a baseball scholarship (Utopia ranks #2 in college baseball). Shortly after he entered college Joe's father died of a heart attack, and it was discovered that the father had a congenital heart condition. Joe and his siblings were tested for heart problems, and Joe was found to have a slight heart murmur. The college prohibited Joe from playing baseball due to fear that Joe would have a heart attack or other heart problem while playing ball. This in turn caused the loss of Joe's scholarship. Joe claims that the college is in violation of ADA Title II.

Does Joe's claim have merit? What factors should the court weigh when determining whether Joe should be held qualified to play baseball?

7. Are students with disabilities entitled to reasonable accommodations in intramural, club, and intercollegiate athletics programs? How would you determine if a requested accommodation in athletics practices or rules would constitute a fundamental alteration in the nature of the athletic competition? What if the requested modification was contrary to a written athletic association rule which the college is required to follow? What if a group of student veterans with substantial physical impairments wanted to form their own wheelchair basketball league? Must the college give the same level of support to a wheelchair league as it accords to its existing intramural basketball program? *See PGA v. Martin*, 532 U.S. 661 (2001); and OCR Dear Colleague Letter (DCL) of January 25, 2013 concerning equal athletic opportunity for students with disabilities, www2.ed.gov/about/offices/list/ocr/ letters/colleague-201301-504.pdf (last viewed on August 25, 2013).

G. INTEGRATED SETTING

The ADA and Section 504 seek to end the isolation and segregation of individuals with disabilities through a preference for integrated settings. In *Olmstead v. L.C.*, 527 U.S. 581 (1999), the Court interpreted ADA Title II to include an "integration mandate" through the provision which requires a "public entity [to] administer . . . programs . . . in the most integrated setting appropriate to the needs of qualified individuals with disabilities." 28 C.F.R. § 35.130(d).

The integration requirement recently arose in the Sixth Circuit. Micah Fialka-Feldman, a continuing education student with mild cognitive disabilities, sought an injunction to require Oakland University to provide him with on-campus housing while he attended a program at the university that was designed to allow students with "mild disabilities" to continue their academic education in a college setting by attending regular university courses and participating in student activities. Because the students were not full-time, degree-seeking students, the university took the position that it did not need to provide housing. Does its housing policy violate the ADA or Section 504? The Sixth Circuit dismissed the case as moot because Feldman had completed his program before the court was able to hear the case on appeal. *See Feldman v. Oakland University Board of Trustees*, 639 F.3d 711 (6th Cir. 2011). The district court's decision is excerpted below. Is its legal analysis correct?

FIALKA–FELDMAN v. OAKLAND UNIVERSITY BOARD OF TRUSTEES

678 F. Supp. 2d 576 (E.D. Mich. 2009)

OPINION AND ORDER

PATRICK J. DUGGAN, District Judge.

Plaintiff initiated this lawsuit against Defendant Oakland University Board of Trustees on November 25, 2008, claiming that Defendant's denial of his request for housing in one of Oakland University's on-campus dormitory living spaces violates the Fair Housing Act ("FHA"), 42 U.S.C. § 3604(f)(3)(B), and § 504 of the Rehabilitation Act of 1973, 29 U.S.C. § 794(a). Plaintiff has since, with the Court's permission, amended his complaint to add University officials Gary D. Russi, Mary Beth Snyder, and Lionel Maten as defendants and the following claims:

(I) disparate impact discrimination in violation of the FHA;

(II) disparate treatment discrimination in violation of the FHA;

(III) disparate treatment discrimination in violation of the Rehabilitation Act;

(IV) denial of a reasonable accommodation in violation of the Rehabilitation Act;

(V) disparate treatment discrimination in violation of the Americans with Disabilities Act ("ADA"), 42 U.S.C. §§ 12101–12213; and,

(VI) disparate impact discrimination in violation of the Rehabilitation Act.

Presently before the Court is Defendants' Motion for Summary Judgment [and] Plaintiff's cross-motion for summary judgment

I. Applicable Standards

[Court summarizes summary judgment standard.]

II. Factual and Procedural Background

Plaintiff is a twenty-four year old male with cognitive impairments that substantially limit a major life activity, specifically his ability to learn. Plaintiff has been attending classes at Oakland University (hereafter "Oakland" or "University") since 2003. He has been enrolled in the University's OPTIONS program since Fall 2007, when the University established the program ". . . to provide a fully inclusive, age appropriate postsecondary education experience for students with mild cognitive disabilities." (Doc. 39, Ex. 6.)

Participants in the OPTIONS program are required to take a minimum of twelve credits per semester and pay the regular University tuition rate for undergraduate students; however, the program is not a degree-granting program. (*Id.*) Students in the program are categorized as "continuing-education" students. The proposal for the program developed and presented to the University by Robert Wiggins, the University's Associate Dean in the School of Education and Human Services, identified the various housing configurations available on-campus as one rationale for University involvement in the program. (Doc. 39, Ex. 3 at 2–3.) When the University approved the OPTIONS program, however, it did not consider on-campus housing as part of the program. (Doc. 45, Ex. 14 at 62–63.)

In Spring 2007, at Plaintiff's Person Centered Planning meeting, housing was discussed as a goal for the coming year. Thereafter, Plaintiff and his father, Rich Feldman, took a pre-arranged tour of Oakland's dormitory housing. At the start of the tour, they were greeted by Defendant Lionel Maten, then the Director of University

Housing. Plaintiff submitted a completed housing application on November 1, 2007. (Doc. 39, Ex. 7.) The "Terms and Conditions" on the back of the application provide, with respect to "ELIGIBILITY": "To be eligible for University housing a student must be enrolled as a student at the University throughout the entire period of the Contract." (*Id.*)

In response to an inquiry from Mr. Feldman on November 8, 2007, Dean Wiggins indicated that he had spoken with Roxanne Fisher in the Housing Department and learned that Plaintiff's application "has been accepted and is being processed." (Doc. 39, Ex. 8.) Ms. Fisher is an Office Assistant in the University Housing Department who is responsible, when applications are first received by the department, for verifying that it is complete and that the required deposit has been submitted. (Doc. 37, Ex. 7.) Ms. Fisher does not determine whether applicants meet the eligibility requirements to live in on-campus housing. (*Id.*)

Mr. Feldman thereafter sent an e-mail to Ms. Fisher, inquiring as to whether there was anything more he needed to do so Plaintiff could begin living in on-campus housing in January 2008. On November 14, 2007, Ms. Fisher responded that "there is nothing else [Plaintiff] needs to do. He is all set." (Doc. 37, Ex. 8.) She then described the University's schedule for making housing assignments, the move-in procedure, and some of the personal items residents can possess in their dormitory rooms. (*Id.*) In an affidavit submitted in support of Defendants' motion, Ms. Fisher states that she did not intend to indicate that Plaintiff was qualified for on-campus housing when she wrote that he was "all set" in her e-mail to Mr. Feldman. (*Id.*, Ex. 7.) Rather, she only intended to convey that Plaintiff's application was "all set" for her purposes (i.e. it was complete and a deposit had been paid). (*Id.*)

On November 29, 2007, Mr. Wiggins sent an e-mail to Mr. Feldman, indicating that he had been told that Plaintiff is not eligible for on-campus housing and that Plaintiff would be receiving a letter informing him of this. (Doc. 39, Ex. 9.) In a subsequent email to Mr. Feldman on January 7, 2008, Mr. Wiggins wrote that he "had a conversation with our university council and found out that it has been university practice for some time that the dorm facilities are restricted to students who are pursuing a degree" and that "they have held to this firmly . . ." (*Id.*) Mr. Wiggins further wrote:

> This is sort of what our VP for Student Affairs [Ms. Snyder] told me initially, but she either didn't explain it as well or I was not really hearing it. I am surprised that the folks in the housing office didn't recognize the conflict before we got so far but Lionel [Mr. Maten] is new and perhaps the others were not aware that OPTIONS was not a degree program.

(*Id.*)

Plaintiff and his representatives lobbied University officials throughout 2008, requesting that the University waive its policy of limiting housing to students enrolled in degree-granting programs and allow Plaintiff to live on campus. Plaintiff's request was denied at various levels. In the interim, in March 2008, the University modified the "Terms and Conditions" on the back of its "Contract for Residence Hall Services" to specify that residents are required to be enrolled as matriculating students. (Doc. 39,

Ex. 13.) Plaintiff filed this lawsuit on November 25, 2008.

On December 15, 2008, Plaintiff filed a motion for preliminary injunction based on his FHA claims. (Doc. 4.) At that time, Plaintiff had only named the Oakland University Board of Trustees ("Board of Trustees") as a defendant. In an opinion and order issued on February 5, 2009, this Court held that Plaintiff's FHA claims against the Board of Trustees were barred by the Eleventh Amendment to the United States Constitution. (Doc. 12 at 12.) The Court also indicated that Plaintiff was not likely to succeed on his FHA claims because his requested accommodation "[was] not necessary to afford him an 'equal opportunity' to use and enjoy on-campus housing because all students not enrolled in a degree-granting program (whether they are or are not handicapped) are ineligible for such housing." (*Id.* at 13.) The Court therefore concluded "that Plaintiff's requested accommodation [was] not necessary to ameliorate the effects of his disability and to afford him an opportunity equal to non-disabled students to use and enjoy University on-campus housing." (*Id.* at 15–16.) The Court now will reevaluate its conclusions with respect to Plaintiff's FHA claims and evaluate Plaintiff's other claims pursuant to the summary judgment standard.

III. Applicable Law and Analysis

As indicated earlier, both parties move for summary judgment. Defendants argue that they are entitled to summary judgment with respect to all of the claims asserted in Plaintiff's Second Amended Complaint. Plaintiff argues that he is entitled to summary judgment with respect to his disparate treatment discrimination claims brought pursuant to the FHA, Rehabilitation Act, and ADA (Counts II, III, and V, respectively) and his reasonable accommodation claim under the Rehabilitation Act (Count IV). At the motion hearing, Plaintiff's counsel informed the Court that Plaintiff is no longer pursuing his disparate impact discrimination claims brought pursuant to the FHA and Rehabilitation Act (*see* Doc. 42). Therefore, the Court is dismissing those claims (Counts I and VI, respectively).

A. Failure to Accommodate

Section 504(a) of the Rehabilitation Act provides that "[n]o otherwise qualified individual with a disability in the United States . . . shall, solely by reason of his or her disability, be excluded from the participation in, be denied the benefits of, or be subjected to discrimination under any program or activity receiving Federal financial assistance . . ." 29 U.S.C. § 794(a). The Rehabilitation Act does not contain an accommodation requirement. *See Wisconsin Cmty. Servs. v. City of Milwaukee*, 465 F.3d 737, 746 (7th Cir.2006). However, the federal regulations implementing the statute specifically set forth such a requirement:

> A recipient [of Federal funds] shall make reasonable accommodation to the known physical or mental limitations of an otherwise qualified handicapped applicant or employee unless the recipient can demonstrate that the accommodation would impose an undue hardship on the operation of its program.

28 C.F.R. § 41.53.

Defendants do not dispute that Plaintiff is disabled. Defendants contend that Plaintiff is not an "otherwise qualified individual" with a disability because he is not enrolled at the University in a degree-granting program and only degree-granting students are eligible to live in on-campus housing. . . .

The relevant question, therefore, is " 'whether some 'reasonable accommodation' is available to satisfy the legitimate interests of both the grantee and the handicapped person.' " *Id.* at 575 (quoting *Brennan*, 834 F.2d at 1261–62). As a result, the "otherwise qualified" and "reasonable accommodation" inquiries merge. *Id.*

One element of the "otherwise qualified-reasonable accommodation" analysis is whether an accommodation is "necessary." *See Smith & Lee Assoc. v. City of Taylor*, 102 F.3d 781, 795 (6th Cir.1996). An accommodation is necessary when " 'the rule in question, if left unmodified, hurts handicapped people *by reason of their handicap*, rather than by virtue of what they have in common with other people, such as a limited amount of money to spend on housing.' " *Sutton v. Piper*, 344 Fed.Appx. 101, 102 (6th Cir.2009) (unpublished opinion) (quoting *Wis. Cmty. Servs.*, 465 F.3d at 749); *see also Smith & Lee Assoc.*, 102 F.3d at 795 (citing *Bronk v. Ineichen*, 54 F.3d 425, 429 (7th Cir.1995)) ("The concept of necessity requires at a minimum the showing that the desired accommodation will affirmatively enhance a disabled plaintiff's quality of life by ameliorating the effects of the disability.") Stated differently, there must be a "direct nexus" or "direct correlation" between the plaintiff's handicap and the barrier to his or her equal access to the program or benefit at issue. *See Schanz*, 998 F.Supp. at 792.

In *Sutton*, the Sixth Circuit determined that an accommodation was not necessary because a federally subsidized apartment complex rejected Plaintiff's housing application due to his poor credit history — which "[a] review of [his] credit report confirm[ed]. . . resulted from his own financial mismanagement and not his disability." *Id.* at 102–03; *see also Schanz v. The Village Apartments*, 998 F.Supp. 784, 791–92 (E.D.Mich.1998) (finding no direct nexus between the plaintiff's disability and the rejection of his housing application because his financial status, not his disability, rendered him ineligible). Similarly, in *Alexander*, the Supreme Court determined that an accommodation to the proposed rule challenged by the disabled plaintiffs was not necessary because it did not impact the plaintiffs by reason of their disabilities. 469 U.S. at 302–03, 105 S.Ct. at 720–21.

The *Alexander* Court wrote:

> The new limitation does not invoke criteria that have a particular exclusionary effect on the handicapped; the reduction neutral on its face, does not distinguish between those whose coverage will be reduced and those who coverage will not on the basis of any test, judgment, or trait that the handicapped as a class are less capable of meeting or less likely of having . . .

469 U.S. at 302, 105 S.Ct. at 720–21. This reasoning, which suggests that an accommodation is not "necessary" whenever it would grant a "preference" to the disabled over the non-disabled, was applied by the district court in *Schanz* and the Second Circuit Court of Appeals in *Salute v. Stratford Greens Garden Apartments*, 136 F.3d 293 (1998). Defendants rely on these cases for that proposition. The Supreme

Court, however, expressly disavowed such a rationale for rejecting an accommodation in *U.S. Airways, Inc. v. Barnett*, 535 U.S. 391, 122 S.Ct. 1516, 152 L.Ed.2d 589 (2002).

In that case, U.S. Airway argued that an accommodation under the ADA's reasonable accommodation requirement should be deemed unreasonable whenever it violates a "disability-neutral workplace" rule (such as a seniority rule) and grants a "preference" to disabled employees. The Supreme Court rejected this argument, explaining:

> While linguistically logical, this argument fails to recognize what the Act specifies, namely, that preferences will sometimes prove necessary to achieve the Act's basic equal opportunity goal. The Act requires preferences in the form of "reasonable accommodations" that are needed for those with disabilities to obtain the *same* workplace opportunities that those without disabilities automatically enjoy. By definition any special "accommodation" requires the employer to treat an employee with a disability differently, *i.e.*, preferentially. And the fact that the difference in treatment violates an employer's disability-neutral rule cannot by itself place the accommodation beyond the Act's potential reach. . . .
>
> The simple fact that an accommodation would provide a "preference" — in the sense that it would permit the worker with a disability to violate a rule that others must obey — cannot, *in and of itself*, automatically show that the accommodation is not "reasonable."

Id. at 397–98, 122 S.Ct. at 1521 (emphasis in original). The Sixth Circuit has applied similar reasoning in holding that an accommodation of a city's zoning law prohibiting more than six residents from living in property zoned for single-family use was necessary and reasonable to provide disabled elderly individuals equal access to housing in single-family residential neighborhoods. *Smith & Lee Assoc.*, 102 F.3d at 795–96. In that case, the court reasoned: "[T]he phrase 'equal opportunity,'. . . is concerned with achieving equal results, not just formal equality." *Id.* at 795.

The second element of the "otherwise qualified-reasonable accommodation" inquiry is whether the accommodation is "reasonable." "[A]n accommodation is reasonable unless it requires 'a fundamental alteration in the nature of a program' or imposes 'undue financial and administrative burdens.' " *Smith & Lee Assoc.*, 102 F.3d at 795 (quoting *Davis*, 442 U.S. at 410, 412, 99 S.Ct. at 2369, 2370). The Supreme Court has indicated that, "in most cases," determining whether an accommodation is "reasonable" will require the district court "to conduct an individualized inquiry and make appropriate findings of fact." *Sch. Bd. of Nassau County v. Arline*, 480 U.S. 273, 287, 107 S.Ct. 1123, 1130, 94 L.Ed.2d 307 (1987) "In cases involving waiver of applicable rules and regulations, the overall focus should be on 'whether waiver of the rule *in the particular case* would be so at odds with the purposes behind the rule that it would be a fundamental and unreasonable change.' " *Jones v. City of Monroe*, 341 F.3d 474, 480 (6th Cir.2003) (emphasis added) (quoting *Dadian v. Vill. of Wilmette*, 269 F.3d 831, 838–39 (7th Cir.2001)). The burden of proving that an accommodation is not reasonable lies with the public entity. *Id.*

Turning to the present matter, Plaintiff has requested an accommodation in the form of a waiver of the University's policy limiting on-campus housing to students enrolled in a degree-granting program. Unlike *Sutton*, the undisputed evidence indicates that this barrier to housing is created "by reason of" Plaintiff's disability (i.e., his cognitive impairments that substantially limit his ability to learn). The University may have denied Plaintiff's housing request based on a characteristic that he has in common with non-disabled students — his status as a continuing-education student and non-enrollment in a degree-granting program. However there is no dispute that, unlike other continuing-education students (except other OPTIONS program participants), it is *because of* Plaintiff's disability (not some other factor) that he is unable to enroll in a degree granting program. In that sense, the Court finds Plaintiff's situation more akin to the plaintiff in the case cited by his counsel at the motion hearing: *Giebeler v. M & B Associates*, 343 F.3d 1143 (9th Cir.2003).

In *Giebeler*, the Ninth Circuit concluded that there was "a direct causal link" between the plaintiff's impairment and the barrier to housing based on the court's finding that "if [the plaintiff] were still able to work in the position he held before becoming ill, he would have met [the apartment complex]'s financial requirements." *Id.* at 1147. The court therefore held that the plaintiff was entitled to the protections of the FHA. *Id.* Similarly, this Court finds that Plaintiff's cognitive impairments prevent him from enrolling in a degree-granting program and therefore the protections of the Rehabilitation Act are necessary to provide him with an "equal opportunity" to live in the University's on-campus housing. The remaining question is whether Plaintiff's requested accommodation is reasonable.

Defendants contend that allowing continuing-education students to live in the University's dormitories will require "a fundamental alteration in the nature of [it's housing] program." (Doc. 45 at 16.) Ms. Snyder, who oversees the University's Housing Department as the University's Vice President of Student Affairs and Enrollment Management, testified during her deposition in this matter that the housing program is "an academic program" that is "focused on the purpose of moving students toward an academic degree." (Doc. 37, Ex. 6 at 9.) Ms. Snyder conveys that allowing non-degree seeking students into University housing will change the "culture" and "the entire nature of the relationship between the university and the people in housing to the point where it's, it's no longer an academic program per se." (*Id.* at 28–29.) When asked to explain how the presence of OPTIONS program students in the dormitories would affect the University's housing program, Ms. Snyder referred to some unspecified impact on "study floors" and "quiet hours." (*Id.* at 31.) She further indicated that expulsion cannot be used as a leverage with continuing-education students like it can with students in degree-granting programs and that there would be "a whole set of issues if the halls were opened to community members who weren't enrolled where the university has limited [housing] space on campus." (*Id.*)

Courts have held that deference should be extended to an educational institution's academic decisions. *See, e.g., Zukle v. Regents of Univ. of Calif.*, 166 F.3d 1041, 1047 (9th Cir.1999) (citing cases). As the Ninth Circuit summarized in *Zukle:*

> These courts noted the limited ability of courts, "as contrasted to that of experienced educational administrators and professionals," to determine whether a student "would meet reasonable standards for academic and

professional achievement established by a university," and have concluded that "courts are particularly ill-equipped to evaluate academic performance."

Id. (quoting *Doe v. New York Univ.*, 666 F.2d 761, 775–76 (2d Cir.1981)). This Court questions whether this reasoning applies equally to a university's decisions with respect to its housing policies and therefore whether such deference should be accorded to those decisions. The Court finds it unnecessary to resolve that issue in this case, however. This is because the rationale Defendants offer for why Plaintiff's requested accommodation is not reasonable is premised on an overstatement of the accommodation the University is being asked to make, is not based on the facts presented, and reflects a failure to engage in an "individualized inquiry."

First, Plaintiff's requested accommodation would not require the University to open its on-campus housing to all continuing-education students. The Rehabilitation Act, like the ADA and FHA, only mandate reasonable accommodations to provide equal access to *disabled* individuals. The University is being asked to provide an accommodation to Plaintiff, only. The Court only is determining whether *he* is "otherwise qualified" for on-campus housing and whether allowing *him* to live in the University's dormitories would impose "a fundamental alteration in the nature of [the University's housing] program."

With respect to the latter determination, the evidence indicates that Defendants did not make an individualized inquiry to determine whether allowing Plaintiff to live in one of its dorm rooms would in some way alter the purported academic-fostering environment of its housing program. As the Supreme Court stated in *Arline*, "[s]uch an inquiry is essential if § 504 is to achieve its goal of protecting handicapped individuals from deprivations based on prejudice, stereotypes, or unfounded fear . . ." 480 U.S. at 287, 107 S.Ct. at 1131. Defendants argue that an individualized analysis of Plaintiff's requested accommodation was unnecessary because it was obvious, without engaging in such an inquiry, that no accommodation would render Plaintiff eligible for on-campus housing. (Doc. 48 at 3–4.) Defendants analogize Plaintiff's case to that of a blind person who seeks an accommodation of a school district's sight requirement for its bus drivers. (*Id.*) However this analogy fails for the reason that, while sight undoubtedly is an essential requirement to drive a bus, Defendants have not shown that enrollment in a degree-granting program is an essential requirement to live in a campus dormitory.

The undisputed evidence undermines any assumption or conclusion reached by Defendants that allowing Plaintiff to live in on-campus housing will interfere with the housing program's "purpose of moving student's toward an academic degree." The evidence shows that Plaintiff contributes to the academic environment, has been praised by professors "for his participation and for the positive effects he had on the classroom environment," that he is not disruptive in class and abides by classroom rules, and that he participates in study groups where he works to understand the material and contributes to the group's efforts to understand the material. (Doc. 39, Exs. 15, 25, 26.) A fellow student at the University, Heather Sterner, states in her affidavit in support of Plaintiff's motion that Plaintiff's "level of participation and interest far exceeds that of most of his peers," that he is "always engaged and asking questions," and "makes it clear to everyone in class that he is clearly there to learn."

(*Id.*, Ex. 26 ¶ 2.) There is an absence of evidence to support Defendants' assumption that Plaintiff's presence in the dormitories will change the academic environment or that he will be incapable of following housing rules. This assessment instead appears to be grounded on prejudice, stereotypes and/or unfounded fear. As a result, Defendants fail to carry their burden of demonstrating a threat to the fundamental nature of the University's housing program if Plaintiff's request for a reasonable accommodation is granted.

For these reasons, the Court concludes that waiving the University's policy of limiting on-campus housing to students enrolled in a degree-granting program is necessary to avoid discrimination on the basis of Plaintiff's disability and reasonable. Defendants violated § 504 of the Rehabilitation Act by failing to provide Plaintiff with this requested accommodation. Plaintiff therefore is entitled to summary judgment with respect to Count IV of his Second Amended Complaint.

B. Disparate Treatment

As set forth earlier, Plaintiff asserts disparate treatment discrimination claims under § 504 of the Rehabilitation Act, Title II of the ADA, and the FHA. The three-part burden shifting test established in *McDonnell Douglas Corporation v. Green*, 411 U.S. 792, 93 S.Ct. 1817, 36 L.Ed.2d 668 (1973), applies to these claims. *Graoch Assoc. # 33 v. Louisville/Jefferson County*, 508 F.3d 366, 371–72 (6th Cir.2007) (FHA); *Jones v. City of Monroe*, 341 F.3d at 477 (Rehabilitation Act and ADA).

First, Plaintiff must demonstrate a prima facie case of discrimination by establishing that (1) he has a disability; (2) he is "otherwise qualified;" and (3) he "is being excluded from participation in, being denied the benefits of, or being subjected to discrimination under the program *solely because of* [his] handicap." *Jones*, 341 F.3d at 477 (emphasis added and citations omitted). A claim under the Rehabilitation Act also requires a showing that the relevant program or activity is receiving Federal financial assistance. *Doherty*, 862 F.2d at 573. As defined in the ADA, an "otherwise qualified" individual is "an individual with a disability who, with or without reasonable modifications to rules, policies, or practices . . . meets the essential eligibility requirements for receipt of services or the participation in programs or activities provided by a public entity." 42 U.S.C. § 12131. As outlined in the preceding section, a similar definition has developed in case law interpreting the "otherwise qualified" element of a Rehabilitation Act claim.

If Plaintiff establishes a prima facie case of discrimination, Defendants must articulate "some legitimate, nondiscriminatory reason" for the University's decision to reject his housing application. Plaintiff then must demonstrate that Defendants' proffered reason is pretextual. In this case, Plaintiff's discrimination claims fail at the first step.

Plaintiff is not able to show that he was denied on-campus housing solely by reason of his disability. The evidence demonstrates that the University followed a policy of limiting on campus housing to students enrolled in degree-granting programs before Plaintiff applied for a room in one of its dormitories. In the Court's view, Mr. Wiggins' e-mails to Mr. Feldman after the University rejected Plaintiff's application are the strongest evidence of this. As Mr. Wiggins wrote, he spoke with university council and learned that "it has been university practice for some time that the dorm facilities are restricted to students who are pursuing a degree" and that "they have held to this firmly . . ." (*Id.*) Mr. Wiggins acknowledged that Ms. Snyder also had conveyed this policy to him. Aside from overnight stays by high school students and one week or shorter stays by summer camp or journalism program participants, Plaintiff presents no evidence of the University waiving this rule. Changes made to the housing application — that the evidence shows were contemplated before Plaintiff applied — do not establish that the rule was enacted to discriminate against Plaintiff because of his handicap.

Because Plaintiff fails to demonstrate a prima facie case of disability discrimination, the Court concludes that Defendants are entitled to summary judgment with respect to his disparate treatment discrimination claims (Counts II, III, and V).

C. Permanent Injunction

In his Second Amended Complaint, Plaintiff seeks an injunction "ordering Defendants to immediately provide on-campus dormitory housing for [him]." An injunction is an available remedy for a violation of § 504 of the Rehabilitation Act. *See* 42 U.S.C. § 2000d–7. As set forth above, the Court concludes that Defendants have violated the Act's reasonable accommodation requirement.

Plaintiff will suffer irreparable harm absent an injunction because he will be denied equal access to campus housing solely by reason of his disability. The Court also finds that there is no adequate remedy at law and therefore a remedy in equity is warranted. Damages cannot satisfy what Plaintiff has lost as a result of Defendants' failure to grant his request for a reasonable accommodation — the opportunity to live in the University's on-campus housing. The only remedy is to grant him a waiver of the housing policy requiring residents to be enrolled in a degree-granting program.

Balancing the equities between the parties, the Court finds that Plaintiff will suffer harm absent an injunction whereas the University will suffer little or no harm. Defendants assert that "Plaintiff completely misstates and oversimplifies the effect a favorable ruling for Plaintiff would have on OU allowing nine OPTIONS students to live in the dorms." (Doc. 43 at 19–20.) Actually it is Defendants who misstate and over-exaggerate the effect of a ruling for Plaintiff when they assert that such a ruling would require the University to make its on-campus housing available for all continuing-education students. (*Id.*) In fact, as indicated earlier, the Court only is finding that *Plaintiff* must be allowed to live in the dorms. In light of the evidence discussed above, and because spaces are available in the University's on-campus housing, the Court cannot find any harm to the University as a result of such a ruling. In comparison, Plaintiff will suffer substantial harm if an injunction is not issued because his opportunity to live in on-campus housing soon will be lost.

Lastly, the public interest is served by the enforcement of federal statutes barring disability discrimination and guaranteeing that disabled individuals are provided equal access to programs receiving Federal financial assistance.

The elements necessary for a permanent injunction to issue therefore have been satisfied. The Court is granting Plaintiff's request for an injunction ordering Defendants to provide on-campus housing for him during his final semester at the University.

IV. Conclusion

Based on the above, the Court holds that Plaintiff is entitled to summary judgment with respect to his failure to accommodate claim brought under § 504 of the Rehabilitation Act. Plaintiff also is entitled to relief in the form of a permanent injunction. Defendants, however, are entitled to summary judgment with respect to Plaintiff's remaining claims.

Accordingly,

IT IS ORDERED, that Defendants' Motion for Summary Judgment is GRANTED IN PART AND DENIED IN PART in that summary judgment is granted to Defendants with respect to Counts I–III, V, and VI of Plaintiff's Second Amended Complaint;

IT IS FURTHER ORDERED, that Plaintiff's Motion for Substitution of Defendant, Summary Judgment and Permanent Injunction is GRANTED IN PART AND DENIED IN PART in that his motion for substitution of defendant is DENIED, his motion for summary judgment is GRANTED IN PART AND DENIED IN PART in that summary judgment is granted as to Count IV of his Second Amended Complaint, and his request for a permanent injunction is GRANTED;

IT IS FURTHER ORDERED, that Defendants are ordered to provide on-campus housing for Plaintiff during the upcoming semester (beginning in January 2010).

NOTES AND PROBLEMS FOR DISCUSSION

1. Because of the injunction entered by the district court, Feldman was able to live on campus for his final four months of school. The university appealed the decision to the Sixth Circuit which concluded that the case was moot because Feldman had already finished his program. *See Fialka-Feldman v. Oakland University Bd. of Trustees*, 639 F.3d 711 (6th Cir. 2011). If the Sixth Circuit had been able to hear the case on the merits, should it have affirmed the district court?

2. What if Feldman had needed assistance to live independently? Would that have rendered him not "otherwise qualified" to live in university housing? Does your answer depend on the kind of assistance he needed?

3. Consider how a court might resolve the following fact pattern:

> Kristy Coleman is a twenty-one-year-old student attending the University of Nebraska, Lincoln. She has cerebral palsy and requires the use of a wheelchair and the services of a personal attendant to assist her with dressing, showering, and toileting. On her house preferences form, she indicated that she desired a double room and a nonsmoking roommate. Pursuant to University policy concerning students with disabilities, she was placed in a double room by herself.

> If Kristy wanted to obtain injunctive relief to obtain a double room with a roommate, how could she best characterize her injury? *See Coleman v. Zatechka*, 824 F. Supp. 1360 (D. Neb. 1993); *Fleming v. N.Y.U.*, 865 F.2d 478 (2d Cir. 1989).

4. While the treatment of Mr. Feldman by Oakland University may have been unlawful, it should not be surprising. Individuals with developmental and intellectual disabilities, as well as persons with disabilities on the Autism Spectrum, present many post-secondary institutions with new challenges, as their numbers in the post-secondary community increase.

Participation by these populations in higher education is a key to independence, self-sufficiency, intellectual stimulation, and skill development. This fact is well-appreciated both by the students and by their parents. They are actively advocating for greater post-secondary opportunities. According to a recent *Forbes* article, "Students with Autism Spectrum Disorder (ASD) have always been on college campuses, but with the lack of screening technologies just a few years ago, they struggled through schooling virtually invisible. Today, however, the number of children on the spectrum has risen from 1 in 150 to 1 in 88 in less than ten years, and colleges are beginning to acknowledge that these young adults are eager to receive their college degrees." *More Colleges Expanding Programs for Students on Autism Spectrum*, www.forbes.com/sites/paigecarlotti/2014/07/31/more-colleges-expanding-programs-for-students-on-autism-spectrum/ (last visited August 1, 2014.)

Despite the magnitude of this trend, how Section 504 and the ADA will apply to these populations is just now being worked out. Moreover, there cannot be a "one size fits all" accommodation for these populations. A wide range of modifications and best practices will need to be developed. Fortunately, according to the Association of University Centers on Disability (AUCD), over 100 colleges, universities, and medical centers are already engaged in developing a wide array of effective service delivery models and practices. *See* www.aucd.org/template/page.cfm?id=1 (last visited August 1, 2014.)

An Internet search reveals a considerable amount of information on this topic. In addition to the above sites other informative sites include:

> www.semel.ucla.edu/tarjan: "The Tarjan Center is a catalyst for collaboration, innovation, and systems change to advance the self-determination and inclusion of people with disabilities. [It] serve[s] as a bridge between the university and persons with disabilities from state, regional and local communities, state and local government agencies and community providers." (last visited August 1, 2014).
>
> http://collegeautismspectrum.com/: "College Autism Spectrum (CAS) is an independent organization of professionals whose purpose is to assist students with autism spectrum disorders, and their families. [It] specialize[s] in COLLEGE COUNSELING (helping students find the right college) and WORK READINESS (skill building for interviews, jobs and work skills)." (last visited August 1, 2014). This site also contains a number of recommended publications on this topic.

TABLE OF CASES

[References are to pages]

A

B

C

[References are to pages]

[References are to pages]

H

I

J

K

L

M

[References are to pages]

N

O

P

R

S

[References are to pages]

T

U

V

W

Y

Z

INDEX

[References are to pages.]

[References are to pages.]

S

T

U